ARMING MILITARY JUSTICE

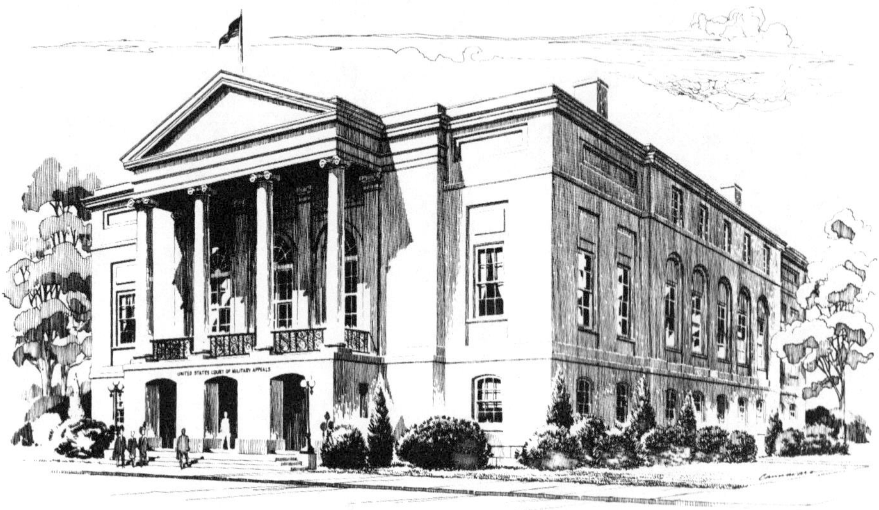

United States Court of Military Appeals building, Washington, D.C.
Illustration by Don Cannavaro.

ARMING MILITARY JUSTICE

VOLUME 1

THE ORIGINS OF THE UNITED STATES COURT OF MILITARY APPEALS, 1775–1950

Jonathan Lurie

PRINCETON UNIVERSITY PRESS PRINCETON, NEW JERSEY

Published by Princeton University Press, 41 William Street,
Princeton, New Jersey 08540
In the United Kingdom: Princeton University Press, Oxford

Library of Congress Cataloging-in-Publication Data

Lurie, Jonathan, 1939–
Arming military justice / Jonathan Lurie.
p. cm.
Includes bibliographical references and index.
Contents: v. 1. The origins of the United States Court of
Military Appeals, 1775–1950
ISBN 0-691-06944-1 (v. 1)
1. United States. Court of Military Appeals—History.
2. Courts–martial and courts of inquiry—
United States—History. 3. Appellate courts—United States—
History. I. Title.
KF7667.L87 1992
343.73′0143—dc20
[347.303143] 91-34737

This book has been composed in Linotron Times Roman

Princeton University Press books are printed
on acid-free paper, and meet the guidelines
for permanence and durability of the Committee
on Production Guidelines for Book Longevity
of the Council on Library Resources

Printed in the United States of America

1 3 5 7 9 10 8 6 4 2

For Mac,

My Counselor in Chief,

and

David, Deborah,

and Daniel

Contents

List of Illustrations

Preface

THE United States Court of Military Appeals (USCMA) is housed in a small but stately building located along with several other courts in an area of Washington appropriately called Judiciary Square. It was erected in 1910 for the use of the United States Court of Appeals for the District of Columbia Circuit. The structure is now listed on the National Register of Historic Places, and has been the home of USCMA since 1952. Upon entering, a visitor sees the ever-present security guard, sitting at a desk in front of a wall on which hang several photographs. One is a portrait of the first panel of judges, who served together from June 1951 to December 1955. There are also four individual portraits which, though labeled, mean nothing to most visitors. In fact, three of these subjects—Felix Larkin, Samuel Ansell, and Edmund Morgan—played major roles in the history of this court; and, as the following chapters will demonstrate, their presence at the main entrance to its building is very appropriate.

The visitor notices the shining marble floors, high ceilings, and the large, well-lighted corridors. On the first floor are located several important offices, such as the Clerk of the Court and the Docket Room, where all incoming cases are first filed. Often these offices are busy, and one hears echoes of voices and footsteps drifting down the hallways. Upon moving to the second floor, however, in front of the entrance to the courtroom the atmosphere changes.

Here, the visitor stands in an impressive foyer, replete with high columns and ornate chandeliers. Two large portraits of George Washington, and Robert Anderson at the battle of Fort Sumter hang on the wall above the marble stairway. In the center of the foyer, and in sharp contrast to its grandeur, is a set of double doors, simply marked "court room." It is set off by two busts, one of Charles Evans Hughes, the other of General W. S. Hancock.[1]

Standing inside these doors, which are actually at the back of the chamber, one sees a functioning courtroom restored to what existed early in this century, when the building was constructed. A large skylight in the center of the ceiling filters light through the entire room. At the far end, one notices a massive mahogany bench, along with several desks for court staff. Directly in front of the bench one also sees a small mahogany lectern. Here the lawyers stand (or lean, depending on their mental state) as they argue their cases before the judges. Because this is an appellate court, there is no jury box.

In back of the large seats behind the bench hang high, heavy, dark red drapes, which can be separated as the judges enter the chamber. On the back

[1] Neither of these gentlemen, distinguished though they were, contributed much to American military appellate justice. Their presence is more a reflection of what was available for decorating the corridors, after USCMA occupied the building in 1952.

walls at the rear of the courtroom are located portraits of the five judges who have died since the court was created in 1951. Two of the portraits, including the first Chief Judge, Robert Quinn, and Paul Brosman—the last of the initial three appointments—are positioned directly facing the current members of the court; looking out as it were, toward their successors. Unintentionally perhaps, the location of the portraits reflects a sense of the linkage between past and present judges, as the court continues to function. One notices the silence in this empty courtroom; an air of both permanence and inevitability seems to hang over it.

At the appropriate time, the Court Bailiff will strike his gavel and demand that "ALL RISE." "Hear ye, hear ye . . . ," he chants. As if responding to a cue, the curtains in back of the bench part and five judges in black robes take their accustomed seats on the bench; the Chief Judge in the center, the next two judges in order of seniority on his right, with the two newest appointments on his left.[2] Like many opening rituals of appellate courts, this is an impressive ceremony to observe. Indeed, there are seats for about 140 visitors; but in fact, they are rarely filled. For most appeals there are more participants present than spectators. With few exceptions, such as a newsworthy case or an admissions ceremony for new members of the Court Bar, the appeals attract little attention. The absence of both jury and witnesses help inhibit any lawyer's tendency toward excessive legal theatrics; and to the general visitor observing an appeal argument, the impression created may be one of legal mumbo-jumbo, of minor interest if not boredom. Such a perception is probably characteristic of appellate courts in general.

But this particular court has special functions, unlike other federal courts of general jurisdiction. It is one of our younger tribunals, having been created in 1950. Though its authority is limited by statute to cases arising from within the armed services, in fact it has jurisdiction over millions of Americans. That is because their service in our armed forces subjects them to the Uniform Code of Military Justice (UCMJ) which, among its many provisions, established a court of military appeals. Authorized during the aftermath of World War II, this court was intended to insure a civilian appellate bench for the military; that it too might function (to cite a famous phrase) as a government of law and not of men to the greatest extent possible—even within the admittedly unique parameters of military life.

Justifiably labeled as an experiment by its creators, the USCMA has been in existence for forty years. Two generations of litigants have appeared before it. More than twenty-seven thousand lawyers have been admitted to its bar. Its decisions now fill over fifty volumes, and its interpretations of the UCMJ and

[2] From its first year of operation in 1951 to 1990, the court had three seats, and all of them had been filled by males. Late in 1989, Congress increased the size of the United States Court of Military Appeals to five judges. At this writing, President Bush has nominated the first woman to serve on its bench, Susan Crawford, and Herman F. Gierke, and Robert E. Wiss.

the Manual for Courts-Martial (MCM) are for the most part definitive. On the federal level, this judicial experiment has become a permanent part of the judicial establishment.

Why did Congress establish this court in 1950? Why not in 1919 or even 1865? What did the legislature intend as its mission? What tradition of military appellate procedure had developed in the armed services? What role did the armed services play in the drafting and ultimate adoption of the statute? How did congressional preferences and the political process affect the new legislation? To what extent did the new tribunal change administration of military justice? How has it operated since 1951? What mandate has the court exercised, and with what degree of success and failure? Answers to the first six questions form the chapters that follow, but some discussion of *how* they were found may be appropriate here.

In 1950, when President Truman signed the statute creating the UCMJ into law, the court of military appeals became a reality. Congress, however, had not set out to establish such a tribunal. Rather, it was a part, albeit an important one, of a much greater legislative effort—a total redrafting and synthesis of existing and heretofore independent bodies of military laws into one uniform code, applicable to all the armed services. One seeking to explore historical origins of this court must accept the fact that it was a by-product of another major piece of legislation. Moreover, when Congress enacted the Code it had to deal with many other critical issues. Indeed, it seems clear that even among military concerns confronting Congress in 1949–1950, enactment of the UCMJ was not a very high priority. In terms of public perception, controversies involving Sen. Joseph McCarthy, military spending, and Korea were all considered much more important.

Furthermore, the bill creating the UCMJ did not originate with Congress, but rather from within the office of Secretary of Defense James Forrestal. A product first of a working committee consisting of judge advocate general (JAG) officers drawn from each service joined by civilian attorneys working in Forrestal's office—each proposed article was then considered by the Morgan Committee, named for its chair, Harvard Law Professor Edmund M. Morgan. In addition to Morgan, this committee included three undersecretaries—Gordon Gray, Army; W. John Kenney, Navy; and Eugene Zuckert, Air Force—plus an assistant to James Forrestal, Felix Larkin, who served as executive secretary. The Morgan Committee considered, altered, approved, or rejected each article of the code. Any disagreements within the committee, and there were several—including establishment of this court—were ultimately decided by Forrestal himself. Only then, and as a finished entity, was the bill submitted to Congress. By the time it became law, a large body of congressional material had indeed been accumulated, but for tracing the history of the code from a proposal to a statute the papers of the two committees would seem absolutely essential for any accurate history of the code, and hence, of this court.

Here, like many historical quests however, the desirable and actual are not the same. There appear to be no formal and complete set of records for either group. But there are a fair number of manuscript collections that were of major importance as research for this study progressed. First and foremost were the papers of Felix Larkin, employed in the General Counsel's office within the newly established department of defense from 1947–1951. Indeed, by the time Larkin resigned to enter private employment, he had become *the* General Counsel. Larkin retained his phone logs and letter books from his years in the department, as well as a number of materials assembled by the working group to use as its members drafted the code. These included various reports of committees appointed to investigate military justice within the several armed services between 1943 and 1948, and an exhaustive comparative study of military justice that served as the basis on which to construct the new statute. Mr. Larkin made both himself and his entire archive available to me for this study; and further, he permitted unrestricted copying so that the great majority of his papers dealing with the court's history will be placed in an archive within its own library.

Edmund Morgan left four boxes of printed material used by his committee in the custody of Harvard Law School, while the bulk of his personal papers are in the Special Collections Library at Vanderbilt University. Because Morgan himself appears to have drafted the first proposals for the appellate procedures under the new code, his papers are important for this study. Morgan's son, Edmund S. Morgan, himself a very distinguished historian, kindly gave me permission to examine and copy from both collections.

Preparation of the UCMJ extended from the summer of 1948 to February 1949 when the finished draft was submitted to Congress. A large amount of inter-service correspondence was generated as the working committee circulated different versions of various articles, accompanied by reactions from the representatives of each armed service. Somehow, much of this material was loosely packed into four cartons, and stored in the basement of the court building, where, in due course, I came across them.

Finally, a number of miscellaneous collections revealed important clues as to the court's origins. The papers of Gordon Gray, who strongly opposed its establishment, contained some valuable information, as did for example, a file in Leverett Saltonstall's papers. Saltonstall, a senator from Massachusetts, served on the Senate Subcommittee that considered the code. Similarly, the papers of his colleagues, Senators Estes Kefauver and Millard Tydings, were helpful. To be sure, no one of these collections was complete in itself. But taken together along with the usual congressional material available to the researcher, the historical origins of the USCMA become easier to delineate and analyze.

In addition to these sources and more traditional published items, I conducted a number of oral history interviews during the course of my research.

Adoption of the code, and creation of this court engendered controversy. It is not surprising that individuals saw the same events very differently. Occasionally it has been necessary to rely on a recollection, in the absence of the written record. Rarely, my subjects requested that some of their comments not be recorded, or that some other written points not be quoted. I have respected their wishes, but the transcripts themselves will become a part of the court's history archive.

It should be emphasized that this study is *not* a history of the entire Uniform Code of Military Justice, a complex document of 140 separate articles. Rather, I have sought to utilize only those materials bearing on the development of appellate procedure within it. Occasionally, I have felt it appropriate to discuss certain other articles as they may relate to this topic, but the focus of these chapters is primarily on the origins and later in the second volume, on operations of the USCMA.

Three themes, separate yet sometimes intertwined, link the following chapters. First is the tracing, over time, of the principle of appellate jurisdiction within American military justice. From the earliest (1775) version of the Articles of War to the UCMJ, some form of review was considered essential. These review procedures, however, were different than the usual recourse to an appellate tribunal.

Second, there is a related theme of the interplay between military justice and civilian judicial activity. Although episodic throughout our history, several such incidents have raised troublesome questions concerning the extent of civilian control over the military. The development of an appellate procedure within the military and the role civilians might play in it, represented an important dimension to this issue. Also, the problem of where any appeals process was to be located, within or outside of the military justice system, had to be confronted. Any review of a court-martial decision by the president as commander in chief, for example, could be considered within the system.

One should also keep in mind the continuing tension between military justice and its civilian counterpart. Military justice is virtually inseparable from military discipline which seeks attainment of specific objectives, gained by a military force prepared for death, if necessary. Our civilian justice system aims primarily to safeguard the rights of property, the community, and the individual. Basic differences between the two systems are immediately apparent, but the extent to which they should be separate from each other remains a source of controversy.

The final major theme that permeates much of this study is the interplay of politics on the course of legislation; not only in its early stages, but more obviously when it reaches Congress. As will be seen, unusual efforts were made to keep the drafting of the UCMJ nonpolitical. But, like most legislative efforts, even this statute was not immune from political considerations. Issues of presidential authority as well as congressional preferences affected the code's final form.

To the extent that the USCMA invited me to undertake this study, and that its judges and staff have consistently supported, facilitated, and encouraged my work, this is an "official" history. When I began research on the project more than four years ago, neither the court nor I had any idea of what materials were available, and where the research would ultimately lead. I had no prior experience with the military of any kind, and what little I had heard or read about military justice left me with the usual "Vietnam era graduate student" viewpoint, that it often was a contradiction in terms. Like most glib generalizations, there was and probably remains some truth in this one. Freely admitting that inexplicable and inexcusable lapses of military justice have indeed occurred, and will again; yet one can still be impressed with changes that have taken place since World War II as well as ongoing efforts to maintain and improve the system.

The conclusions that I now hold will be obvious in the following chapters, and because I am sure that the members of the court may well not agree with all of them, it should be emphasized here that they are my responsibility. Like Professor Jerold Auerbach, I "cannot claim to be a neutral observer." Neutrality, he adds, "is no less partisan than engagement; it is merely an expression of different, but equally partisan values."[3] While my conclusions, of necessity, should be considered somewhat tentative, it seems to me that I have had little difficulty in separating my "objective" or "neutral" accounting of the court's history from interpretive assessments based upon my own views. Only the reader can judge whether or not this statement is accurate.

The history of appellate jurisdiction in military justice has, admittedly, been fascinating for me to trace. I have tried to let the principals in this story speak for themselves. Thus, there are many quotations, some of them extended, and numerous notes. I could have summarized much more than has been the case; but believe, however, that frequently the original tells us more about context and sequence than a historian's summary forty years later. The notes indicate either the source of every quotation or explain why the speaker/writer is not cited. They also are intended to provide some additional points that may be of greater interest to the scholar in military justice than the general reader.

The research and writing of this first volume in the court's history has taken more than four years. I have had support and assistance from many individuals, whose efforts I gratefully acknowledge. I am indebted first of all to the then three members of the court, Walter Cox, Jr., Senior Judge Robinson O. Everett, and Chief Judge Eugene Sullivan, who in June 1987 invited me to undertake this study. At all times, they have been extremely supportive, while

[3] Jerold Auerbach, *Unequal Justice: Lawyers and Social Change in Modern America* (1976), xiii.

consistently letting me discover for myself their court's history. Through the cooperation and support of Dean David Hosford and the invaluable aid from Ms. Sally Zeiss in the Dean's Office, Rutgers University made it possible for me to spend three years of uninterrupted research and writing on this project.

The staff of the court have been unfailingly kind and generous with their help. I am very indebted to Mr. Thomas Granahan, Clerk of the Court; to his Deputy John Cutts; and the following past and present members of his staff: Shirley Bates, Robert Bieber, Gail Bissi, Kathy Cassady, Bethany Miller, Maxine Muller, Barbara Passamaneck, and Alvin Waters. The aid of the Court Librarians, Mary Kuck and Agnes Kiang, has been indispensable. Among the staff attorneys, Robert Miele, Robert Mueller, and James Richardson were always willing to respond candidly to many questions I raised all too often. I am especially obligated to Stephen Wright and Christopher Sterritt for support and advice, and also insights into the dynamics of appellate military review, as seen in the cases considered by the court.

Outside the court, my debts are equally extensive. My good friend and former colleague, Professor Richard Kohn, first encouraged me to consider a project dealing with the history of this court. Dr. Alfred Goldberg, the Historian to the Office of the Secretary of Defense provided counsel and guidance especially in working through the contractual arrangements between me, the court, and the department of defense. Eugene Fidell, Esq., both a perceptive critic of military justice as well as a distinguished member of the bar of this court, shared some of his insights concerning its role since 1951. Another Rutgers colleague, military historian John Whiteclay Chambers II, subjected each of my chapters to a careful examination. His encouraging comments as well as those of the two outside readers from Princeton University Press have been of great value. The support and assistance from Gail Ullman, Social Sciences Editor at PUP and William Laznovsky, my editor, are gratefully acknowledged. The staffs of the National Archives, Library of Congress Manuscripts Division, the Truman Library, and the Pentagon Library were very helpful. Mr. Daniel Lavering, Librarian of the Army Judge Advocate General's School in Charlottesville, Virginia, willingly permitted me to examine and copy from the JAG office records housed there.

I owe a special debt of gratitude to the late Felix Larkin. He did more than afford me access to all his papers and phone logs. He also spent several hours in extended conversations about the history of the UCMJ. His willingness to make these materials available not only to me but also to the court for its permanent archive is gratefully recorded here. Similarly, Professor Edmund Morgan reminisced with me about his famous father, and let me examine not only the Morgan papers at Harvard Law School, but the more extensive collection at Vanderbilt University. Marx Leva, still practicing law in Washington, shared his memories of Morgan's work with me, as did Morgan's daughter, Ms. Roberta Wohlstetter, and two of his former students, Robert Haydock and

Colonel Frederick B. Wiener, USA, ret. Indeed, Colonel and Mrs. Wiener offered me their hospitality for an extended interview/visit in 1987. Mr. Robert C. Quinn, son of the first Chief Judge not only permitted me to examine and copy from his late father's papers, but donated them to the court for its own archive. Dr. Ronald Latimer and George Latimer, Jr, recalled their days in Washington, when their father, Judge George Latimer, became the second judge of this court. In addition, George Latimer made a number of manuscript pages from his late father's unpublished memoirs available to me.

I am also greatly indebted to the following individuals for permission to examine and quote from these unpublished collections: Karin Hardy, *Reva Beck Bosone Papers*, University of Utah; Elizabeth Uhlig, *Enoch Crowder Papers*, University of Missouri—Western Historical Manuscript Collection; Patrick Quinn, *John Henry Wigmore Papers*, Northwestern University; Peggy Haines, *George Earle Chamberlain Papers*, Oregon Historical Society; Jane Jackson, *Robert E. Quinn Oral History Project*, Providence College; Nancy Bressler, *James V. Forrestal Papers*, Seeley G. Mudd Library, Princeton University, and the Forrestal Estate; William Saltonstall, and Louis Tucker, Director, Massachusetts State Historical Society, *Leverett Saltonstall Papers*; James B. Lloyd, *Estes Kefauver Collection*, University of Tennessee; Eric N. Moody, Curator of Manuscripts, Nevada Historical Society, *Patrick McCarran Papers*; Anne Turkos, Assistant Curator, Historical Manuscripts, University of Maryland, *Millard Tydings Papers*; Bentley Historical Library, University of Michigan, *Homer Ferguson Papers*; Richard Sommers, U.S. Army Military History Institute, *Gordon Gray Papers*; Pat White-Williams, Librarian, materials retained by the Army Times Publishing Company.

The following individuals permitted me to record extensive discussions with them concerning military Justice and the Court: William Cook; John Cooke; Robert Duncan; Andrew Effron; Francis Gindhart; Albert Fletcher, Jr.; D. Wayne Hansen; Robert Haydock; Kenneth Hodson; Martin Hoffman; Felix Larkin; George Latimer; George Latimer, Jr.; Ronald Latimer; William O. Miller; Charles Mitchell; Ward Mundy; Leonard Niederlehner; Mathew Perry; Alfred Proulx; George Prugh; Virginia Siegel; Deanne Siemer; Frederick B. Wiener; and Darlene Yarborough.

To gain some familiarity with the military environment, I was able to visit a large number of installations, and observed court-martial proceedings on several occasions. Be it touring on board the nuclear aircraft carrier *Roosevelt*, attending court-martials at Quantico and Camp Lejeune, flying with members of the 82nd Airborne Division, spending three days at sea with the Coast Guard, or receiving some instructions in riflery at Fort Dix—the members of the military in all these branches of the armed services with whom I came in contact, went out of their way to explain their perceptions of military justice in general, and the court in particular. Their candor is much appreciated, and because many remain on active duty, I thank them collectively rather than individually. Professionals all, they demonstrated a pride in what they do that I will long remember. I am especially grateful to Coast Guard Capt. Richard Clark. For making their own collections of materials relating to military justice available to me, I am also obligated to Army Brig. Gen. D. Wayne Hansen, recently retired as Assistant Judge Advocate General of the Army; Lt. Col. John Cooke, Judge Advocate General Dept., USA; and Rear Adm. William O. Miller, JAG, USN (ret.).

I am deeply indebted to all these individuals, and to others who asked not to be acknowledged here. None of them, however, is responsible for the conclusions that follow. I remain grateful to the Research Council of Rutgers University for sustained support not only for this project, but for my long-range research in American legal history. Finally, I would appreciate being informed of any mistakes that might still be lurking in either text or notes. As one author wrote in 1700: ''I must trouble the reader to correct the errata of the press, as he finds them. For I am quite tyr'd.''[4]

[4] Quoted in Howard Mumford Jones, *The Pursuit of Happiness* (1953), xi.

Abbreviations

ABA	American Bar Association
BP	Newton Baker Papers
CP	Enoch Crowder Papers
CUCMJ	Committee on a Uniform Code of Military Justice
Hearings, 1	Hearings, Committee Military Affairs, U.S. Senate, 65th Cong., 3d sess., 1919
Hearings, 2	Hearings, Subcommittee Military Affairs, U.S. Senate, 66th Cong., 1st sess., 1919
HST	Truman Papers
JAG	Judge Advocate General
JAGO	Judge Advocate General Records
KF	Kefauver Papers
LH	Legislative History, Uniform Code of Military Justice
LP	Felix Larkin Papers
LPPL	Felix Larkin Phone Logs
MCM	Manual for Courts-Martial
MPHLS	Edmund Morgan Papers, Harvard Law School
MPVU	Edmund Morgan Papers, Vanderbilt University
SP	Saltonstall Papers
UCMJ	Uniform Code of Military Justice
USA	United States Army
USCMA	United States Court of Military Appeals
USCMAP	United States Court of Military Appeals Papers
USN	United States Navy
WP	Wigmore Papers

ARMING MILITARY JUSTICE

CHAPTER 1

Military and Civilian "Review" to 1815

THE IDEA of an appellate procedure vis-à-vis American constitutional and political history is of venerable ancestry. Between 1650 and 1775, the thirteen original colonies all developed systems of judicial administration that implied, if not employed, an appeals process. The seeds of both a separation of powers doctrine, as well as judicial review can thus be seen in the frequently complex relations between colonial legislatures, royal governors, and the Royal Privy Council. This council in addition to reviewing much colonial legislation, could and did veto certain laws. By the time of the Revolutionary era, from 1775 to 1787, some sort of appellate review had become a virtual given in terms of American *civilian* political institutions.

Of necessity, the colonial figures who orchestrated the revolution in political terms also had to confront governance of the army. Leaders like John Adams and Thomas Jefferson, both acutely aware of the possible contagion of revolutionary sentiment but from very different philosophical viewpoints, were also concerned with the establishment of a workable system of military justice. Indeed, of minor importance were the "rights" of the American soldier; and this included any appellate procedure. Of crucial importance was a set of regulations that would insure discipline and effective control of the armed forces. For all their political and philosophical differences, Jefferson and Adams could both support two early versions of the Articles of War (1775 and 1776) that together constituted the official foundation of American military justice.

TOUGH TALK FROM JOHN ADAMS

Those who drafted the 1775 articles, including John Adams, could draw upon as precedent the Massachusetts Articles of War adopted in early April 1775, even before the battle of Lexington and Concord. Like the American versions soon to follow, Massachusetts drew heavily if not completely upon the existing British rules; rules admittedly harsh but, at least from Adams' viewpoint, historically effective. Thus the regulations provided for both regimental and general court-martials. In certain cases, the latter could serve as an appeals body for the former. Moreover, an officer who felt himself "to be wronged by his Colonel, or the Commanding officer of the Regiment'' could ''complain to the General or Commander-in-Chief . . . in order to obtain justice, who is hereby required to examine into the complaint and see that justice be done.'' Similar provisions were available for ''any inferior Officer or Soldier.''[1] Punishments meted out both by regimental and general courts-martial could not take place until confirmed (and thus presumably reviewed) by the commanding officer.[2] Finally, ''all the Members of a Court Martial are to behave with calmness, decency, and impartiality.''[3]

The Articles of War adopted by the Continental Congress in June 1775 reiterated these provisions. While expanding some of the rules for court-martials, no further details for some sort of review appear to have been adopted. Like the Massachusetts version, a well-defined appellate procedure may not have been considered necessary. In one respect, however, the Congress retained the great severity reflected in the Commonwealth articles. Article 25 provided that ''whatsoever officer or soldier shall shamefully abandon any post committed to his charge, or shall speak words inducing others to do the like, in time of an engagement, shall suffer death immediately.''[4] No provisions for any sort of judicial procedure, let alone inquiry were provided. The new regulations limited the authority of courts-martial, with the exception of the various articles that specified the death penalty, to no punishments ''other than degrading, cashiering, drumming out of the army, whipping not exceeding thirty-nine lashes, fine not exceeding two months pay of the offender, [and] imprisonment not exceeding one month.''[5]

According to Adams, General Washington considered the 1775 Articles insufficient. Assigned by Congress to revise them, Adams observed to Jefferson that ''the least tendency to a necessary discipline of the Army, would be opposed with as much vehemence as if it were the most perfect.'' He therefore

[1] William Winthrop, *Military Law and Precedents* (1920 reprint version), 949. Hereafter cited as Winthrop.

[2] Ibid., 950–51.

[3] Ibid. Of special interest, in terms of the evolving system of American military justice from the 1775 Articles to the 1951 Uniform Code of Military Justice, were articles 46 and 49. One provided for the dismissal of a commissioned officer convicted by a general court-martial ''of behaving in a scandalous, infamous manner, such as is unbecoming an Officer and a Gentleman.'' The other stated that ''all crimes not capital, and all disorders and neglects which Officers and Soldiers may be guilty of, to the prejudice of good order and military discipline, though not mentioned in the Articles of War, are to be taken cognizance of by a General or Regimental Court Martial, according to the nature and degree of the offence, and be punished at their discretion.'' These two articles, often described as ''catchall'' articles have remained part of American Military Justice for more than two centuries. As will be seen in a later chapter, controversy surrounds their continued presence. But the military has consistently, and thus far successfully, insisted on the absolute military necessity for their retention.

[4] Ibid., 955.

[5] Ibid., 957.

proposed that they submit a complete revision, rather than a few remedial measures. "We might as well therefore report a compleat [sic] system at once and let it meet its fate. Some thing perhaps might be gained."[6] Always an admirer of British administrative practices, especially when they worked, Adams proposed to copy the British Articles of War with virtually no changes. Jefferson "cordially concurred in this," and the 1776 revisions were ultimately adopted.[7]

The 1776 revision deleted the article calling for immediate execution, noted above. It also provided that "no sentence of a general court-martial shall be put into execution, till after a report shall have been made of the whole proceedings to Congress, or to the general or commander in chief of the forces of the United States, and their or his directions be signified thereupon."[8] Furthermore, this individual "shall have full power of pardoning or mitigating any of the punishments ordered to be inflicted, for any of the offenses" mentioned in the Articles. On the other hand, the limit on lashes to be inflicted as punishment was raised from thirty-nine to one hundred.[9]

By 1776, Congress had established military courts-martial. They predate our federal district courts by more than a decade, and can thus accurately be said to have been among the first (if not *the* first), federal courts authorized by the United States. They were drawn from a set of military articles, admittedly severe; and thus the question arises why two practical patriots such as Adams and Jefferson—the one with his well-known lawyer's respect for due process, the other with his passionate belief in self government—could both support regulations that can be considered antithetical to much of what they stood for.

The answer probably lay in their belief that governance of the military was based on needs very different from those of a civilian polity. Adams took it for granted that the militia had to be governed by different standards than those applicable in civilian society. His concern for a disciplined army overshadowed the issue of due process within the military itself. In one form or another, although not without some modifications, this concern and its attendant preference continues to the present day. But there was also a practical side to be considered. As a group, revolutionaries generally are not happy with the prospect of losing. The way the army was governed could only affect the way it fought; and whether it won or lost might have overwhelming personal consequences for men like Adams and Jefferson.

"I saw very clearly," wrote Adams, "that the ruin of our cause and country must be the consequence if a thoughrough [sic] reformation and strict disci-

[6] John Adams, *Diary and Autobiography*, ed. by L. H. Butterfield, vol. 3 (1961): 409.

[7] Ibid., 410. "Jefferson in those days never failed to agree with me, in every Thing [sic] of a political nature."

[8] Winthrop, 968.

[9] Ibid., 970.

pline could not be introduced.''[10] Indeed, in his correspondence, Adams made frequent reference to the need for discipline. In 1777, he wrote to his wife Abigail, ''if I were an officer, I am convinced I should be the most decisive disciplinarian in the army. . . . Discipline in an army is like the laws in a civil society. There can be no liberty in a commonwealth where the laws are not revered and most sacredly observed, nor can there be happiness or safety in an army for a single hour when discipline is not observed.''[11]

For Adams, liberty and discipline represented two sides of the same coin. To him, ''the *unum necessarium* to our salvation'' was discipline in the army—together with strong and effective state governments. The two were inseparable. ''There are so many persons among my worthy constituents who like liberty better than they understand it, that I expect to become unpopular by my preaching. But woe is me, if I preach it not. Woe will be to them if they do not hear.''[12]

Although he also supported the new revisions, Jefferson, according to Adams, did not speak about them in Congress. In retrospect, Adams recalled that ''all the labor of the debate . . . was thrown upon me, and such was the opposition, and so indigested were the notions of liberty prevalent among the majority of the members . . . that to this day I scarcely know how it was possible, that these articles could be carried. They were adopted however, and have governed our armies, with little variation to this day.''[13]

Adams's ideas about military discipline were important in legitimating the doctrine that military justice was to be an entity unto itself, separate from civilian practice. Yet the 1776 Articles made it clear that Congress was to play some sort of supervisory/review role in regard to military justice. How closely civilian (congressional) supervision was to be applied to the army remained unclear. Less than three years after the formal conclusion of hostilities between the United States and England, the American Congress had to confront this problem. How much information concerning courts-martial was to be reported to Congress, when, and with what result?

[10] Adams, *Diary*, 433.

[11] Page Smith, *John Adams* (1962), 289.

[12] Ibid., 305.

[13] Adams, *Diary*, 434. Adams took great pride in his ''authorship'' of the 1786 Articles of War. Writing in 1805, he denounced his late rival Alexander Hamilton, killed the year before in the famous duel with Aaron Burr, for accusing Adams of ''being an ennemy [sic] to a regular Army.'' ''I am not obliged,'' he wrote, ''by any principles of morality or religion to suffer my character to lie under infamous calumnies, because the author of them, with a pistol bullet through his spinal marrow, died a penitent. . . . I will not conceal his former character at the expense of so much injustice to my own, as this Scottish Creolion Bolingbroke in the days of his disappointed ambition and unbridled malice and revenge, was pleased falsely to attempt against it.'' When Adams' diary was later published, his grandson Charles Francis Adams omitted these lines. Ibid., 435.

CONGRESSIONAL CONCERNS, 1786–1815

Early in 1786, Secretary of War Henry Knox received a report from Maj. John Wyllys, assigned to a post on the frontier of Pennsylvania. Seeing his command shrink due to blatant incidents of desertion, he convened a court-martial of five officers to try several soldiers for this offense. To be sure, the 1776 Articles called for "a panel of 13 officers for capital cases, obviously impossible in a peacetime army which," according to Richard Kohn, "contained less than 40 officers in toto."[14] The men were convicted, whereupon Wyllys forwarded the findings and sentence to the War Department, as required by the Articles of War. He also made the sentences public, hoping that they would have a dramatic effect upon other members of his command. They did; immediately three more soldiers deserted. This time, Wyllys did not hesitate. The men were promptly captured and executed, with neither trial nor prior notification to Congress. "No desertions," he wrote to Knox, "have happened since & he thinks this instance of severity will probably preclude the necessity for executing the deserters now in confinement." Wyllys was "fully convinced that nothing but such exemplary punishment could produce the desired effect," and he hoped that his course would meet with the secretary's "approbation."[15]

Ultimately, Knox exonerated Wyllys, but he was shocked by the incident. He informed Congress that a commanding officer "cannot inflict the capital punishment of death for desertion contrary to the established forms. To supersede the laws in this respect is to assume the sovereignty and annul the compact, which the public have made with their troops, that they shall be governed by the rules and articles of war."[16] He asked that Congress investigate the entire incident, and pending the outcome, suspended Wyllys "from all command in the troops of the United States."[17]

Congress responded with some revisions to the articles, which were adopted on May 31, 1786. The new rules provided that general courts-martial could consist of "any number of commissioned officers from five to thirteen inclusively." Of greater importance, another article stated that no sentence of a court-martial could be executed "until after the whole proceedings shall have been laid before the said general or officer commanding the troops." Moreover no sentence of a court-martial "in time of peace, extending to the loss of life, the dismission [sic] of a commissioned officer, or . . . either in time of peace or war . . . a general officer [shall] be carried into execution until after the whole proceedings shall have been transmitted to the Secretary of War, to

[14] Richard Kohn, *Eagle and Sword* (1975), 70.

[15] *Journals of Congress*, March 21, 1786, 119–20.

[16] Ibid.

[17] Ibid., 121.

be laid before Congress for their confirmation, or disapproval, and their orders on the case.''[18]

These 1786 revisions also reflected a greater concern for some sort of due process, than had been manifest in earlier versions. To be sure, the judge advocate general or ''some person deputed by him'' was to prosecute the case. But in addition, that official was to ''consider himself as counsel for the prisoner, after the said prisoner shall have made his plea, as to object to any leading question to any of the witnesses, or any question to the prisoner, the answer to which might tend to incriminate himself.''[19]

Whatever was intended by this provision to the contrary, some scholars of military law have minimized its significance. Frederick Bernays Wiener concluded that this requirement reflected ''Blackstonian, common law notion of the judge as counsel for the prisoner,'' rather than a guarantee of the right to counsel. Indeed, the judge advocate apparently could not consider himself ''as defense counsel in connection with the accused's plea.'' Wiener added that a leading American military justice scholar, William Winthrop had gone so far as to call this stipulation ''a most imperfect and ineffective provision,'' one that ''is in the main obsolete and futile.''[20]

In the 1786 changes, Congress also authorized the commanding officer to

[18] Winthrop, 972.

[19] Ibid., 972–73. No doubt with the Wyllys incident in mind, Congress also provided that when faced with desertion, the commanding officer could ''cause the most immediate and vigorous search to be made.'' If that failed, he could advertise in the ''nearest gazette or newspaper,'' offering a reward ''not exceeding ten dollars, for each deserter who shall be apprehended and secured in the gaols of the neighboring states.'' The ''Secretary at [sic] War'' was to pay the advertising charge and reasonable extra expenses. Ibid., 975.

[20] Frederick Bernays Wiener, ''Courts-Martial and the Bill of Rights: The Original Practice,'' *Harvard Law Review* 72 (1958): 22–23. Wiener's two-part article was written primarily to refute claims made by Gordon Henderson. See Henderson, ''Courts-Martial and the Constitution: The Original Understanding,'' *Harvard Law Review* 71 (1957): 293–324. Impressive in its research, Wiener's article nevertheless suffers from a defect for which one can also rightly criticize Henderson. ''There is a temptation to make even the smallest grain of evidence over-probative.'' See J. D. Droddy, ''King Richard to Solorio: The Historical and Constitutional Bases for Court-Martial Jurisdiction in Criminal Cases,'' *Air Force Law Review* 30 (1989): 122. Wiener cited the 1786 excerpt quoted above as evidence that the right to counsel as implied in the Sixth Amendment was intended not to apply to courts-martial. But Droddy notes that this 1786 provision, carried over into the 1806 draft of the Articles of War, make ''it [seem] clear that the article was intended to require the military to provide legal assistance to the prisoner. Indeed, it even levied that obligation upon the Judge Advocate himself. Although the notion of a single individual acting as both the prosecutor and counsel for the accused may offend our modern idea of the substance of the Sixth Amendment, one should note that the amendment itself requires only that the accused ''have the assistance of counsel for his defense.'' Droddy concludes that what Wiener cites as proving that right to counsel was not intended is ''not inconsistent with an argument that the 1806 Congress believed the assistance of counsel [in some form, at least] to be constitutionally mandated in courts-martial. Ibid., 123. He further adds that the issue of the applicability of the Bill of Rights in some form to courts-martial ''is a complicated one. It is an issue that is not likely to ever be settled conclusively.'' Ibid., 124.

establish a Court of Inquiry, and provided that "the parties accused shall also be permitted to cross-examine and interrogate the witnesses, so as to investigate fully the circumstances in question." It should be noted here that the court of inquiry served as the military equivalent of a grand jury proceeding. Yet the right to cross-examine witnesses, as indicated above, went far beyond any comparable privilege granted in civilian practice. Even today, grand jury proceedings are usually secret, and the objects of their scrutiny are not permitted to cross-examine, let alone even hear, other witnesses.[21] In *this* respect, military justice and this before adoption of the federal Constitution—to say nothing of the Bill of Rights—afforded, and presumably still does afford, a greater measure of due process to an accused than in civilian court procedure.[22] It is not too early in this study to caution that one should thus be very careful when generalizing about the comparative merits of military and civilian justice and judicial procedures.

The adoption of the Constitution, replete with the modern system of congressional, judicial, and executive functions came and went with no appreciable impact on the existing Articles of War. The framers delineated two areas from which appellate procedure might derive. They made the president of the United States the commander in chief of the armed services. At the same time, they specifically authorized Congress "to make rules for the government and regulation of the land and naval forces."[23] In large measure, of course, this had already been done with the adoption and revision of the Articles of War. But in the early nineteenth century, it was not clear to what extent congressional authority and power of the commander in chief might overlap.

Clearly Congress could establish rules and procedures for courts-martial. Could the president do the same? Was a court-martial executive or legislative in origin? Not important in 1800, the question would be of much greater concern when a secondary issue arose; the problem of the relationship between actions of courts-martial and other federal tribunals. Were decisions of military courts reviewable outside of the very limited steps under the articles, and if so, by whom? As will be seen in later chapters, much of American military-legal history since the late nineteenth century has focused on the efforts to answer these questions.

President Washington began his term in 1789. Henry Knox realized that

[21] Although it may be highly desirable, there appears to be no requirement for uniformity among the states concerning grand jury procedures. In some states, subjects of a grand jury indictment can request and receive a copy of the transcript.

[22] The 1786 revisions provided that under certain conditions, testimony in a court of inquiry could be used as evidence in a court-martial. But, "as courts of inquiry may be perverted to dishonorable purposes, and may be considered as engines of destruction to military merit, in the hands of weak and envious commandants, they are hereby prohibited, unless demanded by the accused." Winthrop, 974–75.

[23] *U.S. Constitution*, Article I, Sec. 8. Congress also could "provide for organizing, arming, and disciplining the Militia."

military leader—only to return to civilian life after the crisis has passed.[30] With the possible exception of George Washington, probably no American president before or since Jackson has personified this perception with such popularity. Thus, the episode that ultimately involved him as a supreme military commander, a defendant in federal court, and finally as a venerated elder statesman in retirement reflects the peculiar American ambivalence toward military necessity and civilian control in the context of American politics. Its outcome indicates that in the American experience, civilian control of the military cannot always be separated from the political process; a fact that may well render such control less effective than might otherwise be the case.

Prior to the famous battle of New Orleans in January 1815, Jackson had placed the city under martial law. With the incredible victory over a much larger British force, he was regarded as the city's—to say nothing of the nation's—savior. Yet Jackson believed that the great celebrations in his honor had ended neither the war itself, nor the necessity for martial law. Until he received *official* word that a treaty had been signed (as in fact had actually happened even before the battle), Jackson insisted on the retention of the status quo ante. During the next two months, tensions between Jackson and New Orleans' leaders were exacerbated, to say the least. Declining to release the militia, he even went so far as to order the deportation of numerous French-speaking citizens. This order caused his ultimate confrontation with federal civil authority.

In response to his "edict," a French language newspaper printed an editorial very critical of Jackson's conduct. "We do not feel much inclined, through gratitude, to sacrifice any of our privileges, and, less than any other, that of expressing our opinion of the acts of his administration." With the British now in open retreat, Jackson's continued authoritarianism was neither appropriate nor acceptable.[31] The general's response to the editorial was both rigorous and rapid—two characteristics usually associated with military justice.

The editor of the newspaper was brought before Jackson and forced (it is not clear upon the threat of what penalty) to identify the author of the offending editorial. The critic in question was one Louis Louailler, who in addition to his proclivity with a pen was also a member of the Louisiana Legislature. Jackson ordered his arrest both for inciting a mutiny and for spying. In New Orleans, Louailler was picked up a couple of days later by a unit of troops, and apparently yelled to some observers that he was being kidnapped by armed men. A lawyer in the crowd offered his services, and rushed to the home of

[30] This section is based upon material originally presented at the 13th Homer Ferguson Conference on Military Justice in 1988, and later published in *Military Law Review* 126 (1989): 133–45.

[31] Burke Davis, *Old Hickory: A Life of Andrew Jackson* (1977), 155. Robert Remini, *Andrew Jackson and the Course of American Empire, 1767–1821* (1977), 310; hereafter cited as Remini.

Federal Judge Dominick A. Hall, who promptly issued a writ of habeas corpus, returnable in open court the next morning.[32] Jackson just as promptly ordered the judge arrested for "aiding, abetting and exciting mutiny within my camp."[33] The next day found Louailler not before Judge Hall, but rather locked in the same barracks with him; presumably not what the judge had envisaged in issuing the writ in the first place.

Jackson convened a court-martial to try Louailler. But the defendant challenged the authority of the court to try him at all, arguing that in fact he was neither a member of the army nor the militia.[34] As for the charge of spying, what spy would go to the trouble of making his views known through a newspaper column? The court dismissed the charges; whereupon Jackson dismissed the court, and commanded that Louailler be returned to prison.[35] Jackson,

[32] Dominick A. Hall was appointed Judge of the 5th U.S. Circuit Court in 1801 by President John Adams. He retired from that position one year later, when the act under which he had been appointed was repealed. However, at the behest of President Jefferson, in 1804 he returned to the bench when Congress created a district court for the territory of New Orleans. In 1813, he accepted appointment to the Louisiana Supreme Court; but within a year he sought reappointment to the federal bench. Since the vacancy created by his own resignation had not yet been filled, Hall became a federal judge reappointed to his own seat! He remained a federal judge until his death in New Orleans on December 19, 1820. See *Dictionary of American Biography*, 4: 123; *Biographical Dictionary of the Federal Judiciary*, ed. Chase, Krislov, Boyum and Clark (1976), 113.

[33] Remini, 310. Along with Judge Hall, Jackson apparently imprisoned the federal district attorney as well.

[34] Jackson's use of the court-martial in this case was understandable. However, it was far from clear if the Articles of War actually applied to a civilian such as Louailler. What Jackson needed was a military mechanism designed to deal with civilian offenses. By the eras of both the Mexican and Civil Wars, one had evolved—known as the military commission. Unlike a court-martial, a military commission was designed to focus on military wrongs committed by civilians. Many such tribunals functioned during the Civil War, the most famous probably was the panel convened to try the individuals accused of Lincoln's assassination. Military commissions will be discussed in the following chapter.

[35] Under existing rules of war, the verdict of a court-martial was not binding upon the commander, also known as the convening authority. He could, and sometimes did, order the court to "reconsider" its verdict, often indicating whether it was to be increased in severity. He could also disregard the verdict, if so inclined. Since the commander selected the members of the court in the first place, the potential for what is now known as "command influence" was self evident. In 1818, for example, while in Florida campaigning against the Seminole Indians, Jackson ordered the arrest and court-martial of two British subjects—Arbuthnot and Ambrister. According to Remini, Jackson believed that speedy trials and even speedier punishments were warranted. The entire procedure from court-martial to consummation of sentence took two days. The court ordered Arbuthnot to be hanged, and Ambrister to be shot; but at the request of at least one member, the officers reconsidered Ambrister's fate, and ultimately voted for "fifty lashes on the bare back, and confinement with ball and chain to hard labor for one year." Remini, 357–59. Jackson disregarded the recommendation, and ordered both executions. "These unprincipled villains," he later wrote to Secretary of War John Calhoun, "were legally convicted . . . legally condemned, and most justly executed for their iniquities." Their cases, he continued, presented scenes of "wickedness, corruption, and barbarity at which the heart sickens." Ibid.; *Correspon-*

himself a lawyer and a former judge, may well have hesitated over the matter of Judge Hall; for he never convened a court-martial to try the case. Instead he ordered Hall to be marched out of New Orleans "beyond the limits of my encampment to prevent you from a repetition of the improper conduct for which you have been arrested and confined."[36] One day later, on March 13, 1815, Jackson received official word of the peace treaty. He immediately revoked martial law, freed Louailler, and permitted Hall to return to the city. The judge's response was not long in coming. But for the moment, as had also been the case immediately after his initial military triumph two months earlier, Jackson was once again the city's hero; he had won the war and now heralded the peace.

In responding to laudatory remarks proffered by one group of soldiers, Jackson referred indirectly to the recent period of martial law. An extremely able politician, he fully realized the strong opposition that his measures had provoked. When constitutional rights were threatened by invasion, certain basic privileges "may be required to be infringed for their security. At such a crisis, we have only to determine whether we will suspend for a time, the exercise of the latter, that we may secure the permanent enjoyment of the former." Should the legal order sacrifice "the spirit of the laws to the letter," and thus "lose the substance forever, in order that we may, for an instant, preserve the shadow?"[37] Jackson had no doubt that "laws must sometimes be silent when necessity speaks."[38]

---

dence of Andrew Jackson, ed. John S. Bassett, vol. 2 (1927): 367. Hereafter cited as *Correspondence*.

[36] Ibid., 189.

[37] Here, Jackson echoed Jefferson, who only a few years before in 1810 had written much the same thing. Sup., n.29. Jefferson had added that the officer choosing to go beyond established authority took a very real risk. On the other hand, he might ultimately "throw himself on the justice of his country and the rectitude of his motives." Schlesinger, *War and the Constitution*, 11. In 1861, Chief Justice Roger Taney denounced the suspension of habeas corpus by President Lincoln. Later, in justifying his action to Congress, Lincoln sounded very much like Jackson. In the midst of the secession crisis, he asked, "are all the laws, but one, to go unexecuted, and the government itself go to pieces, lest that one be violated?" Lincoln, *Collected Works*, ed. R. Basler, vol. 4 (1953): 430. Although Judge Hall certainly suffered a loss of dignity, he was very lucky, compared to other members of the Maryland Judiciary during the war. One circuit judge, Richard Carmichael, "was arrested while conducting court at Easton, and when he refused to submit, was clubbed over the head with a revolver and dragged off the bench." Walker Lewis, *Without Fear of Favor* (1965), 452.

[38] Remini, 313. This scholar describes Jackson's argument as one that "can justify monstrous misdeeds as well as noble acts of patriotism." Remini is correct, as the course of American military justice amply demonstrates. Reliance on "military necessity" has been used to justify Lincoln's suspension of the writ of habeas corpus in 1861, questionable treatment of American soldiers in World War I, the exclusion of Japanese-Americans during World War II, to say nothing of more recent examples during the Vietnam War and its aftermath. The zeal of military commanders to carry out their mission is understandable. On the other hand, the role of the courts in this process is open to criticism. "Too often," according to the *New York University Law Review*,

On March 21, 1815, Judge Hall issued a show cause order for Jackson to appear before him, to explain why he should not be held in contempt of court for the Louailler incident.[39] Hall probably was determined to punish Jackson for the outrage perpetrated against this federal judge as much if not more than the treatment meted out to the unfortunate columnist-legislator. It would seem that in making himself judge, prosecutor, and jury in a matter involving, again, himself, Hall came perilously close to judicial indiscretion if not impropriety. At any rate, in response to the writ, Jackson appeared before the judge on March 24, accompanied by two attorneys and an admiring crowd of sympathetic spectators.[40]

Jackson's counsel immediately raised a number of legal objections to the entire proceeding. They ranged from the claim that while witnesses against Jackson had been summoned, yet no actual suit had been commenced—to the assertion that because Hall had not been in court when he issued the writ, none of Jackson's alleged contempts were offered in any cause or hearing *before* the said District Court—to the argument that Jackson's response might well require investigation of Hall's conduct, while martial law was in effect; a proceeding over which Hall could not preside "without violating one of the first and clearest maxims of all law."[41] The judge rejected all these challenges; whereupon Jackson sought to read a lengthy justification and explanation of his actions beginning prior to his imposition of martial law.

At this point, Hall temporized. He listed four conditions under which he would listen to Jackson's explanation:

> **1.** If Jackson denied the Court's jurisdiction.
>
> **2.** If Jackson denied the facts sworn to, or if he wished to show that these facts did not constitute a contempt.
>
> **3.** If Jackson wanted to show that under the Constitution and laws of the United

"courts have responded to announcements of military interests with supine deference rather than with a careful assessment of the legitimacy of those claims." Note: "Free Speech in the Military," *New York University Law Review* 53 (1978): 1123. The point will be discussed again in varying contexts, during the course of this study.

[39] The district attorney had urged Hall to cite Jackson immediately after the lifting of martial law. The judge preferred to wait, "stating that the laws would assert their majesty and supremacy in due time, but that, to celebrate the restoration of peace, a few days of public rejoicings should be allowed to pass by without any interruption of an unpleasant nature." Charles Gayarre, *History of Louisiana*, vol. 4 (1885): 616.

[40] According to Remini, one of this number sidled up to Jackson and whispered: "General, say the word and we pitch the judge and the bloody courthouse in the river." Jackson declined the offer, and turning to Judge Hall, who may well have observed the incident with some consternation, intoned "There is no danger here. . . . the same arm that protected from outrage this city . . . will shield and protect this court, or perish in the attempt." Of course, Hall had already received a personal example of Jackson's "protection"! Remini, 314.

[41] "Andrew Jackson and Judge D. A. Hall," *Louisiana Historical Quarterly* 5 (1922): 551–53; hereafter cited as *Jackson*.

States, or in [sic] virtue of his military commission, he had a right to act as charged.

4. If the answer contained "anything as an apology to this Court."[42]

Jackson appears to have made no direct response to these four conditions. His attorney, however, was permitted to begin reading the lengthy explanation. How far he got is not clear; but Hall, convinced at some point that the arguments essentially came down to military necessity alone as justification for Jackson's conduct, refused to hear the complete statement.[43] The case apparently was put off for one week.[44]

When the case came up again on March 31, the government attorney attributed Jackson's "arbitrary proceedings" not to "his conviction of their necessity," but rather to the "indulged infirmity of an obstinate and morbidly irascible temperament, and to the unyielding pride of a man naturally impatient of the least show of opposition to his will."[45] Again, Hall refused to hear Jackson's defense. Instead he asked the general to respond to nineteen specific interrogatories. Now it was Jackson's turn to refuse. He would not answer

[42] Augustus Buell, *History of Andrew Jackson*, vol. 2 (1904): 89–90. Hall seems to have thought through his four conditions carefully. There was little doubt that the Constitution as interpreted in 1815 indicated neither any conditions under which martial law might be imposed, nor who might impose it. He knew full well that Jackson in no way would deny what he had done, and he wanted to leave Jackson an opportunity to apologize in advance of any proceeding. Hall was certainly well aware of the claim that he was serving as judge of his own cause. He candidly admitted that one if not *the* justification for the contempt proceeding "is the imprisonment of the Judge, and the consequent obstruction of the cause of justice." He insisted, however, that the offense itself and *not* so much the judge against whom it was committed remained the important issue. "No personal considerations ought for an instant to induce a judge to abandon the defence of the laws, the support of the dignity of the tribunals, and the rights of his fellow citizens." *Jackson*, 546.

[43] Ibid. Had he listened to the entire explanation, it is doubtful that Hall would have been satisfied. Jackson insisted that "personal liberty cannot exist at a time when every man is required to become a soldier." Not even private property could be "secured when its use is indispensable for the public safety." Moreover, "unlimited freedom of speech is incompatible with the discipline of a camp." As to the alleged unconstitutionality of his actions, Jackson threw the claim right back against Judge Hall. He reminded the judge that the instant proceeding was a criminal prosecution for contempt; yet the Constitution "declares that in all criminal prosecutions the accused shall have the benefit of a trial by jury." Why was this not the case here? Because "courts could not, it is said, subsist without a power to punish promptly, by their own act, and not by the intervention of a jury." Refusing the more subtle method of letting his point pass by implication, Jackson spelled it out. "Necessity then, may in some cases, justify the breach of the Constitution; and if, in the doubtful case of avoiding confusion in a court, shall it be denied in the serious one of preserving a country from conquest and ruin?" As for an apology to the judge, the powers Jackson exercised "have saved the country; and whatever may be the opinion of that country, or the decrees of its courts, in relations to the means he has used, he can never regret that he employed them." Ibid., 560–61, 566–67.

[44] Remini, 314.

[45] Davis, *Old Hickory*, 156.

because the court "would not hear my defense," and thus Jackson awaited sentence "with nothing further to add." On the other hand, "as no opportunity has been furnished me to explain the reasons and motives which influenced my conduct, so it is expected that censure will form no part of that punishment which your Honor may imagine it your duty to perform."[46]

Hall responded with an equally dignified statement. Jackson's service to the country was obvious; a jail term was inappropriate.[47] But for this judge, described by one contemporary as "a magistrate of pure heart, clean hands, and a mind susceptible of no fear but that of God," the only question was "whether the Law should bend to the General or the General to the Law." For Hall, the answer was never in doubt; the most convincing evidence being his own experience. He found Jackson in contempt and fined him $1,000; a sum which the defendant promptly paid. Moreover, Jackson delivered a minidiscourse on civic obedience to the crowd which escorted him from the courtroom. "Considering obedience to the laws, even when we think them unjustly applied, as the first duty of the citizen, I did not hesitate to comply with the sentence you have heard, and I entreat you to remember the example I have given you of respectful submission to the administration of justice."[48]

Why did Jackson pay the fine? He never wavered in his belief that his treatment of Judge Hall was fully justified. Yet it was not in character for him to give in on what he considered an important matter of principle. Remini notes that the conflict had gone on too long, and that Jackson "was not prepared to defy Hall; [and also was] unwilling to blemish his victory with a quarrel he was certain to lose."[49] On the other hand, Jackson may have realized that he was not altogether blameless. After all, it was Jackson who earlier had refused to "render obedience to the laws," upon Hall's issuance of the writ.

Even the federal authorities in Washington took note of the Hall-Jackson incident. On April 12, the secretary of war informed Jackson that reports of his action "require immediate attention, not only in vindication of the just authority of the laws, but to rescue your own conduct from all unmerited reproach." Apparently, he continued, "the judicial power of the United States has been resisted, the liberty of the press has been suspended," and subjects of a friendly government "have been exposed to great inconvenience." At

[46] Remini, 314. Jackson's decision not to respond to the interrogatories apparently had been reached before the court reconvened. Two drafts of his statement to Judge Hall were later published. It is possibly indicative of Jackson's character that the one apparently *not* used contained the nearest thing to a Jacksonian apology. "I may have erred, but my motives cannot be misinterpreted. . . . The law can be satisfied without wounding my feelings." John S. Bassett, *The Life of Andrew Jackson* (1931), 224.

[47] "The Court said that it was becoming to manifest moderation in the punishment of the defendant for the want of it." Charles Gayarre, ibid., 625.

[48] Remini, 314–15; Bassett, *The Life of Andrew Jackson*, 227.

[49] Remini, 315.

this point, Secretary Dallas indicated awareness both of Jackson's reputation and his immense popularity.

"The President views the subject, in its present aspect, with surprize [sic] and solicitude; but in the absence of all information from yourself, relative to your conduct and the motives for your conduct, he abstains from any decision, or even the expression of Opinion, upon the case, in hopes that such explanations may be afforded, as will reconcile his sense of public duty with a continuance of the confidence, which he reposes in your judgement, discretion, and patriotism." In the meantime, "it is presumed that every extraordinary exertion of military authority has ceased." Finally, he stated President Madison's desire "that a conciliatory deportment may be observed towards the state authorities and the citizens of New Orleans."[50]

Jackson promptly sent the text of the explanation he had sought to submit, along with a vigorous denunciation of those who criticized his conduct. But neither Madison nor his cabinet, nor—upon reflection—even Jackson himself had any desire to keep the incident alive. Indeed, during an emotional visit to New Orleans in 1816, the judge and the general crossed paths again. Jackson savored the experience. "When he offered me his hand, I received it and in the gratification of my friends on this occasion my mind receives its reward and tells me I have done right. I have in some measure added peace to his bosom, tranquility to my own[,] and restored him to the social circle of his former friends. . . . On my part the hatchet is buried in oblivion.[51]

Had Jackson retired from the military and resumed his career as a Southern planter, his statement might have been accurate. But he went on to provoke further controversy concerning his military conduct in Florida, entered into national politics in 1824, and ultimately served two terms (1828–1836) as one of the most popular presidents in our history. Externally, with the exception of occasional references during political, partisan debate—the incident was buried in oblivion. Internally, it continued to rankle within Jackson's memory. But not until 1842, with the former president retired, in failing health and serious financial difficulties, did Congress review the episode.

In June of that year, Jackson's congressional supporters introduced a bill to remit the fine levied in 1815, plus accrued interest. They framed their proposal as a simple refund of a fine, without getting into the very controversial question concerning whether either Jackson or Hall or both had been justified in their actions. The proposal immediately fell victim to partisan wrangling. In December 1842, President John Tyler urged that the fine be refunded, again without "any reflection on the judicial tribunal which imposed" it. Tyler, one of our less distinguished presidents, in this case at least showed himself to be

[50] *Correspondence*, 2: 203–4.

[51] Ibid., 259.

well aware of the underlying issues concerning civilian authority over the military.

As Tyler wrote, "The voice of the civil authority was heard amidst the glitter of arms, and obeyed by those who held the sword." Conceding that Jackson had certainly not obeyed the initial issuance of the writ, Tyler still insisted that even "if the laws were offended, their majesty was fully vindicated." Concluding that a refund would be "gratifying to the war-worn veteran, now in retirement and in the winter of his days," he added that "if the civil law be violated from praiseworthy motives, or an overruling sense of public danger and public necessity, punishment may well be restrained within that limit which asserts and maintains the . . . subjection of the military to the civil power."[52]

Delayed by continued partisan bickering, the refund was finally approved early in 1844 by decisive votes, 30–16 in the Senate, 158–28 in the House.[53] From his plantation in Tennessee, the old general felt "truly gratified at the vote . . . reversing the fine imposed by that vindictive and corrupt Judge Hall."[54] On February 27, 1844, Jackson received a check from the Treasurer of the United States for $2,732.90.

From Jackson's point of view, the episode had a fitting and satisfying conclusion. Besides claiming long-delayed vindication for his action in 1815, there was the matter of money. In terms of financial remuneration, he got back more than double what he had paid to the court almost thirty years before. From the vantage point of hindsight in the area of American civilian-military policy, however, the results are less satisfying.

In the first place, the real issue—whether Jackson was justified in detaining Judge Hall and disobeying the writ—received no definitive resolution. To be sure, Hall himself must bear much responsibility for this fact. He refused to hear Jackson's explanation; a step difficult to justify, if only because hearing the statement would in no way have limited his future course of action from the bench. On the other hand, his conduct indicated that he never assumed that Jackson could be immune from a federal writ, or that a citizen could be denied due process by a general any more than by another government official. Jackson declined to appeal the decision, thus depriving a federal appellate tribunal of a great opportunity to explore this important question. Moreover, the ever-

[52] *Abridgment of the Debates of Congress* 14, 609. For his part, Jackson insisted that it was on the basis of "justice alone" that his claim rested. Ignoring his treatment of Hall, he focused instead on the conduct of the judge, claiming that he had "refused to hear my defense, thus depriving me of a constitutional right." *Correspondence*, 6: 155, 157.

[53] The Whigs, typified by John Quincy Adams, whose admiration for Jackson was less than excessive, persisted in their efforts to make political capital out of the inevitable. Adams urged that Congress not set a precedent of "pensioning off an ex president." Rather, Adams would "make up a subscription among the members of Congress to make a present to the old man in his last days." *Debates*, 638–39, 641.

[54] *Correspondence*, 6: 258.

present involvement of partisan interests in policy issues meant that the ultimate solution, remitting the fine with no mention of justification or assessment of responsibility, would be a political resolution in the context of Jacksonian politics.

Thus, it can be said that Jackson imprisoned a judge, defied a writ, and many years later was rewarded for it. Lincoln, who seems to have been much more sensitive to the nuances of military authority than Jackson, nevertheless followed his lead in 1861, when he ignored a writ issued by Chief Justice Roger B. Taney. While there is no way of assessing whether or not Jackson's actions had any specific effect on other judges, there is no doubt that in future cases involving questions of civilian-military jurisdiction, for the most part the bench was very careful not to contribute to a remake of the strange case of *United States v. Andrew Jackson*.[55]

Attention has focused thus far on two distinct modes of review; one within the military system, and the other consisting of some sort of civilian (either judicial or congressional) review of military justice decisions. Both center on the question, to what extent and by whom are such decisions reviewable? The first system, located within the armed services, remained virtually unchanged during the nineteenth century, continuing along the lines indicated in earlier sections of this chapter. In the area of review by civilian judges, however, the opportunity for change was obvious. Of course, Judge Hall would have reviewed Jackson's arrest and imprisonment of Louailler, had he been given the chance.

After 1815, the United States Supreme Court confronted the question of civilian-judicial control over the military. The justices had several opportunities to explore the claim that somehow military justice ought to be beyond *any* level of civilian review. Their efforts are discussed in the next chapter.

[55] An interesting variant to the Hall-Jackson episode occurred in Hawaii in 1943, when that territory was still under martial law. A federal judge determined to hear a petition for habeas corpus raised by two American citizens who were being held without trial by the army. Gen. Robert Richardson declined to appear, whereupon Judge Delbert Metzger ordered him held in contempt. Richardson responded with an order prohibiting Metzger from holding court, and subjected him to "trial by military commission, with a sentence for violation as long as five years at hard labor." At which point, federal officials in Washington intervened. Richardson revoked his order, Metzger lifted the citation for contempt, but fined the general $100 "to make his point." Later, President Roosevelt pardoned him. See the excellent study by Harry N. and Jane L. Scheiber, "Constitutional Liberty in World War II: Army Rule and Martial Law in Hawaii, 1941–1946," *Western Legal History* 3 (1990): 340–78, 366–67.

CHAPTER 2

Military and Civilian "Review" to 1900

BY THE mid nineteenth century, American military justice had become a routinized procedure, thus far at least separate from its civilian counterpart. This separation, however, was not a result of any articulated congressional intention, nor of any statute. Rather, it was due to the exigencies and logic of the military environment. The Articles of War provided for a self-contained system. But they were less than clear on the extent of civilian review in general, and civilian judicial review in particular; while there was *no* provision for any sort of appellate procedure.

Nor does much public attention seem to have been paid to these issues. Indeed, prior to the era of the Civil War, only two incidents involving military justice appear to have provoked any great public interest. The Jackson-Hall episode has already been discussed. Echoes of it were heard during the Civil War, as will be noted shortly. The other occurrence, the execution of Philip Spencer in December 1842, caused a sustained public debate concerning military justice within the United States Navy. Moreover, it led to at least one proposal for creation of an appellate tribunal to review important cases within the armed services.

The court-martial and execution at sea of three crew members on board the U.S. Navy Brig *Somers* might never have come to public attention at all, had it not been for the fact that one of the accused, Philip Spencer, happened to be the son of the secretary of war. Presumably, this latter individual was less than ecstatic when the *Somers* arrived in New York fifteen days after the executions, and Capt. Alexander S. Mackenzie reported concerning Spencer's fate. Outraged, John Spencer urged the navy to convene a court of inquiry. This proceeding concluded that Mackenzie had not acted improperly. In an effort to quiet the resulting controversy, Captain Mackenzie requested that a court-martial be held. Conducted on board a ship in New York Harbor from February to April 1843, this trial also resulted in an acquittal.[1]

[1] The specific details of the alleged "mutiny" need not concern us here. It suffices to note that Mackenzie believed that a mutiny was imminent, with Spencer as its ringleader. Mackenzie, described by one writer as a "sanctimonious, humorless, vain, moralistic, vacillating in time of crisis, and above all, vastly inhuman" individual was singularly ill-suited to command a naval training vessel. On the other hand, young Spencer—described by the same writer as a "lonely, defiant outcast of eighteen"—was as much if not more of a misfit. Obsessed with a love for secret

Officially, the verdict ended the incident. Yet, during 1843–1844 the episode received wide publicity, and there had been extensive commentary both private and public, especially from writers, as the proceedings took place.[2] Like many such observers, James Fenimore Cooper's initial reaction upon hearing that Mackenzie had put down a threatened mutiny by swift execution of the "culprits" was favorable. But after reading Mackenzie's lengthy report, the first account of what supposedly took place, and studying the statements of the witnesses, his view changed.

In 1843, Cooper's favorable reputation as a writer of native American fiction was widespread, especially in Europe. In his own country however, Cooper's criticism of contemporary American society had resulted in a lengthy and bitter feud with leading Whig editors and politicians. The son of a judge, he did not hesitate to sue his many critics for libel; and he seems to have won most if not all of his numerous court battles.[3] The *Somers* incident furnished another opportunity for the type of bitter public feud that Cooper apparently relished.[4] Much of what he contributed to the debate focused on proper legal procedure within the navy, hence its relevance here.

SPENCER AND SCANDAL ON THE *SOMERS*

Never before in American naval history had a captain returned from a voyage with the news that he had executed three members of his crew, and this for a

passwords and rituals, and apparently given to schemes of a "pathetic, juvenile bravura," this "maladjusted eighteen year old," somehow managed to convince the captain that he was scheming to take over the ship. See Frederic F. Van De Water, "Panic Rides the High Seas," *American Heritage* 12 (1961): 22–23.

[2] Among the well-known literary and/or political figures who wrote privately or publicly about the *Somers* incident were James Gordon Bennett; James Fenimore Cooper; Richard Henry Dana, Jr.; Evert Duyckinck; Horace Greeley; Francis Lieber; Henry Wadsworth Longfellow; Herman Melville; Theodore Sedgwick, Jr.; William H. Seward; Charles Sumner; and Thurlow Weed.

[3] Whig writers such as Horace Greeley and Thurlow Weed had all been involved in unpleasant litigation with Cooper. It may have been comments by James Watson Webb that resulted in yet another Cooper lawsuit against him. Webb apparently called the creator of Natty Bumpo "a base minded caitiff who has traduced his country for filthy lucre," a "slanderer [and] a traitor to national pride," the "viper so long nourished in our bosom." See Harrison Hayford, *The Somers Mutiny Affair* (1959), 77, hereafter cited as *Hayford*. This collection of primary sources about the incident remains the best single source of information concerning it.

[4] This point is important because it colored reaction to Cooper's comments about the mutiny. Moreover (as will be seen shortly), Mackenzie had his own cadre of supporters, some of whom were highly regarded literary or intellectual figures. Finally, when Cooper came to write about the *Somers* affair, he had already engaged in a public literary dispute with Mackenzie, who fancied himself a writer and naval historian as well as captain. This fact may explain why Cooper's detailed review of the case, published in 1844, while severely critical remained evenhanded in its conclusions, and free from the type of vituperation in which Cooper had indulged on previous occasions.

mutiny that never occurred. An early article published on December 20, 1842, and signed only with the letter "S," focused on certain disturbing elements of the case, as revealed by Mackenzie himself. The writer noted that the three crew members were arrested on a charge of intended mutiny. In fact, no actual occurrence of a mutinous nature appeared to have taken place during the entire voyage. Nevertheless, Captain Mackenzie convened a court of officers, who in turn recommended that the three be executed. At no time did the court hear from the accused; the prisoners were not allowed to confront any witnesses, nor "to procure any testimony in their own behalf"; nor, indeed, were they even informed that a "trial" was in progress. The writer emphasized that "the laws of Congress prescribing the navy regulations, forbid the taking of human life, even by the sentence of a court martial, before which all parties are heard, without the sanction of the president . . . or, if without the United States, of the commander of the fleet or squadron."[5]

Distinguished legal scholars such as Supreme Court Justice Joseph Story were quick to support Mackenzie. As the Court of Inquiry proceeded, Story's young assistant, Charles Sumner—later to succeed Daniel Webster as a member of the United States Senate—wrote that Story "had not the least doubt that Mackenzie was justified in the alternative he took. . . . The law does not compel a person to stand still till he actually sees the blow descending which is to take his life. He may anticipate it; and the justification will be found in the circumstances which created a reasonable ground of fear for his life."[6] Story probably based his conclusions on Mackenzie's account of the episode, a widely reprinted document written after the fact, full of self justification and pious self righteousness. Cooper, writing to his wife one day after Sumner's comments about Story, dismissed Mackenzie's report as a "medley of folly, conceit, illegality, feebleness and fanaticism."[7]

The Court of Inquiry lasted one month, concluding on January 28, 1843. It

[5] Hayford, 8–9.

[6] Story thought "the circumstances would form a complete defense for a homicide on shore, in the view of an enlightened civil tribune; [and] *a fortiori*, they would at sea, on shipboard, and under the stern laws of war." Hayford, 76.

[7] Ibid., 76. The *New York Herald* described Mackenzie's report as "a singular mixture of folly, silliness and blasphemy." Ibid., 68. Incredibly, Mackenzie admitted that he decided to execute Spencer because he was sure that Spencer's father would make such a step impossible, once the *Somers* had returned to the United States. The *New York Herald* noted "the bad taste in its style—the trivial incidents and horrid execution." The report "does not seem to be written by a human being, with the ordinary feelings of nature." Even those who supported Mackenzie's action, found the report damaging to his cause. Charles Sumner wrote an article in the *North American Review*, based largely on the assertion indicated by Story, that the captain was justified in his ultimate action, if in his judgment, it was necessary to save the ship. Theodore Sedgwick, Jr., a well-known attorney, wrote to Sumner that "we are all under obligations to you." He added that Mackenzie's report "was a diabolical document, and I hope your paragraphs will help to winnow Mackenzie's brain of the notion that he is a Lawyer as well as a Sailor and Historian." Ibid., 171–76.

became clear that fearing some sort of mutiny, Mackenzie had determined to hang the three prisoners as an example to the rest of the crew. Only *after* he had so decided, did he convene a council of officers, all of whom were younger than he and, obviously, subject to his command. Moreover, whatever Spencer had conjured up in his mind, if anything at all, never reached actuality. Somehow, according to the *New York Herald*, Spencer's love of secret ritual and his list of various crew members written in Greek, all combined to presage what Mackenzie saw as a mutiny. "It is probably the greatest farce, ending in an awful tragedy, that ever was enacted since the creation."[8]

But Mackenzie appeared to be guilty of far more than an urge to execute three sailors as quickly as possible. The "trial" was held in secret, with none of the defendants present at *any* time. This meant that any direct testimony from the people with the most to lose, or exercise of other essential due process procedures was impossible. Moreover, when the officers reported that they were unable to reach a verdict, the captain made it clear that he wished the accused to be convicted and sentenced to death. Thus, the convening authority, the only practical source for any sort of trial review, and the perpetrator for the worst sort of "command influence" were all one and the same individual! On February 24, the *New York Herald* concluded that far from demonstrating a mutiny, the *Somers* incident "discloses a tissue of barbarity, insolence, cowardice, farce and folly, that seems unparalleled in the history of human nature."[9]

The role of the navy in its conduct of the two proceedings was also improper. In the first place, during both the Court of Inquiry and the court-martial it permitted Mackenzie to remain in command of his crew. Thus, all witnesses to the events on board including, of course, all those who were to testify were under his control. Moreover, while Mackenzie was given the right to cross-examine every witness, he chose not to testify himself, thus escaping the burden of cross-examination. Instead, according to Frederic F. Van de Water, the navy permitted him "to present written explanations of the points raised by the timid, fusty little prosecutor." A quiet acquittal "became inevitable."[10] The entire episode, depending on one's viewpoint, demonstrated the best and the worst of the military justice system. It had provided Mackenzie, on board a small ship at sea, with a swift but flexible method of discipline. On the other hand, the treatment accorded the three accused was disgraceful; as was the

[8] Hayford, 110.

[9] Ibid., 131.

[10] Van de Water, "Panic Rides the High Seas," 98. The author adds that three days after the acquittal, one of the members of the original court-martial on board the *Somers* shot himself to death. As for the ship itself, three years later in 1846 it capsized during a storm and sank, taking to the bottom almost half of its current crew. Mackenzie went on to command another ship during the Mexican War, and died in 1848 with his dignity, if not his reputation, substantially intact.

apparent inability of the navy to find anything improper with Mackenzie's conduct.

Cooper avoided public commentary until after the court-martial adjourned. But in private, he expressed outrage at the proceedings. Mackenzie, he fumed to one correspondent, "reverses the maxim of the Common Law, which says that if there be a doubt of guilt, the prisoner is to have its benefits; he reasons, if there be a doubt of his innocence, hang him."[11] Moreover, where was the supposed threat of mutiny? Not from the crew who indeed "were so obedient as to hang men contrary to law."[12] Cooper believed that "it is a stain on the American character that a transaction of this nature should be treated as this has been. Three lives were taken without legal process in any form, or manner." Anything, he insisted, was "better than hanging men without trial."[13]

By December 1843, Cooper had finished reviewing the entire transcripts of the case. With his discovery that Mackenzie had first decided to execute the prisoners, and had then convened a council, Cooper concluded that "a serious mutiny now became necessary to escape ridicule." Nothing, he wrote, "is plainer to me than the fact that the testimony was got up as it was wanted."[14] In 1844, his eighty-page analysis of the entire case appeared as part of the published transcript.[15]

Cooper believed that Mackenzie's conduct, and that of the navy in refusing to punish him, represented a serious challenge to the American legal system. "Here is an officer . . . who has used his authority . . . to take the lives of three of his subordinates without a trial—by his own account of the matter, without a hearing—without any overt act of mutiny, violence, or resistance even in the gasp of death." If "the name of an American citizen cannot be a warranty that life will not be taken without the accusation, hearing and condemnation, required by the law, of what use are our boasted rights?" If an American, in this case a member of the crew, "is not assured of this privilege on board an American ship-of-war, which exists only to defend those sacred rights on the ocean, where can he be assured of its exercise at all?"[16] As for

[11] *Letters and Journals of James Fenimore Cooper*, ed. James F. Beard, vol. 4 (1964): 358.

[12] Ibid., 359.

[13] Ibid., 405, 360.

[14] Ibid., 429, 430.

[15] Cooper's motives for agreeing to write the lengthy analysis are unclear. Perhaps he felt a sympathy for Spencer, whose background was in some instances similar to his own. Like Spencer, Cooper had been forced to leave college; like him also, he had gone to sea, and he too possessed an active imagination. On the other hand, Cooper had definite views on the role of law and governmental power in Jacksonian America. It may well have seemed to him that the *Somers* affair was a dramatic abuse of both. He may also have desired to renew his feud with Mackenzie. Whatever the motivation, the final result was impressive. The piece was accurately described by Cooper's biographer as "a masterpiece of quiet sanity." James Grossman, *James Fenimore Cooper* (1949), 190.

[16] *Proceedings of the Naval Court Martial in the case of Alexander Slidell Mackenzie* (1844), 266. Cooper's review may be found on pp. 263–344.

the council of junior officers convened by the captain *after* he had decided upon executions, "were it not for the fearful consequences, they could meet with nothing but pity and contempt from every legal mind on earth."[17]

Cooper was also outraged by the fact that Mackenzie had not conceived of any alternatives to immediate execution, even though a number of options were readily available. These ranged from keeping the three prisoners in irons until the return to the United States, to stopping at a nearby port and requesting assistance. For Cooper, the incident reflected more upon the weaknesses in command leadership than on mutinous elements within the crew.

Some observers doubtless agreed with Mackenzie, that a strong showing of discipline was very appropriate on board a navy ship. Here Cooper had some trenchant comments on the relationship between discipline and military justice. "Discipline," he wrote, "is the result of the authority exercised, in the name of the state, by the few over the many. Its entire virtue exists in its legality, without which it can have no salutary or permanent existence. . . . The essence of all discipline in this country, is strict legality."[18] In short, military discipline and military justice were two sides of the same coin; if the latter was flawed, so too would be the former—to the extent of the imperfection.[19]

Cooper found no justification for Mackenzie's flagrant abuse of due process. If there was such an urgent need for action, why did he permit seven officers to deliberate all day, instead of remaining at their stations? Furthermore, Mackenzie had an obligation to "ascertain not the guilt merely, but the guilt or innocence of the men executed. This . . . could not be done, without giving the party implicated a hearing. In our view of the matter, the violation of justice connected with a departure from this sacred principle, is of more importance to the country, than the preservation of a dozen brigs."[20]

Cooper hoped that "one good effect, at least, will result from this affair. The trial of cases like this, should at once be put exclusively, except in those beyond the reach of the tribunals, into the hands of the civil courts." "Military men," he added, "are not qualified, as a rule, for such investigation. . . . The result of this very case shows how professional men can differ, leaving the strong probability that professional prejudices had more to do with some of their votes, than professional knowledge."[21]

[17] Ibid., 324. The *Somers* incident "leaves a blot on [the American] system of jurisprudence."

[18] Ibid., 330. Cooper added that Mackenzie had clearly misunderstood his situation and his duty. Recollections of the incident would linger. "It will take years to eradicate the injurious influence it must have on the minds of the seamen of the country." Ibid., 331.

[19] As later chapters of this study will indicate, perceptive military commanders have echoed Cooper's views down to the present day.

[20] Ibid., 331. "It is striking at the root of all right, and setting a precedent, which, if sustained and followed, would destroy the social compact."

[21] Ibid., 336. Cooper went on to describe Spencer as a youth of nineteen, ironed hands and feet, whose conversations were reported "to a secret conclave, that only waited for testimony to

1. Currier-Ives lithograph of the USS *Somers*. This contemporary print (c. 1843) is unusual in that it only shows two of the three crew members executed by Capt. Alexander Mackenzie hanging from a yardarm. (Published with permission of the Museum of the City of New York.)

Finally, Cooper noted Mackenzie's insistence that he sought merely to save the ship, his own life, and those of his associates. Perhaps, "but the mental obliquity, so very obvious throughout the whole affair, renders any ordinary analysis of human motives exceedingly precarious. God alone can say how far any selfish feeling was mixed up with the mistakes of this terrible transaction. The act was, unquestionably, one of high moral courage, one of the basest cowardice, one of deep guilt, or one of lamentable deficiency of judgment."[22]

There seemed to be four essential conclusions to Cooper's exhaustive critique: (*a*) civil tribunals were more knowledgeable and, hence, preferable to military courts; (*b*) in certain military cases (Cooper did not define the criteria—but clearly he felt this case to be appropriate) there should be a role for a civil court; (*c*) that the command influence exercised by Mackenzie violated fundamental law; and (*d*) that the navy officials were culpable for not acting responsibly in the subsequent proceedings. Thus, Cooper saw no incompatibility between civilian appellate review for military justice. He also believed that the better the quality of military justice, the better would be the quality of the soldiers and sailors subject to it.

No immediate results can be attributed to his points. As Cooper's own experiences indicated, the *Somers* incident seemed of greater interest to the pamphleteers rather than policymakers.[23] But his views should be kept in mind. In various guises they would be heard again and again, especially in the years following World War I. Today, as later chapters will indicate, even with a civil court of military appeals well established, the issue of command influence continues to trouble military justice.

On the other hand, Cooper may not have been totally fair to the navy. Indeed, the members of the court were less than impressed with the captain's conduct. The verdict of his court-martial was "not proven," rather than "not guilty." Writing in 1886, William Winthrop noted that such a verdict "because of its ambiguity, can hardly fail to have a sinister and injurious effect upon the reputation of the accused."[24] Although Mackenzie was thus acquitted on charges of abuse of authority as well as murder, Winthrop also indicated that his conduct had been less than appropriate. For the suppression of a mutiny, a commander will ordinarily not be justified in "using a deadly weapon and taking life in a case of mutiny unaccompanied by violence or where less

pronounce its doom, and to obtain the concurrence of a commander who had drawn up the programme of the executions, hours before that doom was rendered! We only hope that those who boast of American Justice, and who delight to put it in brilliant contrast with that of other lands, will sometimes recall these facts, in connexion [sic] with the results of this trial." Ibid., 339.

[22] Ibid., 344.

[23] In fact, the episode may well have been instrumental in the founding of the United States Naval Academy at Annapolis; an event that resulted in the removal of young midshipmen from possible mistreatment by commanders at sea, typified by Mackenzie.

[24] Winthrop, 380.

vehement methods will be entirely effectual." The force to be applied depended upon the exigencies of the case, "particularly upon the existing status whether of war or peace."[25] Means, concluded Winthrop "which in war . . . would not only be justified but laudable, might in peace be without warrant and criminal, and commanding officers, in employing them, might become liable, for abuse of authority, not only to trial by court martial but to indictment in a civil tribunal."[26]

MILITARY JUSTICE, 1858–1864

In theory, of course, executive and legislative branches of our government control the military establishment. Civilian control was a well-established and accepted doctrine by the mid nineteenth century. But did it apply to civilian legal review of military justice decisions? To put it another way, did a civil appellate court have jurisdiction over military courts? This issue seems not to have been formally litigated until 1858. While there appeared to be no reason to doubt that in theory federal courts, and the United States Supreme Court in particular, could exercise such authority, the Constitution was silent on the question; and Congress, beyond its adoption of the Articles of War and the Act to Govern the Navy had not clarified the issue. Moreover, the special mission of the military pointed toward an independent system of military justice, but incidents such as the *Somers* case made it clear that some sort of appellate review was necessary.

In 1858, the United States Supreme Court decided the case of *Dynes v. Hoover* (20 How. 65). It may well have been the first case before the Court that involved an actual member of the armed forces, as opposed to a civilian in trouble with military authorities. As such it offered the justices a good opportunity to clarify the parameters of military and civilian judicial jurisdiction.

In 1854, the plaintiff was charged with desertion from the navy. A court-martial found him guilty of "attempting to desert," instead of the original charge. Sentenced to imprisonment, he filed suit on the grounds that the navy court-martial had no jurisdiction to try him for this offense. His counsel argued that the guilty verdict was for an offense for which Dynes had not been originally charged. Furthermore, the rules to govern the navy did not list "attempting to desert" as "an offense within the cognizance of a naval court martial."

[25] More at home with his fantasies, secret passwords, and rituals (in fact, he had been one of the founders of the Chi Psi fraternity) than with a military lifestyle, Spencer chose the wrong time, place, and commanding officer for his "games." No evidence that he had used or even contemplated using force was presented; nor can it be argued that the United States was in any way at war in 1842.

[26] Winthrop, 586. The primary mission of the *Somers* appears to have been a training voyage for its young crew; the majority of whom were teenagers.

Since the court was without authority, the resulting verdict and sentence were null and void.[27]

On behalf of the government, Attorney General Caleb Cushing conceded that "attempting to desert" was not included among the specific offenses forbidden by the statute. But the point was irrelevant. Section 32 provided that "all crimes committed by persons belonging to the navy which are not specified in the foregoing articles, shall be punished according to the laws and customs in such cases at sea."[28] Moreover, Cushing insisted that the decisions of a court-martial, when within its jurisdiction—as was clearly the case here—could not be reviewed by the Supreme Court.[29]

The United States Supreme Court heard the case on January 8, 1858, and handed down its decision on February 1. By a vote of 8–1, with no formal dissent submitted, the justices upheld contentions put forward by the federal government. Justice James Wayne readily conceded that lack of jurisdiction voided a court's action, including a military court.[30] But in *this* case, there was no evidence that the navy had not followed proper procedure; moreover, the verdict had been confirmed by the secretary of the navy. Thus, there could be no doubt in this case about appropriate jurisdiction. A court-martial verdict "when confirmed . . . is altogether beyond the jurisdiction or inquiry of any civil tribunal whatever."

Hence, "with the sentences of courts-martial which have been convened regularly, and have proceeded legally, and by which punishments are directed, not forbidden by law, or which are according to the laws and customs of the sea, civil courts have nothing to do, nor are they in any way alterable by them." Wayne was equally emphatic as to the vague language of article 32. "Not withstanding the apparent indeterminateness of such a provision, it is not liable to abuse; for what those crimes are, and how they are to be punished, is well known by practical men in the navy and army, and by those who have studied the law of courts-martial. . . ."[31] To an observer of the 1980s,

[27] *Dynes v. Hoover*, 20 How. 65 (1854); 15 L. ed. 839–40.

[28] Ibid., 841. The army version of this "catchall" provision has been discussed above in chapter 1.

[29] "Whether they exercise [jurisdiction] wisely or erroneously while they keep within [it], is not the subject of review by other courts." Cushing cited no legal authority for this point. He added that "the question of punishments authorized by the laws and customs of sea, is one purely of fact. Such customs and laws are not written in books, but exist as matters of fact resting in tradition and practice. This court cannot know them as a matter of law, and certainly not as a matter of fact." Ibid., 842. Again, Cushing did not find it necessary to list any citation in support of his claim.

[30] Ibid., 843–44 Wayne added that "Congress has the power to provide for the trial and punishment of military and naval offenses, . . . and the power to do so is given without any connection between it and the 3rd article of the Constitution defining the judicial power of the United States; indeed that the two powers are entirely independent of each other."

[31] Ibid., 845.

this statement verges on the preposterous. Indeed, there can be little doubt that even in 1858 the justices were well aware that abuses of discretionary authority by military officials did occur. How then, can Wayne's statement—of both fact and law—that "it is not liable to abuse" be explained?

In part the answer may lie in the fact that pre–Civil War jurisprudence took a much narrower view of what is today called "due process" than would be true in the twentieth century, especially for the military. Also, historical practice, as the above pages have indicated, resulted in a military justice system isolated from civil influence. Whether this was intentional or not, and there is virtually no evidence that it was, becomes irrelevant. To find for plaintiff in this case would make the civil courts "virtually administer the Rules and Articles of War, irrespective of those to whom that duty and obligation has been confided by the laws of the United States, from whose decisions no appeal or jurisdiction of any kind has been given to the civil magistrate or civil courts."[32]

The decision was almost unanimous, and the view that his brethren readily accepted Wayne's conclusions is strengthened by the fact that the court handed down its opinion less than a month after oral argument. One can accept the claim that in adopting statutes such as the Articles of War, Congress did intend to create a military justice system apart from civil interaction. But it by no means follows from this premise that there was to be absolutely no civilian appellate review of any sort within the military. Nevertheless, *Dynes v. Hoover* remains a landmark holding in American military jurisprudence.

For more than a century, in cases involving a member of the armed forces it was frequently cited as legal support for blocking any meaningful civilian judicial supervision over military justice.[33] Perhaps this sweeping endorsement of military judicial discretion reflected an idea that while in its application principles were preferable, reality required that law be practical and practicable. That the case may well have been based upon a congressional intent possibly apparent but probably unarticulated, seems not to have diminished its appeal. Within the purview of the military, those who claim that the quality of military justice has suffered from such independence, might find a paraphrase of a well-known latin epitaph very appropriate: *Si monumentum requiris, circumspire*. "If you seek its monument, look around."

For better or worse, *Dynes* appeared to bar civilian judicial intervention in a court-martial involving a member of the armed forces. But what if the accused was a civilian, who had no military connection whatsoever? This ques-

[32] Ibid.

[33] The influence of the *Dynes* decision began to wane with the adoption of the UCMJ in 1950. It still occasionally appears in Supreme Court decisions; almost invariably cited by those in opposition to court intervention concerning military justice. See *Parker v. Levy*, 417 U.S. 733, 747 (1974), and *Schlesinger v. Councilman*, 420 U.S. 738, 747 (1975). Both cases resulted in split decisions, with the majority refusing to become involved with the military justice system.

tion arose five years later in 1863. Involving action by President Lincoln, as well as an appeal to the Supreme Court, the case of *Ex Parte Vallandigham*, 1 Wall., 243, can be described as an apt illustration of the American tendency for constitutional law sometimes to reflect an intriguing amalgam of principles and expediency.

The case began in May 1863, when Clement Vallandigham, an Ohio antiwar politician and former congressman running for the Democratic gubernatorial nomination, spoke at a political rally. He declared among other things that the war "was wicked, cruel, and unnecessary," that it was being fought for the "freedom of the blacks and the enslavement of the whites," for the "purpose of crushing out liberty and to erect a despotism." Promptly arrested by army authorities, upon the order of General Burnside, Vallandigham was tried, convicted, and sentenced to prison by a military commission.[34] Very concerned about the effect that the case might have at a critical point in the war, and assuming that Vallandigham's next move would be to seek intervention in federal court, Lincoln seriously considered issuing a special suspension of habeas corpus. However, after receiving assurances from Salmon Chase, his secretary of the treasury who also was extremely well versed in Ohio politics, that Vallandigham's efforts to seek a writ of habeas corpus would probably fail, as indeed they did, Lincoln took a different course. He ordered that instead of being imprisoned for the remainder of the war, as had been the sentence of the military commission, Vallandigham should be transported behind enemy lines and released from custody.[35]

The case aroused much interest in the North, especially among conservative Democrats who supported the Union, but not the inevitable expansion of federal authority engendered by the war effort. Thus on May 16, a group of Albany Democrats led by a local manufacturer, Erastus Corning, forwarded a number of resolutions to Lincoln. They denounced "the recent assumption of a military commander to seize and try a citizen of Ohio . . . for no other reason

[34] Ambrose Burnside was a mediocre Union general whose inability to lead the Army of the Potomac resulted in a transfer to "the Department of the Ohio," where it was hoped that his apparent incompetence would be less detrimental to the war effort. Without consulting Lincoln, he moved to arrest one of the most outspoken Democratic critics of the war. As Charles Fairman noted, "his poor judgment created a situation where . . . Lincoln had either to disavow Burnside and encourage Vallandigham, or defend a measure which he regretted and take the blame for invading civil liberties." See Charles Fairman, "The Law of Martial Rule and the National Emergency," *Harvard Law Review* 55 (1942): 1283–84.

[35] As commander in chief, Lincoln frequently reduced or changed penalties handed down by military tribunals. His treatment of Vallandigham was a variation on an important theme—maintaining the Union without destroying individual liberty; understanding, unlike Daniel Webster who eloquently spoke in 1850 of "liberty *and* Union," that when push came to shove, the Union would be first. Later commenting on Lincoln's "balancing" skills, his former law partner William Herndon noted the policy whereby the president "would keep them in prison a while to keep them from killing the Government." Fairman, "The Law of Martial Rule," 1284.

than words addressed to a public meeting, in criticism of the course of the Administration." The signers expected Lincoln "to be true to the Constitution, and [to] maintain the rights of the States and the liberties of the Union."[36] Lincoln assured the group that he would "give the resolutions the consideration you ask." In the meantime, possibly with unintentional understatement, Burnside telegraphed Lincoln that he had heard that "my action here has been a source of embarrassment to you," and that it "was not approved by a single member of your Cabinet."[37] Lincoln, possibly with intentional understatement, responded that "all the cabinet regretted the necessity for arresting, for instance, Vallandigham, some perhaps, doubting, that there was a real necessity for it—but being done, all were for seeing you through with it."[38]

As will be seen shortly, Vallandigham did not abandon his efforts to gain relief in federal court. In the meantime, on June 12, Lincoln replied to the Corning resolutions. He reminded the Albany malcontents that Vallandigham had been trying "to prevent the raising of troops, to encourage desertions from the army, and to leave the rebellion [Union] without an adequate military force to suppress it." Well aware of the realities of war, he insisted that the prisoner had been arrested not for "damaging the political prospects" of Lincoln's administration, but "because he was damaging the army, upon the existence, and vigor of which, the life of the nation depends. He was warring upon the military; and this gave the military jurisdiction to lay hands upon him." Long experience, he added, has shown that "armies cannot be maintained unless desertion shall be punished by the severe penalty of death. . . . Must I shoot a simple-minded soldier boy who deserts, while I must not touch a hair of a wily agitator who induces him to desert?"[39]

Lincoln then summarized the Jackson-Hall controversy of 1815. He noted, "First, that we had the same constitution then, as now. Secondly, that we then had a case of invasion, and that now we have a case of rebellion, and thirdly, that the permanent right of the people to public discussion, the liberty of speech and the press, the trial by jury, the law of evidence, and the habeas corpus, suffered no detriment whatever by that conduct of Gen. Jackson, or its subsequent approval by the American Congress." Lincoln added that quite possibly he might not have arrested Vallandigham, but that as a general rule, "the commander in the field is the better judge of the necessity in any particular case. Of course I must practice a general directory and revisory power in the matter."[40] As to this prisoner, "I have to say it gave me pain when I

[36] Abraham Lincoln, *Collected Works*, ed. Roy Basler, vol. 6 (1953): 235.

[37] Ibid., 237. Burnside added that "I should be glad to be relieved if the interest of the public service requires it."

[38] Ibid.

[39] Ibid., 266.

[40] Given the state of civil war, it is not surprising that Lincoln reviewed more cases involving military justice than any of his predecessors.

learned that [he] had been arrested,—that is, I was pained that there should have seemed to be a necessity for arresting him."[41]

Although he had been placed behind enemy lines in accord with Lincoln's instructions, and although the Ohio Federal District Court denied him relief—Vallandigham sought a writ of certiorari from the United States Supreme Court as the first step toward his real goal, the writ of habeas corpus. He was represented by the same attorney who had unsuccessfully argued Dynes' case in 1858. There were, however, two important differences between the earlier litigation and Vallandigham's suit. First, he was a civilian with no connection to the military; and second, he had been tried not by court-martial, but rather by military commission.

The military commission was a quasi-judicial military tribunal that differed from a court-martial in that it could deal with civilians accused of criminal acts in time of war. A court-martial, on the other hand, was restricted to dealing with members of the military "and to specific offenses defined in a written code, such as the Articles of War."[42] Both, however, were composed solely of military officers. It was not at all clear in 1864 to what extent, if at all, a military commission had jurisdiction over a civilian, especially in the absence of a declaration of martial law. Vallandigham's case thus offered the Court a good opportunity to clarify an extremely important issue in civilian-military jurisprudence.

It would have been reasonable for the Court to make allowance for the commission's conduct, pointing to the claim that survival of the national government was at stake, and to the fact that the incident took place during the bloodiest war thus far fought in American history. Or, the justices could have attempted some sort of balancing test, trying as Lincoln often did to reconcile the needs of the war with individual liberty. Instead, Justice Wayne reiterated essentially what he had written in *Dynes*, this time for a unanimous bench.

He concluded that a military commission was *not* in fact a court; therefore it was not one of those inferior tribunals over which the Constitution gave the Supreme Court appellate review. Thus, no writ could issue because the Court had no jurisdiction over a military commission. Wayne even admitted that a military commission was exactly like a court in that it had a "discretion to examine, to decide and sentence." Nonetheless, it exercised a "special authority" not reviewable by civilian courts.[43]

It is possible to view the Vallandigham case as being more an exercise in judicial avoidance than sound jurisprudence. Yet, one can understand why the Supreme Court would choose not to confront the United States Army in 1864

[41] Ibid., 269. The excerpts discussed above do not do justice to the astute political realism tempered by a skillful legal sense of the possible that Lincoln demonstrated in this document. It should be read in its entirety.

[42] Winthrop, 831.

[43] *Ex Parte Vallandigham*, 1. Wall., 243 (1864), 243–54.

over treatment of a notorious Ohio malcontent, all the more as Lincoln had already taken final action in the case.[44] On the other hand, by using lack of jurisdiction as the basis for his decision Wayne avoided the much more difficult question of a military commission's applicability to a civilian accused of a nonmilitary offense. He also reinforced a key assumption of *Dynes*, that military tribunals were totally separate from civil courts. Still, the underlying issues raised in the case may well have troubled lawyers in a society where the military had never been dominant. Two years after *Vallandigham*, the Court decided a similar dispute, this time with what appeared to be very different results.

MURDER AND *MILLIGAN*, 1865–1866

Law, and thus legal history, tend to be a responsive rather than an innovative mechanism. It normally reacts to external forces and stimuli such as legislation or public opinion. The famous maxim that "the Supreme Court follows the election returns" may not be phrased in elegant, scholarly prose; yet it remains accurate. The 1866 decision about military commissions can be considered as an excellent example of its validity. From April to August 1865, there seems to have been a good deal of public comment on military commissions and authority over civilians. The cause for such interest was the treatment given the eight individuals accused of conspiracy in the assassination of Abraham Lincoln.

The question of what type of trial the seven men and one woman should receive was raised late in April, shortly after Lincoln's assassin, John Wilkes Booth, had been killed. At least two members of the cabinet, Secretary of War Edwin Stanton and Attorney General James Speed, urged Andrew Johnson to convene a military commission. At this time, there were several other trials of civilians before such commissions in varying stages of completion. Also, use of these tribunals had been common during the war.[45] Finally, the Supreme Court had specifically declined to enjoin their use.

On the other hand, the civil courts in Washington were open and functioning; and there could be no doubt that for the Southeast, the war had ended. Newspaper commentary reflected a basic mistrust of military commissions. They tended, as one writer put it, to be composed "of officers too worthless for field service, ordered to try, and organized to convict."[46] Navy Secretary

[44] See the standard biography of Vallandigham by Frank L. Klement, *The Limits of Dissent: Clement L. Vallandigham and the Civil War* (1970).

[45] Thomas R. Turner, *Beware the People Weeping; Public Opinion and the Assassination of Abraham Lincoln* (1982), 139.

[46] Ibid., 141. See pp. 138–54 for a summary of contemporary opinion both private and public concerning the merits of trial by military commission instead of a civilian court.

Gideon Welles believed that Attorney General Speed had originally favored a civilian trial for the eight prisoners, but that Stanton had "persuaded" him otherwise.[47] Welles also strongly objected to a secret trial, and indeed, after only a few days of closed sessions, public pressure ultimately forced the authorities to make the proceedings public.

What legal advice Speed offered President Johnson was not made public until *after* the proceedings were over, and four of the accused had been executed.[48] The trial of the "conspirators" was controversial at best. In one instance, the commission accepted testimony from a witness whom the prosecutors knew had perjured himself.[49] Moreover, the defendants were not allowed to testify in their own defense; and while this was still common policy in state civilian criminal cases, it was *not* usual practice in court-martials. Most important for this study, however, was the argument presented by defense counsel Reverdy Johnson against the jurisdiction of a military commission.[50]

Johnson took it for granted that the Constitution empowered only Congress to enact rules for governing the armed forces. He cited no less an authority than the late Supreme Court Justice Joseph Story who had written "since otherwise, summary and severe punishments might be inflicted as the mere will of the Executive." Furthermore, "citizens not belonging to the army or navy were not made liable to military law, or under any circumstances to be de-

[47] *Diary of Gideon Welles*, vol. 2 (1911), 303. Edward Bates, Speed's immediate predecessor as attorney general, also believed that Stanton and Secretary of State William Seward had influenced Speed concerning a trial by military commission. "He was caressed and courted by Stanton and Seward, and sank under the weight of their blandishments, into a mere tool. . . . Tho' my indignation rises at seeing the corruption and degradation of the *Law Department* [sic] of the Government, I cannot help pitying my poor imbecile successor!" *The Diary of Edward Bates*, ed. by Howard Beale, in *Annual Reports of the American Historical Association* 4 (1930): 483.

[48] In his diary entry for May 25, 1865, Bates noted, "I am pained to believe that my successor . . . has been wheedled out of an *opinion*, to the effect that such a trial is lawful. If he be, in the lowest degree, qualified for his office, he must know better." Bates considered such a trial "not only unlawful, but it is a gross blunder in policy: It denies the great, fundamental principle, that ours is a government of *Law*." He predicted that "if the offenders be done to death by that tribunal, however truly guilty, they will pass for martyrs with half the world." Ibid. Bates was not the only lawyer critical of Speed's legal acumen. In March 1866, United States Supreme Court Justice Samuel Miller wrote privately about Speed's "utter want of ability as a lawyer—He is certainly one of the feeblest men who has addressed the Court this term." Charles Fairman, *Reconstruction and Reunion, 1864–88*, part I (1971), 201.

[49] Benn Pitman, *The Assassination of President Lincoln and the Trial of the Conspirators*, introduction by Philip van Doren Stern (1954), xx.

[50] Reverdy Johnson (1796–1876) was one of the most distinguished constitutional lawyers of the period. Active in Maryland politics, he strongly supported the Union cause. As a Democrat, however, he opposed many of Lincoln's policies, and thus was not held in high esteem by the Republicans around the president. "Repeatedly he used his eloquence against arbitrary imprisonment and other violations of personal liberty." *Dictionary of American Biography*, 5: 114. His role in the Lincoln Conspirators Trial was limited to an argument against the jurisdiction of a military commission.

prived of any of the guarantees of personal liberty provided by the Constitution."[51] Since there was no proof at all that any of the accused were members of the armed forces, he questioned the authority of military commissions to try civilians. Finally, he denied that martial law provided any justification for such a trial. This condition, he argued, was not in effect in Washington. "It has never been declared by any *competent* authority, and the civil courts we know are in the full and undisturbed exercise of all their functions."[52]

Johnson's argument was submitted to the commission in June 1865, after the prosecution had concluded its case. A lawyer for Dr. Samuel Mudd, the physician who had tended to Booth's broken ankle, also argued against military jurisdiction. Thomas Ewing, Jr., reiterated many of Johnson's points. And with some courage, given the atmosphere surrounding the trial, he urged that the commission be cautious. "If you believe you possess the power of life and death over the citizens of the United States . . . where the regular tribunals can be safely appealed to, still, for the sake of our common country . . . do not press that power too far. Our judicial tribunals, at some future date . . . will be again in the full exercise of their constituted powers, and may think, as a large proportion of the legal profession think now, that your jurisdiction in these cases is an unwarranted assumption."[53]

After the trial had ended, and four of the prisoners had been put to death, Attorney General Speed finally published his opinion, explaining why he believed that "the conspirators not only may but ought to be tried by a military tribunal."[54] He started with the premise that Congress could neither in a time of war nor peace "create military tribunals for the adjudication of offenses committed by persons not engaged in, or belonging to [the armed] forces." Indeed, "this is a proposition too plain for argument."[55] But Speed insisted that Congress had ample authority under *another* clause of the Constitution to create such judicial bodies. He found it in the clause "Congress shall have

[51] Pitman, *The Assassination of President Lincoln*, 252. Congress could "make rules for the government and regulation of the land and naval forces." Johnson insisted that "no artifice of ingenuity can make these words include those who do not belong to the army and navy."

[52] Ibid., 261. Johnson also insisted that the suspension of habeas corpus in no way implied the imposition of martial law. Unlike many of his Democratic colleagues, Johnson conceded the right of the president to suspend the writ. It made no difference to the accused in *this* case. "In what court he is to be tried, how he is to be tried, what evidence is to be admitted, and what judgments pronounced are all to be what the Constitution secures," 257.

[53] Ibid., 266. Here, Ewing demonstrated greater success as a legal prophet than a legal proponent. The commission found all the accused guilty, and sentenced four of them—including Mary Surratt—to be executed. The sentences were carried out on July 7, 1865.

[54] The timing of Speed's opinion did not escape the notice of Edward Bates, who wrote in his diary that "this opinion is . . . dated *after* the sentence, and in fact, after the execution of the accused. . . . ! And thus, it is apparent that the opinion was gotten up (a mere fetch of the War Office) to bolster up a jurisdiction, *after the fact*, so generally denounced, by lawyers and by the respectable press, all over the country." Bates, *Diary*, 499.

[55] *Official Opinions of the Attorneys General* 11 (1869): 298.

power to define and punish piracies and felonies committed on the high seas, *and offences against the laws of nations*.'' (Emphasis added.) Since ''the laws of war constitute much the greater part of the law of nations,'' one ''must look to the usage of nations to ascertain the powers conferred in war.''[56]

Next, the attorney general distinguished between two categories of enemies, one being ''open, active participants in hostilities, [such] as soldiers.'' He described the other as ''secret, but active participants, [such] as spies, brigands, bushwhackers, jayhawkers, war rebels, and assassins.''[57] He had no doubt that an army could defend itself against *both* kinds of enemies. Nor did it make any difference if civilian courts were open. ''The civil courts have no more right to prevent the military, in time of war, from trying an offender against the laws of war than they have a right to interfere with and prevent a battle.''[58] Since the conspirators were obviously active yet secret public enemies, and since they had murdered the commander in chief, it was not only appropriate but, in Speed's view, even mandatory that they be tried by military tribunal.

From his home in Missouri, former Attorney General Edward Bates reacted privately but pointedly to Speed's conclusions. ''This is the most extraordinary document I have ever read, under the name of a law opinion.''[59] The argument contained therein ''would be infin[i]tely rediculous [sic], if it were not so full of danger to all legal government.'' As to the laws of war, ''what are they? Who knows them? Are they written in any book . . . ? There is no such thing as the *Laws of War*. War is the very reverse of law—and its existence always implies (as between the parties to the war) the absence or disregard of all law.''[60]

There is no way of knowing to what extent, if any, the arguments of Johnson and Ewing influenced public opinion.[61] They were published in 1865, and the issue of a military trial was widely debated in the newspapers all during the course of the trial itself. Even as the trial proceeded, the case of another civilian involving a trial by military commission was pending before the United States Supreme Court.

The case of Lambdin B. Milligan was almost a carbon copy of *Vallandig-*

[56] Ibid., 300.

[57] Ibid., 302.

[58] Ibid., 315. ''The civil tribunals of the country cannot rightfully interfere with the military in the performance of their high, arduous, and perilous, but lawful duties.'' Ibid., 316.

[59] Bates, *Diary*, 499.

[60] Ibid., 500–501. Bates added that ''our fathers thought, and taught us to believe that we lived under a government of law. . . . But now, the *first law officer* of the government assures us that this is all a mistake—that in time of war, war with any body, great or small—the laws are silenced, and the *military* at its own caprice, can inflict whatever punishment it pleases, upon any person supposed (by the military) to be guilty of some offense against the (unknown) Laws of war.''

[61] On the other hand, there is no doubt that Edward Bates' views carried virtually no weight at all, because the diary was not published until many years after his death.

ham in two areas. Milligan was also militantly antiwar and anti-Lincoln. A civilian resident of Indiana, he had been arrested, tried, convicted, and sentenced by a military commission. At this point, however, the similarity ended. Unlike Vallandigham, the commission had sentenced Milligan to death. Without actually approving the sentence, Lincoln had ordered the record returned for certain "errors." But before this could be done, he was murdered. President Johnson approved the death sentence, and indeed, even set a date for execution: May 19, 1865. Whereupon Milligan's lawyers sought intervention from the federal Circuit Court, sitting in Indianapolis.[62]

Before the Court took up the case, an unusual development occurred. The two judges presiding over the Circuit, one of whom was a Lincoln appointment to the Supreme Court (David Davis), addressed a confidential letter to President Johnson. They urged that the execution be put off. Milligan had been sentenced by "a new tribunal unknown to the Common Law." Many lawyers "doubt its jurisdiction over citizens unconnected with the military." The judges declined to express their opinion on this point, but added that "it is not clear of difficulty." If Milligan was executed, and the courts should then "deny the jurisdiction under which [he] was tried, the government would be justly chargeable with lawless oppression." Indeed, "a stain on the national character would be the consequence."[63]

Five days later, Johnson commuted Milligan's sentence to life imprisonment at hard labor. But this action did not address the underlying issue raised by the judges, that the question of lawful jurisdiction be resolved *before* a sentence was executed.[64] The case thus went forward in the circuit court. The two judges disagreed on the issue of federal jurisdiction concerning an appeal from a military commission, as well as the authority of the military commission in general over civilians. It was because of this resulting split, that they referred the case to the Supreme Court.

Counsel for Milligan repeated many of the arguments that Vallandigham had raised in vain. Also, there could be no doubt that civilian courts were opening and functioning in Indiana. Indeed, he noted that they had never ceased to function. Indiana had not been an active theater of war since the conflict had begun. Given Milligan's notoriety as a "gadfly" irritant to the

[62] Another difference between the two cases might be noted. Milligan employed some of the best legal talents available, including Jeremiah Black and David Dudley Field. A future president of the United States, James A. Garfield, also participated in the case on Milligan's behalf.

[63] Fairman, *Reconstruction and Reunion*, 198.

[64] It may well be that the judges sent the letter to President Johnson as a respectful and tactful warning, that the legality of military tribunals' jurisdiction over civilians was far from certain. For his part, Johnson possibly believed that by acting to commute the sentence to life imprisonment he could resolve their concern about possible unfavorable consequences, if Milligan was executed. He, of course, missed the point of what the judges were trying to say. On the other hand, he did have the advice of Speed, to say nothing of a unanimous opinion by the Supreme Court in the *Vallandigham* case.

Union cause, his lawyers refused to discuss his guilt or innocence. Instead, they focused primarily on the "competency of the tribunal by which he was judged."[65] Not only did they insist that Milligan's trial had been illegal, but they also denied the power of either the president or Congress to establish military commissions for civilian trials under *any* conditions.

Although the Court heard and decided the case in March–April of 1866, the formal opinions were not filed until December. The justices agreed unanimously that the particular commission involved in this case had exceeded its authority. Its abuse of power was all the more flagrant because civil courts and grand juries had been functioning undisturbed throughout the state during the entire war. But to find that one military commission had acted *ultra vires* in a specific instance, was far from saying that under *no* conditions could Congress establish such tribunals with authority over civilians. This contention carried by a bare majority, with the justices split 5 to 4.

David Davis, whose disagreement with his circuit colleague had sent the case to Washington in the first place, spoke for the majority. Early in his opinion, he hinted at the reason for the lengthy delay between decision and delivery. "During the late wicked Rebellion," Davis wrote, "the temper of the times did not allow that calmness in deliberation and discussion so necessary to a correct conclusion to a purely judicial question." Now that "public safety is assured, this question . . . can be discussed and decided without passion or the admixture of any element not required to form a legal judgment."[66] In other words, with the end of hostilities there was now enough judicial confidence in military obedience to the Court's mandate to justify a ruling contrary to the military viewpoint.[67]

Davis denied that a military commission using the "rules of war," could ever try a civilian where civil courts were in operation and governmental control remained unchallenged, as was the case in Indiana. "No usage of war could sanction a military trial there for any offense whatever of a citizen in civil life, in nowise connected with the military service."[68] Neither the president nor Congress could authorize such a tribunal under these conditions. Certainly the appropriate authorities could indeed proclaim martial law, but not from "a threatened invasion. The necessity must be actual and present; the invasion real, such as effectively closes the courts and deposes the civil ad-

[65] *Ex Parte Milligan*, 4 Wall. 2 (1866).

[66] Ibid., 109.

[67] Clearly such confidence was lacking in 1864, when *Vallandigham* was decided. There, the court refused to consider his case at all—claiming no appropriate jurisdiction. But the question arises if the justices had no jurisdiction in 1864, how could they have it in 1865? Why could they not have claimed jurisdiction, considered the merits in *Vallandigham*, and then decided against the plaintiff? Finally, it should be noted that nowhere in his opinion does Davis cite or mention the 1864 case, even though he had voted with the majority to deny jurisdiction.

[68] Ibid., 121–22.

ministration." Obviously none of these conditions applied in this case, nor presumably to the earlier litigation involving Vallandigham. Martial rule, concluded Davis, "can never exist where the courts are open, and in the proper and unobstructed exercise of their jurisdiction."[69]

At this point, Davis could have ended his opinion—having clearly established that Milligan's arrest, trial, and sentence were all unconstitutional. Instead he added a lengthy paragraph that dealt with a matter not really before the Court: the question of Milligan's guilt or innocence. Davis wrote that had Milligan been found guilty of the alleged offenses by a civil court, "he deserved great punishment." Resistance to those measures "deemed necessary to subdue a great rebellion . . . is wicked." But when this resistance is compounded by formation of an armed, secret political organization, seeking to oppose the laws, it "becomes an enormous crime."[70]

Lincoln's five appointments to the High Court split among themselves in the *Milligan* case. Two of them (Davis and Stephen J. Field) supported the position that under no circumstances could a military tribunal try a civilian. The remaining three (Noah H. Swayne, Miller, and Chase) rejected this claim. Chase insisted that congressional power to establish military commissions represented a fundamental grant of authority, always presumed to be constitutional. Granted that conditions in Indiana were such as to provide "a sufficient reason for not exercising the power, but that fact could not deprive Congress of the right to exercise it."[71] Indeed, the question of deciding when and under what conditions to apply congressional authority was strictly a matter of legislative discretion. In Indiana, Congress had *not* authorized civilian trials by military commission; hence Milligan had to be released. But Congress clearly had the power to establish such tribunals if it so desired. And if it did, protection offered civilians by the Bill of Rights did not apply.

The *Milligan* case has been regarded as a landmark decision that protects a basic civil right of the American people. It should, however, be understood in its context. The decision did not ban imposition of martial law. Moreover, it appeared to apply only to states where civil courts and public administration were in full operation. The finding made no definitive pronouncement, in other words, about the federal government's military authority within the defeated Southern states. Also, the case concerned a civilian. By emphasizing this fact, as he repeatedly did, Davis reiterated the point made in earlier cases: that military commanders when dealing with *military* personnel were beyond the reach of civil federal courts. Hence, as far as the control of military jurisdic-

[69] Ibid., 127.

[70] Ibid., 130. Why, one wonders, did Davis feel the need to add this paragraph? Perhaps he felt it necessary to dispel any sense that the judges were in sympathy with Milligan's conduct. Or, it may have been a concession to some of the other justices in order to keep his majority intact.

[71] Ibid., 140.

tion over the armed forces by civilian courts was concerned, the *Milligan* case established nothing.

Yet in one area, the case has real significance for this study. It indicated that when the Supreme Court wished to do so, it could and would intervene in a matter concerning military justice. To be sure, a trial by military commission was *not* a court-martial. Logically, however, all the self-imposed restraints against intervention in the latter should apply in the former; as appeared to be true in the *Vallandigham* case. Thus, *Milligan* can be interpreted as a message that institutional and political/military constraints are not necessarily a permanent bar to civilian judicial supervision over a military justice proceeding.

END OF AN ERA

Not until the midst of World War II did the United States Supreme Court again take up the issue of civilian jurisdiction over military tribunals. The justices did on several occasions reaffirm the position originally articulated in *Dynes v. Hoover*.[72] But they chose not to clarify the points concerning imposition of martial law and hence of military commissions that had been raised in *Milligan*. Within the military, however, this case remained a source of controversy.

In 1886, for example, a leading textbook on military law summarized the majority and minority holdings. Rollin Ives then added "that the minority opinion expresses the true view of martial law in this country we cannot but believe. The decision of the court was given by the bare majority of one, and, therefore, does not carry the weight of most of its decisions."[73] Similarly, William Winthrop concluded that "the view of the minority . . . is the sounder and more reasonable one, and that the *dictum* of the majority was influenced by a confusing of martial law proper with that of *military government* which exists only at a time and on the theatre of war. . . ."[74]

On the other hand, in 1886 the Judge Advocate General of the Army, G. Norman Lieber, offered a different view. He described the majority opinion

[72] See *Ex Parte Alvin Reed*, 100 U.S. 13 (1879): "If error was committed in the rightful exercise of authority, we cannot correct it." *Wales v. Whitney*, 114 U.S. 564 (1885): "But neither the supreme court of the district nor this court has any appellate jurisdiction over the naval court-martial, nor over offenses which such a court has power to try." *Kurtz v. Moffitt*, 115 U.S. 487 (1885): "In the United States, the line between civil and military jurisdiction has always been maintained. . . . Congress has never conferred upon civil officers or magistrates or private citizens any power over offenders punishable only in a military tribunal." Hence, "a peace officer or private citizen has no authority . . . without the order or direction of a military officer, to arrest or detain a deserter from the army of the United States." *Smith v. Whitney*, 116 U.S. 167 (1886); *Runkle v. United States*, 122 U.S. 543 (1887).

[73] Rollin Ives, *A Treatise on Military Law*, 4th ed. (1886), 13.

[74] Winthrop, 817–18. As to martial law, "it is not—in the judgment of the writer—war alone that may call it into existence."

as one based on necessity. For martial law, "as necessity creates the rule, so it limits its duration." The minority position was based on a constitutional theory, claiming that the power to impose martial law was plenary, and rested solely within the discretionary authority of Congress and/or the president. Lieber added that "I can not but think that the opinion of the majority presents the true doctrine—that of necessity."[75] The judge advocate general was troubled by the open-ended source of congressional power claimed by the minority.

Imposition of martial law carried with it an assumed suspension of constitutional safeguards "which we know are not suspended by war: for . . . the Constitution . . . is a law for rulers and people, equally in war and peace, and covers with the shield of its protection all classes of men, at all times, and under all circumstances."[76] Indeed, "if Congress can declare or authorize a resort to martial law; . . . if it can set aside the safeguards of the Constitution and substitute military power . . . its doing so places the military act which is authorized entirely beyond the reach of the courts, and there is no protection for him who is threatened with it, nor redress for him who suffers by it. It can not be that the law of the land is so impotent."[77]

Other issues besides a theory of martial law were discussed among the military during this period. In 1889, James Fry, a retired Colonel, published a book of assorted essays accurately called *Military Miscellanies*. One of them dealt with a topic central to this study, the proposed establishment of a Military Court of Appeals. Written during the transformation of American legal education, amid growing acceptance of European ideas concerning research and scholarship, Fry based his essay on the idea that "the science of military law is progressive," as is "the science of civil law in a greater degree." Progress in the civil field, "in principles or modes of procedure which are essential to the ascertainment of truth," cannot "be at variance with the objects of the military code, and they ought to be applied to it."[78]

Fry then stated, correctly, that "all available means of ascertaining truth are not invariably resorted to by Courts-martial." Since Congress and the president were the only sources of appeal in such cases, the result was that many "cases are reopened which were supposed to be closed, and are retried by tribunals without legal power and without judicial modes of procedure." He argued that such practices resulted from too great an emphasis on prompt pun-

[75] G. Norman Lieber, "The Justification of Martial Law," reprinted from the 1886 *North American Review* as War Department Document #79 (1898): 4–5.

[76] Ibid., 8–9. "Had the framers . . . suspected that there lurked somewhere in it so dangerous a doctrine as that the safeguards of the bill of rights could be set aside by legislation, the Constitution in its present form would never have become the organic law of the United States."

[77] Ibid., 20. Lieber's words ought to be kept in mind when one considers the decisions of the Supreme Court involving the Japanese-Americans during World War II.

[78] James B. Fry, *Military Miscellanies* (1889), 183.

ishment. Less promptness and more "unquestionable judicial proceedings" were necessary.[79]

Would it not be well, Fry asked, "for the law to transfer the confirming power to a Supreme Court-martial, and leave the President to exercise, in these cases, merely the *constitutional pardoning power*?"[80] It is true, he added, "that the power of Congress and the President's pardoning power would exist with a Military Court of Appeal, just as they do without it, but the temptation and opportunity to exercise these powers would be materially reduced." After all, neither the president nor Congress "can proceed judicially in ascertaining the truth."[81] Fry concluded his essay with the comment that under present conditions, Congress and the president "merely grope for justice, which such a tribunal as that under consideration might make so clear as to prevent their interference, or at least so probable as to give them good grounds for declining to interfere."[82]

One suspects after a close examination of Fry's essay that he was less concerned about the quality of military justice than with the opportunities for civilian interference by Congress or the president. It should be emphasized that his solution was a military court of appeals, *not* a court of military appeals. This distinction is extremely important because a military court of appeals would be *within* the military justice system; whereas a court of military appeals would be outside, and hence presumably more independent in its judgments.[83] Given this bias, Fry still found it necessary to remind his readers that "it is the purpose of this paper merely to present a subject for consideration—not to advocate it."[84]

[79] Ibid., 184, 194. "[I]t has been held by high authorities that the findings of courts-martial are final. The sounder view, it seems to me, is that they are final only in the sense that there is no appointed tribunal to which it is expressly provided an appeal can be taken."

[80] Ibid., 192.

[81] Ibid., 193. Fry also observed that Congress cannot "properly assume to be a court of appeal and revise to acquit or revise to convict a man tried by court-martial." 194.

[82] Ibid., 193.

[83] In support of his point, Fry quoted General William T. Sherman who, during a West Point Commencement address in 1882, had stated, "I am quite willing to see a court of appeals established. It would settle a great many vexed questions and give a legitimate channel for subsequent operations instead of those who make the laws being told the findings are all wrong. . . ." Ibid., 193–94. Examination of the context in which Sherman spoke indicates that he favored exactly what Fry formulated. The speaker just before Sherman had been Senator Harrison, described by a writer in the *New York Herald* as a "large headed man, with a great expanse of forehead, dull eyes and sallow complexion." In urging that the graduating cadets avoid the abuses of alcohol, Harrison had noted "what piteous appeals I have heard of fathers and mothers for erring sons." Sherman picked up on this point during his extemporaneous comments. He, like Fry, would much rather have had a drunken officer appeal to a military court of appeals rather than to a civilian politician like Harrison. See the *New York Herald*, June 13, 1882, 1.

[84] Fry, 186. The March 1882 issue of *The United Service* published an article by Thomas Anderson entitled "Is a Court-Martial a Criminal Court?" Anderson concluded that because a military court of appeals "would only review cases on paper, it could judge no more intelligently as

These discussions of military matters seem in retrospect to have been written in an environment totally oblivious to their content. Nothing came of the debate between Lieber and his colleagues on imposition of martial law; while Fry's essay languished in oblivion until 1919. As the late nineteenth century came and went, there were no innovations or even important changes in the exercise of American military justice. A military society tends to be conservative, and a small peacetime army with very limited federal funding probably more so.[85] If there was to be a dramatic shift in its judicial procedures, it could only come if some major military conflict threatened to bring to public attention the peculiar nuances of the military justice system. In the late nineteenth century, this did not happen. What followed after 1900, however, was a very different matter.

---

to the weight of the evidence than the President or Secretary of War. It could relieve the Executive and the War Department of a great deal of labor, and so far would be a benefit. But unless it could, like the Supreme Court, order a case back for a rehearing on a better interpretation of the law, it would not effect any substantive reform." Thomas M. Anderson, "Is a Court-Martial a Criminal Court?" 6 *United Service* (1882): 300.

[85] An excellent study of the American Army in this period is by Edward M. Coffman, *The Old Army: A Portrait of the American Army in Peacetime, 1784–1898* (1986).

CHAPTER 3

The Ansell-Crowder Controversy, 1917–1918: Round I

LIKE SO MUCH of American society, the military justice system was unprepared for the rapid expansion of our armed forces between 1917 and 1918. With nostalgia if not total accuracy, William Rigby, a member of the Judge Advocate General (JAG) Department, wrote after the war that in 1912 "the country was, and for many years had been, in the enjoyment of profound peace. The army was small and compact, and for the most part removed from centers of population. There was but little public interest, either in the army itself or in military affairs."[1] American entry into the European theaters of war permanently altered this perception. In April 1917, the JAG department consisted of seventeen officers. By December 1918, the commissioned strength of the department had reached 426 officers.[2]

Many of the new members of the JAG department were lawyers fresh from civilian practice. They included, it might be noted, some of the future luminaries of the American law school "establishment," such as Felix Frankfurter, Edmund Morgan, Eugene Waumbaugh, and John Henry Wigmore.[3] The influx of relatively young civilian attorneys and law professors into the JAG Corps had its counterpart in expansion of the army itself. Again, Rigby recalled the "strain" caused by "the sudden multiplication of the army and the inclusion of tens of thousands of new officers, unschooled in Army traditions, unacquainted with each other and the men under them, and unaccustomed to command."

> These new officers, not sitting easily in the saddle, and feeling unsure of themselves (1) are prone as commanding officers to resort too readily to courts-martial,

[1] William C. Rigby, Draft of Report on Court Martial Procedures, in *Records of the Judge Advocate General*, NARC, RG 153, entry 26, box 20. N.p. (1919). The complete report is filed under entry 27.

[2] *The Army Lawyer: A History of the Judge Advocate General's Corps, 1775–1975* (1975), 116; hereafter cited as *History*.

[3] After the war, Frankfurter, Morgan, and Waumbaugh all returned to Harvard Law School, and distinguished teaching careers. Frankfurter later served as Associate Justice of the United States Supreme Court. John Wigmore even before joining the JAG Corps had been Dean of Northwestern University Law School, a post to which he returned after hostilities ended. He was also an outstanding scholar on the law of evidence. Morgan's career after his service in the JAG department will be discussed in much greater detail inf.

and (2) as court martial judges they display ignorance of military law and traditions, uncertainty of themselves, undue fear of showing leniency lest they be thought weak or unmilitary, and a tendency to avoid responsibility by giving severe . . . sentences, accompanied with recommendations to clemency, attempting thereby to shoulder onto higher authority the responsibility for determining the proper quantum of punishment; a responsibility which our system contemplates shall be assumed and discharged by the court martial judges themselves.[4]

Here, Rigby accurately described the context in which arose a conflict between the judge advocate general, and his senior assistant. Beginning in 1917 originally as an internal matter, by 1919 it had expanded into an issue of national interest, a controversy replete with political overtones, extensive newspaper coverage, and lengthy congressional hearings. Before its reverberations had ceased, one participant, Samuel Ansell, had been forced to resign from the Corps, and had become the bitter enemy of the JAG himself (Enoch Crowder); a man who originally had taken much pride in Ansell's earlier successes as his chief subordinate. Personality conflicts, claims of integrity, counterclaims of disloyalty, and lasting enmity all beclouded the original dispute. But in 1917, there was no doubt whatsoever about the basic disagreement between Ansell and Crowder. It involved nothing less than the nature of military justice and the role of the JAG Corps in its administration.

ANSELL AND CROWDER PRIOR TO 1917

Enoch H. Crowder served as judge advocate general of the army from 1911 to 1923. A career officer, he graduated from West Point in 1881, studied law, and gained admission to the Texas Bar in 1884. He also served as a professor of military science at the University of Missouri, where he had received a law degree in 1886. Crowder participated in the final Indian campaigns, and by 1891 had been transferred to the JAG department.[5] In 1901, he became deputy judge advocate general, and a decade later received appointment as *the* JAG from President William Howard Taft. As JAG, Crowder labored for four years to revise the Articles of War; in 1916 Congress finally approved his revisions. Crowder's version provided for the establishment of a third level of court-martial, the "special"; located in terms of authority between the summary and the general.[6] It did not, however, make any substantial changes in court-mar-

[4] Rigby, *Records* sup., n.1.

[5] Felix Frankfurter, who described Crowder as "one of the best professional brains I've ever encountered in life," also commented on Crowder's battle injuries. "The poor man was operated on several times on his head. He often had to hold his head, squeeze the upper and lower parts just to relieve the pain." *Felix Frankfurter Reminisces* (1962), 80.

[6] This tripartite level of court-martial continues to the present day.

tial procedure, and offered nothing in the nature of an appellate process applicable to military justice.

As American participation in World War I drew nigh, Crowder became heavily involved in preparation for administration of the first Selective Service System. The principle author of the new draft law, he also served as provost marshal general during 1917–1918, in charge of the conscription effort.[7] Although Crowder retained his other position, in fact he turned over day-to-day supervision of the JAG department to his senior assistant, Samuel Ansell. And it was in the context of Ansell's activities as an informal "acting" JAG of the army that the controversy arose.

From his letters, Crowder appears to have been a somewhat self-righteous and colorless individual; although he does seem to have had a sense of humor, at least at the unconscious level. In 1918, he wrote to former President William Howard Taft concerning numerous requests from lawyers—often with physical disabilities—for assignment to the JAG corps. "If I do not stop in my tracks, I shall be commanding a Corps of invalids and will have to bring into the department a Corps of trained nurses to take care of my commissioned officers. Every one-armed, one-eyed lawyer and, of course, all the tuberculars, want to serve in my department."[8]

But Crowder's letters to Taft, his benefactor and political confidant, also reflect a deep-seated bitterness about his stature within the military. He very much desired to cap his career with a line field command, something Taft had assumed would be offered Crowder if only because of his very able administration of the draft during 1917–1918. "Nothing," wrote Crowder, "is further from the Secretary's mind. He does not regard such work as I have done during my life as calling for any reward and such too appears to be the service opinion." He noted "a propaganda of organized vindictiveness of line versus staff" that had been going on for almost twenty years. The worst offender was none other than Gen. Tasker Bliss, the senior military aide to Secretary of War Newton Baker. "Bliss leads the movement. If he applied to himself the rule he applies to others, he would today be buying pork and beans for the army instead of being the trusted advisor" to Baker.[9]

[7] The best book on Crowder and the draft is John Whiteclay Chambers II, *To Raise an Army: The Draft Comes to Modern America* (1987).

[8] Crowder to Taft, May 4, 1918; Taft Papers, LOC, reel 193. Crowder added that one general had even succeeded in getting a position for his cousin, "who appears on the firing line with an ear trumpet." Indeed, "if the Field Headquarters should mobilize, there would have to be a squad to take care of an immobile Judge Advocate Corps."

[9] Ibid., September 1, 1917, reel 183. Crowder was publicly respectful, but privately resentful toward his peers who had received line commands. In rank, and more important to him, in stature if not status, they seemed superior. He reminded Taft that Bliss had moved to the rank of brigadier general from within the commissary department, "with less line service than any man ever promoted" to that rank. "Having gotten away with the alleged stolen goods in 1902, he has been crying stop thief ever since."

Crowder realized that, contrary to his hopes, he was destined to end his career as a staff officer, a status akin to that of "swivel chair heroes, a phrase which is easily learned and repeated."[10] Although he was widely honored for his administration of the draft, he retired from the army in 1923 only to suffer another indignity.[11] Congress declined to enact a bill that would have allowed him to leave with the rank and pay of a lieutenant general. Toward the end of his life (he died in 1932), Crowder reflected that "I have lived an average life, and I have confidence unbounded that Divine wrath does not put the heavy hand upon one who lives the average life."[12]

Samuel Ansell also graduated from West Point, in 1899. Five years later, he received a law degree from the University of North Carolina. After teaching military law and history at West Point, he worked for the War Department, and represented the governments of both the Phillipines and Puerto Rico before American federal courts. Assigned to the JAG Corps, Ansell impressed Crowder with his legal ability and enthusiasm. Promotions came rapidly; major in 1913, and brigadier general in 1917. When Crowder became provost marshal general in 1917, his senior assistant, Ansell, took over as acting JAG.[13]

Ansell appears in many ways to have been an opposite to his chief; a point that may help to explain the permanent and bitter rupture to their professional relationship within the corps. Crowder was reflective, somewhat hesitant in manner, and comfortable in a bureaucratic environment. Many years of administrative experience gained from dealing with several secretaries of war had convinced him that military reforms best came from within the army. He might pour out his anguish to Taft and former Secretary of War Henry Stimson in private letters, but he would not be inclined to go public in his criticism either of the system in general or specific officers in particular. Nor would he openly confront senior line officers over disputes concerning military justice.

Ansell was much more aggressive in manner. Articulate and impatient to get results, his statements reveal—to this observer at least—an intense indi-

[10] While the extent of Crowder's discussions with Baker concerning his ambition to hold a line command are unclear, there is no doubt that the secretary was well aware of his sentiments. On August 18, 1917, Baker wrote to Bliss: "I cannot assume that so brilliant and sane an officer as General Crowder and so thoroughly a military man believes that a line command in this kind of war ought to be given as a reward for the service which he has rendered the country as Provost Marshal." Baker to Bliss, August 18, 1917; *Baker Papers*, LOC, reel #1. Crowder might have misjudged Baker's sentiments. It may well be that the secretary believed that a mere line command was less than Crowder deserved, given his service as head of the Selective Service System.

[11] In 1919, Crowder received honorary degrees from Brown, Columbia, Harvard, Northwestern, and the University of Michigan.

[12] David A. Lockmiller, *Enoch H. Crowder: Soldier, Lawyer and Statesman* (1955), 260.

[13] In light of the controversy that was to come, this point is important. According to title, Ansell was *not* acting JAG, but in reality he *was*. His impatience to resolve this distinction is the first documented indication of tension between them. See inf.

2. Samuel Ansell, c. 1917. Courtesy the Department of the Army Judge Advocate General.

vidual who believed very deeply in his causes.[14] He appears to have been a man to whom a cause could become a crusade, more important than a previously established friendship. Thus, one can understand his role in the JAG controversy, and the ultimate severing of his ties to Crowder, the person who not only brought him to the department in the first place, but also facilitated his advance within its ranks.[15]

There is no doubt that between 1914 and late 1917, Ansell and Crowder were very close. Acknowledging some highly favorable comments from Crowder, Ansell wrote that "such praise . . . works in me a new and vigorous inspiration to do all that a limited capacity will permit. Praise from a Discriminating Superior is always gratifying, and it is especially so where . . . it is the expression of a disinterested and appreciative soul." He wrote "to express a sentiment which I could not express orally without embarrassment, and which a sense of gratitude will not permit me to leave unspoken."[16]

Another letter to Crowder, also undated but probably written in 1916, is worth quoting in some detail because it further reveals the intensity of feeling that apparently characterized the man.

> You and your sentiments towards me have [exerted?] a wonderful influence over my life. . . . Without your unfailing kindness, without your confidence in me—which has served as an inspiration—my life in this Army would have been a desert. Under you . . . I no longer remember, much less experience, the restricting influence and environment of military life. Under you, I have had the opportunity of developing intellectual integrity through intellectual liberty. Else than this is the meanest slavery and yet, as I saw it at least, intellectual slavery was my lot before coming to you.
>
> This phase of my service with you means much more than I can express.[17]

[14] In writing to Crowder on November 22, 1917, Ansell discussed whether or not he ought to supercede a lower ranking officer within the JAG Corps. "I should not hesitate to recommend this if I were specially qualified for that place, which frankly, I am not. That requires peculiar personal characteristics . . . which I seem to lack. It requires great patience, considerable tact, and a large acquaintanceship with the Army." JAGO Records, box 4, file 1, folder 1. If Crowder had his burdens, one of whom ultimately was Ansell, Ansell had his demons, one of whom may well have been himself.

[15] Unlike Baker, Crowder, Frankfurter, Morgan, Stimson, Taft, and Wigmore, all of whom figured to some extent in the Ansell-Crowder controversy, Ansell appears to have left no extant body of papers. But sufficient letters from him have been located in various collections to warrant, I believe, the conclusions stated in this paragraph.

[16] Ansell to Crowder, *Crowder Papers* [hereafter cited as CP], University of Missouri, reel 1, folio 14, undated.

[17] Ibid., reel 3, folder 73. In August, 1917, when verbally appointed as acting JAG, Ansell wrote to Newton Baker that "I shall serve you loyally and faithfully, and give you all that is in me." The handwritten letter has the date of August 5, 1917, inserted at the top of the page, but by another hand. Baker Papers, ibid., folder 79.

ANSELL AS "ACTING" JAG

In August 1917, Ansell became assistant to Crowder, actually serving as *the* JAG in Crowder's absence. He did not wait very long before submitting a four-page, single-spaced memorandum to the chief of staff, proposing an organization and expansion of the entire office. He indicated that the JAG Corps was responsible by statute for the "careful revision of records and trials." These actions constituted the "absolute requirements of the statute"; and meeting this responsibility of "revisory and corrective power" was "of the highest importance." Indeed, "this office can and should contribute largely to efficient administration conformably to law." To attain this goal, the "organization here outlined, with the requisite personnel, is considered to be absolutely necessary."[18]

The date of this memorandum is important in tracing the development of Ansell's ideas concerning the role to be played by the JAG Corps in administration of military justice. As of August 24, 1917, he had already determined that this agency was obliged by statute to revise court-martial "proceedings resulting in punishment of a serious character," and that the conclusions drawn from such revisions be "reported for the information of the President, the mitigating and pardoning power." Where did Ansell find the source for this revisory jurisdiction? It came from a law originally enacted during the Civil War, and retained in 1917 as section 1199 of the Revised Statutes. Like many controversial enactments, its brevity contrasts sharply with the controversy it later engendered. "The Judge Advocate General shall receive, revise, and cause to be recorded the proceedings of all courts-martial, courts of inquiry, and military commissions."[19] By implication, later Ansell would make his point explicit, claiming that this section authorized some sort of appellate review.

Today, there is virtual certainty concerning the nature of appellate review in general, whether civilian or military. Professor Daniel Meador has described such action as "to place a case before the reviewing judges in a way that permits them to focus meaningful thought on the contested issues which survive the trial court judgment and to reach a conclusion as to whether, under law, the trial court result should be upheld. Human judgment is the essence of the process. . . . Judgment must be informed, and it cannot be hurried. By its nature it is deliberative."[20] Meador's use of the phrase "under law" should be noted. Historically, American appellate procedure seems to have focused not so much on a review of the case as of the record accompanying it. The

[18] JAGO files, Judge Advocate General's School Library, box 4, file 1, folder 1, August 24, 1917.

[19] 18 Stat., chap. 458. sec. 2, p. 244.

[20] Daniel J. Meador, *Criminal Appeals-English Practices and American Reforms* (1973), 162.

question, according to Roscoe Pound was "not whether the accused was guilty or innocent, but whether the rules of the game had been followed in convicting him."[21]

Lawrence Friedman has written that the "basic problem of review or appeal is how to avoid doing everything over again[,] . . . but at the same time make sure that lower court mistakes are corrected." The search for error "rarely went to the heart of the matter." Echoing Pound, Friedman concluded that American appellate procedure suffered from "record worship." It has reflected "an excessive regard for the formal record at the expense of the case, a strict scrutiny of that record for 'errors of law' at the expense of scrutiny of the case to insure" substantive due process.[22]

The question immediately arises as to the extent that military justice had any procedures similar to those described above. The steps outlined by Meador required time; military justice required promptness. Meador's model assumed adversary appeal proceedings replete with counsel; but in 1917 the military had no facilities for appellate counsel, let alone a formal appellate process. Nevertheless, for many years the JAG department had as part of its statutory authority the section cited by Ansell. Indeed, by 1917 it had developed a uniform procedure for what officers within the department believed to be the type of "revision" mandated by the statute.

When a court-martial record came on for review, it was examined to see if (*a*) there were any "jurisdictional defects appearing in the record," or (*b*) "irregularities occurring upon trial to the prejudice of the substantial rights of the accused."[23] If errors were detected, "it was the practice to write a review and opinion" expressing the findings of the JAG, and to "transmit the record to the Secretary of War through The Adjutant General with the recommendation that the sentence be adjudged null and void and set aside"; and *if* the Secretary concurred, the appropriate order was issued.[24] The essential characteristic of this procedure was that it was advisory only. It was with this approach in mind that the JAG department first considered the Texas Mutiny cases of October 1917.[25]

[21] Roscoe Pound, *Criminal Justice in America* (1930), 95.

[22] Lawrence M. Friedman, *History of American Law*, 2d ed. (1985): 149.

[23] It would appear from this description that during World War I, the JAG department at least attempted to synthesize these two somewhat disparate approaches to appellate review. It was concerned not only with errors appearing on the record of court-martial, but also with possible deprivation of substantive due process.

[24] "Trials by Courts-Martial," in *Hearings before the Committee on Military Affairs*, United States Senate, 65th Cong., 3d Sess. (1919): 165–66; hereafter cited as *Hearings, 1*.

[25] Out of the vast number of available studies on American military history and bibliography during the World War I period, see two books by Edward Coffman, *The War to End All Wars: The American Military Experience in World War I* (1968); and *The Hilt of the Sword: The Career of Peyton C. March* (1966); see also Russell F. Weigley, *The History of the United States Army* (rev. ed. 1984); Jack Lane, *Armed Progressive: General Leonard Wood* (1978); Daniel Beaver,

According to Col. E. G. Davis, one of Ansell's colleagues in his department, these cases arose at Fort Sam Houston when a group of noncommissioned officers were court-martialed on charges of mutiny. It appeared that while under arrest for minor infractions of various regulations, they had refused to attend drill, claiming that one such regulation provided that a noncommissioned officer under arrest did not have to do so. The young commanding officer persisted; so did the defendants—with the result that they were convicted and sentenced to dishonorable discharges as well as various terms of imprisonment.[26] When the cases came on for review, Davis prepared a recommendation that the sentences be set aside.[27] When he submitted the draft for approval, Ansell followed a very different path to a similar goal. Davis proposed that the JAG recommend reversal; on October 30, Ansell himself reversed the verdicts.[28]

He noted that the trial record did not sustain the claim of mutiny, and that the charges against the defendants resulted "largely from the unwarranted and capricious conduct of a very youthful and inexperienced officer." Therefore, "in the exercise of the power of revision conferred upon me by Section 1199," Ansell "set aside the judgment of conviction and the sentence in the case of each of these several defendants."[29] His action differed from the traditional pattern in two ways. Most obvious, on a unilateral basis he undertook to reverse the verdict and sentence of the court-martials. He did not believe that the matter needed to be acted upon by higher authority. Less obvious perhaps, but equally important was the fact that the army practice allowing the defendants to reenlist, to serve out their original term, in no way mitigated against the fact of dishonorable dismissal in the first place. On the other hand, Ansell's order had the effect of vacating the original verdict, of wiping out the dishonorable discharge as if it had never been received.[30]

To senior military officers, Ansell's actions must have seemed like a *coup de theatre*. It was inconceivable to them that by simple fiat a member of the JAG department could rescind an action ordered by a commander.[31] They feared that "the destruction of a division commander's initiative in regard to the discipline of his command might lead to more disastrous results than an actual miscarriage of justice." Indeed, according to one member of the Gen-

---

Newton D. Baker and the American War Effort (1966); and Allan R. Millett and Peter Maslowski, *For the Common Defense: A Military History of the United States of America* (1984).

[26] *History*, 125.

[27] *Hearings, 1*, 201.

[28] "Establishment of Military Justice," in *Hearings before the Subcommittee of the Committee on Military Affairs*, United States Senate, 66th Cong., 1st sess. (1919): 774–77; hereafter cited as *Hearings, 2*.

[29] Ibid.

[30] *Hearings, 1*, 202–3.

[31] In this context, the army reaction to Ansell leads one to recall the reference by Crowder to Taft, concerning the tensions between staff and line command, quoted above.

eral Staff, "as the action of the Judge Advocate General, if permitted to stand, establishes a precedent which may be far reaching in its bearing on the discipline of the Army, I recommend his action be disapproved."[32] For his part, Ansell fully realized that his policy would be debated if not disregarded.[33] He prepared to prove the validity of his claim. But just before submitting his arguments to Secretary of War Baker, he tried to solve a different problem; one that focused on his role in the JAG department.

ANSELL AS ADVOCATE

Since Crowder had become provost marshal general in charge of the draft system, Ansell as his senior assistant had assumed responsibility for the daily operations of the JAG office. The distinction between what he actually did and his title appears to have troubled him. On November 3, 1917, Ansell informed his chief that "I am at times considerably embarrassed . . . by the fact that it is not known to the service at large that you are not conducting the affairs of this office as well as those of the Provost Marshal General; the public conception being that you are, as you legally are, the head of both offices, as in fact you are not." The solution was to have the actual administrator of the JAG Corps "charged with the full responsibility for its policies and for its general administration. That is not the situation now, nor do I believe it can ever be the situation as long as you perform the duties of Provost Marshal General." In other words, "I ought to be designated in orders by the Secretary of War as Acting Judge Advocate General during your practical detachment from this office." Urging that Crowder join in a statement to Baker asking that this be done, Ansell concluded that "I defer to you in this matter absolutely, as I properly should, but at the same time frankly saying to you that I am entirely assured of the correctness of my views."[34]

One day later, Crowder responded that "it would be entirely agreeable to me to have you take up directly and in your own way with the Secretary of War, the subject matter of your letter of yesterday." He also added that since becoming Provost Marshal General, he did not recall being "consulted by outsiders in a single instance respecting any matter pertaining to the Judge Advocate General's Department, except in respect of appointment to the Reserve Corps, except as you yourself have consulted me."[35] Later in 1919, as the Ansell-Crowder feud gathered strength much controversy resulted from this exchange of letters.

What Crowder presumably meant by his first sentence is that while he did

[32] Rigby, *Records* sup.

[33] In terms of this case, he was right on both counts!

[34] JAGO Records, NARC, RG 153, entry 26, box 20.

[35] Ibid.

not intend to discuss the matter with Baker, he would not object to Ansell raising the point on his own. Ansell may well have assumed that Crowder would agree to be associated with the proposed change in JAG command. Nevertheless, absence of opposition to a move is not necessarily the same as supporting it. Had he been a little more attuned not so much to what Crowder wrote and the words he used, as to what he did not write; Ansell might have realized that at best Crowder was uneasy with his proposal. On the other hand, it seems that Crowder was unwilling to articulate his feelings directly on the issue. The ambivalence reflected in his last sentence may also have led Ansell to conclude that he could take action on his own. At any rate, he did. Two days later, on November 6, Ansell sent a memorandum to the chief of staff enclosing a suggested order, and concluded that "I am authorized to say that General Crowder himself is entirely agreeable to my calling this matter to your attention."[36] Having set the formal army machinery in motion, or so he thought, Ansell returned to the issue of JAG authority to revise records of courts-martial.

It is not clear exactly when in November 1917, Ansell decided to submit a formal brief on his position to Baker. In 1919, he recalled that "on October 18, 1917, I had the office begin a study" dealing with the JAG power of revision as drawn from existing law.[37] It appears to have been the subject of internal discussion within his office that lasted for at least two weeks. The brief, dated November 10, and addressed to the secretary of war, "for his personal consideration," may not have been received by Baker until the 12th.[38] Covering almost eight printed pages, this document probably represents Ansell's first attempt to expand on the basic premises set forth in his August memorandum to the chief of staff.

"You, Mr. Secretary," he wrote, ". . . can never appreciate, I think, the full extent of the injustice that has been done our men through" thc inability of the JAG to do nothing about mistakes and abuses of court martials except to "point out the error and recommend Executive clemency."[39] With a tone of urgency that seems to have characterized so much of Ansell's writing, he added that "such a situation commands me to say with all the emphasis in my power, that it must be changed and changed without delay." The basic point of Ansell's brief was built on this premise, buttressed by the fact that the

[36] Ibid.

[37] This assertion is found in a letter from Ansell to Congressman John L. Burnett, 57 Cong. Record, part 4; 65th Cong., 3d sess., February 19, 1919, 3809–10.

[38] A memorandum, dated November 12 by one of the staff "expressing his inability to fully concur in [Ansell's] opinion" indicates that the brief was not submitted to the secretary until on or after November 12th. JAGO Records, NARC, RG 153, entry 26, box 18, February 24, 1919.

[39] *Hearings, 1*, 153. "This, of course, has been utterly inadequate. It has not righted the wrong. It has not made amends to the injured man. It has not restored him, and could not restore him, to his honorable position in the service."

needed change was only one of policy, not law. Here of course, he cited Section 1199. He showed, correctly, that the word "revise" had been applied to the statute since the 1860s.[40] Through copious citations, he further sought to establish the essential legal meaning of the phrase "to revise." For him, revise was equivalent to review, and review could only mean the ability to reexamine, to reconsider and correct if necessary a previous legal decision.

Ansell insisted that "revise" in the context of the JAG statute meant more than "a perfunctory scrutiny" of court-martial records, and "that it in fact vested this office with power to make any correction of errors of law found to be necessary in the administration of justice."[41] He then noted without citing any evidence or examples, that "Judge Holt, the Judge Advocate General [during the Civil War] did revise proceedings in the sense here indicated." Ansell also discussed the reviewing authority common to courts-martial, and claimed that until it had been exercised, the sentence meted out at the trial level, "is incomplete."[42] He was correct in that the reviewing authority could indeed affect the ultimate decision in a court-martial. But it was far from certain whether or not the JAG department was the appropriate reviewing authority.

On the other hand, there was no doubt that in the past verdicts of general court-martials had been set aside, upon *recommendation* of the JAG department, due to "a want of jurisdiction." Without confronting the difficult issue of requiring as opposed to recommending, Ansell argued that "some functionary must sit in an appellate capacity for which there must be some statutory or common law authority." And, he concluded, "no statutory or other authority can be found for the exercise of the power to declare a trial [void] for want of jurisdiction unless it can be found in that provision of section 1199, which confers a general revisory power upon the Judge Advocate General."[43]

As any good attorney would have done, Ansell conceded that there was very solid precedent for the view that "the duly approved sentence of a court martial when the court has proceeded within its jurisdiction and the rules governing its procedure is as final and unassailable as a decision of a civil court of last resort." He probably was well aware of the several decisions of the United States Supreme Court, beginning with the 1859 holding in *Dynes v. Hoover* that affirmed and repeatedly reaffirmed this conclusion. Yet Ansell added, again correctly, that "in each of these cases, the court was speaking of a collateral attack in the civil courts on the proceedings," and did "not have in view the power of the [JAG] department itself to correct court martial judge-

[40] Ansell also noted, correctly, that since the Civil War, the duties of the JAG department had expanded to include much more than simply being military prosecutors.

[41] Ibid., 155.

[42] Ibid., 157.

[43] Ibid.

ment by way of direct revision of it."[44] Ansell concluded his brief with the same point presented in the beginning: "There is a revisory power here, which must be exercised." He also appended a list of his associates each of whom he had asked to read the opinion, "and for the benefit of the record, express his concurrence or dissent."[45] Thirteen officers, including three who later reversed themselves, signed as concurring; none dissented.[46]

CROWDER AS RESPONDENT

Ansell's brief was addressed to Baker. But before it was referred to Crowder, the provost marshal general's attention was called to the matter, still pending, of Ansell's request for formal designation as acting JAG. In due course, the order that Ansell had drafted had gone up the chain of command until it reached Newton Baker.[47] There is no record of what conversation if any transpired between them on this subject, but since it appears certain that Crowder had not alerted his chief to Ansell's proposed change, news of it apparently came as a somewhat unwelcome surprise to Baker. On November 17, he wrote to Crowder acknowledging his awareness that "you would necessarily be

[44] Ibid, 157–58. Ansell added: "I have not found that any authority has ever questioned the revisory power of this office to correct errors in law in court martial procedure when they amount to a denial of justice. And I may be permitted to say that should I find such holdings by any authority other than the highest court of the land, I should not hesitate to question the soundness of the decision."

[45] Ibid., 159. As he prepared his memorandum to Baker, Ansell also had Eugene Waumbaugh, on leave to the JAG department from Harvard Law where he taught constitutional law, draft a set of internal regulations that presumably could be issued by the JAG; assuming that the basic premise of Ansell's brief was accepted. His draft called for "a national military court of revision" to be established within the JAG Corps. It would consist of three officers, to be selected by the JAG, who were to function as appellate judges. The power of revision, flowing from section 1199, did not extend to admitting new evidence; but did include the power to approve or disapprove a finding, as well as the authority "to approve or disapprove the whole or any part of any sentence." The decisions of this court "will not have validity until approved by the Judge Advocate General." The document did not use the word "review," assuming—as did Ansell—that, for purposes of military justice, the word "revise" carried the same meaning. Waumbaugh's draft is dated November 10, 1917, the same date of Ansell's brief; but it is not clear if the proposal was ever forwarded to Baker. *Hearings, 1*, 60.

[46] Lt. Col. Herbert A. White wrote Ansell that "I hardly feel like giving an unqualified concurrence to your opinion . . . regarding the authority . . . to revise proceedings of all courts-martial. While I am satisfied with the logic of the opinion and willing to agree that statutory power can hardly be lost by nonuse, yet I think settled procedure should be departed from only after due consideration." *Hearings, 2*, 846–47. But White added that if the JAG department "had the machinery available to constitute itself a court of review, by which I mean a court of last resort, and the proper officers were available to constitute this court at all times, probably only beneficial results could arise from the office taking full revisory power." He doubted, however, that such a scenario was feasible.

[47] The various documents in the transmittal process are in *Hearings, 2*, 899–901.

withdrawn for a substantial part of your time from the active guidance of the Judge Advocate General's office, where I have learned so confidently to rely upon you.'' Baker praised Crowder's work concerning the selective service law, but added that ''I shall be happy when that work is so far advanced as to be more nearly automatic, and leave you free to return to your task here.''[48]

Crowder wasted no time replying to Baker, informing him on the next day that ''I can resume my active supervision of the work of the Judge Advocate General's Department at once to the extent of giving at least half of my time to that office and continue at the same time an efficient adequate supervision of this office.''[49] For his part, Baker also responded very promptly. Crowder's letter was dated November 18. On November 19, the order drafted by Ansell was summarily canceled.[50]

The timing of these actions, coming even as Ansell had submitted his brief to Baker was extremely unfortunate. Crowder surely knew that sooner or later Baker would learn of Ansell's request. Ansell, on the other hand, might have assumed that the proper way to go was to move through regular channels; all the more as Crowder had declined to join Ansell in a direct communication to Baker. The JAG also had indicated that he had no objection to Ansell taking up the matter directly with Baker, in his own way. He probably did not expect his associate to request a series of endorsements culminating in a sort of automatic approval by the secretary. Baker's action ended the incident with Ansell right back where he had been before.[51] But it may well have troubled Crowder, and engendered an atmosphere of suspicion if not distrust that certainly did not provide an ideal setting in which he could consider Ansell's arguments for revisionary jurisdiction.

The Ansell-Crowder controversy of 1917–1919 was based upon three incidents, two of which have already been discussed: Ansell's effort to have himself named acting JAG, and his arguments—rebutted by Crowder as will be noted shortly—concerning a revisory authority vested in the JAG department. The third incident, and probably the one that provided the final breaking point was the decision by Ansell to bring his internal disagreements into the public forum. Much attention will be given to the public side of the conflict later in the following chapters. Crowder, however, consistently linked the first two episodes together as indicating somewhat surreptitious conduct on Ansell's part. Yet, it has already been shown that Crowder was fully aware that Ansell proposed to have himself named acting JAG. Far from going behind Crowder's back, he had openly sought to enlist his support.

In testimony offered on February 26, 1919, Crowder hinted that he had

[48] Ibid., 901.

[49] Ibid., 902.

[50] Ibid., 901.

[51] Crowder's biographer aptly notes that ''the incident was embarrassing to all concerned.'' Lockmiller, 203.

never seen the document, described by the secretary as a "very powerful brief," before Baker showed it to him.[52] Indeed, during the second series of Senate hearings on military justice held later in 1919, Crowder flatly stated that he had not known about the brief until after he had been made aware of Ansell's attempt to have himself named acting JAG.[53] By this time, Ansell had resigned from the JAG Corps, with the "feud" between the two officers a matter of common knowledge. Rancor may have colored Crowder's recollections; and several points should be noted that raise doubts about his memory.

In the first place, thirteen members of the JAG department immediately supervised by Crowder signed the brief, including three who later supported his views in opposition to Ansell. If Crowder is accurate, he never heard a word from any of them concerning a new interpretation of JAG authority that was not only controversial, but was seen by senior commanders as a real threat to long established procedures involving military justice. In the second place, toward the end of his brief Ansell stated that "it was suggested to me by the present Judge Advocate General himself that the finality attributed by the Articles of War to the power of the several reviewing authorities might be thought to mitigate against or negative the views I advance. This could hardly be true."[54] Since Crowder later wrote into his reply brief what Ansell claimed he had argued, it is difficult to believe that Crowder knew nothing of Ansell's ideas.

Furthermore, in writing to William Howard Taft, a strong supporter of Crowder, Edmund Morgan stated: "I know that the opinion with reference to the right of revision . . . which was the immediate cause of the rupture between General Crowder and General Ansell, was written and submitted only after consultation by General Ansell with General Crowder."[55] A colleague of Taft's at Yale Law School, Morgan served in the JAG Corps with both Ansell and Crowder and was on duty in Washington during the period of October–November 1917, when Ansell's brief was prepared. Finally, it must be noted that Crowder claimed he first saw the brief on November 23, when it was handed to him by Baker. Crowder had frequently emphasized his numerous absences from the JAG office to serve as provost marshal general. Yet, within only four days, he produced an impressive "reply brief," well researched and reasoned—one that effectively rebutted Ansell's arguments. The point is not that Crowder may have been guilty of distorting the truth, as much as the fact that the truth about the controversy—whatever it may be—is not nearly as

[52] *Hearings, 1*, 269. "I have from the Acting Judge Advocate General a very powerful brief on the subject [of revisionary authority], and he seems to argue successfully that this power exists. . . . I wish you would take this brief and read it over and give me your advice."

[53] *Hearings, 2*, 1214.

[54] *Hearings, 1*, 158.

[55] Morgan to Taft, September 19, 1919; *William Howard Taft Papers*, LOC, series III, reel 212.

clear more than half a century later as it seems to have been to the immediate participants.

According to Crowder, Baker handed him Ansell's brief, and asked, "How does it happen that you never advised me that we had here in the War Department a court of appeals that could reverse, modify or affirm sentences of court-martial?" Crowder responded that "we have no such court of appeal," and that if a power of revision "had been discovered in [section] 1199 of the Revised Statute[s] it was an original discovery."[56] Four days later, he produced his reply to Ansell.

At the outset, Crowder responded to Ansell's reliance on the word "revise," noting with some accuracy that "indiscriminate definitions of the words 'revise' and 'review' are quoted throughout the brief." He suggested that revise did not mean the same thing as review, in that revise "imports a purpose of suggesting or making amendments."[57] Surely, if the legislature had intended for a "statutory grant of power so wide as that contended for we should expect, by all the analogies of grants of appellate power, to find something more than authority to 'look over,' or 'to examine.' " Crowder added that he could not point to a single instance where the "power to modify or reverse the judgment of inferior courts is deduced from the words 'review' or 'revise,' without the addition of apt words specifically conferring the power to reverse or modify."[58]

Crowder next turned to the matter of General Holt, JAG during the Civil War. Ansell had claimed without any evidence that Holt had reversed court-martials in the manner endorsed in his brief. But Crowder could not find a "single instance" where Holt on his own authority reversed a court-martial.[59] On the contrary, he found several that contradicted Ansell's contention; and cited one case where Holt noted "fatal irregularities" that render the proceedings and sentence invalid, "and it is recommended that it be so declared by the President."[60]

[56] *Hearings, 1*, 269.

[57] Ibid., 270. "Thus a proof reader revises copy and suggests changes, but he does not effect changes." In the same manner, legislative committees or commissions revise statutes, "but their revisions do not give legal life to the results of their labors. The legislature must enact the revision as a law."

[58] Ibid., 271. "I may add . . . that a rather complete survey of statutes vesting appellate power in tribunals, administrative as well as judicial, fails to disclose a single case where the power to modify and reverse is left to be deduced from such an inapt and single word as the word 'revise,' without the addition of appellate power granted in specific and unequivocal terms." Ibid., 272. For Crowder, these findings only corroborated anew what he already assumed; that if the framers of the statute had wanted the JAG to review court-martials in the sense claimed by Ansell, they would have used the word *review*, instead of the word *revise*.

[59] By dwelling on the Holt matter, Crowder may have intended to cast doubt on the validity if not veracity of Ansell's entire approach, without specifically raising the issue.

[60] Ibid., 273. Another example quotes Holt as stating that "if this opinion is concurred in," the pleadings must be held to be fatally defective. Ibid.

Finally Crowder countered Ansell's insistence that "the power here contended for [has not] been questioned by the civil courts or other civil authority." In this context, he cited *Mason's Case*, decided by a New York Federal Circuit Court in 1882. John Mason had been court-martialed, convicted, and sentenced for attempting to kill Charles Guiteau, the man who had assassinated President Garfield in 1881. The JAG had concluded that the military court did not have jurisdiction, and recommended that the sentence be nullified; a conclusion and recommendation which the secretary of war rejected. Whereupon Mason's attorney sought out a writ of habeas corpus, and cited among other things Section 1199; arguing that under it, the JAG's action had been tantamount to an exercise of appellate authority, and by implication barred any reversal by the secretary.

A unanimous Court denied that "because the statute makes it the duty of [the JAG] to 'receive, revise and cause to be recorded the proceedings of all courts-martial,' the power to reverse is implied. It is not reasonable to suppose that the exercise of such an important power would be conferred in vague and doubtful terms, or that it lurks behind the word 'revise.' " Indeed, "had it been intended by the statute to introduce such a marked innovation into the preexisting functions of [the JAG], and to convert a staff officer or the head of a bureau into a judicial officer having the ultimate decision in all cases of military offenses[,] the power to affirm, reverse, or modify the proceedings . . . would have been lodged in plain and explicit language."[61] Having found a case on all fours with his position, Crowder considered ending his statement at this point. Instead, he informed Baker that he would try to ascertain "whether this power of appellate review cannot be found in the President himself, as the constitutional Commander in Chief; so that, instead of issuing a simple order of restoration, you may by direction of the President, modify or disapprove the findings and sentence."[62]

Crowder's rebuttal to Ansell is dated November 27, 1917. Within twenty-four hours, Newton Baker responded. Himself a lawyer of somewhat conservative inclination, he could not help but be influenced by the very unfavorable reaction within the military command to Ansell's move. Moreover, when the

[61] *Ex Parte Mason*, 256 Fed. 384, 387 (1919). The judges added that it was indeed the duty of the JAG "to revise the proceedings . . . so far as may be necessary to rectify errors of form, and to point out errors of substance which, in his judgment, should be corrected by the proper authorities." Both Ansell and Crowder were aware of this case that, for reasons that are unclear, remained unreported until 1919; when it was published in the current West National Reporter volume "by request." The timing may have had something to do with the public phase of their "feud" that was in full bloom at the time of publication.

[62] *Hearings, 1*, 275. Crowder's statement is important because it indicates that he was not nearly as uncomfortable with the idea of some sort of military appellate review as with Ansell's claim that it ought to be exercised by *his* department. On the other hand, because Crowder, like Winthrop, conceived of a court-martial as strictly an attribute of command, it was logical to vest such review with the highest ranking commander of all—the president.

two briefs were compared to each other, it seems that Crowder's reply was more convincing. Ansell argued for a power which he could not prove existed in law. Nor could he cite relevant examples where it had even been exercised. On the contrary, Crowder could point to almost half a century of consistent practice within the JAG department, to say nothing of a federal civil case which specifically rejected what Ansell had recited. It is not surprising therefore, that Baker decided in favor of his JAG. "Ordinarily," he wrote, "the extraction of new and large grants of power by reinterpreting familiar statutes with settled practical construction is unwise."[63]

ANSELL ARTICULATES ANEW

According to traditional military procedure, Baker's decision should have ended the incident. Crowder, a military superior, had advised; the secretary had acted; Ansell should acquiesce. If anything, however, Ansell seems not to have been a traditional military man.[64] Within two weeks, he prepared a lengthy reply brief, which he submitted to Crowder with a request that it be placed before Baker. The subject, he wrote, "is one of tremendous importance," and if the JAG department could change its view of the law, the results would be "to the great benefit of the administration of military justice." If Crowder and Baker persisted in their views that legislation was necessary, Ansell hoped that "its exercise will not be subjected to General Staff supervision, [which] it seems to me, would necessarily destroy the judicial character of the power."[65]

Ansell's second brief is a remarkable document. On a personal level, it reiterated intensely held convictions. But as an advocate, this time he went further; focusing on the nature of military justice, the status of court-martials, and the difference between army legal practice and civil legal procedure. Furthermore, unlike his first effort, this brief reflected Ansell's growing frustration and personal bitterness toward those army elements he saw as blocking necessary reforms. To the military establishment in 1917, his views seemed pointless; to an observer of military justice in 1991 they seem prophetic.

The basic premise remained unchanged. The JAG possessed statutory authority to revise. "If the revision is worth the name, it should be a revision for gross and prejudicial errors of law that make a [court-martial] conviction bad,

[63] Ibid., 29. If Baker felt this way under ordinary conditions, the fact that Ansell proposed his new interpretation of the law during wartime may well have rendered his position even more unacceptable to the secretary.

[64] In 1919, Ansell recalled that "I was brought up with a good degree of freedom and independence; maybe too much. I was not used to military discipline. I came to it not easily. . . ." *Hearings, 1*, 37.

[65] Ibid., 44.

as well as for those that make the judgement void.''[66] Moreover, both Baker and Crowder were wrong in their assertion that the traditional way of dealing with such cases, to quote Baker, was ''a convenient mode of doing justice.'' The secretary ''has failed to [distinguish] between executive action in the nature of a partial pardon[,] and judicial action which goes to the erroneous judgment of conviction itself and modifies it, reverses it, or sets it aside.'' Restoration can not undo an unlawful conviction. ''The man who seeks a pardon does so upon an express or implied admission of guilt. The pardon itself conclusively implies guilt. A pardon is no remedy for wrong done [to] the innocent.''[67]

Ansell devoted the second part of the brief to an attack on the argument, consistently maintained by the army, that a court-martial essentially was an instrument of command more concerned with ''the support of power rather than . . . the human individual rights offended by an abuse of it.'' Claiming that the views of officials such as the assistant chief of staff and the inspector general ''savor of absolutism,'' Ansell added that ''I poignantly regret the concurrence of the Judge Advocate General, who habitually and constitutionally entertains far more progressive views.''[68] He made reference to the Texas ''mutiny'' case noting that his own ''sense of right and justice and discipline would have impelled me to court-martial not the men, but the officer himself.''[69] It is difficult to maintain, he added, that a court-martial—''the crudest of all courts, exercising such an extent of jurisdiction, is entitled to greater deference than those of the civil tribunals, the review of which, to insure correction, is fundamental in our law.'' Nor did Ansell have any doubt as to who was to blame for this mistaken conclusion. It was none other than the leading writer on military law, William Winthrop.[70]

In his treatise, which by 1917 had been recognized as a standard reference work for American military justice, Winthrop concluded that ''not belonging to the judicial branch of the Government, it follows that courts-martial must pertain to the executive department; and they are in fact simply *instrumentalities of the executive power*.''[71] For Ansell, this was an absolute and obvious ''non sequitur,'' and ''we have all been steeped in the teachings that follow upon that illogical and fallacious syllogism.''[72] The primary source of courts-martial authority could only be Congress. ''Courts-martial are authorized by

[66] Ibid., 45. The inability of the army to comprehend this need ''is symptomatic of more general deficiencies that are the usual concomitants of that institutional formalism which in my judgment so hinders our military development.'' Ibid., 46.

[67] Ibid., 47.

[68] Ibid., 48.

[69] Ibid. ''And I still think that that should be done.''

[70] See George S. Prugh, ''Introduction to William Winthrop's *Military Law and Precedents*,'' *Revue De Droit Penal Militaire et de Droit de la Guerre* 27 (1988): 437–59.

[71] Winthrop, 49. Emphasis in original.

[72] *Hearings, 1*, 49.

Congress. The powers that bring them into being are designated and authorized . . . by Congress. The offenses which they may try and the law which they apply are prescribed and enacted by Congress. Their procedure is regulated under the law of Congress. Their sentences and judgments must be in accordance with the law of Congress.''[73]

Ansell cited a number of Supreme Court decisions which, he claimed, established beyond any doubt that courts-martial were like other federal courts in that they were created by statute, and were ''inherently and exclusively'' judicial in nature. As such, they could not be subject to military command. To be sure, a decision by a commander was required to bring them into existence; but once convened—Ansell implied—they took on a life of their own. On the other hand, Winthrop concluded that while courts-martial were tribunals, and ''their legal sanction is no less than the federal courts, being equally with those authorized by the Constitution''; still, they were not courts ''in the full sense of the term.''[74] This was because of the executive authority exercised by the president as commander in chief.

Ansell strongly denied that ''court-martials are subject to his control.'' When ''Congress does speak out of its power, the President may not speak within the same field. He may not array himself in opposition to the legislative rules governing the administration of military justice.'' In fact, ''Congress has designated what commanders subordinate to the President may convene courts-martial, but when convened they will be subject to all the law of Congress; he cannot, by reason of that power, control courts-martial convened by others.''

Thus, Ansell based his argument on two fundamental propositions: (*a*) that courts-martial were judicial in character, and (*b*) that they were a product of congressional statutory authority, not executive fiat. *If* one agreed with these dual premises, Ansell's conclusions were not unreasonable. Accepting the claim that courts-martial were judicial, ''the power of revision, if it exists, is also judicial and therefore not subject to the power of command.''[75] Since the source of courts-martial authority was Congress, ''only by Congress alone, or by some authority appointed by Congress, can a court martial be controlled.'' Hence, ''judicial revision is not subject . . . to the usual General Staff supervision.''[76]

Several comments can be made about Ansell's points. It is quite true that the Supreme Court on numerous occasions had found that court-martial proceedings were judicial in character, and that such judgments by a court exercising proper jurisdiction were virtually beyond the reach of civilian justice. But in repeatedly drawing this conclusion, the Justices apparently were con-

[73] Ibid., 50.

[74] Winthrop, ibid.

[75] *Hearings, 1*, 51.

[76] Ibid., 51–52.

cerned less with the origins of court-martial authority than with the issue of jurisdiction. It mattered not where original authority for convening courts-martial was found, as how much jurisdiction and authority they might have once they were convened.

Thus, unlike Ansell, it appears that the Supreme Court had not taken a position on congressional as opposed to executive control of courts-martial. It may be that prior to 1917 the question of where executive power concerning these tribunals, and congressional rule making over the armed forces bisected, if indeed they did, had not been raised let alone resolved. Finally, it should be clear that, based on Waumbaugh's proposed draft, Ansell's model of courts-martial review was more conservative than might appear at first glance. It involved no civilian appellate jurists. Nor did it in any way exclude action by a convening authority concerning a verdict and sentence of a court-martial. These steps were considered part of the initial process, unlike any later review that had to be based on the completed record.

The rest of Ansell's brief was mostly a strident reiteration of his earlier insistence that revise meant review. He cited a number of examples where state constitutions employed the word "revise" to describe appellate judicial jurisdiction.[77] Ansell could not accept the contention that in creating a separate bureau (the JAG department), Congress had intended it "for no purpose at all, or, at most, in order that some inconsequential clerical change might be made upon the record." As for the *Mason* case "which perhaps because of its utter lack of authority, I had forgot," the decision represented "the most patent dictum."[78]

In concluding his brief, Ansell predicted in 1917 exactly what Rigby in 1919 admitted had actually taken place. The multiplication of men and officers could only mean vastly increased reliance on courts-martial; and "opportunity for error . . . in the court-martial proceedings themselves will be largely multiplied," if only because they will be administered "by men uninformed in the law." It seems to me, he added before suffering death or other serious punishment, a soldier as a matter of principle should be entitled to have his court-martial proceedings examined not only by the commander "but by a separate and independent authority who, skilled in the law . . . can with the necessary deliberation and considerateness [sic] pronounce the trial free from prejudicial error."[79] After all, "justice under law is as necessary to the American Army as it is to any other American institution."[80]

[77] Ibid., 54. Two such examples were the states of Oregon and Illinois.

[78] Ibid., 53.

[79] Ibid., 58.

[80] Ibid., 59. In the light of public perception concerning military justice from 1918 down to the present day, one of Ansell's points is worth pondering. "This revisory power should exist; and I doubt not that when exercised with judicial wisdom and discretion . . . under proper rules and regulations, it will prove a great help, and never a hindrance, to safe and sound administration,

Ansell may have received some assistance in formulating his reply brief from Eugene Waumbaugh, whose proposed draft of a military court of appeals has already been mentioned. Waumbaugh also prepared a short supplemental brief "in support of the revisory power." Seemingly more familiar with civil practice rather than court-martial procedure, he noted that (unlike a criminal statute), Section 1199 was "a remedial statute, and hence it is to be construed liberally in the light of the perceived evil or danger."[81] Moreover, while Waumbaugh conceded, as did Ansell, the long-established authority of the convening authority to review a court-martial—"it must now be pointed out that the appointing authority, though certainly deserving high respect, can not be said to be ideal for the present purpose." This individual "is a busy military officer[,] whose specialty is not the ascertaining of law and the weighing of evidence."[82]

Ansell emphasized the judicial character of court-martials. Waumbaugh added that these tribunals are "administrative" in their nature; and it was not unusual for due process of law to require "an appeal—whether an appeal to the courts or merely an appeal to a superior officer." Thus, it was not unreasonable to assume that Congress may well have intended to provide through Section 1199 "some sort of appellate procedure, bringing the whole matter ultimately before an expert."[83] Finally, Waumbaugh cited a number of military texts to show that "the power of revision is understood to include a change in the finding and the sentence."[84]

Crowder forwarded Ansell's brief to Baker on December 17, 1917, along with a brief memorandum summarizing the disputed issues. Citing the Texas "mutiny" cases, Ansell "says, I think justly, that there are other cases . . . which demand the exercise of such corrective power; and down to this point I follow him with substantial concurrence without, however, being able to con-

---

and place military justice upon a plane that will cause it to merit and receive, more than it ever has heretofore received, the approval of the American people."

[81] Ibid., 61. Waumbaugh's brief is dated December 1, 1917. Ansell submitted his own brief to Crowder on December 11.

[82] Ibid., 62.

[83] Ibid. The expert would, of course, be the JAG.

[84] Waumbaugh did not discuss the problem of the commander in chief's relation to courts-martial. Moreover, neither he nor Ansell considered whether it was appropriate for the JAG department, already charged with the prosecution of court-martials, to serve as a sort of appellate body that in effect reviewed decisions it had helped to bring about. As will be seen later, this point was not lost on Crowder, and it may be another factor in his opposition to any sort of appeal process *within his office*. Frederick Bernays Wiener called Waumbaugh "the most outstanding" of those JAG officers supporting Ansell, but added that his brief "reflects no familiarity" with long-established military practice, and "quite fails to convince." Frederick Bernays Wiener, "The Seamy Side of the World War I Court-Martial Controversy," *Military Law Review* 123 (1989): 125. Agreeing with Wiener's first point, which I do, does not require acceptance of his second conclusion. Waumbaugh had found a number of military texts that seemed to prove that "revise" did mean to alter or amend—essentially what Ansell had argued.

cur with him that this power has been granted to the Judge Advocate General.'' Crowder had no doubt that Ansell's argument ''presents, about as strongly as it could be presented, the necessity for an appellate power.''[85] His analysis, however, failed to convince the JAG that a change of the character advocated by Ansell was necessary.

The lawyer's mind, according to Crowder, ''is not particularly shocked by the fact that there exists in military jurisprudence no court of appeal.'' Indeed, ''there is no constitutional or necessary right of appeal.''[86] While Ansell had argued to the contrary, there remained ''substantial reasons of expedience and good administration why [current court-martial jurisdiction] should not be disturbed. War is an emergency condition requiring a far more arbitrary control than peace, [and] . . . court-martial procedure if it attain[s] its p[r]imary end, discipline, must be simple, informal, and prompt.''[87] The ''embarrassments'' cited by Ansell and conceded by Crowder could be corrected without resort to a strained interpretation of Section 1199.

Baker responded to Crowder on December 28 that ''it is impossible not to admire the earnestness and eloquence with which Gen. Ansell presents his view.'' His arguments, however, pointed to ''the necessity of the power rather than to its existence''; although ''it may very well be that this power should exist, either in the Judge Advocate General or in the Secretary of War, advised by the Judge Advocate General.''[88] In any event, Baker had no doubt that congressional action was required if Ansell's suggestions were to be implemented. But the secretary had some practical concerns with the actual means needed to satisfy Ansell's goals.

What was the distinction between appellate jurisdiction and jurisdiction in error? Baker cited a hypothetical court-martial record that ''contains radical errors of law.'' Has, he asked, ''the Judge Advocate General the right to set aside the proceedings and direct a new trial to be had before the same or a

[85] *Hearings, 1*, 63–64.

[86] Crowder's point is similar to that made by Justice Joseph Bradley, dissenting in the *Minnesota Rate Case*, 1890. ''It is complained that the decisions of the board are final and without appeal. So are the decisions of the courts in matters within their jurisdiction. There must be a final tribunal somewhere for deciding every question in the world. Injustice may take place in all tribunals. All human institutions are imperfect—courts as well as commissions and legislatures. Whatever tribunal has jurisdiction, its decisions are final and conclusive unless an appeal is given therefrom.'' *Chicago, Milwaukee and St. Paul Railway Co., v. Minnesota*, 134 U.S. 418, 465–66 (1890).

[87] *Hearings, 1*, 64. ''If, for example, all the findings and sentences of courts-martial in France must await finality until the record be sent to Washington, we shall create a situation very embarrassing to the success of our Armies. Such a proposition could hardly be seriously advanced. . . .''

[88] Ibid., 65. ''There is nothing intrinsically abhorrent in the idea of finality in judgments of courts-martial approved by the reviewing authority. Whether or not, however, injustices are likely to arise from such a course which would outweigh in gravity the delays necessary to perfect a complete review on appeal is a question about which differences of opinion may well exist.''

different court, or may he summon the parties before him with the necessary witnesses and become himself a court-martial, or is he remitted to a quashing of the whole proceedings and restoration of the defendants to their original status, protected from subsequent prosecution by the bar of former jeopardy?"[89] Baker concluded by asking Crowder for his views on "the sort of appellate procedure involved in the power to revise."

This tripartite colloquy between Ansell, Baker, and Crowder took place even as a major incident in American military justice also occurred; an event that none of the three participants knew had even happened until after it was over. A second Texas mutiny case involved a number of black soldiers who on August 23, 1917 had rioted in downtown Houston apparently as a result of jeers and insults from white civilians. The result had been a rampage that ended with a number of civilian deaths. Sixty-three soldiers were court-martialed on charges of mutiny and murder. Of this number a few were acquitted; all the rest were found guilty, with four facing short prison terms, forty-one being sentenced to life imprisonment, and thirteen sentenced to death by hanging. The death sentences were carried out the next day in what Wiener called "the first mass execution under American military law since . . . the Mexican War." He added that "until the news of the multiple hangings reached the Washington papers, no one in the War Department had even known of the trial," and there it landed, according to JAG officer Rigby, "with a dull thud."[90] By the time the record reached the JAG department, as one of Ansell's associates—probably with unintentional understatement—later recalled, "If . . . errors of law had been committed or that injustice had been done[,] it would not help the men any to find this state of facts in the record after the man had actually been executed."[91]

In fact, under existing rules what had happened was perfectly legal. Yet the incident received national attention in part because what appeared to be the undue haste with which the military had executed the black soldiers. If the army later found the Houston trial record to be "legally sufficient," it also quietly relieved the commander involved in the case of his command, and reduced him in rank.[92] Baker's response to Crowder was dated December 28. One day later, the War Department ordered that no death sentences could be carried out "until the record of trial has been reviewed in [JAGO] and the reviewing authority has been informed . . . that such review has been made and that there is no legal objection to carrying the sentence into execution."[93]

[89] Ibid.

[90] F. B. Wiener, "American Military Law in the Light of the First Mutiny Act's Tricentennial." *Military Law Review* 126 (1989), 17–18.

[91] *Hearings, 1*, 209.

[92] Wiener concluded that the commander "had exercised his undoubted legal powers with utter lack of judgment." See Wiener, "Book Review," *Cornell L. Rev.* 59 (1974): 752–53.

[93] *Hearings, 1*, 209.

Within three weeks, the JAG department rescinded this regulation, and promulgated a revised and expanded version known as General Order No. 7.

As drafted by JAG officer E. G. Davis, the new order barred execution of a death sentence until the court-martial record "has been reviewed" by the JAG office, "its legality there determined," and "jurisdiction is retained to take any additional or corrective action that may be found necessary." If there were problems with the record, it "will be returned to the reviewing authority with a clear statement of the error, omission, or defect." If this "admits of correction, the reviewing authority will be advised to reconvene the court . . . ; otherwise he will be advised of the action proper for him to take," such as approval or disapproval, remission in whole or in part, retrial "or such other action as may be appropriate." In addition, a JAG department branch office in France was established for the American Expeditionary Force. The head of this branch was to review the records of all courts-martial involving sentences of death, dismissal, or dishonorable discharge, as well as all verdicts reached by military commissions, and "to return to the proper commanding officer for correction such as are incomplete, and to report to the proper officer any defect or irregularity which renders the findings or sentence invalid or void, in whole or in part, to the end that any such sentence . . . shall not be carried into effect."[94]

It can be argued that Ansell deserved much credit for issuance of this order. He had insisted for the last three months that the power of review was inherent in the JAG department. Now it appeared that with Order No. 7, the army establishment agreed. After all, the new procedure mandated that invalid penalties "shall not be carried into effect." In reality, however, Ansell not only opposed the new regulations, but on January 12, 1918, also submitted a memorandum to Crowder detailing his objections. Davis recalled that Ansell "contended vigorously" against his proposed order "because he thought it was based upon a wrong legal theory."[95] In the light of the controversy developing between Crowder and his chief subordinate, Ansell's opposition to a policy that at least appeared to nudge the army toward a goal he strongly favored merits examination.

Ansell described Davis's rule of procedure as "a weak and uncertain step in the right direction," but one "fundamentally wrong as a matter of law." Davis would have the reviewing authority "approve the judgement but suspend its execution until he can be advised of" its correctness; "and if advised of its incorrectness, then to revise it himself."[96] Ansell viewed this as little improvement over what already existed. For him, the *sine qua non* was a re-

[94] Ibid., 209–11.

[95] Ibid., 204.

[96] Ibid., 68.

viewing authority independent of and binding upon the convening authority. He could find no such mandate in Davis's order.

"If the reviewing authority does not take final action, there is nothing for this department to revise. If he does take final action, then the judgment passes beyond his power to revise. . . . Viewed from whatever angle, it is perfectly apparent that the source of the [reviewing] authority is in this department and must be exercised by this department, if exercised at all. No system can be devised whereby the convening authority revises his own judgment at the mere suggestion of this department."[97] In this last sentence, Ansell encapsulated the crux of the controversy, one that would not finally be resolved until the adoption of the Uniform Code of Military Justice in 1950. "What reason can there be," he asked, "to require this office to review for errors of law and then be denied the power of correction?"[98]

Ansell's memorandum to Crowder also indicated that as early as January 1918, he felt disinclined to support any compromise or "halfway" measures such as that embodied in Order No. 7. "I wish I could give concurrence to something which, though less than the full power, would be satisfactory to you and [Baker], and would serve, at the same time, as a partial remedy. I can not." Since Ansell had neither any doubt that the power to revise existed, nor any fears concerning its implementation, such authority "should be exercised in full. Otherwise, it should be entirely denied. Safety lies in taking one course or the other, and not in a compromise." I have given "this question of revisory power the best that is in me."[99]

Ansell's letter to Crowder can be seen as the end of the first phase of their controversy. Thus far, it does not seem to have been personal in tone, as much as a strictly internal debate between two lawyers over an issue more of statutory interpretation than military policy. But problems of personality simmered just below the surface. Ansell's efforts to have himself named acting JAG clearly troubled Crowder, just as his mentor's inability to move away from the

[97] Ibid.

[98] Ibid. "Powers must be located, and they must be powers, not requests." In 1919, Ansell described #7 as "a partial and ineffectual exercise of revisory power . . . [,] simply an administrative makeshift, intended to head off a more thorough and drastic reform." To support this contention, he cited a letter from Crowder to one of the JAG officers assigned to Pershing's American Expeditionary Force. Crowder wrote that prior to the issuance of #7, the inexperience of many officers with courts-martial resulted in "a large number of proceedings . . . which exhibited fatal defects. A congressional investigation was threatened and there was talk of the establishment of courts of appeal. The remedy for the situation was immediate executive action which would make it clearly apparent that an accused did get some kind of revision of his court martial proceedings. . . ." *Hearings, 2*, 115–16. Walter Bethel, the officer to whom Crowder wrote, appeared during these same hearings—and confirmed that Crowder's letter as read into the record by Ansell "is correctly set forth." Ibid., 575. However one may applaud Crowder's candor, his letter strongly supports Ansell's point about the less than enthusiastic desire on the part of the army "Establishment" for genuine reform concerning military justice.

[99] *Hearings, 1*, 69.

status quo irritated Ansell. On the other hand, during 1918 Ansell continued as the senior assistant; and he found several opportunities to continue his drive for a substantial appellate review within military justice. As the United States approached the first anniversary of its entry into the Great War, the Ansell-Crowder disagreement remained buried within the military. When the arena for the dispute became a public forum, rather than the inner offices of the War Department, involving both the press and political figures—what had been discourse over issues became diatribes on individuals. Taking place during much of 1919, these developments—unfortunate for all concerned, but especially detrimental to the goal of reforming military justice—are the subject of the following chapters.

CHAPTER 4

The Ansell-Crowder Controversy, 1918–1919: Round II

ALTHOUGH clearly committed to established procedures, Enoch Crowder was too able a lawyer not to sense some validity in Ansell's strictures concerning military justice. He seems to have spent considerable time during December 1917 trying to draft a proposal for Baker that would remedy the objections while remaining within the existing structure of military command.[1] On December 6, he submitted a lengthy memorandum to the secretary. Based on previously articulated assumptions to which Crowder still adhered, it led to his "firm conclusion that no additional legislation is necessary, but that an ample grant of statutory power already exists for the immediate establishment of a system of military procedure, the practical results of which will be to obviate the objections which have heretofore been made. . . ."[2] Ansell had also argued that no additional legislation was required, finding justification for his views within the existing language of Section 1199. Although sharing this premise, the types of review the two officers envisaged were very different.

CROWDER'S CAUTION

Crowder's analysis of military appellate jurisdiction was based on a simple syllogism: (*a*) the president as commander in chief was the supreme military authority, and (*b*) although judicial in character, courts-martial remained "instrumentalities of the executive power." Since therefore, presidential power extended to all aspects of military justice—(*c*) "the President has ample authority . . . through the office of the Judge Advocate General, to make any revision of the proceedings of courts-martial which may be necessary to accomplish the correct and orderly administration of justice."[3] Furthermore,

[1] Crowder later recalled that after informing Baker why #1199 did not give the JAG the revisionary power claimed by Ansell, "we commenced to look around for an available means to get this power, because Gen. Ansell had certainly demonstrated that it was a necessary power in this World War." *Hearings, 2*, 1205.

[2] *Hearings, 2*, 854. The entire memorandum is on 854–63.

[3] Ibid., 856, 858. Unlike Ansell, Crowder declined to question Winthrop's conclusion on the executive character of courts-martial. Instead he noted that "I do not mean to say that the Winthrop doctrine had the concurrence of all military men. . . . I have always approached the subject

Crowder cited the 38th Article of War which authorized the president to issue regulations "which he may modify from time to time, [to] prescribe the procedure, including modes of proof, in cases before court martials." The JAG found the term "procedure" broad enough to encompass the establishment of "a system of revision and correction."[4]

Unlike Ansell who equated the word revise with review, and thus found Section 1199 sufficient for his purposes, Crowder insisted that this section plus several other articles of war "relate to the same subject matter," and according to established rules of construction, "must be construed together." Hence, *only* the president could breathe life into the provisions of Section 1199. On the other hand, however, Crowder readily conceded that this section provided for some kind of "a statutory appeal." Crowder's conclusion followed inevitably from his premises: "Provision may be made by regulations to be established by the President to bring before the Judge Advocate General for revision such cases . . . as the Commander in Chief should deem it expedient [to] be so revised."

If Baker desired to "rely on the authority here outlined," rules of procedure such as those contained in General Order No. 7 (discussed in the last chapter) were perfectly appropriate. If the secretary had some doubts about such a step, "it may well be that . . . this matter is of sufficient moment to make it advisable to refrain from exercising the authority here outlined[,] and seek instead such a clear grant of legislative authority as will make the President, acting through the office of the Judge Advocate General, a supreme court of review in all military cases, with ample authority to revise, reverse, modify, or set aside any sentence of a court-martial. . . ."[5] Thus, in addition to his memorandum, Crowder also submitted a proposed revision of Section 1199 to Baker, that provided for this type of executive power.

Drafted by two JAG officers, E. G. Davis and Alfred Clark, the proposal reaffirmed that the JAG "shall receive, revise and cause to be recorded the proceedings of all courts-martial." In addition, the JAG shall "report thereon to the President who shall have sole power to disapprove, vacate or set aside any finding, in whole or in part, to modify, vacate or set aside any sentence, in whole or in part, and to direct the execution of such part only of any sentence as has not been vacated or set aside."[6] In a separate memorandum to Crowder, Clark emphasized that the presidential power just described "finds its analogy in the civil courts, in the appellate power lodged in the Supreme

---

with hesitation, . . . and therefore when the necessity of this appellate power became manifest[,] my first instinct was to come to Congress with a proposition to confer it on the President." Ibid., 1196. The "proposition" mentioned by Crowder is discussed below.

[4] Ibid., 860.

[5] Ibid., 863.

[6] *Hearings, 1*, 151.

Court.''[7] Under existing practice, once a court-martial sentence had been reviewed and approved by the appropriate commander—it became final ''and could not be revoked, modified or set aside by the President. . . . All that could be done was to mitigate or remit the sentence . . . and this left the conviction untouched.''[8]

Davis and Clark did more than provide an analysis justifying the revisions for Section 1199. They also drafted a letter for Baker's signature, addressed to the appropriate congressional committee chairmen. In it, the secretary strongly supported the proposed change, and urged ''its early enactment into law.''[9] In so doing however, he (or they) reflected some confusion about the distinction between presidential authority and appellate review.

Baker stated that the president ''bears to the Military Establishment and to the administration of military justice a relation analogous to that occupied by the Supreme Court in the structure of a civil judiciary.'' In actual fact, this statement is something of an exaggeration. In 1919, there was no established appellate review of any consequence within the military. Moreover, it is difficult to equate what the president actually did under existing practice, or even what was proposed in the revision, with traditional appellate process. No lawyers were heard on appeal to the president; no official briefs were filed; with his other responsibilities, one wonders how much reflection and time could be allotted to any presidential review of court-martial records—let alone the judicial deliberation described by Professor Meador in the previous chapter.

Even more striking was the apparent open-ended discretion vested in the president. Unlike many appellate procedures, the proposed revision could be interpreted so as to permit him to increase penalties as well as reduce them; he could even set aside a not guilty finding by a court-martial. Few are the civil appellate judges who can reverse an acquittal in a criminal case.[10] To be sure, under the new changes the president had flexibility and many more options available to him. But in retrospect, the proposed change may well have resem-

[7] Ibid., 185.

[8] Ibid., 183.

[9] Ibid., 149. The proposed changes were ''believed to be both wise and necessary.''

[10] On the other hand, General Crowder insisted that the words ''disapprove, vacate, or set aside any finding'' as well as the words ''to modify, vacate or set aside any sentence'' did not mean that the president could increase a penalty. ''Is there anything said here about the power to substitute a finding of guilty for a larger offense for a finding of a smaller or included offense?'' He conceded that the president might set aside a verdict of not guilty, but even that official could not ''substitute a conviction for the disapproved verdict of acquittal.'' Moreover, Crowder claimed that ''modify,'' especially when used in a penal statute, meant if anything to reduce, rather than expand. In terms of practice, he may have been right. In terms of the actual words used in the draft, however, it would seem that presidential discretion to disapprove, vacate, modify, or set aside in whole or in part any sentence or finding—of necessity embraced any and every finding that a court-martial might hand down. *Hearings,* 2, 1227–28, 1231–32.

bled more an executive discretionary authority, rather than an opportunity for genuine appellate review.

This proposed revision died in the Senate Committee on Military Affairs, which failed even to consider the measure. In February 1919, its chair, Senator George Chamberlain (Democrat from Oregon) stated to Alfred Clark that his colleagues "did not think [the proposed revision] granted any further power than you already had, so that disposed of it. . . ."[11] While he apparently did not speak out in public against the revised section, Ansell also strongly opposed the changes, but for a different reason. In February 1919, he stated before Chamberlain's committee that the bill "in my judgment—and I speak very frankly— . . . was a very imperfect effort, and had it been enacted[,] our second situation would probably have been worse than the first." Either the power should be granted the president, "excluding everyone between him and the Judge Advocate General," or place it in the hands of that officer "solely and independently; and inasmuch as it is a judicial power I believe it ought to be placed not in the hands of the President but in the hands of a judicial officer whose duties are prescribed by Congress, and whom the President himself must appoint."[12]

This step would insure that attorneys within the JAG department would conduct the review. Ansell's goal had consistently been for an independent level of appellate review conducted by lawyers not located within the regular chain of army command, rather than by subordinates to the chief of staff.[13] During 1919 the subject of revising Section 1199 would come before the Senate Committee again, this time in a different version submitted by Chamberlain, but probably drafted by Ansell himself.

ANSELL PERSISTS

By 1918, Ansell appears to have become somewhat obsessed with his ideas on appellate review. To be sure, Baker had refused to accept his interpretation

[11] *Hearings, 1,* 181.

[12] Ibid., 74–75. In August 1919, Ansell in wide-ranging testimony before a Senate Subcommittee returned to #1199 once again. This time, he claimed that "I should like to say that I have never believed, and I have good reasons for not believing that [the revision of 1199] was submitted . . . in good faith." He did not believe that Congress could ever approve "a proposition that is so un-American, so basically illegal, and unjust and unfair, as to permit any man to strike down the judgment of a court to the disadvantage of the accused, substituting harsher punishment, harsher penalties, than the court awarded." He concluded, "It is a good thing that it was never enacted into law, because it would have carried this iniquitous system one step further." *Hearings, 2,* 111–12. By now, Ansell had resigned from the army, and his lengthy testimony was markedly more strident and critical than his earlier comments in February.

[13] It should be noted, however, that nothing in the draft revision precluded the president from delegating to the JAG department the type of appellate review envisaged by Ansell.

of Section 1199. Crowder, on the other hand, strongly supported Order No. 7, as well as the proposed "official" revision of Section 1199—both considered by his associate as ineffectual if not inappropriate. With Crowder heavily involved as administrator of the national draft, Ansell—still listed as his senior assistant—spent much of 1918 trying to establish on paper at least a system of military review; although he conceded frankly that it could only be advisory to the commander. While his formal break with Crowder was more than a year away, the professional gulf between them deepened in 1918, possibly because of the zeal with which Ansell espoused his beliefs.[14]

Even before Order No. 7 had been formally promulgated, Ansell informed the chief of the Military Justice Division "of certain views of mine which . . . must be observed generally in the establishment, if that administration [of military justice] is to be what justice requires it to be and what thoughtful public opinion would like it to be." He wanted to make sure that his views "may not be misunderstood[,] and that they may . . . constitute your authority for action in which you and others may not personally concur."[15] If Crowder advocated the proposition that courts-martial were essentially executive attributes of command, Ansell argued the proposal that they were "*courts*, tribunals for the doing of justice, as much so as any tribunals in the land." Their fairness was to be tested not only by the Articles of War, "but by those principles . . . which are designed to secure a fair and impartial trial and which are applicable to all hearings of a judicial character."[16] Such in part was what Ansell described as the "legal view, now judicially established."

He went on to criticize court-martial penalties levied during the current war "for their undue and inexplicable severity. Frequently they are such as to shock the conscience." Not only do they violate justice, but "they invite and merit public reproach." As to the oft-repeated official response that "nobody expects such punishments to be served," Ansell responded correctly that the truth of this claim was itself an "admission of the injustice of the punishments

[14] On February 17, 1919, Ansell recalled that "in and out of season, whenever opportunity has offered, and at times with an insistence which has strained, if not transgressed, the military proprieties, I have labored to the end that courts-martial might come to be legally established and universally regarded and respected as courts . . . of justice." 57 *Cong. Record*, part 4, 65th Cong., 3d sess. (1919): 3809. Only two days earlier, he had remarked to the Senate Committee on Military Affairs about his own role in the military justice controversy. Said Ansell of himself: "It could probably be said of him that he may have gotten at times unjudicial, that he may have gotten at times too insistent, and may have appeared at times not to integrate very easily with an established order of things. . . ." *Hearings, 1*, 141.

[15] JAGO files, Judge Advocate General's School Library, box 4, file 1, folder 1. The copy is clearly dated January 3, 1918, but it has been altered by hand to read January 3, 1919. It also appears in printed form with this new date. See *Hearings, 2*, 1042–44.

[16] Ibid., 1043. Due process concerning courts-martial "should be determined with less inclination to regard [them] as tribunals sui generis, and with greater regard for those fundamental safeguards with which the law beneficently surrounds every person placed in jeopardy."

and is bound to bring courts-martial into disrepute.'' My sense of applied law and justice, he concluded, ''requires me to enunciate these views clearly and unmistakably and ask you to be governed by them until they may be superceded.''[17]

Ansell later repeated and expanded on these points in a lengthy letter to Secretary Baker.[18] He strongly objected to several courts-martial penalties recently referred to his office because of the courts' failure ''to appreciate the high character of their judicial functions.'' To be sure, he had ''advised'' the commanders that the penalties levied were ''so disproportionate to the offense as to shock the conscience.'' But this was not sufficient enough ''to achieve and establish military justice.''[19]

As he had earlier implied to the chief of the Military Justice Division, here Ansell reaffirmed his insistence that courts-martial must be conducted judicially, as well as judiciously. If such sentences ''are awarded to be served they will bring disgrace by their shocking cruelty; if they are awarded as a sort of 'bluff' they will bring sacred functions into disrepute. From every point of view they are a travesty upon justice''; all the more so because courts-martial fill a judicial function, and the power they exercise so crudely ''is judicial'' in character. The examples described to Baker ''are not in my judgment, isolated examples but are evidence of more general deficiencies in the administration of military justice which I have observed, at least I believe I have observed, during this war.''[20]

To support his contention that courts-martial were judicial in character, Ansell cited two Supreme Court decisions which, he claimed, established this point in law.[21] The first case, *Runkle v. United States*, was decided in 1887.[22] The Court unanimously held that when it appeared that a president had approved a court-martial sentence, the sentence will not be binding ''unless it is authenticated in a way to show otherwise than argumentatively that it is the result of the judgment of the president himself, and that it is not a mere departmental order which might or might not have attracted his personal attention.''[23] When approving a sentence, the president acted in a judicial rather than administrative capacity. What Ansell saw as important was less the actual

[17] Ibid., 1043–44.

[18] The manuscript copy used herein was found in Enoch Crowder's Papers, and is clearly dated January 11, 1918. However, it also appears in the printed hearings with the date January 11, 1919. *Hearings*, 2, 1044–46. As with the earlier example cited above, I have been unable to discover any reasons for the discrepancies in these dates.

[19] CP, reel 3, folder 84, January 11, 1918.

[20] Ibid. Not satisfied with his letter to Baker, Ansell appended a note to Crowder, asking his chief to ''throw the weight of your influence upon the side of getting him interested in the matter.''

[21] He had previously cited but not discussed them in his second brief to Baker, filed in December 1917.

[22] 122 U.S. 543 (1887).

[23] Ibid., 561.

decision, than a description of a court-martial written in 1864 by Lincoln's Attorney General, Edward Bates, and quoted by Chief Justice Morrison R. Waite during the course of his opinion. "The whole proceeding, from its inception, is judicial. The trial, finding, and sentence are the solemn acts of a court organized and conducted under the authority of and according to the prescribed forms of law. It sits to pass upon the most sacred questions of human rights that are ever placed on trial in a court of justice, rights which, in the very nature of things, can neither be exposed to danger, nor subjected to the uncontrolled will of any man, but which must be judged *according to law*."[24]

Ansell's second decision was another unanimous holding, handed down in 1907, *Grafton v. United States*.[25] It involved an American soldier court-martialed in the Philippines on a charge of murder, and acquitted. Whereupon a local court proceeded to retry him for the same offense, resulting in a guilty verdict and a prison sentence of twelve years and one day. When the Supreme Court of the Philippines affirmed the verdict, Grafton turned to the United States Supreme Court; his principle constitutional arguments being that of the 5th Amendment bar against double jeopardy, and also a congressional statute enacted in 1902 that established civil government in the Philippines, providing that "no person, for the same offense, shall be twice put in jeopardy of punishment."[26]

The Court unanimously reversed the second conviction. Justice John Marshall Harlan, echoing the 1859 case of *Dynes v. Hoover*, held that "civil tribunals cannot disregard the judgments of a general court-martial . . . if such court had jurisdiction to try the offense." The prohibition of double jeopardy, whether it came from the Constitution or from Congress, meant that a civil court even if under federal jurisdiction "cannot withhold from an officer or soldier of the Army the full benefit of that guaranty, after he has been once tried in a military court."[27]

Ansell made no effort to explain the significance of these cases either in his second brief, or his letter to Baker. Not until August 1919, in the midst of his testimony before the Senate Subcommittee on Military Affairs, did he discuss them. He seems to have been much less than convincing, although in retrospect it becomes quite understandable why he relied so heavily on these two cases. They were important because the crux of his battles within the JAG Corps focused on what attributes of "judiciousness" attached to courts-martial. If a court-martial was inherently judicial, as indicated in *Runkle*, then it

[24] Ibid., 558. Emphasis in original.

[25] 206 U.S. 333 (1907).

[26] Ibid., 345.

[27] Ibid., 351–52. "We rest our decision . . . upon the broad ground that the same acts constituting a crime against the United States cannot, after the acquittal or conviction of the accused in a court of competent jurisdiction, be made the basis of a second trial of the accused for that crime in the same or in another court, civil or military of the same government."

could be subject to judicial—appellate review, like any other criminal trial; whether it be under civilian or military jurisdiction.[28]

Ansell's use of *Grafton*, on the other hand, is much less satisfactory. When as a civilian, he discussed this case before the Senate Subcommittee in August 1919, he stated that it involved "an issue in which I was then and still am deeply interested, . . . the very character of these courts-martial, and how far those principles of the Bill of Rights . . . are applicable" to them. "I say this was the issue involved."[29] The trouble with his comment is that nowhere in his opinion for the Court did Justice Harlan mention any relationship of the Bill of Rights to courts-martial. Furthermore, while he held that the double jeopardy provision applied in this case, he failed—perhaps intentionally—to choose between the Constitutional provision or the act of Congress as grounds for reversal.

Had this been the extent of Ansell's reliance on *Grafton*, his interpretation might have withstood some scrutiny. It could be argued that just in mentioning the constitutional provision, by implication Harlan recognized its applicability to courts-martial. Perhaps this is what Ansell assumed. However, he proceeded to quote the following "excerpt" from the opinion to the subcommittee. "We base our decision not upon the fact that this clause of the Constitution . . . has been carried to the Philippines by congressional enactment; we do not base this decision upon the fact that Congress has enacted in the old fortieth article of war, an inhibition against double jeopardy. We base it upon the fact that the Constitution . . . applies, regardless of legislation."[30]

As he continued his testimony, Ansell turned to other matters, and *Grafton* apparently was not discussed again until Crowder's appearance before the subcommittee in October 1919. He indicated that he could find no such excerpt in the Court's opinion. Nor, it should be added, can this author. Crowder's reference to Ansell's earlier testimony is accurate.[31] Nevertheless, he specifically declined to "charge Gen. Ansell with having attributed language to the Supreme Court which it did not utter."[32] Where the quotation came from re-

[28] As will be noted later in this chapter, by 1919 Ansell's conception of a proper "review" had changed from his earlier reliance in 1917 on #1199. He now concluded that effective administration of military justice required expanded responsibility and authority for the JAG, that went far beyond #1199.

[29] *Hearings, 2*, 125.

[30] Ibid., 126.

[31] Ibid., 1172.

[32] Ibid., 1173. Crowder added that "I asked another lawyer to come over here to the Capitol and examine the original opinion and briefs of the case, to see if that language was used by the court, or in any of the contending briefs, and he reported back that that language was not to be found." Again, this author also examined the complete briefs and records of this case—with the same result. It might be noted that of all the witnesses who ultimately appeared before the subcommittee—and they included many senior army officers, JAG officials, Baker, Morgan, and Ansell—only one, Enoch Crowder, asked that his testimony be given under oath. Ibid., 1134. Sen.

mains unclear. The point, although admittedly intriguing, is not as important as the fact that Ansell apparently could not cite much convincing case law to support his claim that ample precedent existed for his views concerning the judicial nature of courts-martial.

Ansell's reliance on *Grafton* was not challenged until 1919. In the meantime, though he found it to be less than what he considered appropriate, Order No. 7 had been adopted; and indeed, a branch of the JAG Corps had been established in France to facilitate its implementation. If the new regulation barred Ansell from creating an actual appellate tribunal, it did not appear to ban setting up some sort of JAG advisory board that at least looked like one. But before he could even take this step, both Ansell and Crowder had to deal with Gen. John J. Pershing's objections to the admittedly minimal requirements of Order No. 7, as it applied to his command, the American Expeditionary Force. Ansell's reactions to this incident are of interest because they reveal his growing impatience with a very senior line officer's conception of military discipline.

General Order No. 7 had been promulgated in January 1918, with no recorded objection from Pershing. In March, however, he advised the War Department that "any authority outside of control of the commander in chief will cause delay. . . . Beyond doubt[,] punishment for desertion or misconduct must be summary, if it is to have any deterrent effect. . . . Any thought in minds of men that they can possibly escape punishment for such misconduct would be disastrous. I am very strongly of the opinion that final authority in these cases should rest with the supreme commander here."[33]

In a memorandum to Crowder, Ansell responded first that Pershing's inexplicable delay in objecting to establishment of the JAG branch office "should weaken the confidence the department might otherwise have had in Gen. Pershing's judgment upon the matter."[34] More important, he ignored the requirements of Section 1199. Before the JAG could revise a record of court-martial, he had to receive it. Pershing's emphasis on the need for summary judgment conflicted with the statute. "It is obviously absurd to exercise a revisory power after the execution of death sentences or other sentences finally separating an officer or member of the Military. . . ."[35]

Pershing claimed that JAG review would cause delay. Since such review was mandatory, examination of court-martial records by a JAG officer located not in Washington but with the troops in France "makes not for delay but for expedition." How such a process could cause in Pershing's words a "miscarriage of justice" when justice can not be administered without such a review,

---

Irvine Lenroot responded: "It is not the custom; it is to be taken for granted, but if the witness desires it, I see no objection." Subsequently, Crowder was sworn.

[33] Ibid., 967.

[34] Ibid.

[35] Ibid., 969.

Ansell found "beyond comprehension." Apparently the commanding general believed that "in the administration of military justice[,] mere summariness of execution of sentences is to be preferred to a reasonable assurance of its legality."

Finally, Ansell questioned whether Pershing actually meant that men ought not to escape punishment because of a "trial that is found to be fundamentally illegal." If so, "his attitude could hardly fail to shock the ordinary sense of justice." It was not unreasonable to assume that "the morale of the command would be improved when assured that they will be punished only according to law[,] and not according to hasty and ill-advised judgment." Pershing's "implication that the review of this office must necessarily result in men escaping deserved punishment imposed according to law is thoroughly unjustified."[36]

Crowder, although adopting a much more respectful tone toward Pershing, agreed with Ansell. He first advised that Pershing be informed by the chief of staff that Order No. 7 "must be complied with. Doubtless it will not, when its purposes are thoroughly understood, be objectionable to you."[37] He later added a sentence that "your suggestion that it may result in miscarriages of justice is not concurred in, since it is believed that it will operate to prevent miscarriages of justice by assuring that legality without which no serious sentence should ever be carried into execution."[38]

During the remainder of 1918, on at least three occasions, Ansell sought to integrate JAG practices with traditional appellate procedures. Four months after the Pershing incident, he created within the JAG department a Board of Review. Presumably, he intended it to be the vehicle for the "revisions" mandated by law, as well as those required by Order No. 7. "The duties of such Board will be in the nature of those of an appellate tribunal, and shall be performed with due regard for their character as such."[39] One cannot help but notice how much Ansell modeled his board along the lines of traditional appellate procedure.

Thus, once a JAG officer had examined the court-martial record—it would be transmitted to the board, "and thereupon the members of said Board will proceed to consider the preliminary review . . . in the manner similar to that employed by appellate tribunals on reaching and expressing their decisions." Although this type of board outwardly resembled an appellate tribunal, it differed from the real thing in the most important aspect possible—exercise of judicial power.[40] Sen. George Chamberlain aptly described the realities of An-

[36] Ibid., 969–70.

[37] Ibid., 970.

[38] Ibid., 973. Two days later, Crowder wrote to W. A. Bethel the letter discussed in the previous chapter, wherein he explained why #7 had been adopted in the first place. See, sup., chap. 3, n. 98.

[39] JAGO files, box 1, file 3, folder 1.

[40] Testifying in February 1919, Ansell claimed that the review boards had done "magnificent

sell's review boards. "In theory, that was a review without power to afford a remedy, without power to reverse, without power to modify, without any other power, where the court [martial] had jurisdiction and the proceedings were regular, than the power to advise the commanding officer."[41]

Ansell had no choice but to accept the limitations of Order No. 7. He persisted, however, in his efforts to broaden review authority; whether it actually existed in military practice let alone law, seems not to have troubled him unduly. Thus, on October 25, 1918, he submitted another memorandum to the head of the JAG military justice division, rejecting its position that authority to review courts-martial was "strictly limited . . . to the question of the legality of the proceedings." Employing an unusual interpretation of the regulation, Ansell argued that Order No. 7 "was never intended to operate as a limitation upon the duties of this office."[42] To the contrary, it had been adopted in order to carry out the obligations and responsibilities mandated in Section 1199. Hence the regulation had to be seen as a grant, not a limitation of JAG authority. This office, then, "must be assumed to have the duty, by reason of its powers . . . to speak beyond the strict question of legality authorized by said order."[43]

Obviously undaunted by the earlier refusals of Crowder and Baker to find existing authority in Section 1199, Ansell had no doubt as to how the military justice division ought to proceed now that he had provided the rationale: "[T]here could be no present accomplishment that would operate to the geater good of the Army or meet with greater approbation of those of our people who are interested in the administration of military justice than the establishment in this office of an administrative procedure that would result in rendering the punishments in the military Establishment more nearly uniform, more scientific and intelligent, and better related to justice to the individual upon the one hand and military discipline in general upon the other." Finally, he instructed the department "to make such recommendations in all cases" reviewed under authority of Order No. 7, that "will tend toward the achievement of this result, and [you] will no longer in such cases consider yourselves limited to the sole question of legality of procedure."[44]

---

work. But the opinions are a peculiar mixture of argument and logic and appeals to military power, putting all that you can in language to get a military authority to adopt the view. That is, we were not speaking judicially, and we were not speaking with authority. We were trying to persuade military persons to do what we thought was right." *Hearings, 1*, 141–42.

[41] *Hearings, 2*, 530. William Rigby responded not unreasonably that the persuasiveness of a board's "recommendation" for modification or disapproval of sentence was not to be taken lightly. From October 1917 to August 1919 more than 28,000 cases were reviewed by the JAG department, with 457 recommended for either modification or disapproval. Of this number, JAG recommendations were followed in 447 instances. Ibid., 531.

[42] Ibid., 910.

[43] Ibid., 911.

[44] Ibid.

In November 1918, Ansell issued yet another internal memorandum on the procedures to be followed by the JAG department in its review of reports and proceedings of boards convened for administrative purposes other than examination of court-martial records. Because the "finding is made below and not here[,] accordingly the principles governing appellate review should apply." Hence, "it will be the policy of this office to sustain a finding 'whenever it is thought that an appellate tribunal, under general modern practice, would uphold a similar judgment by a lower court upon a similar issue.' "[45]

Thus, as 1918 drew to a close, Ansell had persevered in his efforts to integrate military justice with civil procedure; apparently with minimal opposition or cooperation from the "establishment." Outwardly there was no dispute between Ansell and Crowder. The arguments over revisionary authority, what with Baker's decision supporting Crowder, implementation of Order No. 7, and the short-lived submission to Congress of a revised version of Section 1199—all had been settled and seemingly consigned to oblivion. Indeed, Crowder even recommended that Ansell receive a distinguished service medal. He paid tribute to his assistant's "exceptionally meritorious service[,] . . . his legal ability . . . personality, energy . . . and vigorous administration." Among "his leading opinions" enunciating "many great principles of law fundamental to military administration," Crowder specifically cited Ansell's insistence that the "Articles of War be construed with more and more regard to the Constitutional principles governing criminal prosecutions."[46]

Even as Crowder prepared the nomination for submission to Baker, a new factor changed the nature of the controversy within the JAG department. Ironically enough, it had been anticipated by Ansell as early as August 1917, when, it will be recalled, he proposed sweeping changes in JAG administration.[47] At that time, he had urged that the process of "revision" be thorough; if only "to provide against the time which will almost inevitably come when the conduct of the War Department will be the subject of Congressional investigation, without which no war has ever been conducted in the history of the United States."[48] Of course Congress had been concerned with the conduct of the war long before December 1918. But not until December 30 was its attention called specifically to problems with the administration of military justice. The speaker was George Chamberlain, Democrat from Oregon, chairman of the Senate Committee on Military Affairs, and a vocal critic both of Wilson's war leadership and Baker's administration of the War Department.[49] Prior to

[45] JAGO files, box 1, folder 3, file 1.

[46] *Hearings, 2*, 1071. The medal was duly conferred on January 18, 1919 only a matter of days before the public side of the feud developed. *New York Times*, January 19, 1919, 5.

[47] See sup., chap. 3.

[48] JAGO files, box 4, folder 1, file 1.

[49] See, for example, Chamberlain's comments in the *Congressional Record* for January 24, 1918 when, for the second time, he stated that the military establishment "has fallen down, [and]

his wide-ranging remarks, only part of which concerned military justice, resolution of the Ansell-Crowder dispute had been improbable; after Chamberlain's speech it became impossible.

GOING PUBLIC

Chamberlain's comments set the tone for the final phase of the Ansell-Crowder controversy, although he discussed neither the issues nor participants. He criticized the role of the commander in the court-martial. "What use of a court if a commanding officer is to practically control its actions?"[50] Next, Chamberlain turned to military justice in general. Court-martials conducted during the recent war "show that we have no military law or system of administering military justice which is worthy of the name of law or justice." If, he stated, "we are to have a democratic Army, military justice ought to be administered . . . by courts which are constituted, whose procedure is determined, and whose action is controlled by law. Courts-martial should be required to accept the interpretation of the law by a responsible law officer in the same manner that a jury in a civil criminal court accepts the interpretation of the law by the judge of the court." Congress ought to "enact a code that would fix the boundaries of these courts, and which would define their jurisdiction and duties."[51] Further, "the sure cure for it all is to have some sort of tribunal, appellate or supervisory that shall have the power to formulate rules and equalize these unjust sentences."

This writer has been unable to find any direct evidence that Ansell and

---

has almost stopped functioning." Wilson responded that the statement was "an astonishing and absolutely unjustifiable distortion of the truth." Privately, he wrote that Chamberlain "is in conference much more often with systematic opponents of the administration than with its friends." 56 *Cong. Record*, part 2, 65th Cong., 2d sess. (1918), 1194–96; Ray Stannard Baker, *Woodrow Wilson*, vol. 7 (1968), 530. As will be seen in the next chapter, the fact that Chamberlain became the leading congressional supporter of Ansell's proposed reforms is of great importance. Aside from genuine disagreement within the army as to their merits, the bitter antagonism between the senator and the Wilson's administration, especially Baker and the war department, made a hostile reception to what he favored a virtual certainty. Indeed, in November 1920, Wilson went so far as to issue a personal appeal to Oregon voters urging that they defeat Chamberlain in his bid for reelection. They did. See also the editorial "The Fight on Chamberlain," in *Portland Journal*, April 27, 1920. *Chamberlain Papers*, Oregon Historical Society.

[50] *Cong. Record* 57, part 1, 65th Cong., 3d sess., 877. Chamberlain added, "It is wholly repugnant to our ideas of the administration of criminal law that any one should have the power to set aside a verdict of acquittal. Nevertheless, this is the power of the commanding officer over a court-martial trial."

[51] Ibid., 878. In the meantime, Chamberlain believed that some badly needed instructions from Baker would produce a more "uniform administration of the law. There is nothing in the world that will make the members of the Military Establishment do their duty in a proper way more surely than to discharge or reprimand an officer once in a while." Ibid.

Chamberlain "collaborated" on these remarks. However, his words resemble many of Ansell's strictures so closely that the senator's familiarity with them may be assumed. Furthermore, by publicly mentioning the problems with military justice, Chamberlain removed it from within the War Department to the outside world. It was one thing to agitate privately for change within the establishment; it was quite another for a senator and chairman of the Committee on Military Affairs publicly to call for reforms. This new component of publicity invariably caused the military establishment to act defensively; seeking to retain, not to innovate. With comments on military justice now spread upon the pages of the *Congressional Record*, the next step was for national press publicity.

This possibility became reality on January 19, 1919. With an American president in Europe for the first time in history, with national attention focused on the preparations for the Versailles peace conference, the readers of the *New York World* (in general a pro-administration paper) found the entire first page of the editorial section devoted to "THE THING THAT IS CALLED MILITARY JUSTICE—CONCRETE OFFICIAL EVIDENCE WHICH ESTABLISHES THAT THE UNITED STATES MILITARY COURTS-MARTIAL INDORSE [SIC] AND APPROVE OF OPPRESSION AND ARBITRARILY IMPOSE GROSS INJUSTICE." The lengthy article was written by Rowland Thomas, who apparently had secured permission of Newton Baker to examine various court-martial records. Besides detailing much of the same material previously discussed by Chamberlain, indeed the senator was quoted in the article, Thomas went a step further. Unlike Chamberlain, he specifically mentioned the Ansell-Crowder disagreement; although he did not identify Ansell by name.[52]

With Chamberlain's speech past history, Thomas reiterated the point that "in the United States Army at present[,] judicial power is only a concomitant and incident of military power." He added that within the JAG department, "there is an irreconcilable difference of opinion about the proper answer" to Chamberlain's question "whether . . . we shall have . . . a system of administering military justice worthy of the name of law and justice, or whether we shall have simply a method of giving effect by courts-martial to the more or less arbitrary discretion of commanding officers." According to Thomas, Crowder believed in the theory that "courts-martial are mere instrumentalities of military command." Such "is not the view held by the officer who, throughout the war, has been Acting [JAG] . . . nor by most of the officers of the department."[53]

The author noted Ansell's earlier attempts at enlarging the power of revision, and Crowder's negative response to his efforts. He described Ansell as "an officer of the highest personal repute in the Army and a lawyer whose

[52] Citations from Thomas's article are taken from *Cong. Record* 57, part 2, 65th Cong., 3d sess. (1919): 1929–32.

[53] Ibid., 1930.

learning and ability are fully recognized at the bar.''[54] He even quoted a lengthy internal memorandum written to Crowder by his assistant, and detailed specific examples of extreme penalties meted out by courts-martial. Thomas concluded that ''the so called military justice of these United States of ours, besides being blundering and senseless, is archaic.''[55]

Publication of this article immediately raised the question of whether or not Thomas had some internal assistance from the JAG department in the research if not the actual writing of his piece. Enoch Crowder had no doubt ''that it was prepared by someone who had access to the records of my office.''[56] Such records would be ''particularly available to officers at work in the Section of Military Justice and in the clemency section.'' Beyond this point, Crowder would say no more. Did he have ''any knowledge as to the identity of the person who prepared it? Absolutely not.''[57]

Chamberlain's speech represented congressional criticism; Thomas's ''exposé'' symbolized emerging popular criticism. Ansell probably had been involved behind the scenes with preparation of both pieces, although the extent to which he ''assisted'' remains uncertain. Shortly after the *World* article appeared, he decided also to ''go public.'' He may have concluded that with both media and political pressure coming from outside, it was now time for evidence from a third source—one representing opposition from within the army itself to the administration of military justice.

On January 25, 1919, the *Chicago Daily News* reported about a luncheon address by Ansell to the Chicago Real Estate Board with the headline ''JUDGE ADVOCATE HITS ARMY COURT SYSTEM.'' According to the writer, he spoke ''frankly of the weaknesses of the court martial system.'' Furthermore, the administration of military justice ''is now the subject of popular criticism.''[58] Noting that as acting JAG during most of the war, he had in effect been in charge of the very system he now attacked, Ansell found it prudent to add that ''I do not regard the criticism as personal or as directed at human agencies

[54] Ibid., 1931.

[55] Ibid., 1932.

[56] *Hearings*, 2, 785. Crowder added that Thomas had indeed visited his office, but also stated his belief that ''the total length of time he was in my office did not exceed an hour, and I feel that it did not exceed half an hour.''

[57] Ibid. Ansell, of course worked in both these offices. Crowder may well have been surprised by some of the article's contents. Especially because, at this point in time, he was doing all he could to help rather than hinder Ansell. The Thomas piece appeared on Sunday, January 19. The next day, he dictated a letter to Lindley Garrison, Wilson's first secretary of war. He asked Garrison's assistance in helping find civilian legal employment for Ansell who ''has steadily grown professionally and in point of usefulness to the Department.'' ''My relations with Ansell,'' he added, ''may be described as fairly intimate. . . . While my motive in writing this letter is a desire to assist a friend, it is broader than that. I have great confidence in Ansell's great ability as a lawyer. . . .'' CP, reel 4, folder 118. Since within about two weeks, Crowder was bitterly referring to a conspiracy against him, arising from within his own office, this letter may well represent the last compliments paid by Crowder to his senior assistant!

[58] A fact, of course, due in great measure to his own involvement.

charged with the administration of the system, but as aimed at the system itself,'' one which ''is in many respects patently defective and in need of immediate revision at the hands of Congress.''

For the first time, Ansell articulated publicly what he had advocated privately to Baker and Crowder for almost two years. Courts-martial were first and foremost *courts*. Yet such a tribunal is the only court ''in all our land that, holding in jeopardy the life and liberty of our citizen soldiery, under existing law, has to proceed to execute that sacred trust without the aid, guidance or control of any person in the least qualified in the law.'' Shocking as it might be, ''the whole system of court-martial under existing law proceeds on the theory that it is to be administered by men who know not one word of law.''[59] The *Chicago Tribune* briefly mentioned Ansell's other speech to the Chicago Bar Association, apparently very similar to the first in content. He ''attacked the system of military courts-martial as unjust to the soldier, and demanded that radical changes be introduced to the end that more exact justice might be meted out to the men in service.''[60]

A few comments need to be made concerning Ansell's public debut as an advocate for reforming military justice. In the first place, it seems clear that he tried to keep the attention on issues, not personalities. There is no indication from the press coverage that he mentioned any names of senior army officials at all, let alone in a critical manner. On the other hand, in calling for congressional changes to the military justice system Ansell publicly pointed to the inability of the army to reform itself. By so doing, he committed an act probably resented more by the ''military establishment'' than his various legal propositions; he did not keep his disagreements within the corps. With a move that is either tribute to his resolve or testimony to his recklessness, in one fell swoop he proposed to challenge the army bureaucracy, leadership of his own department, and the secretary of war; and he undertook this admittedly daunting challenge with his strongest source of support coming from a maverick senator, increasingly isolated within his own party.

CROWDER'S CONCERNS

From his perspective, Crowder saw these several pronouncements about military justice as part of a preconceived scheme. First Chamberlain's speech, followed by publication of Thomas's article, and a few days later the news

[59] *Chicago Daily News*, January 25, 1919, 3. Ansell further observed that when the JAG department sought to set aside excessive or improper penalties, lacking the power to order a new trial ''every such reversal of judgment must operate as an acquittal.'' He added finally, that in an effort to give some assurance of justice, his department had employed ''a resort to extra methods.''

[60] *Chicago Tribune*, January 26, 1919, 6.

3. Enoch Crowder, 1918. Courtesy the Department of the Army Judge Advocate General.

accounts of Ansell's comments in Chicago. By late January, military justice had become a "hot item" for the American press, and it continued to be of popular interest for the next several months.[61] Crowder had reason to be concerned less about the debate itself than its effect on his reappointment to a final term as JAG. Because of a quirk in military personnel procedures, he stood to become a civilian, with corresponding loss of seniority and other benefits unless reappointed and confirmed by February 14, 1919. With Wilson out of the country, the document had to be sent abroad and returned with his signature. It did not arrive in New York until the 12th, and barely reached the Senate in time for favorable consideration on February 13.

Crowder believed that the rash of popular commentary in context with the three episodes already mentioned was clearly intended to persuade Wilson or the Senate against either renomination or confirmation.[62] In fact, neither of these two events appears to have been in any doubt. It is clear, however, that some congressional criticism of Crowder's role or lack thereof in military justice was prevalent. The JAG's sense of beleaguerment although unnecessary was understandable.

On February 4, he wrote his old friend and former secretary of war, Henry Stimson, that "a conspiracy, hatching out in my own office, is responsible for the arraignment . . . of military justice, their purpose being—not to reform the code in aspects where it might be reformed, but to prevent my reappointment. They were working in the interest of another man."[63] As he had done in other instances, Crowder refused to make any specific accusations, but he obviously meant Ansell. Another of Stimson's correspondents, Felix Frankfurter, was a little more candid. Three days later he informed his former chief that Crowder's renomination was on the way. "I think the opposition will . . . peter out, but undoubtedly there is a strong undercurrent. I am sorry to say that I cannot, from the available evidence, acquit Ansell."[64]

[61] Preserved in the JAGO files in the archives is a twenty-page listing of all the newspaper articles dealing with military justice from January 19 to March 1, 1919. While virtually no summaries are recorded, the wide geographic dispersal of the articles from the Eastern seaboard to Salt Lake City is well documented. See *Records of the Judge Advocate General*, NARC, RG 153, entry 26, box 3.

[62] Lockmiller, *Enoch H. Crowder: Soldier, Lawyer and Statesman*, 204.

[63] *Henry L. Stimson Papers* (Yale University), reel 51, frame 547.

[64] Ibid., frame 557. In another letter to Stimson dated the same day, Frankfurter added that "there are fools in the world and people guided by personal ambition, and between the two a good deal of mischief can be done. That is precisely what is happening in the Crowder case." He went on to assure the former secretary of war that Baker supported Crowder. "Baker is 'humping' himself on this matter and is as down right about it as you could wish." *Felix Frankfurter Papers*, February 7, 1919; Library of Congress, reel 63. The next day, Stimson visited Crowder who apparently discussed at some length the entire controversy that had been building between him and Ansell. "The facts stated by him," Stimson wrote in his diary, "reflect badly on General Ansell." Crowder "thought that Ansell was privy to the attack upon him in the *World*[,] . . . and Ansell had stated to someone who told Crowder that if he ever became Judge Advocate General he would

It was not just all the unfavorable newspaper publicity that troubled Crowder. Chamberlain, presumably with Ansell's assistance, had drafted proposed legislative changes not only in the revisory power of the JAG, but in the relationship of that functionary to the court-martial process in general. To make matters worse, Ansell had agreed to be the first witness to discuss Chamberlain's revisions, and the hearings before the Senate Committee on Military Affairs were scheduled to begin on the same day the Senate had to vote on Crowder's renomination.

For his part, Ansell presumably realized that by his actions if not his attitude, he was creating an impossible situation concerning his future in the JAG department. It may well be that by February 1919, this meant little to him. Even as Frankfurter was writing to Stimson, Ansell responded to a letter from a judge, the father of a draftee, concerning military treatment of his son. "Frankly," wrote Ansell, "our military system is absolutely Prussian. I have been very much interested in the subject of military justice, or rather, the system of military injustice. I have striven to establish in it even a little justice. My efforts have been largely in vain. . . . The thing is searing my soul, Judge. I have fought against it. I have fought a good fight; I have kept the faith in the eternal verities of right and truth and justice, the faith which came to me from my forbears and out of my own conscience."[65]

In his December 1918 address to the Senate, Chamberlain had called on Congress to establish the boundaries of court-martials, define their jurisdiction, and their duties. Also, he wanted "some sort of tribunal, appellate or supervisory that shall have the power to formulate rules and equalize these unjust sentences." On February 13, 1919, he opened hearings to consider Senate Bill 5320, "A Bill to promote the administration of military justice." At this stage of his inquiry, Chamberlain did not propose a formal appellate court; rather, he sought to enlarge by statute existing powers of the JAG, much as Ansell had tried to enhance them by implication. Several provisions of his proposed revision should be noted.

A JAG was to be appointed for every general or special court-martial. He "shall not be a member of the court, but shall sit with it at all times in open session and shall fairly, impartially, and in a judicial manner . . . rule on all questions of law properly arising in the proceedings. . . . His rulings and advice, given in the performance of his duties and made of record, shall govern the court-martial." Furthermore, a separate official was to prosecute the case, although it could be another JAG officer. In all court-martial proceedings, "the accused shall have the assistance of and be represented by counsel."[66]

---

not let Crowder into the office." *Diaries of Henry L. Stimson* (Yale University), reel 1, frames 292–93.

[65] *Henry G. Connor Papers*, #175 (Southern Historical Collection, University of North Carolina).

[66] Indeed, "if military counsel be not selected by the accused, the court shall assign military counsel to assist in his defense if such counsel be reasonably available."

Also, the commanding officer was forbidden to refer any charge to a general court-martial unless the appropriate JAG officer "shall endorse in writing . . . that in his opinion an offense made punishable by the Articles of War is charged with legal sufficiency . . . and that it has been made to appear to him that there is prima facie proof that the accused is guilty. . . ." When the court found the defendant not guilty on all charges, "it shall not reconsider, nor shall the appointing authority direct it to reconsider its findings."

Finally, the proposed revision altered Section 1190. First, the traditional power to "receive, revise and cause to be recorded," was to be exercised "only for corrections of errors of law which shall have injuriously affected the substantial rights of the accused." The JAG could disapprove both a finding of guilty as well as the whole or any part of a sentence. After such action, he was to advise the proper convening authority what legal proceedings "may and should be had, if any." If errors of law found in the record caused the sentence to be set aside, the convening authority could order a new trial by another court-martial.[67]

Ansell duly appeared as the first witness; indeed he spent the entire day testifying before the committee. He made public the actual documents generated during his debate with Crowder; including the responses of his chief and Secretary Baker.[68] He discussed at some length the clash between the two opposing interpretations concerning the nature of courts-martial. "Prevention of injustice," he insisted, "is better than any attempted cure . . . after it has once been inflicted, and the way to avoid error is to put the case at the start in the hands of a man who knows what error is. In such a system as ours the errors accumulate from bottom to top, and at the top there is no authority for their correction." In his judgment, no legislation to establish revisory power would have been needed during the war, "if the existing statute [Section 1199] had been properly construed at the beginning of the war."[69]

One senator correctly understood that when Ansell employed the term revision, he meant use of some appellate procedure; and asked Ansell where

[67] *Hearings, 1*, 3–4. Even today, with a military justice at a sophisticated level, and with appellate procedures long established, one is struck by the modernity of Chamberlain's suggestions. In many respects, what he called proposals are now called policies.

[68] "Of course," he added, "I disclaim any desire to read these views of my own for the purposes of accentuating any difference that I may have with any officers of the Army or with any persons in authority." Furthermore, when asked by Chamberlain, "Is there any personal difference between you" and Crowder, "or is your only difference on the proper construction of the statute?" Ansell replied, "We have no personal differences in the world." Ibid., 59. Like Justice Jackson in the famous *Everson* case in 1947, Ansell's protestations also remind one of Julia, who according to Byron's reports, "whispering, 'I will ne'er consent,' consented." *Everson v. Board of Education*, 330 U.S. 1 (1947).

[69] *Hearings, 1*, 7, 16. Perhaps Ansell was being a little disingenuous here. After all, in his opinion *he* had long construed the statute properly. It was to his superiors, Crowder and Baker, to whom he made this oblique reference.

such power ought to be vested—in the JAG or in the "President, he to be advised" by the JAG. Ansell replied that "inasmuch as it is inherently a judicial power, it ought not to be confused with or located by any considerations of military command."[70] As a matter of fact, "It does not shock me to say that there shall be some judicial authority, some independent law officer, some skilled man, some man who has been designated by Congress and appointed by the Chief Executive for this purpose, to determine whether or not, in the subjection of this individual to this system of penalties, the law of the land was complied with, even to the point of restraining any power, however high, if it is simply executive power or the power of military command."[71]

His answer may appear ambiguous, if only because it was not clear in 1919 exactly what authority a line command had over a staff position, such as the JAG. Ansell was surely aware that traditionally, commanders were not compelled to follow JAG "recommendations." On the other hand, as the Senate committee would learn from another witness, there were inherent problems in vesting such authority within the JAG department; and Ansell did not discuss them.

He returned for a second day of testimony, much of it repetitive. Two themes, apart from his legal arguments, seem to stand out when Ansell's testimony is considered as a whole. First, his regret that this type of public airing concerning military policy had become necessary. "This is not a pleasant duty for me to perform. I realize, if I may be permitted to say it, that I am arraigning the institution to which I belong—not the institution, but the system and the practices under it."[72] Second, his refusal during *these* hearings, to make his disagreement with Crowder into a personal feud, even though he probably knew that it would end as such; and more for what he said and did, rather than Crowder.

"I think it is always unfortunate in war to have a divided responsibility. My views were known, and they were not accepted. All well and good. But two officers can not control the same establishment to the very greatest advantage when one insists that the existing institution and order of things are wrong and ought to be changed. You may say I am a good soldier, and I am going to do what my chief says. . . . But, at any rate, I am not so compliant."[73] The "views" which he had reiterated numerous times were simply that "we

[70] Ibid., 39.

[71] Ibid., 41. Although he did not actually propose a court of military appeals for several months, the similarity between what Ansell described and what exists today is noteworthy. Further, Ansell continued to insist that lawyers play a major role in any appellate review. "The trouble is we have got to examine the record as lawyers. Lawyers must examine the record. . . . We have got to get down to the record as judges and lawyers and see what that record reflects." Ibid., 86. Today, in the United States Court of Military Appeals, the first step for a case after it has been received and assigned a docket number is to refer it for examination by a staff attorney.

[72] Ibid., 81.

[73] Ibid., 146.

should have authority somewhere, and I contend it should be in a judicial officer, to order a new trial. . . .'' The current system ''depends on the view of [a] man, not governed by law. The law does not govern.''[74]

CROWDER'S CONVICTIONS

Even as Ansell appeared before the Senate committee, Crowder had prepared a detailed and lengthy rebuttal to Chamberlain that duly appeared in the *Congressional Record.* It took the form of a letter to Baker, dated February 13, 1919, the very day of Ansell's testimony.[75] Although he considered many aspects of the senator's speech, two points were important for the debate over the reviewing authority. First, far from receiving no real review, in military justice proceedings according to Crowder the accused received ''an automatic double appellate review''; first from the JAG officer who examined the record, and next from a board of review. Crowder even went so far as to say of this ''thorough scrutiny,'' one that also included a third inspection of the record by the JAG himself, that it was superior to civilian justice. In the second place, while it was true that the judgment expressed by the JAG ''in his appellate capacity is customarily phrased in terms of a recommendation to the commander,'' such suggestions ''are given practical effect in the same manner as the trial courts in civil justice give effect to the mandate of the supreme court of the state.'' In other words, the commanders were under no statutory compulsion to accept the JAG findings, but invariably they did.[76]

Chamberlain's committee recessed for more than a week, and did not reconvene until February 26, 1919, when it received testimony from several JAG officers including Crowder, all opposed to Ansell's contentions. In the meantime, the *Washington Post* criticized military justice, noting that ''it is a violation of the principles of justice . . . under which the right of appeal is denied

[74] Ibid., 107.

[75] Unlike Ansell, Crowder seems to have felt it inappropriate as the JAG to make public speeches concerning a now public dispute within his own office. On at least two occasions lengthy letters to Baker, which generally found their way into print, served to make his views known. In addition to testifying before congressional committees, Crowder also did not hesitate to make use of his private correspondence, which was extensive, to justify his views. He also encouraged his old acquaintances to write ''public letters'' to various newspapers on his behalf. Former Secretary of War Stimson and former President William Howard Taft were among several who did so.

[76] *Appendix to Congressional Record* 57, 65th Cong., 3d sess., 252, 256. ''The judgment of the Judge Advocate General . . . is practically enforced and put into effect by the commanding officers with virtually the same effect as the decision of an appellate civilian court.'' Ibid., 257. Crowder's description may be contrasted with Ansell, who said, ''We created some boards of review, consisting of very eminent lawyers, and made these reviews very formal and impressive, and they must have impressed everybody who read them. But again, they were only advice, carrying no authority, and I do not mind saying that when you are hedged in by limitations of that sort, you are bound to go at things rather timidly.'' *Hearings, 1*, 141.

to no man convicted of an offense.''[77] Within a week, the paper noted that Ansell ''may get out,'' and that his disclosures were said ''to be deeply resented.'' Indeed, such revelations have created a situation which ''will force his retirement.''[78]

When it reconvened, the Senate Committee first heard from Alfred Clark, one of the JAG officers who although originally supportive, ultimately was unpersuaded by Ansell's claim of revisionary authority within Section 1199. But Clark had a more fundamental problem with Ansell's approach, and it concerned the relationship of the JAG office to the power of revision. From 1917 to the spring of 1919, Ansell had argued that revisionary or review authority was inherent within the JAG department. He assumed that Congress ''could provide for a court which would have just as much power over the complete proceedings as the trial court itself has.''[79] But he also assumed, thus far at least, that the logical place for such a body was within his own ranks. Perhaps this was a bit egotistical; Ansell probably had no doubts that with officers like himself reviewing cases, military justice would indeed be well served.

Clark, although he fully agreed that ''there should be a military judicial appellate tribunal,'' denied that it should be either the JAG or officers under his jurisdiction. He observed that the JAG was ''the head of the whole prosecuting organization of the Army.''[80] It would be inappropriate to have such an officer in charge of appeals, just it would be unacceptable that the ''Attorney General . . . should finally review all cases tried in all the Federal Courts . . . by his assistants. The proposition is entirely inconsistent with the conception of an impartial appellate tribunal.'' Such a judicial body ''ought to be . . . constituted by Congress, which should provide for the appointment of the members thereof in the usual manner by the President and confirmation by the Senate, leaving to the President, the discretion as to selection—whether he shall select distinguished lawyers from the Army, or distinguished lawyers from civil life, or distinguished lawyers in part from the Army and part from civil life—and constitute the personnel so appointed a judicial body subject to no military control.''

Clark believed his proposal to be ''the only way you will get an appellate tribunal that would function impartially as such.''[81] Under Ansell's interpre-

[77] *Washington Post*, February 15, 1919, 6. Of course, added the editorial writer, military law must be sufficiently strict to enforce discipline. This is a ''prime necessity.'' But the existing military law and procedure as set forth by Ansell ''are grossly un-American.''

[78] Ibid., February 21, 1919, 4. Ansell, according to the writer, had already been ordered to return his car to the Motor Transport Corps ''at once.''

[79] *Hearings, 1*, 130–31.

[80] Ibid., 175.

[81] Ibid. When, as will be discussed in the next chapter, Ansell had an opportunity to draft a major revision to the Articles of War, he tried to act on Clark's comments. In retrospect, Clark

tation of Section 1199, "the Judge Advocate General was the Supreme Court of the Army; he could reverse, revise, and modify, or make such disposition as he saw fit of any case when it came up to him."[82]

E. G. Davis, who together with Clark had drafted the 1918 revision of Section 1199 that had been ignored by Chamberlain, was also "unalterably opposed to vesting in the Judge Advocate General any such authority." Not only was the JAG "a subordinate officer of the War Department" detailed to his position for a four-year term; but "he has no certain tenure of office, and it would be clearly wrong to invest in any subordinate officer . . . the control of discipline for which the President . . . is ultimately responsible."[83] As to the new proposals affecting court-martial procedures, "this legislation is both unwise and unnecessary." Davis insisted that any needed changes, and he conceded that some were desirable, "can be inaugurated by regulation," rather than congressional enactment.[84]

The final witness before the committee was Enoch Crowder. Since his dispute with Ansell about Section 1199 was well documented, with himself clearly the winner, Crowder focused on a more fundamental flaw with Chamberlain's revision, the new role for the JAG. Part of the draft held that the ruling and advice given by the JAG during a trial "shall govern the court-martial." The authority of the court was thus reduced, and Crowder thought "that is rather a weighty matter to consider, whether you want to do it or not." The proposal would ultimately place the JAG "in a position to administer the discipline of the Army."[85]

Senator Francis Warren observed that "it is rather unusual for an officer to come before a committee and plead against having more authority."[86] Crowder recognized that "there is an opportunity here to aggrandize myself to such a point where I would have about all the authority there is." But he sincerely believed that a provision to permit an individual appointed by the JAG to have such control over the direction of a court-martial "would be in derogation of the constitutional authority of the President."[87] Clearly, Crowder was troubled by a potential clash between congressional authority to adopt rules for the army, and presidential authority as commander in chief. It

---

rather than Ansell may have better anticipated the future direction that military appellate jurisprudence would take.

[82] Ibid., 174.

[83] Ibid., 212. Not surprisingly, Davis still believed that revisionary power should be vested in the president, as his earlier draft had sought to do.

[84] Ibid., 219.

[85] Ibid., 243–44.

[86] Warren was familiar with military matters, if only because his son-in-law was John J. Pershing.

[87] *Hearings, 1*, 245. Crowder assumed that the president "is the national and proper depository of the final appellate power, in all judicial matters touching the police of the Army." Ibid.

could be avoided, he insisted, by lodging an appellate power within the executive.[88]

"I deprecate very much [a] departure from so fundamental a theory as would be presented if you lodged in a staff officer outside of the hierarchy of command the authority to control the President . . . in his action upon any court-martial proceedings." With Chamberlain's proposed statute, Crowder emphasized that "the President is absolutely concluded by the opinion of his Judge Advocate General."[89] He believed that under such a law, if in 1865 the JAG had found the proceedings under which the Lincoln conspirators were tried to be irregular, he could have "recorded his decision to that effect, and concluded Andrew Johnson from the execution of any one of them. That is the power you are conferring in this statute. Do you want to do it?"[90]

Military judicial authority, concluded Crowder, "should be vested in the constitutional commander in chief[,] and . . . all appellate procedure should be in his name." Under these conditions, he was "in favor of an appellate power in the President[, and] I have been in favor of it always." When asked by one senator if such power should be excercised "by some officer of your department, or, possibly . . . to have an appellate tribunal independent," Crowder responded, "I do not think so."[91]

Crowder's convoluted interpretation of Chamberlain's draft did more than "conclude the President" vis-à-vis JAG authority. It apparently precluded him from conceptualizing any appellate procedure except one coming from the president. It seemed that Congress could not create such a tribunal, presumably because it would interfere with the constitutional mandate of the commander in chief. Thus, Crowder "concluded" himself into a corner somewhat analogous to a "catch-22" situation. One sought an appellate tribunal independent of military command, but the only possible way to have it was through the highest ranking military commander of all. Moreover, if the president wished to create such a judicial body, how could it be free of military influence when, in reality it would be administered by lower ranking military functionaries?[92]

[88] By 1919, Crowder readily conceded that there should be an appellate procedure within the army; the issue on which he and Ansell differed was *where* it should be located. Crowder's intellectual inability to separate the existence of a military appellate system from the general grant of presidential power seems to have resembled a straw man, worth more in theory than actual results in American history. He agonized over the potential for conflict, perhaps not realizing that historically the two disparate grants of constitutional authority have complemented rather than collided with each other.

[89] Ibid., 278.

[90] Ibid., 279.

[91] Ibid., 281–82.

[92] Unlike Ansell, Crowder recognized that in 1919 JAG officers acting judicially were as susceptible to military control as any other branch of the service. Followed to their logical conclusion, his ideas implied an independent JAG Corps, one with its own criteria for promotion, free

As Congress rushed toward adjournment during the last week of February, Chamberlain's bill disappeared. One is tempted to dismiss Crowder's objections as anachronistic, unrealistic, and trite, if not trivial. And in the light of almost forty years under the UCMJ, such temptation is hard to resist. Yet it would be a very serious error to underestimate the depth of his conviction concerning the proper constitutional location of military appellate jurisdiction. In 1919, other high ranking officials, civilian as well as military, agreed with him; and his views were very influential in shaping the changes in the Articles of War that ultimately were adopted in 1920.

The Senate Committee on Military Affairs did not return to the topic of military justice until August 1919. With Congress out of session, between February and July the Ansell-Crowder battle resumed in the press and the corridors of the War Department. As will be seen, Ansell lost the battle; but whether Crowder would win the war was far from certain as Congress adjourned.

---

from line command interference. Such a policy was little discussed, if at all conceived in 1919. After adoption of the UCMJ, however, it would become a reality.

CHAPTER 5

The Ansell-Crowder Controversy, 1919–1920: The Outcome

THE PUBLIC PART of the Ansell-Crowder controversy began with the January 19, 1919 article in the *World*, and accelerated with testimony before the Senate committee in February. From this point on, what had been a private discussion became a public debate—and usually in more contentious tones.[1] By February 21, the *Washington Post* predicted that Ansell's "courage" would cause serious difficulties with Baker and Crowder.[2] Clearly aware of the unfavorable reaction to his chosen course, but possibly unaware of the depths of resentment it had caused within the "establishment," on March 1 Ansell addressed a personal, hand-written letter to Baker.

CROWDER'S COUNTERATTACKS

"It is the gossip of the Street . . . as well as of my own office," he wrote, "that you are to demote me." Noting that Crowder had been detailed to special assignment in Cuba to work with the Cuban government on political reforms, Ansell had heard that Baker would name a different officer as acting JAG, "and I be made to suffer the humiliation of serving in subordination."[3] He informed the secretary that "I myself can suffer such humiliation . . . and shall not complain. But it seems to me that in matters affecting military justice you are being impelled by forces beyond you to do wrong—wrong to yourself, the Army, the Country; above all, wrong to justice." He believed that Baker "wanted to be helpful" in obtaining a system of court-martial procedures "that assure justice." If such was the case, "let me plead with you to help now; to lend your great influence on behalf of legislation to liberalize the unjust system." Ansell urged the secretary "to forget me, all men, and look at measures. The Congress wants to do something. The people want you to do

[1] This was especially true in the case of Ansell, whose comments during his August appearances before the Senate Subcommittee were markedly less restrained than his earlier testimony in February.

[2] *Washington Post*, February 21, 1919, 4.

[3] Crowder spent several months in Cuba from March to June 1919. From Havana, he kept an anxious eye on the dispute over military justice. His absence, however, seems not to have hindered his support, as will be seen later in this chapter.

something." Could you not find time, he concluded, "to let me present you with my views of the requisite remedial legislation?"[4]

There is no indication that Baker even acknowledged this note. On the same day, however, he signed a letter to Crowder drafted by John Henry Wigmore that indicated outright opposition to Ansell's position.[5] Baker emphasized that the "recent outburst of criticism and complaint" upon our system of military justice "has been to me a matter of surprise and sorrow." More important, however, was his conviction that in spite of the "highly colored press reports of certain extreme statements" the system remained "essentially sound." Yet officials of the War Department "have not been in a position to make any public defense or explanation and have refrained from doing so." In other words, it was now appropriate to rebut Ansell's comments in public. Thus, Crowder should "draft a concise survey of the entire field and . . . furnish the main facts in a form which will permit ready perusal by the intelligent men and women who are so deeply interested in this subject."[6]

Crowder's response to Baker's request, dated March 8 and apparently also written by Wigmore, was promptly published in the JAG Official *Bulletin*.[7] Crowder fully agreed with Ansell that under existing procedure, "there is no further appellate body or officer who can review the appointing officer's review and modify, affirm, or reverse his action." He reminded Baker that more than one year ago, he had proposed a revision to Section 1199 as a remedy for this admitted defect. The secretary had not only strongly endorsed the change, but also accepted without question Crowder's narrow interpretation of the revisionary power granted to the JAG department.[8] The dispute was not over the *existence* of an appellate power, but its *location*. Ansell claimed that it should be vested in the JAG, and that "a complete judicial system with faithful analogies to the organization and procedure of civil courts should be substituted

[4] *Newton Baker Papers*, LOC, reel 6, March 1, 1919.

[5] John H. Wigmore was one of Crowder's staunchest supporters within the JAG Corps. On temporary duty to the war department, in civil life, he was Dean of Northwestern University Law School and already a distinguished legal scholar on the law of evidence. In addition to Baker's letter, Wigmore appears to have authored two "refutations" to Ansell's charges, both of which were signed by Crowder, as well as written other speeches on his behalf. Very much at home in legal disputation and accustomed to controversy, Wigmore possessed none of the inhibitions that had prevented Crowder from speaking out concerning the dispute with Ansell. See inf.

[6] *Hearings*, 2, 921.

[7] Ibid., 920. It, along with a speech by Wigmore delivered the same day, and another much expanded statement from the JAG to Baker on March 10 comprise the first "official" reply to Ansell, after the Senate hearings. Late in March, Wigmore publicly admitted that he had also drafted Baker's letter to Crowder. See *Wigmore Papers*, Northwestern University Library, *New York Times*, clipping undated although a notation at the top of the page reads "probably Mar. 30." "The drafting of official letters for busy superiors . . . is a common practice in all the departments of the Government."

[8] *Hearings*, 2, 1037–38. "Countenance of a plan to play ducks and drakes with a statute of the United States, you refused."

for the present simple and direct system of Army discipline.'' His own department maintained that ''the power should be vested in the President. . . . These are the real issues and the only ones.''

Crowder further noted that purposes of the military and civil codes are diametrically opposed. One ''is designed to encourage, permit and protect the very widest limit of individual action consistent with the minimum necessities of organized government.'' The other ''is designed to operate on men hurriedly drawn from the liberal operation of the civil code, and to concentrate their strength, their thought, their individual action on one common purpose, the purpose of victory.''[9] In time of war, an army in the field cannot function with ''two commanders—one in charge of the discipline and one in charge of its strategical and tactical maneuver.'' Such a structure is ''nothing less than ridiculous.''[10] As to the claim that severe, unjust, and excessive punishments had been meted out during the past war, Crowder's response [as drafted by Wigmore] was eloquent. ''Why should the offenses by a soldier of sleeping on a post of the guard, desertion, disobedience of orders be punishable by death? Because cities and fortifications and armies have been lost through the drowsiness of sentinels; because armies have been disintegrated and nations humbled by desertion; because battles have been lost and peoples sold into captivity by the disobedience of soldiers.''[11]

Crowder next turned to Ansell's conduct ''as one of the most promising and trusted officers in my office.'' Why, he asked, had Ansell never advanced the changes he now supported during 1916 and 1917, when the Articles of War were revised; a project on which Crowder had worked diligently since 1912.[12]

[9] Ibid., 1038. ''Therefore individual liberty of action inconsistent with that common purpose must be restricted.''

[10] Ibid., 1039.

[11] Ibid., 1040. Wigmore's conservative attitude toward military justice was matched by the patriotic fervor with which he worked in the JAG department. ''He was in a colonel's uniform; and his pride in it was evidenced by his abrupt correction of anyone addressing him as Dean. He fully radiated the military tradition; and he bore himself as a soldier.'' His views of military justice, his martial spirit, and his anger toward any cause that in his judgment impeded the war effort—all complemented each other. See Richard Polenberg, *Fighting Faiths: The Abrams Case, the Supreme Court, and Free Speech* (1987), 251. Supreme Court Justice Oliver Wendell Holmes felt the sting of Wigmore's invective after he dissented in *Abrams v. United States*, 250 U.S. 616 (1919). Wigmore described the case as a matter less about freedom of speech than ''freedom of thuggery.'' For his part, Holmes considered Wigmore's critique as ''bosh,'' while Felix Frankfurter—later denounced by Wigmore for his defense of Sacco and Vanzetti—concluded that Wigmore had become ''one of the casualties of the war . . . increasingly violent and recklessly indifferent to facts.'' Polenberg, 396, 257; Michael Parrish, *Felix Frankfurter and his Times* (1982), 186.

[12] Ibid. Crowder might have cited Ansell's comments in the *New York Times Magazine* in September 1917. Crowder, wrote Ansell, had ''made it his lifework to secure an intelligent revision and modernization of these ancient articles. . . . [T]he revision was done so thoughtfully and with such prevision [precision?] that it applies admirably to the maintenance of discipline in our armies now abroad.'' Ibid., September 30, 1917, 4.

Furthermore, he recounted Ansell's attempt to be named acting JAG. This episode, plus the quality of the brief submitted on expanding the revisory authority in Section 1199 led to one result. "From that time forth the feeling of trust and confidence that I had in Gen. Ansell was shaken."[13]

Finally, Crowder mentioned the organized campaign of printed criticism concerning military justice. It was "too consistently connected and too instinctively based on distorted accounts of matter on record in the [JAG] office to allay the thought that a bitterly partisan propaganda rooted in this office was being conducted." As had been his public position all along, Crowder declined to accuse Ansell by name. "But I do say with the utmost confidence that . . . the propaganda was being fed into the hands of the press by those seeking not a reformation of the code, but the accomplishment of ulterior motives."[14]

Thus, Crowder again alluded to the apparently intentional series of attacks against him and his department, beginning with the Chamberlain speech in December 1918. By March 1919, it may well have been Ansell's turn to feel the effect of an organized response; this time, against him. First, there was Baker's letter of March 1, followed by Crowder's reply of March 8, wherein for the first time, he publicly mentioned his loss of confidence in his senior assistant. On the same day, John Henry Wigmore—still in the JAG department but soon to return as Dean of Northwestern University Law School—delivered a public address to the New York County Lawyers Bar Association. He offered a vigorous defense of military justice and excoriated its critics. Two days later, what Ansell had predicted Baker now promulgated; Ansell was reduced to his "permanent" rank, that of lieutenant colonel in the JAG Corps. From the viewpoint of his cause, worse was yet to come. It may not be unreasonable to conclude that if Ansell had sown, Crowder had reaped.

ANSELL, BAKER, AND CROWDER

In his speech to the New York lawyers, Wigmore had listed fourteen current criticisms against military justice.[15] "The coincidence of these fourteen points," he observed, "with another celebrated fourteen is fortuitous, but . . .

[13] *Hearings*, 2, 1041.

[14] Ibid., 1042. From Crowder's viewpoint, one such motive would be the timing of the criticism vis-à-vis his reappointment and confirmation as JAG.

[15] "1. Arbitrary discretion of military commander. 2. Archaic criminal code. 3. Charges without inquiry [investigation]. 4. Large number of trivial charges. 5. Court martial ignorant of military law. 6. Prosecutor and judicial advisor the same man. 7. Second lieutenants defend serious cases. 8. Plea of guilty [sometimes accepted] in capital cases. 9. Commanding Generals directing reconsideration of acquittals. 10. Judgment [verdict] kept secret. 11. Sentences severe. 12. Sentences variable. 13. Judge Advocate General's Office severe. 14. Judge Advocate General's action ineffective." *Wigmore Papers*, Outline of Speech, March 8, 1919.

I am sure that military justice will win out on at least as many and perhaps more than the United States will secure of the other fourteen points.''[16] The charges ''are nothing short of reckless defamation.'' Most were totally groundless, while a few with slight basis in fact were cited in support of ''grossly false inferences.'' Wigmore reiterated Crowder's insistence that ''there is an automatic appeal from every court martial.'' Nor was it true that courts-martial were conducted by men not acquainted with military law. ''Every officer who graduates from West Point [or from training camp] is required to study and pass an examination based upon the system of military law as embodied in the Manual. . . .''[17]

Wigmore conceded that, especially in cases dealing with a sentence less than death, ''the proportion of officers of lower grade who act for the defense is probably a substantial one.'' But he saw no way to remedy this situation, and refused to call it a defect. Senior officers, he noted, ''must, of course, be taken for the members of the court; and the number of available officers from whom to select counsel . . . is limited, and the main object of an Army is victory and not trials.'' Similarly, Wigmore refused to fault those military officers who handed down excessive sentences. ''They were charged with the task of building the Army. That signified an absolute perfection of discipline before the men went overseas to be tested amidst the hardships of the trenches and the horrors of gun fire.''[18]

As Crowder had done, and since he had drafted both pieces the similarity is not surprising, Wigmore noted that the defamatory charges against military justice ''are repeated with such frequency as to give the impression that there is somewhere a deliberate effort to discredit all those who have been concerned in the administration of military justice. What the motive is, and who has organized that effort,'' Wigmore declined to hypothesize. But he predicted that ''when all the ramifications of intrigue are permitted to be disclosed, our system of military justice will be amply vindicated.'' Moreover, such vindication would include Enoch Crowder, ''whose reputation as a wise organizer and a sympathetic administrator has once [and] for all been established in the hearts of the legal profession.''[19]

Ansell reacted to the release of the Baker-Crowder exchange with a seventeen-page letter to the secretary dated March 11, 1919—one day after he had been reduced in rank. He probably was responding to the incidents just de-

[16] Ibid., 6.

[17] Ibid., 3, 8. Ansell's concern went to the quality of the appellate process, not the issue of its existence. Wigmore's glib assertion about the legal training received at West Point in no way rebutted Ansell's claim that as legal proceedings, defendants before a court-martial were entitled to a trained lawyer, not someone who had passed an exam on customary practices of military justice.

[18] Ibid., 8, 12.

[19] Ibid., 15.

scribed. Unlike his earlier letter of March 1 written more in a poignant rather than polemical tone, this document reflects indignation, frustration, and anger. He accused Baker of giving the public "a bitter attack upon me," and stated that the secretary's opinion of military justice was "based upon inadequate evidence, very limited observation, and the statements of biased witnesses." Ansell demanded that he be given an opportunity through Baker's office to reply to "the same intelligent men and women" who had been given the Baker-Crowder version. The reality was that the system "does not do justice. It does injustice—gross, terrible, spirit-crushing injustice. Evidence of it is on every hand to those who will but see. The records of this office reek with it."[20]

Ansell distilled the essence of his differences with Crowder into one sentence. "The issue is whether the convening authority, the court and the officer ordering the execution shall be a law unto themselves, or whether they shall be restrained by and required to keep within the limits prescribed by established principles of law; whether military justice shall be governed by the power of military command or whether it shall be the result of legal principles."[21] He further accused Crowder (accurately, as it turned out) of describing Order No. 7 as a mere administrative palliative, designed to head off a threatened congressional investigation, replete with talk about a proposed system of military appeals. Moreover, Ansell insisted that Crowder had not only known about the proposed reinterpretation of Section 1199 from the beginning, but had actually supported Ansell in his attempt "to put it over." Later, the JAG opposed his assistant "out of a mistaken notion of the necessity of self protection and a desire to soothe his wounded pride."[22] Ansell also strongly denied any surreptitious action on his part to displace his chief.

If there was any maladministration of military justice, primary responsibility for it "must be located first upon the Secretary of War." After all, it was he who had assigned Crowder to "more duties . . . that were in no sense related, than a man of greater capacity than General Crowder could carry. This was bad administration; operated to the great injury of this department. It proved an insuperable obstacle."[23]

Finally, Ansell turned to an order from Baker that the inspector general investigate the dispute within the JAG department, and its possible effects on the administration of military justice. Because he considered that officer's views to be "reactionary and savor of professional absolutism," he would not submit to "such unfair, partial, and unjust" inquiry from this office. Of course, however, "this subject ought to be investigated." The part that Baker and Crowder played in it "should be investigated, and I myself do not ask to be excused from such an investigation; on the other hand, I welcome [a] fair

[20] *JAGO* files, box 1, folder 4, file 2.

[21] Ibid., 4–5.

[22] Ibid., 8, 10.

[23] Ibid., 13–14.

and impartial and helpful investigation,'' but such a proceeding ''to be helpful and impartial must come from without the War Department.''[24] ''It is obvious to me,'' Ansell concluded, that ''I am under attack because I stood for a principle, because I opposed the existing system, and because I have expressed my opinion of it, that it is unjust, un-American, and ought to be destroyed.''[25]

Baker did not reply to Ansell until March 27, 1919, possibly because he was on an inspection tour of army camps in the western United States. In the meantime, Senator Chamberlain requested and received a copy of the letter from the War Department, ''furnished me confidentially and for the information of the Military Committee alone.'' The senator immediately telegraphed Baker, asking that Ansell's letter be released promptly to the public.[26] Reaffirming his strong support for Ansell, he stated (according to press reports) that this officer ''shall not be made a second Major Dreyfuss,'' because he had exposed the evils of court-martial practice.[27]

On March 27, Baker wrote to Crowder in Cuba, that ''I have now had an opportunity to read the Ansell letter, and have determined that because of its obviously improper character I shall return it to General Ansell without other comment.''[28] He also telegraphed President Wilson in France that he believed the whole controversy about court-martial procedure was ''now clarifying.''[29] Finally, he addressed a curt note to Ansell. The letter of March 11 ''herewith returned is not only obviously useless and improper for publication, but in its present form improper to be received by the Secretary of War officially.'' Personal conflicts ''between Colonel Ansell and other officers can not be properly discussed, or at least determined by newspaper publicity.'' On the other hand,

[24] Ibid., 16–17.

[25] Ibid., 17. During the spring of 1919, the Inspector General did indeed conduct an exhaustive investigation of the entire controversy, but without Ansell's participation or cooperation. He submitted his report to Baker on May 8, 1919. It appears to have been impartial in character, and intensive reexamination of the controversy undertaken for this study reconfirms its main conclusions. ''Until recently, what was first a mere difference of opinion went no further. The opposing views were urged with force, but with dignity. Such opposition as existed was an opposition of opinion, of judgment, and not of personality. There was no diffusion of energies nor conflict of loyalties. . . .'' When Ansell testified in February before the Chamberlain Committee, ''he performed his full duty and rendered a real service to the Army and to the Country.'' However, later statements made by Ansell ''were exaggerated and misleading,'' and references to Baker and Crowder were made in terms that were ''intemperate, disrespectful and insubordinate.'' *Hearings, 2*, 768–69. The report of the entire investigation, together with the accompanying appendices, may be found therein on pp. 726–1121.

[26] CP, reel 28, folder 01063, clipping from the *Washington Herald*, March 17, 1919. Chamberlain added that he regarded Ansell's letter as a public document, ''one which you should be as quickly disposed to give to the public as you were the statement made in defense of the system.''

[27] Ibid., *Charleston American*.

[28] Ibid., reel 104, folder 132. Baker added that Crowder should not concern himself with the flap over military justice. ''Whatever is wise about it will ultimately prevail, and I have no anxiety left in the matter, and do not want you to have.''

[29] *Tasker Bliss Papers*, LOC, box 245, cablegram N.D.B. March 27, 1919.

Baker "will welcome" any observations that Ansell desires to make "either through ordinary military channels or directly, looking to amendments or modification of legislation or procedure affecting military justice."[30]

What Baker probably did not welcome was more public comment from Ansell. Before that officer responded to the secretary's invitation, he delivered a public address to the North Carolina Society. Not surprisingly, he focused on military justice. But he also had some comments on military discipline that indicated the depth of the split between his views and those of the army. "Discipline," Ansell stated, "is a quality that is but little controlled by law. [It] is not the result of the application of legal power." On the contrary, "it is founded upon respect for self, a respect for others, a respect for duty, a respect for obligation."

Of course, obedience to orders was absolutely essential. But "if legal restraint must be imposed to prevent delinquency upon the part of the soldier, like restraint must be imposed to prevent the capricious and oppressive use of power upon the part of the officer. There can be no discipline in our army without justice." Ansell reiterated his belief that the current system "does not lead to justice." The fault "is a fault of the system, and of no particular person." Probably with himself in mind, Ansell concluded that the only way to assure justice under the status quo is through "the interposition of strong personalities intent upon justice[,] and intent upon extorting justice out of the system."[31]

From Cuba, Crowder read about Ansell's comments, and warned a fellow officer that "if the Army wishes to remain silent and leave the fight wholly with me, I shall not make it." If the Chamberlain proposal, with the sweeping powers given to the JAG was acceptable to the military, so be it. "I have no objections to presiding over the discipline of the Army and the largest Staff Department in the Army—as my Department will certainly become if the bill passes in its present form." As for Ansell's public comments, I have "no doubt" that his remarks (along with those of his congressional supporters) "are being applauded in all the anarchistic centers of our country."[32]

[30] *JAGO* files, box 1, folder 4, file 2.

[31] CP, reel 28, folder 01068. *Raleigh News and Observer*, March 27, 1919. One day earlier, Ansell had given yet another speech reiterating his critique of military justice to the National Popular Government League, in Washington. In both instances, he avoided comment on personalities, expressing criticism of policies not people. Ibid., *New York Tribune*, March 26, 1919.

[32] Ibid., March 28, 1919; reel 4, folder 132. Crowder added that in 1879 Gen. William Sherman had warned the army that "it must be on the defensive when civil lawyers undertook to engraft upon the military procedure of courts martial the essentials of civil procedure. I verily believe that if [his] remarks were read into the Congressional Record . . . it would produce a riot, so far have we drifted from professional ideals." In his memoirs, Sherman noted that "the presence of one of our regular civilian judge-advocates in an army in the field would be a first-class nuisance, for technical courts always work mischief." William T. Sherman, *Memoirs*, vol. 2 (1957), 397. Sherman's comment remains a frequently cited example of the supposedly vital

Baker had invited some sort of response from Ansell that presumably would be in a more "appropriate" format than his rejected letter of March 11. On April 2, 1919, Baker received a four-page memorandum listing a number of key requirements for an effective system of American military justice. They were all based upon Ansell's now familiar claim that courts-martial were essentially courts, and thus inherently judicial in character. Ansell used this premise as the foundation on which to propose dramatic if not drastic changes. Even today, these points remain a valuable guide by which to measure the transformation that has taken place in military justice since 1919. Thus, they should be specifically noted:

1. Federal laws should, "under penalty if need be, forbid the [War] Department and the Army to disregard the sacred character of these judicial duties and functions."

2. Military justice should require "that the system be law-controlled, and not controlled as it is now by men, and military men at that, whose training is rather away from judicial appreciations."

3. Organic law "should require that the fundamental rights of an accused, declared in our Bill of Rights, be recognized and protected throughout the proceeding." Indeed, it "should compel, by applying penalties if need be, a recognition of the substantial rights of an accused at every stage of the proceeding."

4. The "do-as-you-please character" of the punitive Articles of War should be abolished. All too often, they "neither define the offense nor the penalty," and rely instead on phrases such as "as the court-martial may direct," and "with death or as the court-martial may direct. . . ." Congress "tells the courts to do as they please and the courts tell the convening authorities to do as they please. Such delegations of penal power are intolerable."

5. The statute should require that "no charge be referred to any inferior court-martial until the commanding officer convening the court shall have made a thorough investigation of the charge[,] . . . nor until he shall have certified that, in his judgment, the case cannot be properly disposed of without trial by court-martial."

6. No charge should be referred to a general court-martial "until after the judge advocate . . . shall have certified on the charge that the papers show that a thorough investigation has been made and that, in his opinion, the charge suffi-

---

distinction between military and civilian judicial procedure. See, for example, Edward Sherman, "The Civilianization of Military Law," *Maine Law Review* 22 (1970): 4–5; Walter T. Cox III, "The Army, the Courts, and the Constitution: The Evolution of Military Justice," *Military Law Review* 118 (1987): 17–18. Crowder continued to believe that a conspiracy to deny him reappointment lay at the base of the entire controversy. Thus, for example, on May 2, 1919, he wrote to Forrest Cooper that "I do not know whether the conspiracy which is back of this defamation will ever be revealed or not; but, if it is, you will find the most highly developed piece of Army politics that has ever been attempted." CP, reel 15, folder 143.

ciently alleges an offense triable by court martial, and that the evidence is prima facie sufficient to sustain the charge.''

7. The position of the judge advocate as prosecutor should be abolished, and a statute ''should require the assignment of a specially qualified officer to prosecute in the name of the United States.''

8. A statute should ''make it mandatory that an accused should have military counsel before special and general courts-martial, and authorize him to have civil counsel,'' should he so desire. Moreover, when the convening authority assigns counsel, he should have to certify that ''he has assigned to that duty that officer within his command whom, by reason of legal qualification, experience and rank, he deems best qualified therefor.''

9. The statute should require that a JAG officer ''be assigned to sit with every general court martial,'' and be empowered ''to rule upon all questions of law raised during the proceeding, to sum up the evidence for the court, and to perform generally those functions which are usually performed by a judge sitting with the jury'' in a criminal case.

10. The statute ''should require that the court and judge advocate general shall function independently of the convening or any other authority, and it should forbid the convening or any other authority to return to the court any record for reconsideration,'' except when such action will ''operate to the benefit of the accused.'' Reversing a not guilty verdict, or changing a guilty finding on a lesser offense to a different offense or one of higher degree, and increasing the punishment were all to be forbidden by law.

11. The convening authority should be forbidden by statute ''to act upon the proceedings of a general court martial until he shall have the views of his [JAG] thereon in writing, and no convening authority shall approve any proceeding or sentence of a court martial pronounced illegal or void by his judge advocate.''

12. The statute ''should place beyond question the revisory power of [TJAG], who should be specifically authorized on a question of law raised (*a*) to pronounce the proceedings, findings of guilty, or sentence, in whole or in part, invalid, (*b*) and in a proper case to recommend to the proper convening authorities that a new trial may be had.''

13. Finally, a statute should so establish the office and duties of TJAG that ''in their performance he shall not be subjected directly or indirectly to military supervision of any kind, but kept free from that military influence which I regard as offensive to justice.''

In submitting these recommendations, Ansell also asked that Baker rethink his decision to reject Ansell's earlier letter. How, he asked, could readers judge the validity of Crowder's statements if they were denied an opportunity to consider them in the light of these criticisms. ''Unless my statement is published, the people will not be in a position to judge whether or not the information contained in General Crowder's statement is worthy of public credit.''[33]

ANSELL'S ACTIONS

Before Baker could respond, the complete text of Ansell's March 11 letter that the secretary had refused to receive was published in the *New York Times*, on April 3, 1919. Referring to it as ''the suppressed letter,'' the anonymous writer specifically mentioned that it had not been given out by Ansell. But no information that might reveal the source of the leak appeared in the article.[34] Two days later, Baker replied, through the adjutant general, to Ansell's memorandum.

His suggestions ''merit earnest consideration, which they shall receive.'' Indeed, Baker heartily concurred with many of them, ''if, in fact, existing statute law is defective in the particulars suggested by the proposed changes.'' Furthermore, he ordered Ansell ''at the earliest possible date'' to prepare and submit a draft of a bill that would ''carry into effect'' the ideas expressed in his various suggestions. But Baker would have nothing to do with the letter of March 11, now published. ''There is . . . no point in seeking to use the Secretary of War as a medium of publicity.'' He reminded Ansell that ''the resort to personal comment . . . was not begun by General Crowder.''[35] It ''plainly would have been more fitting and appropriate if never begun by anybody. It has certainly been carried far enough by everybody.''[36]

Ansell immediately set to work and, as will be seen shortly, with impressive results. In the meantime, public discussion about military justice continued

[33] JAGO files, box 1, folder 4, file 2. Ansell's response was published in the *Washington Post* on April 6, and editorially endorsed on the next day. CP, reel 28, folder 1075, 1076. It should be noted that in none of his suggestions did Ansell specifically call for an appellate court of military appeals. He may have thought that such a tribunal might result logically from the JAG revisory authority, which he did discuss.

[34] WP, *New York Times*, April 3, 1919.

[35] In this swipe at Ansell and his supporters, perhaps Baker was a little unfair. If Crowder had not been the first to resort to personal comments, he displayed great ease with the practice—but usually in private correspondence. On April 24, for example, he wrote that ''Ansell is of an unstable mentality, brilliant in the extreme but without any poise; he is essentially destructive in character, personally inordinately ambitious, and utilized his incumbency of the office of Judge Advocate General to gather around him a bunch of snakes whom he allowed to warm at that very hearth-stone plotting every minute of the time how they could defeat my reappointment and put Ansell in charge.'' CP, reel 4, folder 140, April 24, 1919.

[36] JAGO files, box 1, folder 4, file 2. Baker assumed ''Ansell's earnest desire to concentrate public [and official] attention upon the improvement of the system of military justice.'' A ''single-minded and unbiased consideration of that subject can best be assured by the abatement of further personal discussion.'' Baker's statement was discussed in both the *Washington Herald*, and the *Washington Post* on April 6, 1919. See CP, reel 28, folder 01076.

during the spring and summer of 1919, but at an increasingly desultory level. There were occasional indications, however, that some disputants still felt strongly about the issues. Thus, John Wigmore—commenting on the military justice experience of some pro-Ansell JAG officers—noted that they had been in the corps only a few months, assigned to the "War risk Insurance Section, which has no more to do with military justice than kalsomine [sic] has to do with the stability of a skyscraper." As for Senator Chamberlain's claim that a court-martial system represented a system neither of law nor justice, Wigmore concluded that "if a man, after any rational inquiry whatever, holds to that view, he is hopeless."[37] On the other hand, Edmund Morgan, JAG officer and strong supporter of Ansell, and soon to join the faculty of Yale University Law School, stated on April 3 that defendants in courts-martial are often prosecuted by "officers of low rank who wouldn't know a law book from a bale of hay, and as frequently are defended by a chaplain who is hardly able to distinguish between a rule of evidence and the Apostle's Creed."[38]

Wigmore and Morgan, both law professors and scholars on the law of evidence, debated military justice once again in June 1919, when they appeared together at the Maryland State Bar Association Meeting. For his part, Wigmore assumed that "the prime object of military organization is victory, not justice. . . . If it can do justice to its men, well and good. But justice is always secondary and victory is always primary."[39] Next, Wigmore expanded on a point that Crowder had also raised in earlier statements. Rather than defend military justice, Wigmore attacked civilian criminal procedure as inferior in certain instances to the military version. Military justice, he insisted, was far ahead of its civilian counterpart in at least five areas, three of which warrant mention: (*a*) centralized supervision of all criminal courts, (*b*) verbatim record of trial—something, Wigmore observed, that was common practice in general courts-martial,[40] and (*c*) automatic appellate scrutiny for every accused's case.

[37] CP, reel 28, folder 0170, *New York Times*, March 29, 1919; WP, *Washington Post*, April 24, 1919. Crowder's bitterness toward Ansell continued unabated. On April 11, he wrote to his old boss Henry Stimson that with the way Ansell had changed, "I begin to doubt my judgment of men. He has ability—very great ability. He was deficient in character always, and lately I have doubted his sanity. . . . That he is disloyal, I know." *Henry Stimson Papers*, reel 52. J. Easby-Smith's comment to Crowder a few months later about Chamberlain and Ansell was equally pointed. "One is crazy and they are both crooks." CP, reel 5, folder 160, July 31, 1919.

[38] WP, clipping from the *New York World*, April 4, 1919. Crowder was furious at Morgan's comments. More than six months later, he cited Morgan's statement to a correspondent. Morgan must, he added, "have some mental aptitude[,] but he is primarily a school man with no practical sense. I have no hesitation in saying that he is the smallest man from the standpoint of character that I have ever come into contact with[,] and three minutes [of] conversation with him shows this littleness of his soul." CP, reel 6, folder 182, November 4, 1919.

[39] *Report of the Twenty-Fourth Annual Meeting of the Maryland State Bar Association* (1919), 188.

[40] In urging such a practice upon the states, Wigmore added that "in common fairness such a report should be made at the expense of the State." Ibid., 192.

Here, Wigmore glorified the "review" system practiced in the military, claiming that "every record of every case goes up to at least one higher authority."[41] Records in general courts-martial "go up two stages, to the Judge Advocate General or the President." Every convicted man, he wrote, "thus obtains an appellate scrutiny without any cost. . . . This is an idea of which civilian justice has been dreaming ever since Magna Charta. Complete justice to the poor man is still a dream in our civilian courts. In the military courts it costs not a cent."[42]

Morgan denounced the system that Wigmore "seems to consider well-nigh perfect." In fact, it was a system designed for professional soldiers serving an empire for hire, applied to an army of civilians, temporary soldiers, "protecting the republic." Military justice actually was governed by the whim of a commander rather than the rule of law. Moreover, all too often, the military court, the prosecutor, and defender were "all untrained and incompetent," thus making a "fair and impartial trial almost impossible."[43] Morgan argued, contrary to Wigmore, that in actual fact there was no judicial supervision of a military justice proceeding "at any stage."[44] Unlike the Dean of Northwestern Law school who spoke in generalities, Morgan offered numerous specific examples of incredible sentences meted out by military courts.

He noted that the Special Clemency Board created by the army had recommended reduction of sentences in cases that came before it "by more than 77 percent, and remitting a total of over 18,000 years" of confinement. These cases were "a travesty upon common sense." And "woe be unto him in the service who dared oppose this sacrosanct system. Everybody knows what has happened to Ansell." Morgan knew that Ansell had been preparing a revision of the Articles of War, as Baker had ordered. He predicted that the War Department would try to kill the proposal before it became law. "It will offer all sorts of substitutes by way of regulation and reform from within. It will predict bolshevism and the destruction of discipline." Morgan concluded with a challenge to Wigmore and supporters of the current system "to produce a single specific case wherein the granting of a fair and impartial trial under a judicial supervision, in the stead of the travesty upon justice actually granted, would have injured discipline or morale one whit."[45]

[41] Wigmore failed to note that this review was rarely if ever carried out by a superior legal officer, or indeed by a military officer with adequate legal training.

[42] Ibid., 192–93.

[43] Ibid., 197–203.

[44] Ibid., 210. As for the so-called "automatic appeal" that according to Wigmore "costs the accused nothing[,] in the vast majority of cases it is worth to the accused exactly what it costs."

[45] Ibid., 215–18. Morgan's observation that defenders of the status quo would "predict bolshevism," is of interest when one notes Wigmore's response to Morgan's presentation. "As I listened to his speech, I thought I was listening to the kind of speech which must have been delivered somewhere before a Russian Soviet just before the Russian Army went to pieces." Ibid., 218. He

By April 12, the press reported that Ansell had completed his draft of revisions to the Articles of War. If the dates on the various pieces of correspondence and press accounts are accurate, Ansell produced his draft in less than two weeks. One reporter stated that Ansell's proposed changes "are so drastic that it is difficult to predict what their reception will be [either] at the War Department or on Capitol Hill." The draft, however, "will be submitted to Congress whether it meets with [Secretary Baker's] approval or not."[46]

Even as Ansell prepared his revision, the JAG department had presented seven amendatory orders for approval by Baker, all dealing with reform of court-martial procedure. Several of them clearly reflected Ansell's concerns. One required a convening authority to consider a written opinion of a staff JAG "before ordering a case to trial." Another called for "one specially qualified member" of a general court-martial who would serve as the "law member." While not mandated to attend every sitting of the court, "no serious, difficult or complicated case" was to be tried without his presence. The law member also had the duty and responsibility "of advising his fellow members as to the law of the case." Finally, regulations were proposed that would bar "reconsideration of acquittals" and "increasing sentences on revision proceedings."[47]

On March 26, Crowder described these proposed changes to Baker. "I very much desire," he wrote, "that the orders be issued at as early a date as is practicable." Thus, the Senate Committee would be made aware of how much could be accomplished by executive order, rather than congressional statute. Furthermore, Crowder wanted it known how much Ansell could have undertaken on his own while he administered the JAG office, had he been so inclined.[48]

When exactly Baker received Ansell's revisions is not clear, but on May 14 he established a three-member Board of Officers to "consider all recommendations looking to the improvement of the present system of military justice, and recommend . . . any changes which they believe necessary."[49] Drawn from the regular army and chaired by Maj. Gen. Francis Kernan, an officer well known for his devotion to the existing forms of military discipline, Bak-

went on to insist that the advances in military justice that *he* had discussed made it possible to correct the abuses cited by Morgan.

[46] CP, reel 28, folder 01080; excerpt from the *Cleveland Plain Dealer*, April 13, 1919. Crowder may have had some doubts concerning Baker's position on the Ansell reform. On April 17, he asked a friend "to see that the right men write letters to . . . Baker and stiffen up his backbone a little bit. . . . He is very likely to yield points here and there where he ought to make a fight." Ibid., April 17, 1919, 1. In this respect, the JAG, even though he felt isolated and neglected in Havana, had nothing to worry about.

[47] *Baker Papers*, reel 7, March 26, 1919.

[48] Ibid.

[49] *Proceedings and Report of Special War Department Board on Courts-martial and Their Procedure*, GPO (1919), 3; hereafter cited as *Kernan Report*.

er's committee reflected his reaction to Ansell's proposed reforms—many of which were aimed at lessening the influence of officers typified by those now assigned to evaluate them. Also, the secretary's response can be seen as an effort to undercut congressional initiative. From the army viewpoint, Kernan's report as the basis for legislative inquiry would probably be much more desirable than Ansell's bill. Crowder, of course, well understood the motivation behind Baker's decision, and wrote to him the next day that the announcement of the Kernan Board had brought me "the greatest satisfaction."[50] Given Crowder's enthusiasm, Ansell's response was predictable. After his resignation from the army, he commented that "If [Baker] had gone out designedly to appoint the most reactionary set of men in the United States[,] he could not have improved upon his selection."[51]

A few days after appointment of the Kernan Board, the *New York Times* reported that Chamberlain would introduce Ansell's bill "to establish military justice and cure defects in the existing army court martial system."[52] An examination of the text shows, not surprisingly, that it incorporated the basic principles previously discussed in this chapter. But Ansell went beyond the issues of appellate jurisdiction, and proposed additional changes in the Articles of War. As will be seen, many were doomed to failure in 1919–1920. Even today, in a more progressive era of military justice, some of his proposals have yet to receive military and congressional sanction.

Ansell suggested that military justice procedures be called courts, rather than courts-martial, with three levels of tribunals: summary, special, and general. A general court was to have eight members; if the defendant was a private or noncommissioned officer, three members were to be of this rank. In the special court, which included only three members, one had to be drawn from the rank of the accused. Ansell further provided that, unless Congress decided otherwise, these courts were to use rules of evidence generally followed in federal district courts. Cruel and unusual punishments "of every kind, including flogging, branding, marking or tattooing on the body" were prohibited.

Ansell's bill also established limitations on penalties that traditionally had been at the discretion of the military court. Thus disrespect toward the president, Congress, and other public officials carried a maximum prison term of

[50] Sup., n. 48; May 15, 1919.

[51] *Hearings, 2*, 215. Although invited to give his views on military justice to Kernan's committee, Ansell refused. "I knew what the report of this Board would be, and I was not going to waste any time in arguing before a prejudiced forum. . . . It was a foregone conclusion what that report would say." Indeed, "nobody, even on the other side, anticipated that it would be so reactionary as it is. I have just one bit of respect for it. . . . It is a good exposition of the reactionary view." Ibid., 215–16. The Kernan report which prompted Ansell's comments is discussed below.

[52] *New York Times*, May 19, 1919, 16.

one year, while disrespect toward a superior officer was punishable by confinement "for not more than six months." He restricted the famous "catch-all" article penalty to the same period of time. But Ansell went beyond just limiting punishments that could be meted out by the military. He provided that officers who failed to make required pretrial investigations were themselves subject to imprisonment.[53]

Finally, Ansell specified operation of the revisory authority that he considered so vital to military justice. It was in the form of a proposed court of military appeals (*not*, it should be noted, a military court of appeals) "which for convenience of administration only shall be located" in the JAG department. The tribunal would be composed of three judges, "each of whom shall be learned in the law," appointed by the president, approved by the Senate; each to serve during good behavior, with the salary, "and emoluments including the privilege of resignation and retirement upon pay" of a United States Circuit Judge.[54] Unless clearly not desired by the accused, it would review the record of every general court or military commission wherein a sentence of death, dismissal, dishonorable discharge, or confinement for more than six months had been rendered.[55]

The court could disprove a finding of guilty, as well as the whole or any part of a sentence. In light of such action, it could advise the convening authority "of the further proceedings that may or should be had," and if all the findings and sentence were disapproved by the court, the commander could order a new trial before another court. Also, the judges could recommend presidential clemency in any case where they considered the sentence, though valid, to be "unjust or unduly severe." The members of the court would select the presiding judge themselves. All these provisions were prospective. But Ansell included a retroactive provision whereby the court could revise and review sentences that had already been handed down since April 1917, if so requested by the defendant up to six months after Ansell's bill became law.[56]

[53] The complete draft of Ansell's proposed revisions is in *Hearings, 2*, 5–23. The best discussion of the difference between his proposals and what has since become part of military law is found in Terry W. Brown, "The Crowder-Ansell Dispute: The Emergence of General Samuel T. Ansell," *Mil. Law Rev.* 35 (1967): 1–45.

[54] Given the later history of the United States Court of Military Appeals, it is noteworthy that Ansell saw no constitutional impediment to Congress creating such a court, and providing life tenure for the judges without reference to their political affiliation. In his proposal, the issue of an Article I court contrasted with an Article III tribunal was conspicuous by its absence. He did not even discuss the possible clash between congressional and presidential authority that troubled Crowder.

[55] The review would be for the correction of errors of law evidenced by the record that injuriously affected the substantial rights of the accused. It made no difference whether or not such errors were subject to objection or exception at trial.

[56] Such a provision was necessary, according to Senator Chamberlain, "because clemency at best is inadequate to correct unjust convictions and almost completely fails in the face of an

Crowder had already indicated his fundamental difficulty with any revisory authority unless in the name of the president.[57] He opposed Ansell's "court" because, as he wrote privately to Baker, it would "divorce the President from his disciplinary relations to the Army by erecting between him and [it] a Court of Appeal with power to conclude him upon every question of discipline arising in [the] Army. I deny the Constitutionality of such legislation, and I also doubt its expedience." As for the rest of Ansell's reforms embodied in the Chamberlain bill—"some of them are silly, some ridiculous, but none vicious. We can stand for all of them."[58]

ASSAULTED BY THE ARMY

Although submitted by Chamberlain to the Senate early in May, Ansell's bill was not discussed in committee until August.[59] In the meantime, the Kernan Committee published its report to Baker on July 17, 1919—a few days before Ansell resigned from the army.[60] It had been assigned to evaluate various proposals to reform military justice, and also to submit its own recommendations for change. While the report claimed to be an objective assessment of current commentary on military justice, in reality it represented the response of senior

unsympathetic attitude on the part of the military authorities." *New York Times*, May 19, 1919, 16.

[57] On April 25, Crowder wrote to a friend about the "hostile critics who have attacked the system, which they would abrogate and substitute by a system bearing faithful analogy to trials in civil courts. You have too much military blood in your veins not to know that such a system transplanted into the Army would destroy the discipline and make us a Bolshevist Army. . . . You might as well adopt a referendum among the enlisted men on the question of when, where and how a battle was to be fought." CP, reel 4, folder 140, April 25, 1919. For Crowder, the idea of making the JAG into some sort of an appellate court was equally absurd. In order for it to be effective, such a tribunal would have to supersede the president and all persons "under him in the hierarchy of command, in respect of discipline of soldiers. I doubt the constitutionality of such legislation, and I certainly doubt its expediency even if it were constitutional." Ibid., reel 5, folder 145, May 6, 1919.

[58] At this point, Crowder added a sentence that reflected his belief that the JAG department was not on the level of a line command. "Although I should, out of deference to my military training, deprecate any provision which would undertake to say to General Pershing—You may try Division Commanders in France only when your Judge Advocate approves." *Baker Papers*, reel 7, May 14, 1919. Although beyond the scope of this volume, the relationship of the military command to the JAG Corps, particularly since 1919 is worthy of study. Ansell's aggressiveness about JAG authority and Crowder's ambivalence in a sense represent the two poles of a controversy that may be incapable of total solution. As will be seen in the second volume of this project, recent cases in military justice indicate that Ansell's view may be closer to the mark than Crowder's.

[59] Herbert F. Margulies, "The Articles of War, 1920: The History of a Forgotten Reform," *Military Affairs* 43 (1979): 86, 89.

[60] *New York Times*, July 20, 1919, 4. His resignation—"I hereby resign as an officer of the army"—was, according to the reporter, "the shortest resignation on record."

officers and the military establishment to Ansell's suggestions; and it becomes quite clear why Crowder—weeks before he even read the report—could write to Baker of his "greatest satisfaction" in the committee's composition.

The report, based upon comments and suggestions solicited from about 225 officers, opened with the observation that officers "who served with fighting units and had brought home to them the overwhelming importance of discipline in a command when it was subjected to the supreme test of battle," favored the present regulations and procedures. On the other hand, those officers "whose duties kept them remote from the scene of battle, and perhaps entirely disassociated from actual service with troops view the system with a more critical eye," comparing it with "criminal practice in the civil community to the advantage of the latter." There was no need to note that Ansell and his supporters were in this latter category of critics who wanted to transfer administration of military justice from "those who are soldiers first and lawyers second only in a mild or secondary degree, if at all, to those who are lawyers first and soldiers by title and courtesy only, if at all."[61]

This view was widely shared in the regular army, where critical reaction to Ansell's draft had been evident even before Kernan's committee was created. On May 10, for example, Maj. Gen. David Shanks had expressed opinions to the adjutant general that were probably typical:

> Courts-martial should be free from wrangling of lawyers and hair-splitting technicalities. . . . While I have great respect for lawyers[,] I have recently noted on the part of some of them such a lack of discipline and loyalty, considering the opportunities that they have had, that it is not only remarkable but it is absolutely astounding. . . . Nothing can be more discouraging to the seasoned officer who knows the difficulties connected with the control and management of soldiers than to find that all of his experience which has taken him a lifetime to acquire is set aside to the whim of some lawyer who has a hobby to ride. . . . When the sentence is reached[,] it should be imposed by men who know the soldier and not by a bookworm who knows a little law."[62]

The Kernan Report next turned to "the fundamental doctrine that the constitutional authority of the President as Commander in Chief can not be abridged by Congress in the exercise of its power to make rules for the government of our armies."[63] The committee argued that in fact, his authority to appoint such courts predated the Constitution itself. Ansell would create "a

[61] *Kernan Report* (1919), 5. This "radical change" would take control of courts-martial "out of the hands of those, who, as soldiers, know much of discipline and something of military law," and place it "in the hands of those who as lawyers know much of law but little of soldiering, or the discipline indispensable to successful soldiering." Ibid., 6.

[62] JAGO *Records*, NARC, RG 153, entry 26, box 1.

[63] Without even citing him by name, the committee explicitly accepted Winthrop's interpretation of a court-martial as an instrument of command, emanating from presidential authority.

new functionary with powers so extensive . . . as to constitute him the administrator of discipline, though he is not himself of the hierarchy of command.'' Is it not possible that such a proposition that takes away presidential authority from the court-martial ''may be unconstitutional?'' Is it not ''in effect an attempt to withdraw from command an essential part of that which belongs to it historically and in sound reason? Is it not open to be questioned as an attempt by law to emasculate the legitimate and heretofore undisputed authority of the President?'' Indeed, ''in the opinion of this board the unwisdom of this new departure, assuming it to be legally competent, is startlingly apparent.''[64]

Implicit in Kernan's report was a subtle emphasis that military justice be judged not in the abstract but in practical terms consonant with reality. It ''is carried out at times under great urgency and stress, where the nice deliberation and finish of the civil procedure is utterly impossible.'' The report also conceded, however, that the president's ''pardoning power does not remove the moral stigma of conviction[,] nor otherwise make completely good the judicial wrong.'' The only solution, given the committee's insistence on the causal links between executive command, military discipline and courts-martial was, of course, ''that the appeal should be in the sequence of the hierarchy of command—never outside of it.''[65]

Having come out in total opposition to the proposed court of military appeals, the Kernan report next considered other specific reforms suggested by Ansell. There was no need to change the name of ''court-martial'' to ''court.'' The former title ''is an old term, well understood, and indicates by its name that it is a military or martial court.'' Whatever abuses there were, would not

[64] *Kernan Report*, 6–9. The committee discussed a hypothetical case where in France, for example, a verdict and penalty handed down by ''fellow officers, duly equipped by special knowledge and antecedent training to judge fairly and sanely, could be set aside upon a legal technicality construed by three civilians sitting in Washington to be an error of law injuriously affecting the substantial rights of the accused. . . . The power to discipline effectively, inseparably bound up with the power of effective command, would be in this particular case paralyzed. The requirements of effective command as determined by the Commander in Chief, be it observed, are thus halted by an independent agency outside the Army.'' Ibid., 8. That this hypothetical case included such judicial qualifiers as ''duly equipped by special knowledge and antecedent training to judge fairly and sanely'' may be in one respect a backhanded compliment to Ansell. It can be argued that if most military judges were so equipped, the outrageous verdicts so offensive to him would not have been in evidence, thus obviating the need for a special appellate tribunal.

[65] Ibid., 13. The report also criticized reliance on the record of trial as a basis for appellate review. ''No written court-martial record is anything more than a partial reproduction of the case in its fullness.'' Officers of the court, plus the local convening authority possessed ''fuller relevant knowledge of the whole case and of the requirements of discipline, and represents justice as a whole better than does the later opinion of the distant reviewer limited to a reading of the written record in a Washington office.'' Ibid., 11. Here, Kernan's report did more than reflect a lack of understanding about the nature of appellate review. In one sense, it undercut the very rationale for presidential review, or indeed any review within the military hierarchy beyond the local convening authority. For all these reviews could only be based on the record, which, according to the committee, was inherently deficient.

be corrected by a mere name change.[66] The proposal that men of the same rank as the accused sit on the court "is out of harmony with the American conception of democracy. . . . The change would seem to be more in harmony with that form of discipline which in Europe recently resulted in the establishment of soldiers' and workmen's councils." With intriguing if not convincing logic, the report claimed that the current procedure of having only officers serve on court-martials was inherently more democratic, because "under the democratic tests made and applied for the creation of officers, the enlisted men who possess such qualities in the fullest measure become officers."[67]

Ansell's proposal that federal rules of procedure be followed in court-martials received predictable rejection. His plan "would require continued study on the part of officers. . . ." The idea "illustrates vividly the impracticability of suggestions made by officers and others who have had little or no experience in the field, men whose military experience has been largely limited to permanent offices elaborately equipped with libraries and with abundant leisure to pursue the niceties of legal subtleties."[68]

In place of the proposed court of military appeals, Kernan's committee came up with a synthesis involving expanded power for the convening authority, and the major provisions in the old (1918) bill to vest appellate review in the president. When the confirming authority believed that the rights of the accused had been injuriously affected, he could order a retrial before a new court—only upon those charges of which the defendant was found guilty. Nor could this new trial result in any greater penalty than the original sentence. In addition to all the review powers given the president, he could also "set aside the entire proceedings in any case," grant a new trial, "or he may restore the accused to all rights as if no such trial had ever been held."[69]

[66] Ibid., 17.

[67] Ibid., 18. Also, it was these officers who should fill the need for more lawyers to serve as defense counsel in courts-martial—a deficiency conceded by the committee. But it did not propose to increase the number of civilian lawyers on temporary duty with the JAG, but rather to have the JAG department enlarged, "to be detailed from the line of the Army." Such officers should be provided the opportunity for legal education; and "coming from the line and serving for a period of four years . . . these officers . . . should retain their knowledge of the service, of matters of discipline, and of all the intimate details which can only be kept fresh by a recurrence to duty with the troops." Ibid., 22–23.

[68] Ibid., 27.

[69] Ibid., 30–31. Because this proposal did not set up a review system independent of the military, it was unacceptable to Ansell. In the committee's view, however, because it gave the president plenary power to do more than pardon or remit the sentence, their suggestion solved the problem that Ansell had been discussing for two years; and it kept the entire procedure within the army. It "meets all reasonable suggestions of amendment and at the same time preserves unimpaired the disciplinary power of the Commander in Chief."

THE LINGERING CONFLICT

Crowder was delighted with the Kernan report, understandably if not unnecessarily seeing in it personal vindication. "I get my greatest comfort," he wrote, "out of the report of the Kernan . . . Board. . . . I think that it is the last word in the argument. It is the voice of the Army in France speaking through its most experienced officers." Crowder anticipated strong support from General Pershing, and had "no doubt that I shall be sustained on every question of fundamental differrence."[70] He was correct, except that by August 1919, when the Senate Subcommittee began hearings on the Ansell-Chamberlain bill, popular and political interest in military justice had waned.[71] Crowder had already won.

Conducted before a subcommittee consisting of two and occasionally three senators, the hearings began early in August, and continued on a very irregular basis through November 8, 1919. The focus was supposed to be on the Chamberlain-Ansell bill, but in fact the testimony ranged far and wide and became a rehash of the entire controversy. Ansell testified for five days, even as Baker announced his endorsement of the Kernan Report. Now free from whatever military constraints he may have previously felt (and by the spring of 1919 they could not have been many), Ansell lashed out at his critics.[72] In retrospect, his performance can be seen as a furious epilogue to a futile exercise.

Yet there is ample evidence that, personalities aside, the question of military appellate jurisdiction had become an issue that by the fall of 1919 aroused more ambivalence than antagonism—as becomes clear upon examination of the testimony offered by Crowder and Baker. By the time they appeared (the former late in October, the latter in early November), the subcommittee had received Ansell's original proposal (as embodied in the bill), the Kernan re-

[70] CP, reel 5, folder 166, August 26, 1919.

[71] As early as June 3, 1919, Wigmore had advised Crowder that "so far as concerns military justice, I find that the public in general, and the legal profession in particular, seems to have regarded the matter as no longer one of active pending interest. They seem to be satisfied to let the matter drop." Ibid., reel 5, folder 153.

[72] See Wiener, "The Seamy Side of the World War I Court-Martial Controversy," *Mil. Law Rev.* 123 (1989): 109–28. While in general this author does not disagree with Wiener's very critical comments about Ansell, as these several chapters hopefully have shown, the issues are more complex than Wiener indicates. Moreover, Crowder was every bit as vituperative as Ansell, but only in private. At the same time that he wrote to Baker as a loyal subordinate, he could also privately comment about the secretary's supposed lack of backbone. He denounced Ansell's "slander" in meticulous detail to the Senate Subcommittee, but he wrote privately to Wigmore that none of Ansell's friends of former years retain "any faith in his loyal or honest motive or action." Crowder still entertained "the highest estimate" of his former assistant's "legal ability and reasoning powers . . . but Benedict Arnold was not lacking in some of these regards, and yet possessed the capacity to be disloyal to his country and flag." WP, October 19, 1921.

port, and commentary from numerous military officers—much of it repetitive. Unlike Kernan, Crowder at first did not wish to argue the issue of whether a civilian court for the military would be an unconstitutional interference with executive power as the commander in chief. ''I am not,'' he stated, ''predisposed to question the constitutionality of laws: and I am more in the attitude of assuming, and I am at present in the attitude of conceding, that Congress, in the exercise of its power to make rules and regulations for the government [of the armed forces], may establish a court of appeals.''[73]

The JAG believed, however, that Ansell's bill would ''take away from military men the discipline of the Army and transfer it to civilians.'' Such a policy ''offends my sense of what is right much more than it would if the proposition were to turn over to civilian control common law and statutory felonies committed by persons within the Military Establishment.'' Moreover, under the Ansell proposal if the president himself convened a court-martial, his authority would be severely circumscribed by the JAG's power. When one added to this an exclusively military court of appeals functioning independently of the president, the result ''is wholly untenable from my point of view.''[74]

At this point, Senator Irvine Lenroot asked Crowder if the jurisdiction of the proposed court was ''limited to passing upon prejudicial errors and jurisdiction, but was in no sense permitted to substitute their judgment for that of the court[martial] upon the facts,'' would this mitigate his objections?[75] The JAG responded that ''there is no jurisprudence that needs, so much as the military, an appellate review on both the law and the facts.'' He hoped that ''it will not be the final judgment to create an appellate jurisdiction for the errors of law alone.''[76]

Crowder emphasized that since he was able to appoint extremely well qualified officers to the various Boards of Review, and since they could scrutinize records for errors of both law and fact, and present to the secretary and the

[73] *Hearings, 2*, 1208–9. Instead, Crowder wished to rest his entire case on the ''expediency and advisability of locating power in such a way as to shut the President and the commanding generals under him off from considerations of questions vital to the discipline of the Army.'' Another reason why he did not feel it necessary to raise the constitutional question is that Kernan, a senior line officer, had already done so in his report.

[74] Ibid., 1263.

[75] Lenroot, a new Republican senator from Wisconsin, was the second of the two Republicans on the subcommittee. His senior colleague, Francis Warren, was also chairman of the Senate Appropriations Committee, and thus frequently absent from the hearings. Because the Republicans now controlled Congress after the 1918 elections, Chamberlain was no longer chair of the Senate Committee on Military Affairs; hence, Lenroot took a more dominant role in the hearings than might have been expected. See Margulies, ''The Articles of War,'' sup., 86–87.

[76] *Hearings, 2*, 1264. ''I can not emphasize too greatly this view.'' Crowder to the contrary not withstanding, from its inception the USCMA has been limited in its review authority to matters of law; while the lower military appellate courts (now called Courts of Military Review) whose members are appointed by the JAG of each service retains jurisdiction over issues of both law and fact.

president any possible grounds of reversal, there was no need to change the system. Senator Lenroot observed that while such a board might indeed be exercising a supervisory authority, in fact "you have no jurisdiction to do so." In reality, these boards (and Chamberlain had made the same point earlier in the February hearings) exercised supervisory power in an advisory capacity. Crowder agreed, and added that in practice the president relied on the advice of his civilian lawyer, his secretary of war. Indeed, Crowder went even further, and claimed that the president is not "qualified to exercise command independently; he acts upon the advice of experts." And "I assume that the [JAG] and the Secretary . . . his legal experts, will advise him in the exercise of this appellate authority . . . and that he will follow their advice." This point may have been what interested Lenroot. On the one hand, numerous witnesses had voiced concern about possible interference with the executive command authority, but in reality "you are creating an appellate tribunal in name that you do not expect will independently exercise the powers that are given [it]."[77]

Although the Wisconsin senator was attempting to get Crowder to see this inconsistency, his point may have been too subtle for Crowder, who reiterated that the president would exercise appellate authority "upon a legal review" prepared by the JAG. "I believe it would be 100 percent effective." It was more the possibility that an appellate court might "interfere with discipline if such a court is superior to the President," rather than the probability that the chief executive might choose not to exercise appellate review directly that troubled him. In addition, although he declined to oppose an independent appellate court on constitutional grounds, Crowder predicted that if such a tribunal emerged from Congress, "I have no doubt that in time of some great crisis, the constitutional question will arise." Such a prospect failed to daunt Lenroot. "I see no more reason why, upon questions of law, [the president] should not be governed by a military tribunal as Commander in Chief; he certainly is, just as a civil officer is, by the very men he appoints to the bench, and they control his action and find [it] invalid in a given case." Crowder could only fall back on an old theme: "I am afraid that this question of military relations is *sui generis*[,] and that it does not aid you much to invoke the analogies of our civil jurisprudence."[78]

Newton Baker also had to confront Lenroot's questions, and his answers were even more contradictory than Crowder's—so much that he felt it necessary to write an explanatory note before the transcribed hearings were published. The secretary readily conceded that, in spite of all authority flowing to the commander in chief, the president remained unable to "quash a trial and order a new trial de novo." There ought to be an opportunity "for reversal on

[77] Ibid., 1265.

[78] Ibid., 1267–68.

either the facts or the law.'' But such appellate jurisdiction should remain within the military establishment, ''supervised by the civilian authority, which is the President, and the Secretary of War for him.''[79] He cited three reasons why an independent appellate court was unacceptable. First, the constitutional command that ''discipline shall flow through the President to the Army.'' Second, 88 percent of the cases tried by court-martial are military not civil offenses, and ''military men are better able to judge the facts and circumstances.'' Finally, that the military justice system should work in an emergency as well as in peacetime, and ''that any necessity for an appellate tribunal remote from the field of action, with the consequent delay, is not adopted to the emergencies of actual, active field operations.''[80]

Baker insisted that if Congress gave the president power to reverse, modify, or affirm court-martial decisions, there would be no need for an appellate court. But this jurisdictional might did not reach the ability to order a trial de novo.[81] With Baker, just as he had done with Crowder, Lenroot tried to explore the perimeters of authority in a court that could supplement rather than supplant the president. If, he asked, an appeal from a court-martial could be taken to a tribunal whose jurisdiction was limited to questions of law, its duty being either, in the face of error to transmit the record back to the convening authority for a new trial, or otherwise for further action—''could there be any possible objection from the standpoint of controlling superior authority?'' Baker replied, ''None, and in time of peace, it would be a most desirable arrangement.''[82]

Adding that in actual fact most of the civilians in the JAG department were ''a very high type of lawyers,'' the secretary agreed with Lenroot that such men would be logical candidates for such a court; and because they would devote themselves only to military cases for a term of years, they would become especially qualified. Moving to his main point, Lenroot asked if this court would be ''much better qualified to pass upon these questions than . . . for instance, the convening authority?'' Baker answered that ''I think such a court . . . would undoubtedly bring to bear upon a record a higher degree of skill than can be looked for from convening authorities acting upon the record.''[83] Lenroot pushed ahead. ''You would say . . . that unless pressing necessity exists for reposing authority in the President, or somebody who may not be qualified to pass upon the law, or who, because of his other duties, finds it physically impossible for him to give his consideration to the cases individ-

[79] Ibid., 1340, 1344.

[80] Ibid., 1347.

[81] Ibid., 1356–57. The Kernan substitute for Ansell's proposed court, it will be recalled, included explicit language to give the president authority in this matter.

[82] Ibid., 1363.

[83] Ibid., 1364.

ually, it would be very much better to place that authority in the hands of qualified persons, who would give that attention to it?''

''Surely,'' replied Baker. And, added Lenroot, if a court did not interfere with the discretion of the reviewing or confirming authorities, ''but to confine it solely to passing upon questions of law, you would see no objection to such a court?'' Baker answered, ''none whatever.'' What if such a tribunal could be established in the field of operations during war, ''would there be any objection then?'' For a third time Baker responded affirmatively, ''none that I can see.''[84]

Before the transcript of the hearings was published, Baker had the opportunity to review his testimony. He found himself ''perplexed at the inconsistency between my answers'' to the questions of Chamberlain and Lenroot ''with regard to the creation of an appellate power,'' so much in fact that he felt it necessary to add an explanatory memorandum to the printed record. Again, he feared that ''any extraneous and independent appellate power'' would ''inevitably weaken and might conceivably gravely imperil'' authority of the president. While the idea of an appellate power ''is wise, and our experience in this war shows its propriety,'' there should be no case of army discipline ''beyond the reach of the [president] for correction.'' Therefore, the commander in chief should vest authority in the Boards of Review within the JAG department ''to review court martial proceedings and upon the detection of errors of law, . . . to return a record to the convening authority, pointing out the error of law and directing a retrial or disapproval of the proceedings and the restoration of the accused to his previous status.'' The entire process, however, ''should be systematically organized under the direction of the President and at all times under his control.''[85]

The Senate Subcommittee finished its hearings in early November 1919; but seemed in no hurry to act on reforming military justice. In all fairness to Lenroot and Warren, their time was taken up by other issues (especially the battle over the League of Nations) that if not of more political import, were certainly of greater public interest than military judicial procedure. The Senate voted on a revised version of Chamberlain's bill in April 1920. After further changes in the House, the revised Articles of War were finally signed into law on June 4, 1920.[86]

Debate persists about how significant the changes were. Edward Sherman,

[84] Ibid. Possibly Chamberlain may have assumed that he had not heard Baker correctly; for he immediately discussed the exact point with Baker again, only to hear the secretary state, ''I can see no objection to that at all.'' Ibid., 1365.

[85] Ibid., 1369–70. Inconsistency seems to have plagued Baker even in his effort to explain it away. As stated above, he held that the boards of review should set convictions aside for errors of law. But later in his statement he added that ''the appellate power should be able to reach errors of fact as well as errors of law.''

[86] Margulies, ''The Articles of War,'' 88.

a distinguished military-legal scholar concluded that they "can hardly be considered an important reform of military justice."[87] On the other hand, Frederick Bernays Wiener, a noted military-legal historian, recently described them as "genuinely enlightened."[88] Whether of minor or major consequence, there is no doubt that the revisions provided for a new military review procedure; but it was far from what Ansell had proposed.

Article 50 1/2 established within the JAG department a board of review consisting only of officers. They would review records of all cases that normally had to be approved by the president, but they were not an appellate court in any real sense. Counsel did not appear before them; briefs were not presented. Indeed, the article did not even employ the word "court." Moreover, far from being independent of the military, the board was truly a subordinate body. Appointed by the JAG, the members served at his pleasure and in an advisory capacity. Only if he agreed with their recommendations for reversal, was the record returned to the convening authority for dismissal or retrial. If the JAG did not concur with the board, or if he agreed with a recommendation for affirmance, the case was referred to the secretary of war for action by the president. While the chief executive had numerous options, unlike the wording in the Kernan Report the final version of the article did not give him the power to order a new trial de novo.[89]

Many of Ansell's other suggestions were similarly emasculated. A pretrial investigation was now required before a general court-martial could proceed, but resulting recommendations were not binding upon the convening authority. Defense counsel was indeed provided, but there appears to have been no requirement that he be an attorney. A law member could now sit with the court, and he did have to be a lawyer from the JAG Corps, but with the sole exception of ruling on admissibility of evidence, his instructions or findings were not binding upon the court.[90]

[87] Edward F. Sherman, "The Civilianization of Military Law," *Maine Law Rev.* 22 (1970): 27.

[88] Wiener, "Tricentennial," 25. The present author tends to agree with Sherman.

[89] "Courts-Martial, Amendments to Article of War," *Hearings before a Special Subcommittee of the Committee on Military Affairs*, House, 69 Cong., 2d sess., May 4, 1920, 18. The president "may confirm the action of the reviewing authority or confirming authority below, in whole or in part, with or without remission, mitigation or commutation, or may disapprove, in whole or in part, any finding of guilty and may disapprove or vacate the sentence, in whole or in part."

[90] These "modifications" of Ansell's bill not withstanding, some officers remained unimpressed with what had been enacted. Thus, George Marshall wrote in 1925 that "Ansell has imposed a harmful system on the Army. . . . Practically all of our Judge Advocates are men . . . whose point of view is not at all that of a soldier." He was unhappy with the "vicious phases of the present system." In reality, "we are deliberately squelching the soldierly spirit and developing a tribe of legal quibblers. . . . It is very depressing." In a paragraph submitted for inclusion in a formal Post Report, Marshall added that under current court-martial procedure and practice "the real issue is befogged in the ineffective form of ceremony and quibbling over minutia." *Papers of George Catlett Marshall*, ed. Larry Bland, vol. 1 (1981): 278, 280. Twenty-six years later, as

Thirty years later, in 1951, a staff member in the office of the secretary of defense informed an assistant to Sen. Estes Kefauver that "there is nobody that I can find around the Department of Defense who has a clear recollection of the facts of the famous Ansell-Crowder controversy."[91] This indication of slight interest in a significant controversy is unfortunate. Actually, the episode was highly important to the future of American military justice. It may indeed have had, as Wiener put it, a "seamy side," but it also has great relevance in several areas for this study.

For the first time the army, and to some extent the American polity, debated the issue of a military appellate procedure. Prior to Ansell's agitations, according to Crowder, "there was no such thing as appellate review."[92] To be sure, Ansell raised many questions that he failed to answer. Yet, he forced the military establishment to consider the complex relationship between command structure and an independent source of trial review; while the lengthy hearings revealed a perceived incompatibility between the totality of command and civilian norms of appellate jurisprudence. Definitive answers were not forthcoming in 1919, but the first step was taken.

The episode also offered another example of the important role that politics plays in the formulation of military policy. Political figures such as Sen. George Chamberlain, though their concerns for the American soldier may indeed have been genuine, saw the issue through partisan eyes. Chamberlain's antagonism toward Wilson, and his harsh criticism of Baker as secretary of war, when matched with his equally vigorous support for Ansell, made it highly improbable that the reforms could have been considered in nonpartisan terms. Moreover, Ansell's complex relationship with Crowder, together with his own conduct and the resulting split within the JAG department, had more to do with their ultimate rejection than did reasoned discourse on their validity. His plan for an appellate court was unacceptable both to civilian leaders of the military establishment such as Baker, as well as to the army hierarchy. Finally, in 1919–1920, public interest in military justice proved to be fleeting. Independent of each other, these factors might not have been important, but taken together they were dispositive.

The characters in the controversy went their separate ways, and military justice continued to operate as provided in the 1920 Amendments. Oregon voters rejected Chamberlain's bid for reelection.[93] After he retired from the

---

secretary of defense, Marshall presided over the inauguration ceremonies of the first judges selected to sit on the newly established Court of Military Appeals.

[91] *Kefauver Papers* (hereafter cited as KP), University of Tennessee Library, Special Collections, February 21, 1951.

[92] Sup., Courts-Martial Hearings, 10.

[93] Ansell wrote to Chamberlain: "You are to be congratulated on your defeat. You are not defeated: only the things you have fought were defeated. Nobody expects the public to be over discriminating." George Chamberlain Papers, November 15, 1920.

army, Crowder served a term as ambassador to Cuba; he died in 1932. Wigmore and Morgan returned to teaching at law school. In 1925, Morgan became professor of Law at Harvard, where he stayed for the next twenty-five years, until his retirement. Ansell resigned from the army in 1919 to establish a law practice in Washington, D.C. He was still alive in 1949, when he received a copy of a proposed new military code, drafted by a committee chaired by none other than his old supporter, Edmund Morgan. Contained in that new proposal was a provision for a court of military appeals, and in Morgan's last evidence class before he retired from Harvard Law School was a future chief judge of that court, although neither knew it at the time.[94]

Americans have a proclivity to reargue old conflicts in new contexts. In 1919, reform of military justice became a political issue that split the military. In 1949, reform of military justice was proposed by the secretary of defense on behalf of the armed services. In 1919, a dissident JAG officer drafted a reform bill. In 1949, a committee dominated by civilians, but working closely with the several JAG departments, drafted a bill. Only when the civilians were satisfied with the measure, was it submitted to Congress. In 1919, the proposed reforms largely came from the military; in 1949 they came for the military.

History, observed Mark Twain, does not repeat itself, but it does sometimes rhyme. When Morgan resigned from the JAG Corps in 1919, he believed that he would not see major changes in military justice during his lifetime. But in fact, both Morgan and Ansell lived to see the Court of Military Appeals in actual operation. How these changes came about, and what factors led to failure in 1919 but success in 1949–1950 are discussed in the following chapters.

[94] Robinson O. Everett, a member of the Harvard Law Class of 1950, was appointed by President Carter in 1980 to a ten-year term as Chief Judge of the United States Court of Military Appeals. The unusual circumstances surrounding his appointment will be discussed in the second volume of this study.

CHAPTER 6

Renewed Calls for Reforming Military Justice, 1943–1948

IN 1922, ANSELL published a short article in the *Yale Law Journal* commenting on "Some Reforms in Our System of Military Justice." Written apparently to note the enactment of the 1920 "revisions" concerning the Articles of War, the piece also reflected ambivalence about the extent to which the new enactments represented real reforms. Ansell observed the American allegiance "in our first war, as in our latest, and in all the years of our national existence between," to the "Arkansas Traveller philosophy: when war was on we could not change the Articles [of War] and when it was over we no longer needed [to change] them."[1] The American Articles, "at utter variance" with our political ideals, had been adopted "as an incident of emergent circumstance rather than the result of free intelligent consideration."[2] Ansell recalled that "those who saw the daily grist of injustice" pointed out from time to time, in official memoranda and otherwise, vices which they aptly characterized as "destructive of every assurance of justice." These efforts had culminated in the submission to Congress of the Chamberlain Bill in 1919 "to establish Military Justice."[3]

Ansell recognized that many of his key proposals, including establishment of a real appellate court within the military, had been cut from the bill—which in fact he, rather than Chamberlain, had authored. Nevertheless, he still believed that the revisions "properly administered" would "establish military justice." This was because the new version "accepts the general principles and for the most part the specific revisions" in the original draft as submitted by Chamberlain. On the other hand, Ansell conceded that administration of the new provisions "by reason either of uncontrollable circumstances or a lack of sympathy—apparently the latter—has not been in accord with the letter, spirit or purpose of this highly remedial legislation."[4] Ansell's comments were probably as accurate at the end of World War II as when they were written in 1922.

[1] Samuel Ansell, "Some Reforms in our System of Military Justice," *Yale Law Journal* 32 (1922): 147.

[2] Ibid., 148.

[3] Ibid., 151.

[4] Ibid., 155.

REFORM SEEMS THE NORM

The essence of the complaints raised by critics about military justice in World War I can be distilled down to six key abuses: (*a*) There was an extremely high number of convictions, about 88 percent; (*b*) the penalties meted out by courts-martial were excessive, resulting in later reductions by review boards of at least 75 percent of the noted cases; (*c*) there were incredibly wide discrepancies in punishments for the same offenses (inappropriate language merited a prison term of three months imposed by a U.S. Army court in England, but up to twenty-five years from a similar tribunal in France, while punishments for "common absence offenses" could range from a few months to a ninety-nine-year term of confinement); (*d*) rights of the accused were not protected during a court-martial proceeding; (*e*) defense counsel was often incompetent; and (*f*) sentences as rendered by the court could be increased before the court-martial was formally ended.[5] If these problems were troublesome during the relatively brief period of actual American conflict in World War I, how much greater was the potential for complaint during the three and a half years of fighting in World War II.

Ill prepared to cope with what was considered in 1917–1918 to be a major increase in American armed forces, the military justice system was in a much worse position to meet the dramatic needs engendered by the Second World War. The army expanded from 1,460,000 personnel to more than 8,000,000. By 1945, the navy's ranks had doubled in size to over 4,500,000. In all, at least 12,000,000 people were subject to military justice; and at the height of the war, approximately 600,000 courts-martial were convened per year. Over 1,700,000 trials were held, more than 100 executions were carried out, and at the end of the war in 1945, some 45,000 members of the armed forces were in prison.[6] Given these numbers, plus much greater public awareness of the war through advances in communication (e.g., radio and motion pictures) it is not surprising that severe criticism of the military justice system resulted.[7] The

[5] Robert J. White, "The Background and the Problem," *St. John's Law Review* 35 (1961): 200.

[6] Ibid.

[7] While there may not have been a modern version of the famous *New York World* exposé of military justice during World War I, nevertheless as was true in 1918–1919, so during the aftermath of World War II the popular press featured numerous articles critical of military justice. Many of them mentioned the 1919 controversy, and recalled Ansell's role. (His reaction, [he was still living in Washington], can only be imagined. As will be seen, Ansell was involved, albeit to a minimal extent, in the debate over military justice as the UCMJ was drafted.) A representative sampling of these pieces may be found in *80th Cong., 1st sess., Subcommittee of the Committee on Armed Services, Hearings "to Amend the Articles of War" (1947) #125, 2166–2175*. Moreover, members of Congress publicly criticized military justice after the war had ended. Following his late predecessor George Chamberlain, Oregon Senator Wayne Morse stated, for example, that military courts "have been guilty of the grossest types of miscarriage of justice." His colleague,

dimensions of American involvement exacerbated weaknesses which, as the last three chapters have demonstrated, were repeatedly raised but not resolved more than a generation before.

Unlike the Ansell-Crowder era which focused attention primarily on the army, during the period from 1943 to 1948 it was the navy's turn to receive extensive critical scrutiny. In view of the not unreasonable conclusion that without changes similar to the 1920 reforms the navy court-martial system "was even more inadequate than that of the Army," the success of the navy in avoiding extended external inquiry during the earlier controversy is noteworthy.[8] Nor, indeed, had the contrast between public treatment of the two branches been lost on Enoch Crowder. Why, he wondered in 1919, "has not the storm broken out against the Navy?[9] The answer is, I imagine, because the Judge Advocate General of the Navy was more alert in instructions and admonitions given courts than ourselves."[10]

On the other hand, Frederick Bernays Wiener while conceding that prior to 1948 the navy military justice system "had never been modernized in any significant respect," has offered a different explanation. Service in the navy during both world wars, he argued, "did not involve rearrangement of the individual's position in society." During World War II, however, army officers were competitively selected through "the rigorous proving ground of the Officer Candidate School." Hence, to quote Wiener, as in the play *The Admirable Crichton* so too in the U.S. Army, "the butler rather than the country club member frequently wound up as the commander who issued the orders. Necessarily, the inescapable social inversion thus created brought out loud, articulated, and widespread unhappiness."[11]

Wiener may well be right, yet a few additional points can be noted. Unlike World War I, American entrance into the 1941 conflict was precipitated by a

---

William Jenner, accused the army of "stacking the courts against defendants in courts-martial," and Representative Charles Elston believed that "under present law[,] command has an abnormal and unj[u]stified influence over military justice." While disputes over military justice tended to be less partisan than other controversies, in this case all three speakers were Republicans. *New York Times*, November 7, 1945, 8; July 9, 1947, 1, 16.

[8] Sherman, "Civilianization of military law," 29. Sherman cites at least seven different studies of naval military justice carried out in the four-year period between 1943 and 1947.

[9] CP, reel 5, folder 144; May 5, 1919. "They have no law officer of the court to decide questions of law. They have gotten along without the military court of appeal or other form[s] of appellate jurisdiction." Actually, as will be seen below, the two military justice systems although basically similar had some fundamental differences. The authority of the Secretary of the Navy concerning review of courts-martial, for example, appears to have been greater than that of his counterpart, the Secretary of War.

[10] Ibid. "We [and presumably Crowder meant Ansell] had the same opportunity to escape criticism that they had. We seem to have made less use of our opportunities than they with the result that with practically the same system in both services, the Navy is applauded and the Army submerged with vindictive criticism."

[11] Wiener, "Tricentennial," 25–26.

dramatic navy/air attack. Indeed, much of the war—especially in the early period—was primarily fought at sea. Understandably therefore, beginning with the attack on Pearl Harbor public attention focused on the navy, and interest in or complaints about the quality of its military justice were to be expected. Judging from the fact that seven different reports, some from within the navy, others from externally appointed commissions, on the subject of naval military justice were submitted to the service within a four-year period (1943–1947), the navy was not unaware of the problem. Why it took such an effort, with the inevitable duplication of findings and recommendations is unclear.[12] It is not surprising to discover that in 1943 and thereafter, comments about naval military justice were similar to those made about the army's system, twenty-five years earlier.[13]

In addition to the numerous official investigations into military justice, voluntary organizations such as the American Legion, the New York County Bar Association, the New York City Bar Association, and even the American Bar Association—all were interested in reforming the system. Compared with the work of the ABA in 1919, these groups had much more input—if not influence—in 1947–1948.[14] Nevertheless, the historian's efforts to get through the

[12] One explanation might be based upon the navy's desire for thoroughness before determining to change its judicial procedures. A less charitable analysis could rely on the dilatory tactics of a bureaucracy encrusted with tradition. Not without reason, apparently, was the cumbersome volume *Naval Courts and Boards* (the navy's version of the Army Manual for Courts-Martial) generically known as "Rocks and Shoals."

[13] This point is all the more interesting because navy officials were well aware of some underlying issues in the Ansell-Crowder dispute. Indeed, in 1919, the Navy JAG urged the navy to establish a permanent JAG Corps. He also suggested that a "law member" sit at all general courts-martial, and that his "advice upon legal questions arising in connection with the hearing shall be binding upon the court." The law member, however, would have no vote upon questions of fact. Although these proposals apparently received support from the secretary of the navy, they do not appear to have been incorporated into the Act to Govern the Navy (the naval version of the Army Articles of War). LP, *Report of the [NAVY] General Court-Martial Sentence Review Board* (1947), 77; hereafter cited as RGCMSRB. A few words about this report, apparently the last of the seven studies already mentioned, are appropriate here. Originally convened by Navy Secretary Forrestal in 1946, this board was charged with reviewing some five thousand prison sentences. It consisted of six officers and two civilians. The board president was Arthur J. Keeffe, professor of law at Cornell University. Much of the actual direction for the commission, however, came largely from the vice-president, Felix Larkin, a young lawyer who had been an assistant to Judge James Wallace of the Court of General Sessions in New York City. After completing the numerous specific recommendations on reduction of sentences, Larkin received approval from Forrestal to present an expanded report of more than three hundred pages. It was, in fact, an analysis of naval justice that frequently compared and contrasted earlier findings. Larkin's evident ability to organize and synthesize a group effort was so impressive that later in 1947 he was invited to join the legal staff of James Forrestal, who had just become secretary of defense. As will be seen, Larkin played a leading role in the drafting of the UCMJ and its ultimate enactment into law.

[14] William Generous, Jr., *Swords and Scales* (1973), 23–24, 208–9, nn. 8, 19.

reports, memoranda, and recommendations, in an effort to track any resulting legislation is hampered by the fact that primary legislative interest, as had also been the case in 1919, focused elsewhere.

Between 1946 and 1950, when the Uniform Code of Military Justice was signed into law, along with the inevitable political issues such as the presidential election of 1948, Congress also had to deal with such difficult questions as the unification of the armed services, the establishment of the department of defense and the administrative machinery to run it, and the Berlin blockade/airlift, to list only a few. As was clearly demonstrated in 1919, thirty years later military justice was not high on the congressional list of priorities. Nevertheless, out of such a plethora of proposals came a revised code that included a real appellate court. The initial bills reforming military justice focused on either the army or the navy. But once the services were better coordinated (perhaps "unified" is too strong a term), improving army and navy justice through separate revisions of their already complex legal systems made less and less sense; while the need for a single uniform system became readily apparent, even as the specific congressional proposals were pending. The role of the armed services in the ultimate enactment of a unified code, however, would be very different in 1949 than thirty years earlier.

In 1943, the navy received the first of a number of reports that examined naval judicial procedures. A board headed by former Undersecretary of the Treasury Arthur Ballantine concluded that "nowhere do we find a requirement of law that any member of a general court martial shall be skilled in the law." It was true that navy practice required that the JAG be such an officer, one who was supposed to advise the court "in all matters of form and of law." Yet his primary responsibility was "to act as prosecutor." Recognizing anew that these two functions in the same official were seemingly incompatible, Ballantine's committee proposed that "as a matter of policy, wherever practicable at least one member of each general court martial should be skilled in the law."[15]

Ballantine's report also commented on the tendency for navy courts to hand down severe sentences, and then at the same time to recommend clemency from the reviewing authorities. Of course, earlier critics of army military justice had objected to the same practice because "it throws a responsibility upon others which properly belongs to the court."[16] An even more serious issue for the committee was the extent to which the navy system was able to "distinguish between the maintenance of discipline and the administration of justice," providing "a workable plan under which the two factors are accorded

[15] LP, *Ballantine Report*, "Organization, Methods, and Procedure of Naval Courts" (1943), 11. This suggestion might be compared with Ansell's 1919 recommendation, one far less tentative in tone.

[16] Ibid., 15. For comments on the army practice, see William Rigby's statement cited above in chap. 3, n. 1.

proper relative importance.''[17] Here the committee found much room for improvement.

The navy procedure ''might well provide greater independence to the judicial function.''[18] Because the convening authority not only ordered the accused to trial, but also selected his ''judges,'' and because they supposedly would not convene a court-martial ''unless reasonably convinced of his guilt, acquittal may be considered tantamount to an expression of disagreement with a superior officer.'' Having pointed to the underlying tension between a justice system and a well established command structure, the report emphasized that its statements were ''without any criticism whatsoever of the integrity and sense of fairness of officer personnel[,] and with the belief that substantial justice is generally effected.''[19]

Finally, the Ballantine Report pointed (not unreasonably) to the connection between the quality of naval justice and the qualifications of its administrators. They should, it emphasized, be trained in law, and while experience can substitute for training ''to a degree,'' legal work in the navy was generally performed either on temporary assignment or on intermittent tours of duty, neither of which ''is hardly conducive to the accumulation of experience.'' Even worse was the committee's finding that ''competence in law does not appear to be a factor of particular importance contributing to a successful career in the Navy.'' Nor should it be expected ''when it is neither influenced by instruction, nor developed by experience, nor rewarded when acquired by independent effort.''[20]

The recommendations made in the Ballantine Report were in the form of polite suggestions, a tactic that may have undercut its impact. In November 1945, another committee presented its version, and the contrast between the two documents is striking. The panel, headed by Federal District Court Judge Matthew F. McGuire, introduced its written evaluation with the comment: ''It may be said categorically that the present system of military justice is not only antiquated, but outmoded.''[21] Based on the needs of a navy ''where bread and water was routine, and flogging not an unusual occurrence,'' current navy judicial procedure is unable ''to meet the demands of a modern'' service. Ac-

[17] *Ballantine Report* (1943), 23.

[18] Ibid. ''There is a substantial risk that members of courts, judge advocates and defense counsel may not be altogether free from pressure and restraint by superior authority.''

[19] Ibid., 24.

[20] Ibid.

[21] LP, *McGuire Report* (1945), ''Articles for the Government of the Navy and Courts-Martial Procedure,'' 1. McGuire's active role in changing the military justice system apparently was limited to preparing this report. In 1948, he declined to expand his views when invited to do so by Edmund Morgan who, as will be seen, had agreed to chair a committee charged with preparing a uniform code of military justice, applicable to all the services. Whether by accident or appropriate intent, when the three new Judges of the Court of Military Appeals took their oaths of office in June 1951, they were administered by Judge Matthew McGuire.

cording to McGuire, "certain basic rights vital in our viewpoint as a people, and by virtue of that fact inherent in, and essentially a part of any system, naval or otherwise that purports to do justice, must be accepted and safeguarded." Here also, "the present system fails."[22]

McGuire reiterated the point made in the earlier Ballantine Report about the incompatible duality in the JAG's office. The trial judge advocate was "to inform the Court as to the law," but "he is told in the same breath that he *must* never forget he is the prosecutor—two positions diametrically opposed and mutually exclusive."[23] Moreover, the navy mandated no provision for the most rudimentary procedures in criminal trials.[24] Nor was this blatant omission remedied by requiring the judge advocate "to advise the Court in all matters of form and law." In fact, "it is advice with no sanction—it is not binding—and coming from one whose primary function is so completely diverse emphasizes the necessity for change. Humanity simply does not admit of such perfection."[25]

Recognizing that grave miscarriages of justice can result when basic requirements of due process are not followed, McGuire appears to have been well aware of the standard military response to such criticism. "Nor can it be argued with any degree of persuasion or cogency that provision for such instruction interferes in any way with the function of command, and the maintenance of discipline. It *simply means* that if there are to be trials for violation of naval law, the rights of the individual accused are to be scrupulously respected and safeguarded—as they ought to be—which is emphatically not done under the present system of naval justice."[26] Neither was the cause of

[22] Ibid., 2.

[23] Ibid., 3. Emphasis in original.

[24] These included instructing the court as to the primary elements of an offense that must be proved, what is meant by reasonable doubt, presumption of innocence, etc. "These are essentials of due process and Americans, called upon to fight for their preservation, ought to find them in their Navy." Ibid., 3.

[25] Ibid., 3–4. Another member of McGuire's Committee, one who also served on the Vanderbilt panel, was Judge Alexander Holtzoff, of the District Court for the District of Columbia. Holtzoff echoed McGuire's concern that the navy Judge Advocate had contradictory functions. "Like Poobah he combines a number of functionaries in one person" The navy practice "completely ignores the canons of legal ethics in concentrating in the same person the inconsistent functions of a prosecutor and of a legal advisor to the court,"—an advisor who was supposed to be impartial. Furthermore, although the Army Articles of War called for the law member to be from the JAG department except when not available for that purpose, "in actual practice it is understood that [such] officers . . . are rarely detailed to courts-martial[,] and unfortunately officers without any legal training whatsoever are often designated as law members." These two conditions made it clear to Holtzoff that "in the armed forces, the law is not fully recognized as a profession and legal work is frequently entrusted to laymen, at times with results that are either ludicrous or disastrous." Alexander Holtzoff, "Administration of Justice in the United States Army," *New York University Law Review* 22 (1947): 5–6.

[26] McGuire, 4. This situation was only exacerbated by "the reported practice of regarding

justice aided by verdicts in a large number of cases that "strangely comports to what is felt is the desire of the convening authority."

McGuire's proposed reforms included making the JAG "as independent as is conceivably possible, and outside the control and the influence of the convening authority." He also provided for the creation by the secretary of the navy of boards of review composed of three members, one of whom had to be a civilian. The relevant articles were reduced from seventy to eleven, and incorporated "major procedural and practice reforms together with others suggested in the so-called Ballantine Report"; something according to McGuire "which most officers charged with the responsibility of administering naval justice state they never heard of." Courts-martial should follow the "law of evidence as interpreted by the United States District Courts," thus providing "uniformity hitherto appallingly lacking."[27] Finally, McGuire described *Naval Courts and Boards* (the navy equivalent to the army Manual for Courts-Martial) as "unprepossessing in format," and suffering from the "same lack of modernity as the Articles on which it is based." This volume is "hopelessly inutile [sic], and apart from decided defects of prolixity, unfortunate choice and sequence of subject matter . . . is more confusing and harmful than helpful."[28]

As was seen in a previous chapter discussing the Kernan Report in 1919, when confronted with serious criticism of its military justice system the army responded in a defensive tone. One unofficial reply to the McGuire Report from the navy reflected the same tendency. To be sure, the blunt, even acerbic tone of McGuire's criticisms may have contributed to such a reflexive reaction.[29] Marine Col. John Curry, a member of the navy JAG department, submitted a rebuttal to the recommendations, "lest it appear that the report has full concurrence." As naval spokesmen had argued from the 1840s in the wake of the Spencer incident, so too Curry claimed that sometimes ships had

---

lawyers as surplus, and the consequent appointment of incompetents . . . as defense counsel in serious cases."

[27] Ibid., 8.

[28] Ibid., 8–9. McGuire also called for a separate navy JAG Corps, "with promotion dependent on legal merit without any reference to sea duty." He insisted that legal and related problems "*are not* an integral part of the command function any more than those involving medicine or engineering. Efficiency demands their separation." The report ended with the observation that "halfway measures simply will not do." Ibid., 10–11. Emphasis in original.

[29] On the other hand, the markedly restrained tone of the earlier Ballantine Report appears to have been of mimimal value in convincing naval authorities, with the possible exception of Secretary Forrestal, that changes were essential. Forrestal's important role in moving the military toward a unified code will be discussed in detail later. Unlike Secretary of War Newton Baker in 1918–1919, Forrestal, as secretary of defense, was more evenhanded in his reaction to the calls for changes in military justice. As Forrestal stated, "I do not believe it is as bad as it has been painted, nor as good as some of its defenders claim. Many of the criticisms have seemed to me to be without foundation, but many of them have seemed to me to be justified." White, "The Background and the Problem," n. 5, 202.

to operate "for long periods without direct contact of superiors,"—the implication being that naval justice had to leave much flexibility and discretionary authority to the ship's commanders.[30]

Nor did Curry see any intrinsic difficulty with the fact that the judge advocate combined both the functions of legal advisor to the court and prosecutor in the same person. "The duality of the position . . . is of no danger so long as his views, both argument and advice, are legally sound. . . . It is believed that it is more accurate to state the two positions of the judge advocate are mutually exclusive but not diametrically opposed."[31] As to command interference, "the criticism of the report is extravagant in this matter." When interference with the courts occurs, other "injustices and administrative defects are usually present." While "influence is often attempted, it is not often successful."

Finally, Curry strongly rejected a proposed separate navy JAG Corps. "It would present new evils without a cure." Moreover, there is "no assurance that a corps of lawyers will deal more fairly and justly than a corps of line officers." Legal matters were related to discipline, an essential ingredient of command. To claim, as did the McGuire Report, that "legal and related problems are not an integral part of the command function" was from Curry's viewpoint dead wrong.[32]

CONGRESS CONSIDERS

In retrospect, these multiple investigations into American military justice during World War II represented an unfortunate though understandable waste of resources. Had there been some mechanism for coordination of such activities between the army and navy, much duplication might have been avoided. Moreover, neither the Ballantine nor McGuire reports appear to have consid-

[30] LP, *Memorandum*, "MacGuire Report, Comment on," July 22, 1948, 1, 2. Even as he wrote this response, addressed to no specific officer or department, Curry was serving as the representative from the Navy JAG to a working committee within the office of the secretary of defense, charged with the task of drafting a uniform military code.

[31] Ibid. Having established, at least to his own satisfaction, that current naval practice remained acceptable, Curry added "it is freely agreed that a legal authority on the court, separate from the prosecution, is most desirable."

[32] Ibid., 5. There remains in military justice an ongoing tension between those who insist that legal issues must be handled by a separate trial system (albeit one within the military), and those who claim that the unit commander can never afford to be insulated from the operations of the military justice system. As will be seen in the second volume of this study, the United States Court of Military Appeals has tended to increase the authority and independence of the military trial judge, often at the expense of the convening authority's jurisdiction. For a well-articulated criticism of this trend, see Donald W. Hansen, "Judicial Functions for the Commander," *Military Law Review* 41 (1968): 1–54.

ered the lengthy materials that had accumulated during the army hearings in 1919. Not until 1947 did the navy receive a comprehensive, comparative analysis of military justice—one that not only compared other military systems, but drew heavily on the earlier army experiences.[33] In the meantime, Congress as well as the army prepared their own proposals for change.

Between 1945 and 1946, the House Committee on Military Affairs conducted an extended examination of "the National War Effort," and spent more than a year studying both the court-martial procedure as well as the entire judicial system of the army. On August 1, 1946, it presented a number of recommendations to the House.[34] Seen in the light of the Chamberlain Bill in 1919 and the 1920 revisions of the Articles of War, the proposals reflected a desire to consolidate what existed, rather than to construct new procedures. Thus, rather than create an appellate court, the committee urged that the JAG be vested with appellate powers. Although similar to what Ansell had envisaged, the 1946 recommendations would have given the JAG even more authority than he had proposed.

The committee suggested that the JAG "be empowered to consider appeals from general courts-martial both as to law and fact," and that he be able "to retry any case de novo, [or] order any case retried de novo."[35] In addition, he should have the power "to void any original proceeding, or to alter any sentence, or to issue an honorable discharge . . . or to take other action as may be required to correct any injustice and so far as possible to make whole the part or parties injured." Moreover, enlisted men when tried by special or general court-martial would have the right for a number of their peers to sit on the court, to the maximum of one-third of the total membership. "Failure to comply with this provision shall be a jurisdictional error."[36]

The committee further proposed to require that the law member, as well as the trial judge advocate and the defense counsel, were either to be officers of the JAG Corps, or officers who are members of the bar of a Federal court, or of the highest court of a State. The law member would not vote either on the findings or any resulting sentence. The convening authority would be forbidden to "censure, reprimand or admonish any member of a court-martial . . . with respect to the findings or sentences adjudged by such court." Failure to conduct a thorough and impartial investigation before a court-martial was to be considered "a jurisdictional error."[37]

[33] See above, n. 13. Recommendations of the RGCMSRB concerning appellate review are discussed in a later section of this chapter.

[34] 79th Cong., 2d sess., House, Committee on Military Affairs, *Report No. 2722* (1946), 1. It might be noted that one of the members of the House Committee was Paul Kilday, Democrat from Texas. In 1961, he would be appointed to the U.S. Court of Military Appeals by President Kennedy.

[35] This legal term simply means trying a case all over again, from the beginning.

[36] House Report 2722, 2.

[37] Ibid., 2–3.

Even as the committee sent these recommendations to the House, the army had selected its own advisory committee—nominated by the American Bar Association—to study military justice. Appointed on March 25, 1946, it consisted of nine civilians with Arthur Vanderbilt, Dean of New York University Law School and soon to become Chief Justice of the New Jersey Supreme Court, as chair. On paper, the committee's investigation appeared impressive. It held regional hearings in nine cities throughout the country, accumulated more than twenty-five hundred pages of testimony, and received several hundred answers drawn from all ranks of the army to a questionnaire dealing with military justice.[38]

In the light of later history concerning establishment of a formal court of military appeals, two excerpts from the testimony received by the Vanderbilt panel are of interest. While he insisted that in the military, "we cannot indulge the view that all men are created equal," Frederick Bernays Wiener called for some system of permanent courts available to the armed services. A former sergeant-major went even further, and urged that "an appellate system should be established. . . . There should be a separate legal department responsible only to Washington. Defense appeal briefs should be used. The Army appellate system would follow the New York [State] system of appeals. The appellate courts would consist of ranking officers of the legal department, and would sit either in the theatres or in Washington. They would be appointed by the JAG or the President."[39]

There is little doubt that this panel received an accurate picture concerning many of the flaws in military justice. Indeed, earlier investigations and hearings had already exposed them. Thus, in retrospect the findings of the Vanderbilt Committee were to be expected, and their recommendations were not very innovative. Had the army, to say nothing of Congress, not already undertaken inquiries of similar import based upon similar complaints in 1919, they might have been more impressive. In actuality, however, they indicated the tenacity of tradition, and the fact that in 1946 the military establishment seemed unwilling to make changes first recommended more than twenty-five years earlier. For the reader familiar with the Ansell and Crowder controversy, a sense of déjà vu rather than doctrinal initiative hung over the Vanderbilt Report.

It found, for example, that "the command frequently dominated the [military] courts in the rendition of their judgment"; that "defense counsel were often ineffective because of (*a*) lack of experience and knowledge, or (*b*) lack

[38] One source *not* utilized by the committee was "testimony of convicted men or their friends." This was because the army, like the navy, had established a separate committee to examine excessive sentences. Chaired by former United States Supreme Court Justice Owen Roberts, soon to become Dean of the University of Pennsylvania Law School, the committee had reduced a large number of prison sentences that it considered unnecessarily severe. *Report of War Department Advisory Committee on Military Justice* (1946), 2–3.

[39] MPHLS, Harvard Law School, vol. 1 (containing the Vanderbilt Report): 12–13, 70.

of a vigorous defense attitude''; that sentences ''were frequently excessively severe and sometimes fantastically so''; that military justice afforded enlisted men and officers differed ''as to the bringing of charges[,] . . . convictions and sentences''; and that the pretrial investigations called for in Article 70 (a result of the 1920 amendments) ''were frequently inefficient or inadequate.''[40] As Ansell had repeatedly noted during 1918–1919, so also the committee emphasized the need for the soldier to know that ''if he is charged with an offense, his case will not rest entirely in the hands of his accuser, but that he will be able to present his evidence to an impartial tribunal with the assistance of competent counsel and receive a fair and intelligent review.''[41]

Not only did the committee suggestions reiterate what Ansell had frequently repeated; they also echoed the Congressional Report presented only a few months before. Thus, the convening authority should be forbidden to reprimand members of the court or its members in any way. Enlisted men should be able to serve as members of a court-martial.[42] Both the defense counsel and law member should be trained lawyers; the ruling of the latter on legal questions should be binding on the court, ''except as to the sufficiency of evidence.''[43] Reviewing authority should be vested in the office of the JAG. ''This reviewing authority shall have the power to review every case as to the weight

[40] Ibid., 4. Precisely the same point had been raised by Ansell in 1922. As to legal representation for the accused, one witness before the committee noted that ''defense counsel were inadequate. When an accused got a good defense counsel[,] his chances were good. But good counsel were transferred out.'' The committee also received samples of what was known as ''skin letters.'' The term was commonly applied to letters from a commander to members of a court-martial regarding a verdict which he did not like. One such letter stated that had an acquittal been warranted by the facts and the applicable law, according to the commander, ''I would have dismissed the charge without referring it to you for trial in the first instance; therefore, I simply cannot fathom your reasoning other than [to] conclude that you were either activated by some fact not disclosed in the record of trial, or else arbitrarily refused to perform your duty.'' Sup., n. 39, 18–19.

[41] Ibid., 6.

[42] Here, however, the committee seems to have hedged. ''Qualified enlisted men should be eligible to serve as members of general and special courts-martial and should be appointed thereon to the extent that in the discretion of the appointing authority, it seems desireable to do so.'' There was, in other words, no absolute right of an enlisted man to procure one or more of his peers as members. Ibid., 12.

[43] Ibid., 8. This exception had some justification. As the committee noted, ''an adverse ruling . . . on the sufficiency of the evidence would result in an acquittal[,] and this question should therefore be left to the whole court.'' Although the navy was by far the worst offender, both services had failed to recognize ''law as a profession in the same sense in which they recognized medicine.'' Judge Alexander Holtzoff recalled that a retired army colonel testified before the Vanderbilt Committee, and ''stated in his opinion that the law member of a general court-martial did not have to be a lawyer, since he was given a manual which he could study and which would guide him in making his rulings.'' Holtzoff, who happened to be presiding at this particular session, asked the witness ''whether he would be willing to designate a layman as a regimental doctor, if the latter would study a brief pamphlet on medicine. Naturally, the witness had no answer to make.'' Holtzoff, ''Administration of Justice in the United States Army,'' 11.

of the evidence, to pass upon the legal sufficiency of the record and to mitigate, or set aside the sentences and to order a new trial.''[44]

In at least two respects, the committee went beyond the House Report. It confronted and rejected the claim that local convening authorities were best able to select appropriate members to serve on courts-martial. Rather, the members urged that commanders establish a panel of available officers, ''subject to change from time to time, from which the selection of members of the court may be made.'' The absolute power of the convener to summon the court, as well as his authority to approve or disapprove the sentence remained inviolate. But, ''further than that the command should not go.'' Indeed, the ''time is past when a court-martial might be deemed merely as an advisory council to the commander.'' In point of fact, the court-martial ''is an independent tribunal; and if the commander controls the prosecution, the appointment and functioning of the court may safely be left to the legal department of the army.''[45]

Furthermore, the committee implied that the JAG Corps ought to be a separate unit within the army. The House recommendation, while calling for the enlargement and reorganization of the department, had merely proposed that JAG jurisdictions within the army were to be ''independent of the immediate commands in which cases arise.'' As had the McGuire Report for the navy, so too the Vanderbilt summary urged that members of the JAG Corps ''be governed as to promotions, efficiency reports and specific duty assignments in the chain of command of the Judge Advocate General's Department[,] and not by the commanding officer of the organizations in which they may be serving.''[46] Although the report was not as explicit as its naval counterpart, the committee clearly believed that an independent JAG department would alleviate if not eliminate abuses of command influence.[47]

The Vanderbilt Report was delivered to the War Department on December

[44] Vanderbilt Report, 9.

[45] Ibid., 10.

[46] Ibid.

[47] The point was made even clearer in the 1947 House Report from the Committee on Military Affairs that accompanied the favorable recommendation that a proposed revision to the articles be approved, one that among other things called for a separate JAG Corps. ''At the conclusion of a trial, under the present system, the same officers who conducted the case return to the command of a line officer who has full authority over their efficiency ratings, promotion recommendations, leaves and duty assignments. These officers, many of whom have families and have chosen the Army for a career, would be less than human if they ignored the possibilities of such influence.'' The same difficulty applied to officers who conducted any reviews, appellate or otherwise. ''We contend that those who are charged with the impartial administration of military justice must have sufficient freedom of judicial determination to meet the responsibility.'' 80th Cong., 1st sess., *House Report No. 1034* (1947), 9. From the military viewpoint, a separate JAG Corps removed a key *staff* department from *line* supervision; something considered inappropriate by senior military officials. When an independent JAG Corps was ultimately established, it seems to have been the result of civilian preference, not military policy.

13, 1946. Within about two months, Secretary of War Robert Patterson announced through the public relations division of the department that he "had approved the principal recommendations" of the committee. And indeed, to a much greater extent than Newton Baker in 1919, he did endorse various changes. These included enlarging the JAG Corps, the prohibition against any sort of reprimand to members of the court from the convening authority, the requirement of legal training for the law member, as well as the expanded appellate authority within the JAG office.[48] From this list, as well as the title of the release itself, one could easily get the impression that substantial reforms were now inevitable.

On the other hand, the last three pages of the release contained information on what the secretary, presumably after discussions with his military advisors, including Undersecretary of War Kenneth C. Royall, had declined to approve.[49] These included the suggestion that the JAG (presumably from Washington) be empowered to appoint members of a court instead of the convening authority; that the JAG, rather than army commanders, be responsible for evaluating members of his department, and that there be a separate promotion list for the JAG Corps.[50] Also, the Vanderbilt recommendation that defense counsel should always be lawyers received short shrift. Not only was it impractical because there were not enough lawyers available; but also "in many simple military cases line officers are equally effective as counsel as are lawyers." Instead, Patterson suggested that "where the trial judge advocate is a lawyer[,] the defense counsel must also be a lawyer. This proposal insures equal advantages to both sides."[51]

One month after the press release, the War Department submitted a bill to Congress that amended the Articles of War along the lines noted above. It was assigned to the Committee on Armed Services, which held hearings on the measure. Unlike the proceedings of an earlier era, in 1947 the most controversial issue did not deal with appellate jurisdiction. The War Department proposed that a three-member board of review be established within the JAG's

[48] LP, Press Release, "Secretary Patterson announces action on Military Justice Report" (1947), 2–5.

[49] Royall, an able lawyer and administrator, would soon become secretary of the army in the new department of defense. A man of imposing stature, he had received the nickname of "Dumbo" from his associates. Royall was no stranger to the military justice system. See inf.

[50] Royall opposed creation of a separate JAG department. He wrote an article published shortly after the war department submitted a bill to Congress amending the Articles of War along the lines indicated in the press release. In it, Royall conceded only recognition of the fact that the JAG Corps "is composed of professional men and that their situation requires peculiar treatment, [and that] special privileges should be accorded them with respect to promotion"—within the overall control of the regular army. Kenneth C. Royall, "Revision of the Military Justice Process as Proposed by the War Department," *Virginia Law Review* 33 (1947): 269–88.

[51] Press release, 6–7. Patterson's proposal can also be said to have insured that trial incompetence would be more equitably distributed!

department. Called a "judicial council," it was to consist of three officers. Neither the proposed version nor the committee's amended draft that ultimately became law made any reference to civilian membership on the council.[52] Moreover, neither version envisaged any formal rules of appellate pleading. The council did, however, have some expanded jurisdiction over the existing review boards. Further, a clause provided that "all actions taken pursuant to [army appellate proceedings] shall be binding upon all departments, courts, agencies, and officers of the United States."[53]

The committee made two additional changes, including one that disturbed the military establishment much more than the creation of a judicial council, which remained under the control of the JAG department at all times. In his article, Kenneth Royall had heralded the proposed change to permit enlisted men to serve on courts-martial "at the option of the appointing authority."[54] To the committee, such an option undercut the force of the proposed change. The choice whether or not to have enlisted men on the court should be "at the option of the defendant," not the commander.[55] The other change involved the decision to establish a separate JAG Corps with a promotion list independent of line command—a step strongly opposed by the army.[56]

[52] House Report 1034, 7. With commendable understatement, the committee noted that "any system of judicial review is complicated, technical, and difficult to understand." Indeed, the military establishment apparently found the old article 50 1/2 so difficult to comprehend that they replaced it. With what success, however, is not clear. One student of military justice wrote in 1970 of the 1947 revised article that it "is nearly incomprehensible, and the specific powers of the Judicial Council are not clear to me, if they ever were to anyone." Generous, *Swords and Scales*, 209. Frederick B. Wiener stated that the creation of the Judicial Council added "an extra layer of further examination over the existing boards of review. The details of this expanded reviewing process were fully as complex as the wiring diagram of a large automobile's dashboard." Wiener, "Tricentennial," 31.

[53] Ibid., 22. It is not clear whether this wording was intended to block the traditional route of appeal from a court martial verdict to a civilian tribunal through collateral attack. Nor is it clear if this section was ever tested judicially although the statute, better known as the Elston Act, was in effect from 1949 to 1951.

[54] Royall, "Revision of the Military Justice Process," 273–74.

[55] House Report 1034, 14. But it remained unclear whether or not the convening authority *had* to appoint enlisted men, if so requested by the accused. According to the committee's words, he could appoint "those officers of the command and when eligible those enlisted persons of the command who, in his opinion, are best qualified for the duty by reason of age, training, experience, and judicial temperament."

[56] Some indication of the opposition can be seen in the fact that Under Secretary of War Royall and Lt. Gen. J. Lawton Collins, testified against the proposal before the subcommittee that first considered the war department measure. In spite of their appearance, the subcommittee urged creation of a separate corps. "When the matter was brought before the full committee," Secretary of War Robert P. Patterson and Chief of Staff Dwight D. Eisenhower voiced "their strenuous objections[,]" but to no avail. It seemed apparent to the committee that the "command" considered the JAG department "to be composed of a nonprofessional group, whereas we are of the opinion that [it] must be a professional group, specially trained." According to the committee, some 90 percent of the field work undertaken by JAGs related to military justice, with 50 percent

THE KEEFFE-LARKIN PANEL

In 1947, James Forrestal received the Report of the General Court-Martial Sentence Review Board, dealing with naval military justice. A thoughtful analysis of almost four hundred pages, replete with scholarly citations, appendices, and references to the other reports submitted since 1943, it came from a committee chaired by a professor of law at Cornell University, Arthur J. Keeffe, but actually administered by Felix Larkin.[57] Because Larkin later played such an important role in the drafting of the UCMJ, as well as the specific proposal for an appellate tribunal, some of the specific comments and recommendations made in the report should be noted.

At the outset, the report strongly endorsed an earlier conclusion that "it can no longer be expected that [naval] legal affairs can be handled competently except by qualified, full time experts."[58] While it specifically eschewed "considerations relating to possible unification of the armed services" (something that while imminent had not yet happened), most of its proposals "can be readily coordinated with any proposals for reform of the Army court-martial system."[59] Both systems had retained the automatic review of court-martial findings and sentences by the convening authority. But Larkin's committee insisted that such a procedure be seen exactly for what it was.

It was not an appeal "in the true sense, and the analogy if pressed too far, is misleading." In fact, such review "is a condition precedent" to the implementation of the court's "findings and sentence. It is a procedure peculiar to our military and naval law, deriving directly from the concept that the court is the arm or agency of the commander, and it has no real counterpart in Anglo-American civil law."[60] Moreover, dispassionate analysis revealed major weaknesses with the practice, however it was labeled.

In the first place, "the reviewing authority is usually the same officer who convened the court and referred the case to trial." It is "humanly impossible for a person, no matter how high his purpose, to dissociate himself from his prior actions and opinions . . . [,] and to view it later as though he were seeing

---

of their work in Washington being of the same nature. "It can hardly be expected that unqualified personnel can handle these assignments. If they could, this subject would not be before us today." Ibid., 9–10. Eisenhower and Patterson believed that a separate JAG corps "would hurt discipline by reducing the power of the line commander." See *80th Cong., 1st sess., House, Committee on Armed Services, Hearings on Sundry Legislation Affecting the Naval and Military Establishments (1947)*, 2:4415–37; *New York Times*, July 16, 1947, 11.

[57] Sup., n. 13.

[58] RGCMSRB (1947), 7. Moreover, the court-martial "can no longer be regarded as a mere instrument for the enforcement of discipline." It is this, but "it is also much more: it is a criminal court [capable of] applying highly punitive sanctions." When so functioning, "considerations of law and justice become paramount." Ibid.

[59] Ibid., 8.

[60] Ibid., 20.

it for the first time.''[61] Furthermore, as indicated above, the review actually undertaken was ''not really analogous to an appeal.'' Technically speaking, defense counsel could submit briefs; but ''he does not often do so, and rarely, if ever resorts to oral presentation of the case to the convening authority.'' Even while conceding that—in theory—objections raised concerning evidence and rulings were weighed as though on appeal, and also that the record could be carefully scrutinized for jurisdictional errors, ''it is difficult, [with] such a procedure, to detect all the errors which may exist, sometimes serious ones.''[62]

The ''practical result'' of these proceedings was ''that the reviewing authority rather than the court'' fixed the sentences; and while he could extend clemency, all too often such action consisted ''merely [of] reducing the sentence to something approaching what it should have been in the first place.''[63] Such a practice inevitably gave the reviewing authority ''a large measure of indirect control over the court and its actions.''[64] Members of the court, usually of inferior rank to that of the reviewing authority, would be less than human if they were not aware of his preferences concerning penalties.

Larkin's committee further concluded that the solution lay in strengthening the initial court-martial proceeding, not in relying ''on subsequent [internal] reviews to correct deficiencies therein.'' The best ways to accomplish this goal were to separate the reviewing officer from the one ordering the case to trial, and/or ''abolish the initial review altogether . . . [,] making the court's sentence self executory, subject however to being set aside by a Board of Review or other higher authority.''[65] To be sure, a step that eliminated control of a convening authority over the sentence ''might be destructive of discipline.'' To their credit, the report's authors did not flinch from the implications of these recommendations. Once a case has been referred to trial, ''it ceases to be a mere disciplinary matter, and from that time on the process of law should be paramount, and command control should cease.''[66]

Moreover, the form of review beyond the convening authority in many instances was less than satisfactory. In fact, the secretary of the navy might receive a case from the JAG's office, or from the Bureau of Naval Personnel. For the most part unable to examine these cases personally, he would refer

[61] Ibid., 192. ''This is recognized . . . in the rules followed everywhere with respect to disqualification of judges in civilian appellate courts. It is anomalous not to recognize it in the single case of the authority who reviews court-martial cases.''

[62] Ibid., 193.

[63] Ibid.

[64] Ibid., 194.

[65] Ibid., 195. This, of course, is precisely what Chamberlain (in reality Ansell) had proposed in his 1919 bill to ''establish military justice.'' The advantages of a self-executory sentence were obvious: control over its functions would be placed squarely in the hands of the court, and the problem of the same authority convening and reviewing would be eliminated.

[66] Ibid., 203.

them to other officers—with the possibility of receiving several distinct and varying recommendations. Thus, the final action taken by the secretary frequently might be a "compromise of half a dozen views. Administratively, and from the standpoint of justice, such a result is deplorable."[67] Also, the secretary was ill equipped to distinguish between the need for "legal review, for legal sufficiency of the proceedings, findings, and sentence; and sentence review, for appropriateness of the sentence, clemency factors and the like."[68]

Building on similar suggestions put forth by the Ballantine and McGuire reports, Keeffe's committee recommended that a Board of Legal Review be established by statute, and that it be housed in the office of the secretary rather than in the JAG's department. Although there seemed to be general agreement on a three-member board, "five would be equally satisfactory."[69] At least one member should be a civilian.[70] But possibly more important was that all members "be highly qualified for their important duties and that they be appointed on a long term, semi-permanent basis." The civilian member should have a term of at least six years, and should be "a well qualified civilian lawyer or judge of long experience. He should not be a naval officer or civilian official who has been retired for age." He should "be appointed by the President, as the Commander in Chief of the Navy, on the recommendation of the Secretary." Finally, in terms of salary, "there is no reason why he should receive less than a federal District or Circuit Judge." In short, "the goal should be the establishment of a Board of Legal Review occupying the same place in the scheme of naval justice as the Circuit Court of Appeals does in the system of federal courts, and having the same dignity, standing and importance."[71]

The report further suggested that this tribunal review "automatically, all convictions by general court martial, and any conviction by [an] inferior court which is appealed to it." Moreover, it should have the authority to review both questions of law as well as fact—although [the latter] power "would rarely be exercised, for in most cases the Board . . . would defer to the [lower] court's conclusions on issues of fact." Also, it should be able to consider errors in the record, whether raised or not by appellant or his counsel. Moreover, the committee considered the degree of finality, "if any," to be accorded decisions from this board.

[67] Ibid., 214.

[68] Ibid., 222.

[69] Ibid., 225. When it began operations in 1951, the U.S. Court of Military Appeals had three members. In 1989, Congress expanded the court to include five judges, effective October 1, 1990.

[70] "While this feature has perhaps been overemphasized, it could do no harm and would probably go a long way in convincing the general public that naval justice was as fair as civilian justice." Ibid., 223–24. However, the Keeffe-Larkin Committee seems to have been ambivalent on whether or not the head of the board should be a civilian.

[71] Ibid., 224–225. The suggestions of this panel serve as a very good basis of comparison with what ultimately emerged in 1950 as the Court of Military Appeals.

Ansell, it will be recalled, had advocated that his proposed court of Military Appeals have final authority on questions of law. The end result, after the Kernan Board had acted and Congress had reacted, was a complex, cumbersome, and confusing system that "obviously represent[ed] a compromise between a desire to give a certain amount of finality to the findings of the Board of Review, and a desire to make them advisory only."[72] The committee cut through the confusion with a simple proposal that the "Board of Legal Review's determination of matters of law should be final and conclusive, subject to the reserve power of the Secretary to set aside any conviction at a later date."[73]

Finally, the committee turned to the relationship between the findings of its proposed Board of Legal Review and civilian appellate courts. As earlier chapters have noted, collateral attack—often on jurisdictional grounds—remained an acceptable route to civilian judicial review of court-martial decisions. This approach however, while viable was also cumbersome. The committee suggested in appropriate cases "authorizing a petition for review of the findings and decisions of the [proposed] Board of Legal Review to be filed directly with the United States Supreme Court."[74] Granted that the High Court, already burdened with a heavy calendar of cases, might not welcome such a change, its adoption "might improve and strengthen the system of naval justice."

Even more important, "from the standpoint of full justice, it is important that this ultimate right of appeal be granted to every accused," especially "in cases involving constitutional privileges and due process." Just as the highest civilian state courts were not infallible, "it is not to be expected that the Naval Board of Legal Review would be entirely free from error." The report noted how promptly the cases of the Nazi saboteurs and the Japanese generals had received review before the Supreme Court.[75] "The granting of such an ex-

[72] Ibid., 226–29.

[73] Ibid., 230. The committee was not being inconsistent here. "Despite the comprehensive powers which it is proposed be conferred upon the Board of Legal Review, and despite any degree of finality which might be given to such review, it will still be possible for mistakes to occur and injustices to arise." Ibid., 239–40. Larkin's report further urged that the Board of Legal Review examine sentences "only from the standpoint of their legal sufficiency, reserving matters of appropriateness of sentence to another authority. The two functions are distinct, and cannot be well performed by a single body." The head of a proposed Sentence Review Board should be "a civilian lawyer of similar qualifications, experience, and compensation as the head of the Board of Legal Review." Ibid., 231.

[74] Ibid., 251–52. Larkin saw several advantages to such a procedure. It would provide "a final and conclusive answer" to "every difficult jurisdictional, constitutional, and due process question" arising in a court-martial. And, it would eliminate the "necessity of petitioning the various district courts for writs of habeas corpus," with further appeals through the system culminating in the Supreme Court.

[75] As defense counsel for the Nazi saboteurs in 1942, Col. Kenneth Royall had not hesitated to

traordinary privilege of appeal to a nation's enemies has been applauded, and properly so.''[76] However, ''we should be no less ready to grant similar privileges to our own military and naval personnel, when substantial questions of jurisdiction and due process arise in court-martial proceedings.''[77]

THE NAVY BECALMED

The navy's ''official'' reaction to the plethora of proposals for change took the form of a congressional bill. Presented at the request of the service about five months after receipt of the Keeffe Committee's report, the bill to amend the Articles for the Government of the Navy[, and] to improve the administration of naval justice, was introduced in the Senate on May 26, and the House on June 2, 1947.[78] There is no doubt that the navy ''brass'' seriously considered some of the suggestions for change previously put forward. But on the whole, the generalization that tradition dies hard in the military, and hardest in the navy received little challenge from this suggested legislation. All commanders were still required to ''show in themselves a good example of virtue, honor, patriotism, and subordination.'' Unspecified penalties could still be meted out by courts-martial for more than fifty-five specified offenses. These included ''profane swearing, falsehood, or gambling,'' as well as the act of ''send[ing] or accept[ing] a challenge to fight a duel or act[ing] as a second in a duel.''[79]

---

carry their cause to the United States Supreme Court, claiming (unsuccessfully) that their trial by military commission violated the Constitution.

[76] In an earlier section, the report had noted a number of cases wherein substantial jurisdictional or constitutional due process issues should have been raised before a civilian tribunal. In many instances, these convictions ''might have been invalidated.'' But ''the accused were apparently not advised of the questions involved, nor did their defense counsel carry these cases beyond the trial proceedings. The probabilities are that the accused in these cases are not aware that the questions exist and can still be raised by petition for writ of habeas corpus.'' Especially when compared with the cases of the Nazi saboteurs, ''this represents a failure to do full justice.''

[77] Ibid., 253. On behalf of their Nazi clients, experienced military lawyers like Kenneth C. Royall ''took every step to present the full case of the accused'' to the Supreme Court. Apparently ''they did so because with their high rank and greater experience, they were more aware of the avenues of appeal open to them than is the average defense counsel.'' That they failed is not the issue. ''What is important is that these defense counsel secured for the accused . . . every right and privilege known to our law. If this can be done for our enemies, provision should be made to insure that it is done for our military and naval personnel, not merely as a matter of theoretical right, but as a matter of deed and fact.'' Ibid., 91–92.

[78] 80th Cong., 1st sess., S. 1338, H.R. 3687. For convenience only, all citations are from the Senate version.

[79] 80th Cong., 1st sess. (1947), S. 1338, 1, 8. Acting upon a suggestion made in the Keeffe-Larkin report, this bill included a navy version of the ''catchall'' articles found in the Army Articles, and discussed above in an earlier chapter. Court-martial punishment could be levied for

Navy officials did recommend some changes. The Keeffe Report had urged that "qualified officers who are lawyers should be provided to act as prosecuting lawyers and defense counsel for every general court-martial."[80] The proposed bill stated that the convening authority shall appoint "a prosecutor and a defense counsel who shall be persons qualified to perform such duties."[81] Did this language mean that the prosecutor and defense counsel *had* to be lawyers?

In an article published only a few months after the bill had been submitted to Congress, Larkin and Robert Pasley, Jr., a staff member of Keeffe's Committee, so concluded.[82] The actual language of the navy version, however, does not seem to support this interpretation. The word "lawyer" has a definite meaning to it, especially in terms of qualifications to practice. Had the navy wished to require that its prosecutors and defense counsel be lawyers, it could have employed the specific term (as did the Keeffe Report) instead of the language used.

The Report had also suggested that the convening authority be required to appoint as judge advocate, an officer so certified by the navy JAG. This individual would be responsible *not* to the convenor but to TJAG. The navy bill accepted both these proposals, but with a change that reflected the service's traditional concern with command.[83]

The committee had favored a trial procedure where the ruling of the judge advocate on matters of evidence and interlocutory questions were to be binding upon members of the court. The navy supported this recommendation so far as that the judge advocate should indeed advise the court on this and other matters as well, but added that he "may be overruled by a majority vote of the court in which the reasons therefore shall be spread upon the record." Larkin and Pasley explained that "the Navy's reasons for [this proviso] are understood to be based upon the feeling that an anomalous situation would be created if the judge advocate, who might be a junior officer, could impose his judgement on the rest of the court, who might all be senior to him. The navy believes as a practical matter, the judge advocate will rarely be overruled, because of the requirement that in any case where he is overruled, the reasons therefor[e] be spread upon the record."[84]

"any disorder or neglect to the prejudice of good order and discipline or any conduct of a nature to bring discredit upon the naval service." Ibid., 14.

[80] RGCMSRB (1947), 92.

[81] S. 1338, 22.

[82] Robert Pasley, Jr., and Felix Larkin, "The Navy Court Martial: Proposals for its Reform," *Cornell Law Quarterly* 33 (1947): 195–234.

[83] Ibid., 23.

[84] Ibid., 209–10. Two points might be noted: (*a*) the navy position did not address the fact that in terms of legal training and experience, the Judge Advocate would probably be senior to members of the court, regardless of their rank, and (*b*) the subtle effect that this provision might have on a Judge Advocate, not so much in being overruled, but in so deciding various questions that

The Keeffe Committee had desired that the traditional post-court-martial review be undertaken by an authority other than the convenor, who presumably had brought the case to trial in the first place. The navy declined to accept the change, probably concluding that it repudiated "the importance of the command function." On the other hand, it proposed restriction of the convenor's authority "to a clemency function solely."[85] Finally, the navy draft made no mention whatsoever of the proposed Board of Legal Review. Instead, it included a provision that "under such regulations as may be prescribed by the Secretary . . . [,] the proceedings, findings, and sentence of a court martial shall, upon good cause shown, if requested by the person convicted, within one year after such person has been informed that the review of his case has been completed, again be reviewed."[86] The draft was unclear as to who would review, the extent of such a procedure, and the composition of its members.[87]

Pasley and Larkin prepared their article during the summer of 1947. When Keeffe saw the draft, apparently he was less than enchanted with its treatment of the navy response to his committee's report. "It gives me great pause," he wrote to Larkin. "I think it is dull as dish water and picked clean of any conviction. If we [presumably Keeffe was referring here to the *Cornell Law Quarterly*] publish it, I think I will precede it with 10 hot pages as to what is really wrong with the navy bill. Want to join me?"[88] Larkin promptly replied from Washington where he had recently become a full-time member of Forrestal's staff.

He reminded Keeffe that the aim of the article, undertaken "at a great sacrifice of time and effort" was to take "an approach quite different from the critical approach we took when we examined the navy system and, hence, called for no propaganda." He was "considerably disturbed by your idea of writing a ten page blast. I think the time for that kind of thing is past, and I

---

there would be no desire to overrule him in the first place—was not resolved, even if considered, in the navy's wording.

[85] Ibid., 221. The navy draft further provided that the secretary was to issue regulations to insure that "members of every court martial shall be free to perform their sworn duties without any coercion or influence, directly or indirectly, on the part of any person in the naval service." Unlike his army counterpart, the secretary of the navy had long possessed "the power to set aside the proceedings and findings, or remit, or mitigate, or commute the sentence in whole or in part."

[86] S. 1338, 29–30.

[87] For reasons which remain unclear, Larkin and Pasley somehow concluded that these words pointed toward "review by a board of appeals appointed by the Secretary . . . to serve in his office," with "power to take any action which could have been taken by the Judge Advocate General upon initial review, or by the clemency board." The navy bill "did not preclude civilian membership on these boards." Pasley, Larkin, 229. But neither did it mandate any such policy. My reading of the draft as submitted to the Senate is that the secretary had wide latitude to establish whatever type of review system he thought appropriate. He *might* have been able to appoint along the lines set forth by Pasley and Larkin, but there appears to be no specific language compelling him to do so.

[88] LP, October 21, 1947.

have neither the inclination nor opportunity to join you on any such fiery project."[89] Somehow Larkin had assumed that the committee, including Keeffe, "[was] one on our criticisms of the navy system and that we all agreed that the Navy Bill incorporated 98 percent of our recommendations." What "has changed your mind about the Navy Bill . . . ? Maybe you have been eating too much red meat."[90]

The perturbed professor's response, if indeed he wrote one, has not been located; and the Pasley-Larkin piece was duly published in the *Cornell University Law Quarterly* without any prefatory comments from Keeffe.[91] Larkin sent a copy to his friend and former employer, Judge James Wallace. The article, he admitted, "isn't very spicy reading." Quoting Keeffe's unflattering description of it, Larkin added that "Keeffe's objection, of course, stems from the fact that we refrained from stirring up every controversial issue and we did not break a lance for all his pet theories." Nor was Larkin surprised that the ten-page diatribe "never materialized. I was confident that it wouldn't because that would mean that Keeffe would have to sit down and write something."[92]

With the submission of the navy bill, even as the Armed Services Committee had voted to report major reforms in military justice, Congress now had two separate plans to consider as 1947 drew to a close. But it had recently enacted legislation that "unified" the armed services, and established the office of the secretary of defense. Indeed, by the time Larkin sent out reprints of his articles, although he may not have realized it, the time for changes applicable to a single service had passed. To the greatest extent thus far in our military history, unification was now a fact, and a uniform approach to military justice seemed to make very good sense. In the spring of 1948, both the chairman of the Senate Armed Services Committee as well as James Forrestal were ready to move in this direction.

[89] Ibid., November 6, 1947. "Of course, I am somewhat amazed at your statement that you think the Navy Bill should be blasted."

[90] Ibid.

[91] Shortly thereafter, however, Keeffe did publish a piece in the same journal, and criticized the navy's response to his committee's proposals. See inf., chap. 8.

[92] LP, February 24, 1948. On the same day, Larkin also sent a copy of the piece to Robert Smart, a lawyer serving on the staff of the House Armed Services Committee. He noted that "we tried to avoid controversy and adopted a matter of fact, expositionary style."

CHAPTER 7

Forrestal Creates a Committee, 1948

AS AMENDED by its Committee on the Armed Services, on January 15, 1948, the House passed the bill to revise the Articles of War. However, its counterpart—a companion bill dealing with naval justice—lay pending, with no hearings scheduled. Although Congress had previously enacted legislation to unify the armed services, the proposed law applied only to the army. This fact may have led some members of Congress to consider it anachronistic even before being taken up by the Senate. More important, however, was extensive criticism from segments of the legal community that the changes did not go far enough in reforming military justice. At least one former JAG officer agreed. Thus, Charles Dickson wrote to Texas Sen. Tom Connally that the bill was "fatally defective," due to the "lack of effective appellate review"; and he drew this conclusion in spite of his concession that the law would "improve the administration of military justice."[1] Connolly may not have realized it, but Dickson—now permanently retired from the Army JAG Corps on medical disability—had become obsessed with what he saw as defects in military justice.

DICKSON'S DIATRIBES

A former member of an Army Board of Review, Dickson claimed, "My realization of the wholly inadequate powers of appellate review was the greatest tragedy I ever experienced."[2] He appears to have written approximately three thousand letters to a wide variety of politicians, judges, and JAG associations, calling for a new military appellate tribunal. Indeed, Dickson's perseverance is reminiscent of Ansell's efforts in an earlier era. On February 25, the secretary to Harry Vaughan, a retired army major general serving as President Truman's Military Aide, wrote to one such recipient, "while Mr. Dickson may have had an excellent idea to begin with, I am afraid he is defeating his own purpose by sending copies of this letter to about half the population of the country[,] and they are all finally reaching us."[3]

[1] LP, January 31, 1948, 1. Later, Connally would claim some credit for creation of the Court of Military Appeals.

[2] *Truman Papers*, Official File, box 984, file 303, February 28, 1948; hereafter cited as HST, followed by box and file number, if different.

[3] Ibid.

But Dickson did more than just write letters in support of his proposal. Early in March, he wrote to Army Secretary Kenneth Royall urging the creation of an "Armed Forces Supreme Court of Appeals. I prefer to talk with you informally as one lawyer to another, any time you can talk with me."[4] Royall replied the following day that "I find myself unable to give you an appointment for a personal conference at this time."[5] Undaunted, Dickson sought a meeting with Vaughan, and stated that "the record made by General Royall in the performance of his duties in the matter of military justice is highly unsatisfactory." Any fair-minded competent judge, he added, after examining court martial records, would conclude that "the supervision of [army military justice] should be immediately taken out of the hands of General Royall."[6]

Perhaps the most dramatic indication of Dickson's obsession with his cause was a proposed executive order he drafted for Truman's signature. As commander in chief, Truman would direct that this tribunal be established.[7] Its members had to have the same qualifications as judges of the United States Supreme Court, and would hold office "during good behavior." The court would establish and promulgate "all rules of procedure and regulations to govern the trial of any person by any court martial," and all such rules "shall be observed and obeyed by all persons subject to military law." Severe sentences were to be suspended until this court had reviewed them. If the judges found such punishments "not to be just or legal," they were to recommend alternatives to the president.[8]

When Dickson wrote to Connally, apparently he had not yet reached the extreme positions just described. He reminded Connally that boards of review were "mere adjuncts" of the JAG. Not only did that officer control the ratings and promotions of these members, but in most cases their findings of fact as well as of law were "merely advisory" to him. Dickson saw very little distinction between the review boards and the new "judicial council" called for in the statute. Indeed, he wrote, "I am inclined to believe that the creation of these judicial councils will further impair the effectiveness of appellate review."[9]

He urged that the Senate eliminate "all provisions relating to judicial councils . . . [,] and abolish all Boards of Review." In their place, Congress should "create an entirely new and separate tribunal in the nature of an Armed Forces

[4] Ibid., March 2, 1948.

[5] Ibid., March 3, 1948.

[6] Ibid., March 16, 1948. Earlier, on February 7, Dickson had sent a handwritten letter of eleven pages to Vaughan on the same subject.

[7] Ibid. In his draft, Dickson made no mention whatsoever of Congress, or legislative authority.

[8] Ibid. The copy of Dickson's draft order originally stated that "the Commander in Chief will cause any such recommendations to be put into effect." The word "will" has been crossed out, and the word "may" has been inserted. Of course, such a change would have vitiated exactly what Dickson had demanded—an independent appellate tribunal capable of enforcing its decisions.

[9] LP, Jan. 31, 1948, 3.

Supreme Court,'' that would have ''full and final appellate jurisdiction in cases involving sentence by general courts-martial.''[10] Further, this court should be able to adopt and promulgate rules of procedure governing such trials, and its decisions ''should be absolutely final . . . regardless of whether such decision is to approve, modify or reverse.'' The members of this new court ''should be nominated by the President and confirmed by the Senate,'' as was the case with other federal judges. Most important, these individuals were to be totally independent.[11]

Dickson admitted the absolute necessity for discipline but, as so many other critics of military justice had done, insisted that the authority to command combat troops ''is a wholly separate and distinct thing from a judicial procedure to determine the guilt or innocence of one . . . charged with violation of a military or civil law,'' and subject to ''the loss of his reputation, or his liberty or his life.'' Only judges who were free from every aspect of command influence could properly exercise such responsibilities. For, a ''judge who is subject to command from any source is not a judge.''[12]

Although the way he went about presenting his ideas may have worked against him, Dickson's comments had some merit.[13] Moreover, he was not alone in his concern. Less than a month after his letter, the Association of the Bar of the City of New York submitted a formal report, calling for major changes in the House bill. It accused the army of disclaiming on the one hand, ''any desire to subject the decisions of military courts to command influence,'' while insisting on the other ''in retaining in the command that combination of powers which deprives the courts of independence.'' The Bar Committee found this an unacceptable contradiction. ''If it be concededly wrong for command to exercise the power to influence . . . the court, what possible justification exists for the retention of that power in command?''[14] Echoing Dickson, the committee concluded that ''if the bill is amended to check command control, it can still become an effective instrument of reform. Failing amend-

[10] It is interesting to compare Dickson's letter with the draft of Truman's proposed executive order drafted for Vaughan, sometime in March 1948. He no longer found it necessary for Congress to be involved at all.

[11] Dickson argued, as the remainder of his letter makes clear, that as currently constituted Military Justice could not provide for such independence. He insisted that ''a judicial body empowered to administer justice to the individual citizen charged with crime should not be under the domination or command of any one, not even the President of the United States.'' He did not deem it necessary to add that the president was also the commander in chief of the Armed Forces. Ibid., 3–4.

[12] Ibid.

[13] As will be seen in the second volume of this study, Dickson would be heard from again concerning the new Court of Military Appeals.

[14] Association of the Bar of the City of New York, *Report on Pending Legislation for the Revision of the Army Court-Martial System*, February 27, 1948, 2. ''This question the proponents of the present and prospective system have never answered[,] and can never answer satisfactorily.''

ment, there will be the appearance, but not the substance, of reform; and the opportunity to create a fair and impartial system of military justice will have been frittered away.''[15]

The House bill, later known as the Elston Act (named for its sponsor, Charles Elston of Ohio), languished in the Senate from January to June 1948. The chairman of the Senate Armed Services Committee, J. Chandler ''Chan'' Gurney had been deeply involved in the congressional drive toward unification. With that goal accomplished, he preferred to wait on the House measure, seeking a broader military justice revision that would be applicable to all the services—not just the army. Moreover, it seemed clear that the chair, if not the full Senate Armed Services Committee, was not nearly as enthusiastic about a separate JAG Corps, as had been the House. Thus, Gurney had at least a two-part justification for not moving forward quickly. Whatever his reasons, this lengthy delay for Senate consideration of Elston's bill irritated not only numerous members of Congress who had labored over its provisions, but also segments of the legal community who saw it as an important move toward court-martial reform, albeit only a first step.

Gurney's dual dissatisfaction with the House enactment may have convinced him to propose a shift in the stage for court-martial reform to, as it were, another theater. On May 3, 1948, he wrote to James Forrestal concerning both the Elston Bill and the naval counterpart. Because these pending proposals ''do not provide a uniform system of military justice applicable alike to all three services, I think it would be well to have an over-all study made, and defense establishment proposals ready for the convening of the 81st Congress.'' Gurney assured Forrestal that ''this letter is a personal one from me and gives only my thoughts in the matter. It does not in any way reflect any action that has been taken by the Senate Armed Services Committee.''[16]

Three days later Forrestal replied to Gurney's letter, and indicated that internal discussions within his office had already been held ''concerning the feasibility of such an approach.'' After congressional adjournment, the three services ''could profitably look into the matter.'' He added that ''I offer the foregoing as my personal and interim comment.''[17] The question arises why both men were so careful to hedge their comments.

In actuality, Gurney was suggesting to Forrestal a radical departure from previous practice. His innocuous words concealed a proposal that Forrestal's office (the ''defense establishment'') prepare some sort of legislative draft that *it* would present to Congress on behalf of *all* the armed services. The army and navy had traditionally been treated separately by Congress. As the Ansell-

[15] Ibid. See also the letter by Richard Wels, a member of the committee in the *New York Times*, June 30, 1948, 24.

[16] LP, May 3, 1948.

[17] Ibid., May 6, 1948.

Crowder episode well demonstrated, the army had not hesitated to involve itself in the legislative process. Similarly, the army and navy had each taken the lead in preparing their drafts of the legislation under consideration in 1947–1948. Gurney's idea that a civilian official undertake to speak for the armed services also reflected his awareness that unification was now a political reality. Here, past practice merged with his political preferences. He possibly believed that his suggestion to Forrestal would undercut the need for Senate consideration of the pending House measure.

Forrestal's next step, on May 11, was to meet with the secretaries of the several services. They agreed to establish an ad hoc committee, consisting of a representative from Forrestal's office as chairman, and one civilian undersecretary from each service—Gordon Gray, W. John Kenney, and Eugene M. Zuckert—representing respectively the army, navy, and the recently created air force. The task of this committee would be "preparing a uniform code of military justice which would be applicable alike to all three Services, and which could be submitted to the 81st Congress as the recommendation of the National Military establishment."[18] At this date, the chairman had not yet been selected, nor had the drafting of the "final terms of reference" (the instructions for the committee) been completed.[19]

The appointment of this committee was followed promptly by the creation of another panel, known as "the Working Group." It consisted of one military representative selected by each member of the main panel, plus a number of lawyers and civilian researchers within Forrestal's office. Felix Larkin, now a full-time member of Forrestal's staff, was named chairman of this group as well as executive secretary of the first committee. It would be the responsibility of this panel to cull through all the reports and investigations that had been prepared; compare and contrast the present army and navy rules and procedures; and finally to produce a working draft of each article in a proposed new uniform code of military justice, applicable to all the services. Each article would be submitted to the ad hoc committee, as yet without a chair, for modification, rejection, or ultimate final approval.

[18] Memorandum from John H. Ohly, Special Assistant to Forrestal, May 24, 1948; LP. For reasons unique to the military, Gray and Zuckert were assistant secretaries of their services, but Kenney was the under secretary of the navy.

[19] Forrestal wrote to his friend and fellow Princeton classmate, Representative Walter G. Andrews, that "such a uniform code, if enacted, will of course have the effect of superseding existing legislation in this field, as well as any legislation which may be enacted at the present session of Congress." Because Andrews at this time was chairman of the House Committee on Armed Services, Forrestal's implied warning about the House Bill then pending in the Senate is of interest. Unfortunately, Andrews—known as one who "runs offense for Forrestal's defense" —did not live to see the final enactment of the Uniform Code. Forrestal to Andrews, May 21, 1948, LP; Speech by Arthur Krock at Princeton Alumni Day, February 21, 1948, in *Forrestal Papers*, box 80.

SENATORS AND SELECTIVE SERVICE

By May 22, it was clear to members of the House Armed Services Committee that Senator Gurney was not about to move on the Elston Bill. Forrestal received a phone call from its chair, Congressman Walter Andrews, who informed him that "they are upset that Gurney never did anything on the bill, and they realize now he's never going to do anything on the bill." Elston accepted this fact, and therefore, according to Andrews, "he will cooperate and welcome anything that's done over in your department[,] trying to bring them together."[20] Having already received Gurney's encouragement, Forrestal was thus assured that—although for very disparate reasons—both Houses of Congress would be inclined to support the idea of a complete code being submitted to them by the "defense establishment" for consideration.

For his part, however, Gurney appears to have underestimated his colleagues' desire to reform military justice. When, early in June 1948, the Selective Service Act came up for Senate action James Kem, a first-term senator from Missouri, moved to attach Elston's bill as a rider to the measure establishing the first postwar draft in American history. Indeed, according to a member of Larkin's staff who had also worked on the Keeffe Committee Report, some members of the Senate refused to provide crucial votes for the Selective Service bill unless it was accompanied by immediate reform of the court martial system.[21]

Gurney was uncomfortable with Kem's motion. To adopt the Elston Bill, applicable only to the army, "would amount to piece-meal legislation, and would not accomplish the true purpose envisioned by the Congress when it passed the unification legislation." Furthermore, the question of "fundamental control of the Military Establishment is of such consequence that it cannot

[20] Excerpts of telephone conversation between W. G. Andrews and J. Forrestal, May 22, 1948, in LP. Andrews also strongly suggested to Forrestal that he utilize the talents of his staff member Robert Smart, a lawyer who "really did the work on this Court Martial bill." Andrews was concerned that staff members, to say nothing of his colleagues, not feel bitter that their many hours of work on the Elston bill had been wasted, simply because Forrestal's office now was going to prepare a uniform code. Robert Smart did ultimately serve as liaison between the House Committee and the committee to draft the code. Andrew's phone call is even more important in that it established from the very beginning the preference that the code project would be linked to the Congressional Armed Services Committees—as indeed turned out to be the case. This meant that when it came to implementing some provisions of the new code, such as appointment of judges to the Court of Military Appeals, approval of their nomination would come from the Armed Services Committee, *not* the panel on the Judiciary. As will be seen in the second volume of this study, this fact has had great significance for the court's subsequent history.

[21] LP, January 18, 1971. Responding to a request from William Generous, Jr., at that time preparing his dissertation at Stanford University, Robert Pasley further characterized Kem's action as "a surprise move."

be lightly considered by the Congress.'' It certainly should not ''be hastily tacked onto a bill of such importance'' as the draft. Gurney told his colleagues about Forrestal's new committee, and read into the Record the various communications between himself and the secretary dealing with it. The Senate should wait for ''careful and complete consideration of the entire problem,'' rather than rush to ''enact a piece of legislation which will be repealed by other legislation—soon, I hope.''[22]

Kem was not impressed. Why, he wondered, had Gurney's committee been unable to hold even one hearing on the House measure, a proposal, he added, that had been unanimously approved by that chamber? Kem further noted the lengthy hearings that had been held by Elston's committee, and the wide public support the resulting legislation had received.[23] Gurney responded that the House bill was in fact a composite proposal that ''might be better and it might be worse. [His] committee has a right to change the language of a House passed bill.'' Gurney's colleague on the Armed Services Committee, Massachusetts Senator Leverett Saltonstall added that it should not be ''attached blindfold'' to the Selective Service bill.[24]

Kem insisted that if Congress had time to reinstate the draft, it had time to revise the Articles of War. By a margin of only five votes (44–39) the Senate agreed.[25] According to the *New York Times*, its action was ''by a generally unexpected vote.''[26] With minimal discussion, the House accepted the amendment. No further hearings were held, and when President Truman signed the Selective Service Act of 1948, the provisions dealing with courts-martial became law—to go into effect nine months later. As far as Forrestal was concerned, this fact made it all the more important that a uniform code be drafted within this period of time.

Even as Truman approved the bill that enacted the Elston Act into law, Arthur John Keeffe returned to the subject of military justice. It will be recalled that the Cornell law professor originally had proposed submitting some ''hot pages'' detailing what was wrong with the bill to reform naval judicial procedure. In the June 1948 issue of the *Cornell Law Quarterly* he published an article on ''Universal Military Justice with or without Reform of Courts-Martial.'' Essentially a rehash of the original report prepared by his committee, the final note in the piece mentioned the very recent Congressional Ac-

[22] 94 *Cong. Record*, part 6, 80th Cong., 2d sess., Senate, June 9, 1948, 7520.

[23] Ibid., 7521–22.

[24] Ibid., 7522. Sen. Wayne Morse strongly supported Kem's move. He noted that for two successive Congresses, he had been unable to gain even a hearing from Gurney's Committee on his own resolution calling for an investigation of the court-martial system. ''The fact is that we have been delinquent . . . in not taking action on court-martial legislation long before this.'' Ibid., 7523.

[25] Generous, *Swords and Scales*, 29.

[26] *New York Times*, June 10, 1948, 2.

tion. If further changes could be made in the law between June 1948 and February 1949, when the new law became effective, Keeffe had no objection. However, "what is everybody's business is nobody's business. The time for sporadic voluntary effort is past[,] and the Army and the Navy do not want any more committees. Neither does the country."[27]

With the ad hoc committee selected, and the working group ready to construct an outline for a systematic revision of army and navy rules into a single code—the need to select a chair for Forrestal's committee had to be addressed. Between the middle of June and July 17, 1948, Forrestal's General Counsel, Marx Leva, considered several possibilities.[28] There were a number of distinguished lawyers/scholars who had been very active in the drive to reform military justice since 1943. Several had authored one or more of the numerous reports now available. Ballantine and Vanderbilt, to say nothing of Arthur Keeffe, were among this group.[29] And, as will be seen shortly, Keeffe certainly was considered, at least in his own opinion, as an appropriate candidate.

Yet Larkin believed, and so ultimately did Leva, that the chair should "be one who had not previously engaged in a study of any one service." Since each service viewpoint would "be represented through the individual [under or assistant] secretary," it was all the more important that the chair be unconnected with the recent spate of investigations and reports. "On this basis," as Larkin tactfully wrote Keeffe, "which I am sure you will agree is logical, such stalwarts as Vanderbilt . . . and yourself were disqualified."[30] In addition, Owen J. Roberts—a former Justice of the Supreme Court and recently named Dean of Pennsylvania Law School—was at least mentioned, if not seriously considered as a candidate.[31]

There seems to be no doubt that Leva first proposed Edmund Morgan as a possible chair for the committee.[32] He had been a student of Morgan's at Har-

[27] Arthur John Keeffe, "Universal Military Training with or without Reform of Courts-Martial?" *Cornell Law Quarterly* 33 (1948): 465–87. One obvious reason for Keeffe's insistence that yet another committee was unnecessary lay in his belief that—largely because of the insights contained in the 1947 report—all Congress needed to do was merely to follow its recommendations!

[28] Graduating from Harvard Law School in 1940, Leva clerked for Supreme Court Justice Hugo Black. He served in the navy during World War II, and later filled several legal positions including counsel to Secretary of the Navy Forrestal. When Forrestal was appointed to the new position of secretary of defense, Leva went along as the first General Counsel, and also as one of the first assistant secretaries of defense.

[29] It might also be noted that Samuel Ansell was still living in Washington, where he continued to practice law.

[30] LP, July 29, 1948.

[31] On August 11, 1948, Forrestal asked Leva to draft a letter of congratulations to Roberts on his new appointment as law school Dean. Leva wrote on his chief's behalf that "I imagine it was the possibility of your acceptance of the Deanship which precluded your heading up our study in the field of military Justice." *Forrestal Papers*, August 11, 1948.

[32] In addition to having Morgan as his professor, Leva recalled that he also knew Morgan

vard Law School in 1939, although that professor did not determine Leva's final grade because Morgan withdrew from the evidence course in mid-1939 to fill in for his close friend Felix Frankfurter whom President Roosevelt had just appointed to the Supreme Court. Another of Forrestal's assistants, John Ohly, also had been a Morgan student, as had John Kenney—who was to represent the navy on the code committee.

Fully aware of Morgan's interest in military justice during World War I and his strong support for Ansell in 1918–1919, Leva believed that far from being a handicap, these factors were positive justification for Morgan's candidacy. Moreover, it is very clear that Forrestal and other defense officials were well informed of Morgan's past activities involving military justice. Thus, Leva told Larkin on July 13 that "he had talked to [army secretary] Royall about Morgan for Chairman of the [new committee], and Royall thought he would be good."[33] Because Forrestal agreed with Leva that an outside figure, a sort of—as Leva put it—"stormy petrel" would be most suitable as a strong chair of the committee, by the middle of July he was ready to talk with Morgan.[34]

Morgan, at that time seventy years old and soon to be retired (not by choice) from Harvard Law School, had been at that institution for almost a quarter of a century, including two stints as acting Dean. During World War II he served as chairman for one of the war shipping panels with the War Labor Board. This diminutive academician (standing barely five feet tall) seemed to resemble something of a pixie rather than an intimidating professor. Yet he was known for the demands he made upon his students, and opinion concerning his skills as a teacher of law—aside from his undoubted distinction as a legal scholar—was far from unanimous.[35] It can be said that in terms of age, to say nothing

socially at Harvard Law School ["it was much smaller in those days"], and that he was well aware of Morgan's support for Ansell during the 1918–1919 controversy. Interview with Marx Leva, December 21, 1987, Washington.

[33] Larkin Phone Logs, July 13, 1948; hereafter cited as LPPL. On August 3, a representative of the navy inquired "about Morgan's testimony before the Subcommittee of the Senate [in 1919], and his article in the *Yale Law Journal* . . . on military justice" in the same year. Ibid., August 3, 1948.

[34] LP, November 16, 1970. There is no indication that Forrestal or Leva somehow sought to insure that Ansell's ideas would be incorporated into the new code through Morgan's appointment. On the contrary, he would be only one of a four-member committee, with three of the four well able to speak on behalf of a particular service. Gray and Zuckert were graduates of Yale Law School, while Kenney (as well as Army Secretary Royall) graduated from Harvard Law School. Like most strong committees, give-and-take and ultimate compromise, rather than domination by the chair, characterized the workings of this Committee on Military Justice.

[35] Among Morgan's papers was a five-page handwritten letter from one of his students in civil procedure during 1936. At the outset, the writer—identified only as "J.R.D."—informed Morgan that "you are the world's worst expounder of the law." If he was teaching torts, "we would not mind so much since there are abundant sources of clear exposition, we could ignore everything you said." If "you are really trying to make things reasonably clear (this may be an erroneous

4. The Morgan Committee, 1948. *Left to right:* Felix Larkin, Gordon Gray, Edmund Morgan, John Kenney, Eugene Zuckert. Courtesy the U.S. Court of Military Appeals.

of a legal career at Yale and Harvard that spanned more than thirty years, Morgan certainly stood out.

Such was the man to whom Forrestal wrote on July 17, 1948. "I sincerely hope that your personal affairs will permit you to accept the Chairmanship which I now offer to you on behalf of myself as Secretary of Defense, and on behalf of the Secretaries of the Army, Navy and Air Force."[36] Even before seeking approval from his Dean, Morgan informed Forrestal about his support for Ansell and his opposition to Crowder during 1918–1919. Pending Forrestal's response, Morgan contacted Erwin Griswold, then on the threshold of what would turn out to be a very distinguished tenure as Dean of Harvard Law School. Although Griswold was troubled about the proclivity for some of his faculty to spend a lot of time in Washington, he also realized that Morgan soon would have to retire from Harvard. Moreover, "you are old enough to know what you want to do, and I feel very clear that the School should be happy to have you take the leading position in this task." It "is an important one, and you are surely well qualified to deal with it. I think it is an honor for you, and an honor for the School."[37]

Meanwhile, Forrestal reassured Morgan that "I was already familiar with your service during World War I, but it was very thoughtful of you to mention it in your letter. The part which you played in connection with the necessity for reforms in the military justice system at that time should be an asset rather

---

assumption), the only fair thing for you to do would be [to] go back to practice." Morgan should realize that he is "a terrible instructor." Perhaps, added the student, "you do not care whether your students respect you or not—but whether you do or not it is clear that they don't." We all "like you as a man, but a lot of us still think you are the world's worst expounder of the law." *Morgan Papers*, Vanderbilt University, hereafter cited as MPVU. Morgan carefully preserved this letter in his personal file, along with others of a more recent date. In June 1950, for example, he wrote to a student in one of his last courses that "I was considerably disappointed in the quality of the papers. . . . I lectured altogether too much this year, partly because with so large a class and with so many men failing to prepare adequately, it involved too great a waste of time to discover and call upon men who had given the problems involved any previous consideration." Ibid., June 28, 1950. Conversations with several of Morgan's former students, as well as interviews with both his children indicate that he was indeed regarded as a very "tough" instructor. Edmund S. Morgan informed me that after his father had flunked several students in his evidence class, they arranged to retake the course in the summer at the University of Denver Law School. Unknown to them, however, Morgan had agreed to teach that evidence course at Denver—and the reaction of the students upon walking into the classroom and learning the identity of their "new" instructor can only be imagined. *Interview*, Edmund S. Morgan, February 9, 1988. When Morgan retired from Harvard in 1950, a comment in the *Harvard Law School Bulletin* was both accurate and apt. "His kindness and deference mitigate in part the medieval horrors to which he subjects his students." It was cited again in the same journal as part of a tribute to Morgan after his death, sixteen years later. *Harvard Law School Bulletin*, March 1966, 3.

[36] MPVU, July 17, 1948. Forrestal added that a "unified code of military justice would be a major step both in unifying the armed services[,] and also in the work of modernizing the military justice structure[,] many of whose roots may be said to be too deeply involved in the past."

[37] Ibid., July 22, 1948.

than a liability.''[38] But Morgan was still concerned about the possible effects that his earlier criticisms might have on his relationship with the other members of the committee. Thus, on July 24, he notified Forrestal that he would accept the position ''provided that inspection of my service record in 1917–1919 has not raised doubts in your mind as to my fitness for the position.''[39] Morgan immediately followed this letter with another to Leva, his former student.

He had accepted, Morgan wrote, ''with the proviso that he [Forrestal] has not had doubts about my fitness after inspection of my 1917–1919 record. I should hardly be satisfied to have him and you rest the decision on my previous writings. I think you really ought to know what the record shows—which is more than I know. But I do know that it contains some unfavorable entries by or under direction of General Crowder.''[40] Forrestal, according to Larkin, ''was delighted'' with Morgan's acceptance.[41] Duly appointed on July 29, 1948, as an ''expert advisor on the military justice study being undertaken by OSD'' [office of the secretary of defense], Morgan was to be paid $50 per diem.[42]

MORGAN AND LARKIN

Before Morgan had accepted the appointment as chair, and the instructions (the Precept, or Terms of Reference) had been drafted, Larkin proposed a new approach to committee deliberation and decision-making that turned out to be of great importance. Because of his work on the Keeffe Report, he had necessarily become familiar with the voluminous prior reports, hearings, and investigations concerning military justice. He also knew of their usual fate, one not unique to most studies of the government by committees. After they had been completed, they had to be returned to the originating department for review and reaction. Frequently, the reports never appeared again. They were,

[38] Ibid., July 24, 1948.

[39] Ibid. Morgan's handwritten note is undated, but was probably written on July 24, 1948, the same day he wrote to Leva.

[40] Ibid.

[41] ''I told Morgan . . . we would issue a press release announcing his Chairmanship of the Committee and asked if there was any pertinent information he would like included. He said everything of interest could be found in *Who's Who*.'' LPPL, July 27, 1948.

[42] Personal Service Contract, MPVU. On September 20, a Pentagon secretary ''asked Mr. Larkin if he would mind asking Morgan to sit down for a few minutes and talk with her about the proper way in which to make out pertinent forms, etc., in connection with his travel.'' LPPL, September 20, 1948. Forty years later, this writer while undertaking to gain reimbursement for some of the travel expenses related to this study ran afoul of a current incarnation of a Pentagon secretary, and immediately developed a lasting sense of sympathy if not déjà vu with the spirit of Edmund Morgan!

in reality, almost always exercises in futility. The last thing Larkin wanted was to spend a lot of time on a comparative study, and have the judge advocates from the three services "review it, and have it interminably debated and nothing ever happen."[43]

He pointed out to Forrestal that the services were well represented on both the Working Group panel as well as the committee of the three undersecretaries—each of whom could draw on whatever legal or military expertise he felt appropriate from within his own service. Once this committee had agreed among itself, Larkin urged that the resulting decision not be reviewed again by any of the services, nor even by the office of the secretary of defense—but that it be *final*. In those instances where the committee could not reach consensus, he suggested that Forrestal himself have the last word. The secretary accepted Larkin's proposals with the result that in more than three-fourths of the articles, approval by the committee would be the last step prior to the process of submission to Congress. In those few areas where the committee could not agree, Forrestal's decision would also be final. Unlike the Ansell-Chamberlain proposals in 1919, the military in 1948 could discuss and even debate—but they could not derail.

Larkin submitted a draft of the Precept and Terms of Reference for the Committee on a Uniform Code of Military Justice (hereafter called the CUCMJ) to Forrestal on August 12, 1948. As he saw it, three objectives could be met by drafting a uniform code in time for submission to the 81st Congress: (*a*) the integration of the three military justice systems into one, "on as uniform a basis as possible"; (*b*) modernization of substantive and procedural aspects of military justice should be undertaken with a view [both] to protect "the rights of those subject to the code," and to increase "public confidence in the military justice system"; and (*c*) the language and draftsmanship of both the army and navy military justice procedures should be improved, and matters of jurisdiction or substance should be organized "in a logical and orderly manner." The CUCMJ should "take advantage of the studies, reports, articles, recommendations and proposed legislation which exists in the field of military justice."[44] It should be able to "consult with such persons in the armed forces as it may wish[,] and to call as witnesses such individuals and organizations from outside the National Military Establishment as the committee desires."[45]

With one important exception, Forrestal accepted most of Larkin's draft. He deleted the section empowering the committee to call witnesses. Instead,

[43] Larkin, Interview, December 17, 1987.

[44] Draft, Precept and Terms of Reference for CUCMJ; LP, August 12, 1948, 1. Larkin also noted that the new code "should not impede any service from carrying out its military functions." Since 1951, as the second volume of this study will discuss, there has been ongoing debate within the military as to the extent to which the code has or has not impeded the armed forces in their operations.

[45] Ibid., 2.

"the committee shall . . . invite the views of such individuals and organizations from outside the National Military Establishment as it may desire."[46] Forrestal, possibly on advice from Marx Leva, may have concluded that given the very limited time in which to draft the code, as well as the vast amount of prepared material already available, it would not be necessary for the committee to take testimony, as much as to insure that interested parties could submit their views in writing. This, it did.[47]

With the first meeting of Morgan's committee scheduled for August 18, Larkin submitted a progress report to Forrestal. He informed the secretary that the Working Group had already been meeting since June. Representatives from the Armed Services Committees of both House and Senate would participate. Again, he saw three major aspects to drafting a uniform code between August 1948 and January 1949: (*a*) to recodify "in a logical, sensible form, new articles applicable to the three [services]." At present, he added, "the Articles of War and the corresponding Articles for the Government of the Navy are so mixed up [that] it is difficult to find anything in them." Indeed, a recodification "without change would be a major contribution in itself"; (*b*) the differences between the three services had to be addressed; and (*c*) there was also the need to consider the wishes of Congress as indicated in the Elston Act, to say nothing of "other criticisms which have been made over the years." In conclusion, Larkin reminded Forrestal that Morgan's committee "will require a maximum amount of delegation of authority from you and the three departmental secretaries, because I am certain that time will not permit a restudy by the Departments of the uniform code."[48]

Morgan presided over the first meeting of his committee on August 18, 1948. It agreed that the proposals prepared by the Working Group "are to serve as a basis for the Committee's deliberations."[49] Moreover, "the members of the Committee will reflect to the extent they desire the viewpoint of their respective departments [services] and have authority to bind them." Zuckert of the air force noted that "it might be helpful to have the views of key represen-

[46] Ibid., August 18, 1948.

[47] On August 11, 1948, the Working Group agreed that "since most of the research is already done, such [public] hearings are unnecessary. Even before Forrestal's Precept had been distributed, Morgan had indicated his desire that invitations for written views should be sent to interested groups and individuals," including Vanderbilt, Ballantine, Keeffe and McGuire. Memorandum on Working Group Meeting of August 11, 1948; LP.

[48] Memorandum for the Secretary, August 17, 1948, LP.

[49] At a later meeting, Larkin was a little more candid concerning how the Morgan Committee planned to use the Working Group. "It is their overall desire that we solve everything and come up with recommendations[,] and see if they meet [with] their approval. . . . They fully insist that we sit by the hour and do this kind of work." *Transcript*, Working Group Meeting, September 21, 1948, 6–7. Perhaps, Col. John Dinsmore had this point in mind when he later noted that "I wouldn't want to limit the freedom of discussion, but I do think perhaps we could curtail the number of words we use." Ibid., 20.

tatives of the services on certain controversial issues. It was [decided] that they would be invited to appear personally before the Committee in that event.''[50] As to the code to be drafted, it should ''be uniform in substance[,] . . . in interpretation and application.''[51]

In response to the press announcement concerning formation of Morgan's committee and his request to various interested parties for comments and suggestions about military justice reforms, numerous letters were received at Larkin's office during the fall of 1948.[52] They, together with the copies of documents and reports previously given him by Larkin, represented a valuable introduction to the Harvard professor's new role. All this material makes it clear that when the panel came to draft the actual provisions of the new code, Morgan's committee ratified more often than it innovated.

One writer, for example, urged that ''only men who have passed a state bar exam and are qualified to practice before a federal court be permitted to sit as a judge in a military trial.'' These judges were to be responsible to no one but their branch of service headquarters in Washington, and were to move from ''post to post as does a circuit judge.'' Moreover, they were to wear robes, and procedures were to be established that would give ''the military trial the dignity and justice found in our State and Federal courts.'' The writer had been both an enlisted infantryman and an infantry officer, and further informed President Truman that he had been disciplined six times.[53]

John Finn who had been involved with the earlier McGuire Committee on Navy Justice suggested to Morgan that there should be one review board, ''responsible only to the Secretary of Defense and consisting solely of civilian lawyers, which would review the law, facts and sentences and have power and authority to reverse, remand, or set aside'' certain military justice verdicts. Also, Finn urged that ''Board [members] should be appointed for sufficiently long periods of time, and be paid salaries substantial enough to afford them that independence of the military, in the performance of their functions. . . . One who reviews cases should be as impartial as humanly possible. It is unusual and difficult to be impartial, completely, if one is aspiring to higher office or rank[,] and his promotion is dependent upon his personal standing with his superiors.''[54]

A committee from the New York County Lawyers' Association reminded Morgan that for all its supposed reforms, the Elston Act—to go into effect in

[50] Although one cannot be certain because of the paucity of records from the committee, it seems that few, if any, such representatives actually came before it.

[51] CUCMJ, Minutes of Meeting, August 18, 1948; LP.

[52] These documents were carefully copied and bound for distribution to both the Working Group and the committee.

[53] Indeed, Ernest Wolfe, Jr., ended his letter with a P.S. ''To the clerk who bothers to read this letter. Please see that the President gets at least an inkling of the material in this letter. It was plenty tough to see my buddies 'railroaded' on courts-martial.'' *Comments on a Uniform Code of Military Justice*, December 7, 1948; LP.

[54] Ibid., September 1, 1948.

February 1949—still vested review power strictly within the military. Prosecutors and defense counsel were to be members of the JAG Corps or otherwise qualified lawyers only "if available—a qualiication which realistically leaves the situation in status quo." So far as the basic "fundamental matters at which the movement for court martial reform has been aimed, little is accomplished by the Elston Act." The "torturous" system of review it set up "is completely at odds with American concepts of justice."[55]

The collection of comments contained one letter from William Hastie, at that time governor of the Virgin Islands, and soon to be named by President Truman to the United States Court of Appeals. Hastie urged that military trial judges "should be persons of the temperament and professional training considered essential for judges of civil courts. Moreover, through tenure and freedom from responsibility to field commanders, military judges should be relieved of pressures which now affect their work."[56]

A different view came from a 1932 graduate of Harvard Law School. Allen Miller wrote to Morgan that "we have noted the resolutions of the Vanderbilt Committee, and the suggestions of other lawyers' committees composed of lawyers, many of whom never spent a day in the Army, much less a day involved in military matters, and we are quite concerned lest overemphasis of the individual's rights as an approach to military justice undermine the paramount purpose, that is, administrative control in a war organization as the chief mission of a disciplinary code."[57]

The disparity of viewpoints illustrated by these excerpts represented only one of several challenges confronting the CUCMJ. In addition to the difficulty of constructing a code that could insure due process for the military and at the same time not impede the armed services in their functions, both Morgan's panel and especially the Working Group had to consider the political preferences already demonstrated by the Congress as well as differences between the services—primarily the army and navy—in their military justice procedures.[58] A third problem lay in the larger context within which the new code would be drafted.

At an early stage in its work, Larkin told the working group that since 1947, there had been a dramatic increase in habeas corpus petitions filed on behalf of federal prisoners—many of whom had been convicted by courts-martial. Both the implication and impact of this trend were clear. Larkin emphasized

[55] Ibid., undated, but probably between September and November 1948.

[56] Ibid., November 16, 1948.

[57] Ibid., August 13, 1948.

[58] Thus, Morgan wrote to R. Dressler, "I am afraid that your proposal for a series of district courts-martial and a Supreme Court-Martial will prove too radical for complete adoption." The committee's final recommendations "will, I hope, eliminate improper command influence in the operations of courts-martial and provide for an ultimate impartial review in such a way as to make the application of the reformed Articles of War uniform in all three services." MPVU, September 21, 1948.

the desirability of "keeping [these cases] out of the federal courts." This could only happen if military justice in fact represented "a system which would[,] perhaps[,] bend over a little backwards to fulfil" basic requirements of due process. If the military establishment was unable to draft such a procedure that worked, one would ultimately be created for it.[59]

Larkin had never served in the armed forces, and spoke from the position of a young lawyer who had found much to criticize in military justice. It is interesting therefore, that a representative of the army at the meeting of the Working Group, Col. John Weber, agreed with him. With the advent of the draft, Weber explained, "military service is no longer contractual; it is quite to the contrary. It has become an additional duty of citizenship." The connection of the soldier with the government "is sort of like the relationship between the court and juror—that the court must protect that individual." What Weber saw as significant in the spate of cases cited by Larkin was "that [military] justice must be administered in a fundamentally fair way. It shifts from the whole contractual basis to what we regard [as] the soldier having a fiduciary relationship, and it is our duty to look after them."[60]

Although the committee achieved a surprising extent of unanimity on most of the provisions of the uniform code (there were ultimately over 140 of them), consensus broke down concerning three issues. Linked to the problem of both appearance and reality of fairness in military justice procedure, they also well reflected the challenges just described. The three areas of difficulty concerned the question of (*a*) enlisted men serving on court-martials, (*b*) the role of the law member as a judge, and (*c*) the nature of the review/appellate process.

It will be recalled that the Elston Act had provided enlisted soldiers with the right to have a limited number of their peers as members of a court-martial tribunal. Larkin accurately characterized the army viewpoint as "we don't like it, perhaps, too much, but actually we don't object." He further suggested that the committee take the same position vis-à-vis the other services. "I don't think it would cause any great harm and I am frank to say I am quite sure it won't do a heck of a lot of good."[61] John Curry, representing the navy, ob-

[59] *Transcript*, Working Group, September 21, 1948, 28. It can be argued that the decision to establish dual committees, both dominated by civilians, to construct a uniform code, was recognition that the military had been unable to impose on itself the type of military justice reforms sought by the external legal order.

[60] Ibid., 28–29. In this context, one of the early decisions reached by the CUCMJ was that in general courts-martial, "the law member, the prosecutor, and the defense counsel should be lawyers." Moreover, "the Committee agreed with Professor Morgan that no qualifying language such as 'if available' should be inserted into the uniform code with respect to trial judge advocates [prosecutors] and defense counsel." CUCMJ, Minutes of Meetings, September 30, October 1, 1948, 2; LP.

[61] *Transcript*, Working Group, August 19, 1948, 4–5. Unfortunately, although this panel had a few of their early meetings transcribed, for reasons that remain unclear they abandoned this practice. All quotations from the meetings that were recorded are taken from the volume in the library of the Court of Military Appeals.

jected expanding this policy to his service. The congressional decision to adopt it for the army underlined the fact, in his opinion, that "we should not yield to expediency here. . . . We are not a political branch of the government. . . . Congress is, and if they properly feel they must do it as a matter of expediency, I do not feel it is up to us to anticipate that and to do something."[62] Larkin reminded Curry that Congress had already spoken on this subject, and "they are going to expect[,] and we are going to try to come up with something uniform."[63]

A second example where consensus failed was the question concerning the law member of the court-martial, and whether or not he should function strictly as a judge, or retire to deliberate with the other members of the court, and actually vote on the case. The army and the newly independent air force supported the latter option, in part because they apparently lacked the personnel to support a panel of judges who did nothing else but preside at trials. Moreover, according to Col. Stewart Maxey of the air force, if the law member had to give instructions in open court, they would have to be drafted to withstand legal challenges. This would lead to numerous errors for other courts to review. If, on the other hand, he retired with the other members, he could explain the law in simple layman's terms that could be clearly understood—thus increasing the chances for a legally acceptable verdict.[64] This time, Larkin found himself supporting the navy.

What Maxey was actually saying, Larkin argued, was that there were many errors in informal layman's language that the law member uses, "and if they were to be spread on the record [in open court], they would have to be disclosed . . . and as I see it, we don't want to catch those errors because it slows up the system." Maxey responded that errors are not committed by the law member. Numerous questions are asked, "which he answers, and we don't have the errors in law. Actually, there are few errors." Larkin replied, "Of course we don't know, do we?" In fact, "what he [the law member] tells them in layman's language is not preserved. We know nothing of what he tells them."[65] In turn, Maxey pointed to the outcome of the trials as evidence that the great majority of verdicts were properly determined.

[62] Ibid., 8.

[63] Robert Smart candidly conceded that the House Armed Services Committee did not believe that "it will do a bit of good to have them there, but I think that the better compromise is to have them on at the option of the enlisted man because we feel in due time it is going to wear itself out, and will not become attractive to enlisted men, and they will cease to use it." Ibid., 19. At a meeting on September 16, 1948, Larkin found it necessary to remind his Working Group that it would "have to think in terms of not only the position of their own Service[,] but in terms of unification." Modification of previously held views would be inevitable, but the committee "has to come up with a uniform provision." After all, "we think in terms for the Navy, for the Army and for the Air Force." Ibid., September 16, 1948, 28.

[64] Ibid., September 10, 1948, 14.

[65] Ibid., 15. Maxey's reasoning "persuades me that there is considerable necessity to catch

Larkin: But you don't know what he told them, what is the law[,] on the basis of which they found the facts and applied them.

Maxey: I won't concede that there is any error being committed now.

Larkin: I don't charge that there is because I don't know. I don't think anybody else knows because they never see what he does say.[66]

The army representative emphasized that "the glory of the court-martial system has been its freedom from technicalities. . . . we are apprehensive that this proposal . . . will give rise not to justice, but to innumerable injustices from the government's point of view by affording loopholes and technicalities on which men clearly guilty will escape."[67] Larkin ended the discussion by noting that this issue would have to be solved by Morgan's committee. He could not see any compromise between the two positions. "I'd be delighted to recommend one but I can't see one. There isn't any. I dislike sending up something that is split, but I . . . think it is inevitable that we'll have to do this at times."[68]

When Morgan's committee considered the question of the law member, it reflected the same split apparent in the Working Group. Larkin and Kenney supported the idea of the law member acting as a judge. "Any errors he may make in charging the jury will be reviewable if placed on the record[,] and since instructions on the law to the jury are a source of a great number of reversible errors[, they] should be subject to review."[69] Moreover, "if the judge does not vote with the jury, his position as a judicial officer is more clearly established."[70] Morgan agreed, but Gray and Zuckert remained uncon-

those errors on the grounds that the less error there is or the more error you catch, the end product is greater substantial justice." Ibid., 16.

[66] Ibid., 17–19.

[67] Colonel Dinsmore added, "The acid test here is the evidence and here are the findings and here is the sentence—and all that is spread on the record, so what difference does it make [that] the discussion was in closed session." Ibid., 22–23. Although he did not do so, Larkin might have asked Dinsmore how the accused who might well be innocent would fare under his court-martial system so free from "technicalities."

[68] Ibid., 25. Morgan's group would have to "take the bit in their teeth on some of these problems and take up the responsibility. . . . They don't expect us to predigest and spoon-feed them on every question."

[69] Larkin, statement attached to agenda for meeting of September 17, 1948; LP. In the first draft of the minutes for that meeting, Larkin wrote "Great importance was attached to this problem [the role of the law member] and, in view of [Morgan's] suggestion that the purpose of the Committee is to fashion, where practicable, the proceedings of courts-martial along the lines of the civilian courts, the members thought that it involved a basic philosophy about which they would like to give additional thought." Significantly, the committee voted to delete this entire sentence from the final version of the minutes. See *Minutes*, Meetings of September 17–18, 1948, drafts I and II; LP.

[70] Statement, 5. The army and air force maintained their view that if the law member's instructions were placed upon the record, "it will not only be an administrative burden, but it will also

vinced. As with the issue of enlisted men serving on court-martials, so here with the question of the judicial role of the law member, Forrestal would have to make the ultimate decision.[71]

The problem of what sort of appellate review should be implemented for all the armed services represented the most difficult challenge for the CUCMJ, if only because of the disparity between the two existing models, army and navy. The Elston Act, for example, had rescinded the old Article of War 50 1/2, and replaced it with a confusing system that included the establishment of "judicial councils." Whatever the functions of these new tribunals, one characteristic of the army policy remained unchanged. The entire review process stayed within its purview. All Boards of Review were to be composed of JAG officers, with the Judicial Council to include three "general officers" from the same department.

The navy proposals for appellate review had been embodied in a bill that never passed the Congress, and since the Elston Act applied only to the army, no changes were imminent. Thus, important differences remained between the two services. The Navy Board of Review, for example, was only advisory to the Navy JAG, while the functions of the army judicial councils were specifically defined by the statute, which gave these boards at least some measure of judicial independence. Unlike his army counterpart, however, the secretary of the navy had full power concerning both clemency as well as other legal aspects of a court-martial. He alone among the three service secretaries, for example, had authority to convene a court-martial.

The Keeffe Report had called for a Navy Board of Legal review, to be created by statute and administered through the JAG department. It would include at least one civilian, with total composition to consist of not less than three nor more than five members. In most cases, its decisions on matters of law would be final. The Keeffe Committee also recommended the establishment of a separate board of sentence review.

When the Working Group first took up the issue of a uniform appellate procedure, Larkin acknowledged that "the review should be as expertly done as possible from the legal standpoint[,] and from the disciplinary standpoint" as well. Thinking possibly from a view of practicality, he indicated that perhaps reviews of legal issues as well as the severity of sentence should be undertaken by the same tribunal. But the real challenge was less overcoming technical difficulties than obviating interservice parochialism. His language might have been awkward, but Larkin's meaning was very clear. "I think your own mind

---

make the trial of a court-martial much more technical[,] and it will tend to complicate the trial of cases to an unwarranted extent." Ibid.

[71] Larkin's Minutes stated that "while the Committee's vote was split, the members reserved the right to change their respective decisions as work progresses on the code. There was a feeling that it might be possible to avoid forwarding a split decision to [Forrestal] for resolution." *Minutes*, CUCMJ, September 30, October 1, 1948, 2; LP.

is based on all you see of merit in your own system, and now if you would see if you can see any merit in the opposite system . . . for instance in the Army [and] Navy . . . and see if you can't work out a relatively uniform system for everybody[;] and not think of your difficulties as a representative of your own Department but as a justice of defense, maybe we can come up with something workable.''[72]

The normal procedure was for the Working Group to present both suggestions and actual drafts of proposed articles to Morgan's committee. However, it was evident that the Working Group was far from any sort of agreement, and Morgan's panel was ''impressed by the complexity of the review procedures.'' Larkin's minutes indicated that a change in approach was coming. This time, Morgan would not wait for the Working Group. ''He had given considerable thought to this very important problem, and, after additional thought, will reduce his ideas to writing for distribution to the members of the Committee.''[73]

It is difficult to assess the extent to which Morgan influenced his committee, even though all of its other members were both much younger than he and law school graduates as well. On the contrary, writing to William Generous, Larkin recalled that in the give-and-take of drafting, Morgan ''lost the argument in many cases and had to recede from some of his pet ideas.''[74] However, Larkin also stated on another occasion that Morgan ''was a most dynamic factor in our deliberations. His erudition carried most arguments.''[75] What Morgan proposed to his committee concerning a uniform appellate review system, and whether Larkin's generalization was accurate concerning it, is discussed in the following chapter.[76]

[72] *Transcript*, Working Group Meeting, September 28, 1948, 24–25; LP. ''It may mean, from a functional aspect, getting a good appellate review, a good legal review, a good sentence review.''

[73] Sup., n. 71, 4.

[74] LP, November 24, 1970. In this context, a letter from Morgan to an Army JAG officer is of interest. Morgan wrote that ''the job which I have taken on seems to me particularly important, although as merely one member of the Committee, my influence may not be great, and my limited experience in the Army may lead me to underestimate the importance of the command element in the administration of Military Justice.'' MPVU, September 2, 1948.

[75] Larkin, Lecture, ''Uniform Code of Military Justice,'' Fordham University Graduate School of Business, January 11, 1983, 13; LP.

[76] Even as Morgan prepared to present his proposal, he received a letter from Arthur Keeffe. He wanted to ''wish you well[,] and to express the hope that the reforms you proposed in the morning of your days, you will put into effect in the evening of your days without any compromise with principle.'' Indeed, he concluded, ''I guess the answer is that right and reason will always win if we can only be patient and live long enough.'' MPVU, September 29, 1948. Keeffe's comments should be kept in mind when his reaction to the UCMJ as finally enacted is discussed below in a later chapter.

CHAPTER 8

The Committee, the Code, and the Court, 1948–1949

BY EARLY OCTOBER, Edmund Morgan was ready with his proposal for a uniform system of appellate review. On October 5, he sent a copy of it to Felix Larkin for distribution to the committee. However, he had already discussed his ideas by telephone with Larkin, and the Working Group spent several sessions on the plan before the chairman met with his panel. From Morgan's letter, it is clear that he assumed from the outset that his proposals would be controversial. He was absolutely correct.

MORGAN'S "BOMBSHELL"

Originally, Larkin had invited the various JAGs to meet with his group for a discussion concerning a uniform appellate review system. However, the army JAG, Gen. Thomas Green, wished to take up this topic only with Morgan's committee, causing Larkin to cancel a joint meeting scheduled for October 6.[1] Instead he decided to acquaint the Working Group with Morgan's plan, sent from Cambridge the previous day. Enclosed, Morgan had written, please find a "copy of the bombshell which I threatened to let go concerning the plan for appellate procedure." Morgan added that the working group should take up his proposals, and "suggest a substitute for each part of the proposal with which they do not agree." Larkin should "emphasize that mere disagreement without a suggested substitute is not particularly helpful to our Committee."[2]

Because he was concerned with a uniform code, applicable to all the services, Morgan proposed a uniform review system of similar scope. His first level of review was by the convening authority who would receive "the entire record, including findings and sentences of every trial by general court martial." This officer "shall have the record examined by his staff judge advocate or legal officer." After that advice had been received, he had four options:

1. To "set aside any proceeding, finding or sentence or part thereof, as he finds legally insufficient, with the power to return the case for a rehearing."

[1] LPPL, October 5, 1948.

[2] MPVU, October 5, 1948.

2. To "remit or mitigate, but not commute, all or any part of a sentence, if he deems such action for the best interests of the service."

3. To combine "two or more" of these two options.

4. To "approve the findings or sentence."[3]

If the commander chose not to set aside the entire sentence, or to return the case for a rehearing, Morgan's second stage called for submission to a board of review, that would be established in the JAG's office. Here too, Morgan appeared to be echoing army procedure that had been in effect since the 1920 amendments to the Articles of War. Examination of the section indicates, however, that he would have gone much further in allocating powers to this board than existing practice. Under his proposal,

> The Board of Review shall examine the whole record to ascertain whether the court has committed any error which has injuriously affected the substantial rights of the accused; it shall have the authority to weigh the evidence, judge the credibility of witnesses and determine controverted questions of fact, bearing in mind that the court saw and heard the witnesses who testified before it, and the Board shall determine whether the findings or sentence or both insofar as heretofore approved by the convening authority shall be set aside in whole or in part or affirmed in whole or in part, or modified, and whether the charges shall be dismissed or the case reheard.

If the board of review decided that any action "other than affirmance of any part of the sentence should be taken," the case was to be returned to the convening authority "for appropriate action."[4] This tribunal would be appointed by the judge advocate general, to consist of not less than three JAG officers.

Morgan's third level of review was the most radical of all, although, as with the other two parts of his plan, he described it in traditional terminology—in this instance as a "judicial council"—the exact term that had been employed in the Elston Act. But his council was a very different tribunal from that envisaged in the legislation.

> The Secretary of Defense shall constitute in his office a Judicial Council composed of not less than three members, each of whom shall be a member of the bar ad-

[3] In Larkin's papers, the draft of Morgan's original proposal was attached to the agenda for the CUCMJ meetings of October 14 and 15, 1948. Actually, Morgan's first stage represented two reviews, one by the staff Judge Advocate, the other by the CA, a point not missed by Larkin. As far as the army was concerned, this first level of review replicated what had long existed—and Larkin was correct in stating, "I daresay our services are in accord with this much of it[,] so far." *Transcript*, Working Group Meeting, October 11, 1948, 4.

[4] Morgan Proposal, 2. Morgan did not spell out the implications of this second level, but they must have troubled senior officers comfortable with the existing procedures. Could the board of review supercede the judgment of a commander? Was the commander compelled to obey the mandate of the panel? My reading of Morgan's draft indicates an affirmative answer to both these questions.

mitted to practice before the Supreme Court of the United States (and of at least ten years' experience in the practice of the profession of law). Each member shall be nominated by the Secretary of Defense and be appointed by the President[,] and shall receive a salary equal to that of a United States Circuit Judge. . . . The term of a regular member would be long, probably for life.

Morgan specified that in three types of cases, "the entire record, including findings, sentence, action by the convening authority and the opinion of the Board of Review, shall be forwarded to the Judicial Council for further review:

1. All cases in which the sentence affects a general officer, or in which the sentence is death.

2. All cases which the judge advocate general orders forwarded to the Judicial Council for review.

3. All cases in which a petition for review by the Council is filed by or on behalf of the accused and in which after considering the petition[,] the Council determines that the petitioner has shown that there is a reasonable ground to believe injustice has been done to the accused[,] or that the determination of the Board of Review is in conflict with that of a Board of Review of another service; or that the best interests of the service will for some other reason be furthered by a review."

In its review, according to Morgan, the Council "shall have authority to weigh evidence, judge the credibility of witnesses, determine controverted questions of fact[,] and to order such disposition of the case as the demands of justice and the best interests of the service require." Morgan further augmented this broad mandate with another section. "At any time within one year after a sentence which includes dismissal, or dishonorable discharge or bad conduct discharge has been executed, the accused may move the Judicial Council to order a new trial on the ground of newly discovered evidence; and if such motion is made[,] the Council shall hear and determine it in accord with the rules usually applied in such motions in the [federal] District Courts." Finally, Morgan proposed that the JAG appoint members of his department "as defense counsel[,] whose duty it shall be to represent the accused before the Judicial Council, and in such cases before the Board of Review as the Judge Advocate General shall direct."[5]

In several instances, Morgan's three-part appeal plan represented a radical departure from existing practice in 1948. Beside the basic change to one uniform appellate system applicable to all the services, Morgan gave each level an unusual degree of independence. Possibly because he himself was uncertain, it was unclear from his first draft what relationship the Board of Review and the Judicial Council would have to the JAG. In the Elston Act, they apparently had been intended to function more in an advisory capacity. Morgan's

[5] Ibid., 2–4.

plan clearly put the judicial findings of both panels beyond the purview of the JAG to approve or alter them. Moreover, Morgan took the judicial council out of the JAG's office entirely, and opened its membership to *civilian* lawyers with life tenure.[6] Finally, he gave that panel broad discretionary jurisdiction over what cases it could hear. Compared to existing military appellate practice in 1948, Morgan's proposal could well be described as a "bombshell."

MILITARY REACTION

After the initial meeting with Larkin to consider the Morgan plan, the navy representative, Marine Col. John Curry, prepared a report for his JAG—Adm. George Russell. Dated October 8, 1948, the summary noted army opposition to the proposal that would require defense counsel at the appellate level as "needless and cumbersome."[7] In addition, the army deplored "any diminution of the position of the Judge Advocate General or of his influence with the Secretary of War."[8] Curry further commented that the air force proposed "exploring the possibilities of providing one supreme judicial counsel for the armed services in order to resolve legal conflicts; [it] might consist of each Judge Advocate General or a deputy nominated by him."[9] As for the navy, all Curry was prepared to report at this point was "it is believed that the Navy

[6] From Morgan's choice of words in this first draft, it is not certain that originally, he intended to preclude members of the military from serving on the Judicial Council. There were numerous officers in the JAG department who met the criteria he listed. On the other hand, Larkin and members of the Working Group assumed from the outset that the judicial council would be dominated by if not consist totally of civilians. Furthermore, the fact that the council would be appointed by the secretary of defense, himself a civilian, lends credence to the view that Morgan wanted a civilian board. Later, as the committee considered the ultimate form of the council, Morgan made it very clear that he had intended a court *only* of civilians. See below, sections 5–6. Thus, later drafts—including the one ultimately enacted—employed the term "from civilian life."

[7] Curry to [Navy] JAG, October 8, 1948—in United States Court of Military Appeals Papers, hereafter called USCMAP. Curry added that according to Larkin, "Professor Morgan contemplated that [appellate] counsel should be provided . . . in view of a feeling that the public lacks confidence in the present system, and [also,] it is often uncertain whether all points in favor of the accused have been freely considered, if at all."

[8] Ibid. Under usual procedure, the secretary of war had "receive[d] no other legal advice on any court martial case than that presented by the Judge Advocate General." The army did not yet see exactly how the Judicial Council would affect this pattern, but it was apprehensive.

[9] Ibid., 3. From the military viewpoint, the idea of a supreme judicial counsel composed of JAGs from all the three services may well have appeared a very desirable alternative to Morgan's "bombshell." It would provide a uniformity of judicial interpretation, but one that would be strictly controlled within the military establishment. From Morgan's perspective, of course, such a tribunal would represent little, if any improvement over what already existed.

will favor preservation in some form of the residual power of the Secretary to direct a further review.''[10]

The working group met again on October 11, and Colonel Dinsmore on behalf of the army emphasized that ''we are opposed . . . very strongly [to] cutting the Judge Advocate or our Secretary out of the picture.''[11] The army also opposed Morgan's plan for a judicial council, calling instead for what had already been enacted under the Elston Act. Dinsmore did not ''think that the Office of the Secretary of Defense ought to get into the picture except as a matter of policy.'' Indeed, ''we would have no objection to a policy body in the Secretary's Office.'' When pressed by Larkin as to exactly what such a group could do, Dinsmore replied that ''they'd be a judicial council in the sense of the Keeffe report—make a continuing study of the operation of the system with a view to improvements and . . . to correction of defects which are observed as time goes on.''[12]

It is doubtful, therefore, if Dinsmore supported the Morgan judicial council which, in reality was an appellate court with civilian judges. Col. Maxey of the air force emphasized also that ''military justice is a service function and action should be final in the service concerned.'' A judicial council for all the services might go too far in the direction of enforced uniformity. ''We wish to approach uniformity as closely as possible[,] but absolute flat uniformity is not a judicial matter at all.'' Larkin responded that ''I think what we are striving for is uniformity of technique . . . [,] uniformity of interpretation of the same substantive law.''[13]

Maxey further reiterated that the air force, like the army, did not support a judicial council in the secretary of defense's office. On the other hand, ''if there is a method of improving the appellate system within ou[r] service, we'll buy it.'' The air force representative was also troubled by the fact that the Elston Act, to go into effect in a few months, had produced a series of changes

[10] Ibid.

[11] *Transcript*, Working Group Meeting, October 11, 1948, 8. Larkin observed that under Morgan's proposal, if he disagrees with a decision from the board of review the JAG ''cannot automatically as a matter of writ send it to the Judicial Council . . . , but he can ask for a writ, and if the Judicial Council takes it, then it is the same as his opinion being sent on; and if they don't take it, of course he is out.'' The army insisted that their JAG should have an inherent right to send cases on to this tribunal without prior approval. Ibid., 10.

[12] Ibid., 11. The army did not want to put the secretary of defense ''in the operating game.'' Dinsmore's idea of judicial council would be ''a body composed of the three JAGs and two outstanding civilian lawyers.'' The army representative did not explain *who* would appoint the two lawyers, but probably assumed that it would be the secretary of the army. Dinsmore added that work on this panel ''would be a part time job, I take it, if they come down here like Professor Morgan comes on this thing—maybe not as often—to monitor the operation of the system.'' When Larkin asked if this group would ''have the authority to promulgate a manual, for instance, or changes in the manual,'' Dinsmore replied, ''I don't think so, but I think that kind of a body would be able to effectuate changes.'' Ibid, 12.

[13] Ibid., 14.

in military justice, including the appeals process. Why employ a new system now without giving the one just adopted at least a trial period? "Just to throw it out the window and put in a new system doesn't impress us as being desirable."[14] Although Larkin mentioned only the air force, he might well have had all the armed service representatives in mind when he stated that Maxey's group seemed "opposed to a supreme court in the office of the Secretary of Defense, whether it be civilian or general officers or anybody else."[15]

These viewpoints reflected an important distinction that troubled the several service representatives to the Working Group. They were concerned less with some sort of advisory council than with the fact that it would be housed in Forrestal's office. At this time, unification was not even one year old. The relationship between the new secretary of defense and the three undersecretaries was still in a very amorphous state. What new authority Forrestal possessed and what powers the three service secretaries still retained was not yet clear. The services could envision their respective secretaries with some role in the military justice appeal system. But Morgan's plan housed his Council in Forrestal's office, and apparently left the three undersecretaries virtually out of the picture. Thus, the various adjustments and changes to the proposed code that are discussed below, must be seen in the context of an emerging Department of Defense, with centralizing authority that appeared to diminish the traditional roles of the three service secretaries.

Later that afternoon, Larkin phoned Morgan and reported to him that while some of the Working Group were sympathetic to his plan, "the departmental JAGs are opposed to it." As to the JAGs appearing before his committee, Morgan raised no objection "if they expressed a desire to be heard, but otherwise he thought it was unnecessary and did not want to request them to appear."[16] Larkin sent out the agenda for the CUCMJ meeting for October 14–15, and simply informed its members that "the discussions of the Working Group . . . have not resulted in the resolution of the differences between the [army and navy] appellate systems. . . . In favoring their proposed system . . . the Army, necessarily, opposes the proposals of Professor Morgan," as does the air force, while the navy "generally favors its own system and opposes [that] of the Army."[17]

[14] Ibid., 15–16.

[15] Ibid., 18. Larkin found further discussion by his group useless. "I don't see any profit in saying one more word on the whole thing. I think we have reached a complete impasse on it. . . . The final decision . . . in connection with this whole problem is very obviously up to the main board." Ibid., 22.

[16] LPPL, October 11, 1948.

[17] *Agenda*, Meeting of CUCMJ, October 14–15, 1948, 1–2; LP. On October 13, Larkin was informed that the Navy JAG, Admiral Russell, "wanted to argue against the Morgan plan." One day later, it was decided that Dinsmore and Maxey could join Gray and Zuckert at the CUCMJ meeting. Secretary Zuckert suggested that "the Committee get out a letter to the JAGs telling them we would be glad to hear them on any point they wish." LPPL, October 13–14, 1948. Probably

In the meantime, Edmund Morgan wrote to Forrestal offering to resign from the committee. The episode is of interest in that it reflects Morgan's continuing concern that his past activities in no way impede work on the uniform code.[18] This time, it was the publication of a book that he had coauthored on the famous Massachusetts trials of anarchists Sacco and Vanzetti. Morgan had "completely overlooked the fact that this book, then in the press, would be published while [his] Committee was at work." Because Morgan found that in his judgment the two accused Italian immigrants had not received a fair trial, Forrestal might well conclude that his continuing as chairman "will not only not be helpful to you in your efforts to accomplish a very desirable object, but on the contrary may be harmful." If so, Morgan would be glad to resign.

"I regard," he wrote to Forrestal, "the enactment of a uniform code of military justice with proper safeguards for the accused and without impairment of military efficiency as of the highest importance and desirability. I would not want to be a party to any activity which would in any way hinder the accomplishment of this objective."[19] Morgan gave the letter to Leva, for transmittal to Forrestal. The secretary replied on February 15 that "I do not feel that the publication of this book will in any way affect the value of the very real contribution you are making, through your work as Chairman."[20]

Although there appears to be no surviving transcript of the October 14 meeting, Larkin's minutes make it clear that Morgan's original proposal received major alterations. It should also be noted that Gordon Gray was absent from the meeting, and the consensus reached by those present was "subject to an expression of Mr. Gray's views and a draft of the [revised] proposal."[21] It would seem, therefore, that whatever changes were made caused the air force and navy to drop their opposition.

At the outset, Larkin noted that the Working Group had been in error when it assumed that under Morgan's plan the JAG could only appeal to the Judicial Council through seeking a writ. In actuality, his proposal provided that the JAG "in cases of disagreement with the Board of Review can, as a matter of right,

---

drafted by Larkin, and duly sent out under Morgan's signature on October 14, the letter informed the three JAGs that his committee "has reached the point where it is making decisions on the various portions of the uniform code." Morgan was only too well aware that "the opinion of your office is reflected by the Service members of the Working Group. However, there may be occasions when you would prefer to present your opinion directly to the Committee. The Committee would be happy to have you do so at any time you desire." LP, October 14, 1948. In spite of Larkin's information that at least one JAG desired to speak, there is no indication from the Minutes—which lists the persons present—that any JAG even attended, let alone spoke, at the meeting of October 14.

[18] It will be recalled that earlier, Morgan expressed similar concern that Forrestal be informed about his role in the Ansell-Crowder dispute.

[19] MPVU, October 13, 1948.

[20] LPPI, October 14, 1948; MPVU, October 15, 1948.

[21] *Minutes*, CUCMJ Meeting, October 14, 1948, 1–2; LP.

have the Judicial Council hear the case.'' The first major change involved the composition of the Judicial Council. No less than three ''qualified civilians'' would be appointed by the secretaries of the three services, instead of the secretary of defense—each secretary to appoint one-third of the council. While the members were to be paid a salary comparable to that of a federal circuit court judge, each would serve at the will of the secretary by whom he had been appointed, rather than for the long terms that Morgan had originally suggested.

A second modification dramatically curtailed the authority of the council. Now it would be limited to a legal review in only four categories of cases; (*a*) death sentences, (*b*) dismissal from service, (*c*) appeals by the accused, and (*d*) referrals by the JAGS. The council would be without authority to weigh evidence, judge the credibility of witnesses, or determine controversial questions of fact. Instead, these functions were to be vested in the Boards of Review, appointed—it will be recalled—by the JAG of each service. The final change restored a good deal of authority to the respective secretaries, including residual clemency powers.[22]

A comparison of Morgan's original draft, and the changes just noted reveals how much the Harvard law professor had to compromise. He had sought a council of civilians, appointed by the secretary of defense for extended terms. Instead, each secretary would appoint one-third of the tribunal. Since council members would hold office at the discretion of that official, and since service secretaries were political appointments, rarely serving more than four years, and often less—the outlook was for a frequent turnover of council members, something Morgan had wanted to avoid. Moreover, he had vested the council with very broad powers, including authority to decide matters of both fact and law, as well as extensive jurisdiction in the area of rehearing. Instead, his council would be limited to a legal review only. On the other hand, the categories of cases that the council might hear remained essentially unchanged. And all these alterations had yet to receive endorsement from the army through Gordon Gray. Nevertheless, Larkin and one of his assistants agreed to redraft Morgan's plan into separate articles that embodied these changes, and to have them available for further discussion at the next meetings of both the Working Group and the CUCMJ.[23]

[22] Ibid; *Memorandum to [Navy] Judge Advocate General*, October 18, 1948, USCMAP.

[23] Morgan, as some of his letters cited in the previous chapter indicate, realized from the outset that military tolerance for radical change was very limited. He also knew, better than many lawyers who had called for reforms, that compromises would be inevitable. Thus, he supported Larkin's suggestion that the committee not make public any of its proposals or their ultimate fate until the entire code had been approved by Forrestal and submitted to Congress. Larkin did meet informally with members of the ABA commission on military justice, including Vanderbilt and McGuire. But when they asked if their committee could be informed about the course of Morgan's work, Larkin replied that his conversation was ''completely unofficial[,] and the [CUCMJ] feels that it would not be practical to publicize the interim steps of its activities.'' LPPL, October 15,

Although both the Working Group and Morgan's panel had agreed to keep their deliberations confidential, given the numbers of observers and "consultants" who participated in various meetings, to say nothing of the controversial issues being discussed—some leaks to the external military community were inevitable. Larkin possibly concluded that it would be better for him to make some public comments, if only to prevent unnecessary and unsettling rumors. Thus, he decided to discuss the UCMJ project at an open meeting, and on October 25, he spoke to the Reserve Judge Advocates Association. The internal disagreement concerning Morgan's proposed appellate process may well have been on his mind, because he drafted two versions of his address—and the one he presented is of interest more for what he deleted than for what he delivered.

At the outset, Larkin declined to comment about the specific "virtues and defects of military justice. I have found that I can maintain a relatively serene existence if I limit the expression of my views on this subject to the deaf and dumb only."[24] After a description of the background developments leading up to the Morgan Committee, and the interconnection between the two panels, Larkin turned to the appellate process and military justice. "I have always felt that the term 'military justice' is self-defining. It involves military problems and . . . problems of justice. Neither should be eliminated and both must be given due weight. I think there is widespread agreement that an independent court with qualified personnel is essential. The means to achieve that objective are in dispute."[25] For reasons which remain unclear, in the final draft Larkin deleted these four sentences, and made no reference to the proposal for appellate review.[26]

Morgan had originally proposed a tripartite review system. During the last part of October, Larkin—assisted by Cornell Law Professor Robert Pasley (who had worked so well with him on the Keeffe Report)—revised Morgan's suggestions into a series of separate articles. Although they "tightened up"

1948. Larkin and Morgan also met informally with the members of the New York City Bar Association's military justice group during the weekend of October 29–30. Ibid., October 29–30, 1948. How much specific information they made available to the committee is not known, but one can imagine the reaction of outside lawyers had they been informed of the changes in Morgan's plan from its original draft to the tentative structure as noted above.

[24] LP, draft of address, October 25, 1948, 1.

[25] Ibid., 9.

[26] His caution in deleting them may be because he realized that the army was far from ready to endorse the idea of an independent court. Indeed, the next day Larkin informed Gordon Gray that during his speech before the Reserve JAG Association, General Green (TJAG of the army) remarked "to the effect that he knew nothing whatsoever about the work or decisions" of Morgan's committee. LPPL, October 26, 1948. Larkin reminded his audience that "each and every provision [in the forthcoming code] won't please everyone. . . . However, I believe it will be a code that will have some of the best ideas of everyone." Finally, Larkin could not give out details or copies of the proposed UCMJ because "I am afraid the complete code will not be ready until 15 minutes before the deadline."

some of Morgan's prose, with two minor exceptions, Larkin and Pasley left his first two levels of review—i.e., by the convening authority and the board of review essentially as he drafted them.[27]

Article 56 redrew the new Judicial Council along the lines agreed upon at the October 14 meeting, with one key difference. Larkin's minutes for that meeting indicated that the council members were to serve at the pleasure of each secretary who had nominated them. Somehow, that provision was dropped from the Larkin/Pasley revision. Indeed, no term limitation of any sort whatsoever appears in the new wording.[28] It may well be that Morgan's committee decided to leave the decision as to the length of years up to Congress. In any event, as will be seen, its final decision was not what Morgan had envisaged.

Larkin and Pasley also clarified the establishment of defense counsel in the JAG office, something Morgan had denoted but not developed. Now the JAG was to select *both* appellate defense counsel and appellate government counsel to appear ''in all cases before the judicial council.'' Moreover, these officers could also appear before boards of review (*a*) when the judge advocate general shall direct, (*b*) when the Board of Review shall request their appearance, and (*c*) when the Appellate Defense Counsel shall deem it necessary.[29] Morgan found this version inadequate. He added the words ''or the accused shall request'' to the first section, and supported if not initiated further revisions that resulted in the following wording:

> It shall be the duty of Appellate Government Counsel to represent the accused before the Board of Review or the Judicial Council—
>
> (1) When he is requested to do so by the accused; or (2) When the United States is represented by counsel; or (3) When the judge advocate general has requested

[27] In the new article establishing the Board of Review, Larkin and Pasley specified two provisions that Morgan had probably assumed would be included: (*a*) neither the revised 1920 Articles of War, nor the Elston Act as adopted by Congress in 1948 established any criteria for membership on the Boards of Review, except that the members were to be drawn from the JAGs Office. The Larkin/Pasley draft added that each board of review would be composed of ''not less than three [JAG] officers, each of whom shall be a member of the Bar of a Federal Court or of the highest Court of a State of the United States,'' and (*b*) Morgan had originally provided that when the Board of Review took action other than affirmance of the lower court decision, the record would be returned to the convening authority ''for appropriate action.'' Larkin and Pasley added that when the record had been returned, ''in any case where the convening authority finds a new trial impractical because of the unavailability of witnesses, or for other good reason, he may dismiss the charges.'' LP, draft of Proposed Article 55, 2, October 22, 1948.

[28] This cannot have been accidental because at least four versions of the revised article have been preserved, one of which was prepared by Morgan at Harvard Law School. None of them mentions anything about this provision. It seems reasonable to conclude that Morgan acquiesced in this deletion.

[29] LP, Draft, Article 58, 1, October 22, 1948.

the reconsideration of a case before the Board of Review or has transmitted it to the Judicial Counsel.[30]

MORGAN'S "READJUSTMENTS"

Although Morgan, Kenney, and Zuckert had tentatively endorsed what Larkin called "the Morgan plan as amended in many respects," they had also agreed to discuss the appellate process again at the meeting of October 28, 1948—when Gray would be present.[31] On the morning of October 28, however, the JAG of the air force wrote to Zuckert in opposition to a judicial council "composed of civilian lawyers." Maj. Gen. Reginald Harmon reminded Zuckert that

> the administration of military justice is a function of the Military Establishment[,] and not of the Federal Judiciary. There should be no division of authority between the military and civilian branches of government. . . . It is questionable . . . whether a civilian lawyer, unfamiliar with military justice and the customs of the service, will be more competent to discharge the functions of appellate review than will those lawyers [in] the Judge Advocate General's Department. In my opinion, the judicial counsel should be composed of officers from each service.[32]

Harmon failed to convince Zuckert, who remained committed to the Morgan plan as amended.

When Morgan convened the meeting, Gray "regretfully but firmly" dis-

[30] This wording appears in the final draft of the UCMJ as presented to Congress in the spring of 1949. Morgan's committee had much less difficulty with providing for counsel before its judicial council than with the establishment of the council itself.

[31] *Transcript*, CUCMJ meeting, October 28, 1948, 2. This seventeen-page excerpt is one of the very few partial transcripts from Morgan's committee—as opposed to the Working Group—that has survived. It was found in Gordon Gray's papers at the U.S. Army Military Institute Library, Carlisle Army Barracks. Apparently, at Gray's request Larkin sent him the excerpt "which covers your views on the problem of an appellate system . . . so that you could refer to them in writing a memorandum" concerning Morgan's plan. LP, November 4, 1948. This author has been unable to locate a complete transcript of any Morgan Committee meetings.

[32] *Memorandum for the Assistant Secretary of the Air Force*, October 28, 1948, USCMAP. As for the companion provision for appointment of appellate counsel, Harmon believed that "this provision, while theoretically desirable, is unnecessary." As will be seen below in chap. 11, when Harmon testified before the Senate Subcommittee considering the UCMJ, he endorsed Morgan's court. Nevertheless, Harmon, who served three consecutive terms as TJAG of the air force from 1948 to 1960, believed he had been consistent in his opposition to an appellate court. In 1987, he recalled that "I had some strong feelings about that development and still do. I don't think we needed it, and I don't think we need it now." Moreover, "I wouldn't have an independent judiciary[, and] I wouldn't have an independent prosecuting staff or an independent defense staff." As for the UCMJ, "I was not for the Uniform Code of Military Justice, and I am not for it now." USAF, Oral History Program, *Interview of Major General Reginald C. Harmon*, March 5, 12, 1987, 46, 50.

sented from "the agreement you all agreed to."[33] In the first place, he argued that the plan was contrary to the National Security Act of 1947. Reflecting the tension discussed earlier, Gray emphasized the statutory provision that the army, navy, and air force "shall be administered as individual executive departments by their respective secretaries." He held that until such time as Congress might decide to merge the three services into one, an unlikely eventuality, the secretary of the army "has and must have independent responsibility as to all matters pertaining to the Army, including courts-martial." He "strongly objected" to Morgan's "radical change" because it deprives "the Secretary of the Army of judicial authority, and lodges ultimate judicial authority in a tribunal composed of members without military experience and without responsibility for results."[34]

Morgan replied that the judicial council "carries out both the letter and the spirit of the National Security Act. I'd be prepared to argue that before any court in the land." Earlier, Morgan had prepared a short brief dealing with the "Legality of Judicial Council under [the] National Security Act."[35] By virtue of that statute, he wrote, the secretary of defense must "establish general policies and programs for the National Military Establishment and for all departments and agencies therein," as well as to "exercise general direction, authority and control over such departments."

"It seems too clear for argument that, in establishing a general program and exercising general authority and control . . . the Secretary . . . may set up a uniform system of military justice, and establish as the instrument for exercising his control a tribunal of civilians for the uniform construction and application of . . . a code of military justice." Morgan conceived of his judicial council as "the final interpreter of the law for the National Military Establishment" as embodied in a new uniform code. Functioning like a circuit court of appeals, "it would be like a court of last resort over a group of states, applying a uniform statute governing matters as to which their separate state courts had theretofore not been in harmony."[36]

[33] *Transcript*, 2. These paragraphs dealing with Gray's arguments are based both on this partial transcript and his expanded analysis, submitted on November 26, 1948.

[34] *Transcript*, 2–3; *Memorandum*, 1–2. Gray also believed that Morgan's proposed tribunal would be swamped with appeals, since convicted defendants would want their cases reviewed by the highest authority, "especially since such an application will involve no expense [to them]."

[35] Found in his papers dealing with the UCMJ on deposit at Harvard Law School, it probably was the basis for his rebuttal to Gray at the October 28 meeting.

[36] *Transcript*, 4–5; Morgan, *Legality of Judicial Council*, 2–4, MPHLS, undated. It is not clear for whose eyes Morgan intended this memorandum. In it, he was probably much more candid than he could have been in meeting with senior civilian representatives of the three services. Morgan added that the entire thrust of the recent legislation that unified the military was toward "a central integrating authority; otherwise there will be uniformity only in the written word, and diversity in interpretation and application. There will be reiterations of claims of discrimination as between services and . . . various branches of the same service; there will be continuing com-

However, Gray's objections went beyond his belief that Morgan's judicial council violated federal statute. The proposal was bad enough as Morgan had drafted it. But John Kenney's revision, accepted by Zuckert and Morgan in Gray's absence, was even worse. The change would have the three secretaries each name one member of the council—to serve at their pleasure. If, according to Gray, "it was done on the basis that . . . the secretaries retain some sort of control[, you] cannot in theory have an independent Judicial Council. If they are removable at the will of the appointing secretary for what he might consider bad judgement or conduct that doesn't agree with his point of view, then you are really in trouble."[37]

Gordon Gray did more than merely criticize the appellate procedure under consideration. It seemed to him that Morgan's judicial council "seeks to serve two purposes—uniformity of application and civilian participation in review of cases."[38] If this was so, he proposed a two-part alternative plan that would accomplish these goals but in a way that would not involve an independent civilian tribunal. On the contrary, it would involve only a change in the existing boards of review as set forth in the recently enacted Elston Act.[39]

Gray suggested that these tribunals be reconstituted to consist of three senior JAG officers, or two officers and one senior line officer—plus three "especially qualified civilian lawyers, who would be well paid." If the JAG disagreed with a board's finding, he could take the matter to the service secretary. Similarly, if the board split 3–3, the JAG could then present the record to the secretary.[40]

---

plaints of disregard by the military of the mandates of a civilian Congress with no check by a tribunal having the qualifications of a civil court." The alternative would be a return to conditions Morgan had denounced as a young assistant to Ansell, thirty years before. The new congressional emphasis is for "unified direction of the three military departments under civilian control. This emphasis is as applicable to the administration of military justice as to any other aspect of the establishment. Indeed it is in this respect that the necessity for the imposition of civilian, as distinguished from military, concepts has been most strenuously advocated. The creation of such a tribunal will tend not only to accomplish one of the specific objectives of the Act[,] but will do much to restore public confidence in the administration of military justice."

[37] *Transcript*, 3. In his later memorandum, Gray added that Kenney's change might result in the "implications of [a] lack of independence on the part of the members of the Judicial Council. Furthermore, it seems to me that it might invite political pressures upon the three Secretaries." *Memorandum*, 3. Morgan could only have agreed with Gray on these points, but he realized that Kenney's revision was probably the price he would have to pay for getting a judicial council at all. Moreover, as noted above, the fact that later drafts of the appropriate article deleted all mention of limitation on terms may indicate that *sub silentio* the committee decided to leave final decision on this question to Congress.

[38] Ibid., 3.

[39] Gray further claimed that "one of the outstanding virtues of the Army court-martial . . . is its freedom from the technicalities which encumber and often defeat justice in the civil courts." A judicial council composed entirely of civilians could well result "in a body of technical rules and decisions upon technical grounds." I sincerely believe, he emphasized, "that our concern ought to be with justice rather than legal niceties."

[40] Memorandum, 3–4; *Transcript*, 7–8.

He saw several virtues in this proposal that were all absent from Morgan's plan. First, it involved civilian judges but *only within* a military appellate procedure. Second, these judges could contribute important input, but by themselves they could never obtain a majority. Third, the secretary of the army would be kept in this appellate review system.

To achieve some uniformity in sentencing, Gray advocated an advisory council to consist of the three service JAGS, plus a representative from the office of the secretary of defense. This body would review the court-martial activities of the three services in order to comment on "inconsistencies of sentence, the effectiveness of appellate review . . . and [it] would be charged with recommending policies and changes in policies to bring about uniformity where there are appearances of lack of uniformity."[41] This advisory council would, however, be powerless to intervene in any way with actual courts-martial or appeals.

Gray failed to convince his three colleagues that his alternative was preferable to Morgan's plan as amended. They agreed, therefore, to disagree—and left it to James Forrestal to decide the ultimate form of the appellate process.[42] But before turning to other articles, Gray asked Morgan if he would consider substituting judges from the circuit court of appeals for his judicial council. Morgan's answer is of interest, especially in the light of USCMA history since 1951.

Although the Harvard law professor strongly favored civilian judges as the basic part of a court-martial appeals system, he drew a sharp distinction between an external civilian court, and his proposed civilian court to be established under auspices of a military code. Morgan had noted "an increasing tendency, particularly in the District Courts, to interfere with the court-martial on the grounds that their proceedings were too far off. I think if you had a council like [the one he proposed] at the head, you'd find a tendency to trust that council. Say, if it had gone through them and you had the opportunity to have certiorari there[,] the judges would be much more likely to keep their hands off."[43] Morgan's answer was prophetic. As will be discussed in the second volume of this study, from its first sessions in 1951 to the present term, the United States Court of Military Appeals has been notably free of interference from other courts. Not until 1984 did Congress provide for appeal from certain of its decisions directly to the United States Supreme Court, and that tribunal has been very selective in accepting such petitions.[44]

While the CUCMJ had tentatively approved a much amended appellate procedure for the new code by a vote of 3–1, the members agreed that Gordon

[41] *Transcript*, 5–6.

[42] *Minutes*, CUCMJ, October 28, 1948, 1–2, MPVU.

[43] *Transcript*, 14–15.

[44] From 1984 to 1990, this author is aware of only two such cases, and one of these resulted in an unsigned (per curiam) decision.

Gray should have an opportunity to present both a written critique of Morgan's Judicial Council, and the army's suggested alternative. This would come at the meeting scheduled for November 29. In the meantime, preparation of other articles continued, and those dealing with the appellate review were revised again for submission at the November meeting. They indicate not only flexibility on Morgan's part, but also his ability to distinguish between components of a code essential for it to serve as a constitutional framework for military law, and more detailed provisions better suited for enactment through regulation rather than congressional statute.

The CUCMJ had already restricted the judicial council to ruling on matters of law. Possibly to insure continued support from Zuckert and Kenney, Morgan agreed to even narrower wording in the latest revisions—language that further diminished what little discretionary authority it still retained. The new section provided that

> in any case reviewed by it, the Judicial Council shall act only with respect to the findings and sentence as approved by the convening authority[,] and as affirmed or set aside as incorrect in law by the Board of Review. In a case which the Judge Advocate General orders forwarded to the Judicial Council, such action need be taken only with respect to the issues raised by him. In a case reviewed upon petition of the accused, such action need be taken only with respect to issues specified in the grant of review. The Judicial Council shall take action only with respect to matters of law.[45]

There may be several factors that explain why Morgan acquiesced in restricting his proposed court only to matters of law. Like any good lawyer, he was fully aware that such a limitation rarely restrained a resourceful appellate court from intervening in a case it wished to hear. Further, he had prevailed in his insistence that the council would have the right to review "all cases in which, upon petition of the accused and good cause shown, the Judicial Council has granted a review." This very broad discretionary jurisdiction could well mitigate against the narrow restriction to matters of law. Finally, Morgan may have concluded that by insisting on what he had originally proposed, he might split his committee even more on this issue than it was already.

Morgan also had to accept the fact that the Boards of Review, the second level in his tripartite review system, had emerged with the broad authority to review matters of fact and law that he would have placed in his judicial council. To be sure, under Morgan's plan these boards had greater independence

[45] MPVU, draft of Article 57, November 26, 1948. While further alterations of this article were forthcoming, this language remained unchanged, and would be part of the code as submitted to Congress in 1949. It will be recalled that in the October draft, Morgan had also included authority for the council to grant new trials on the grounds of newly discovered evidence, under rules comparable to those in effect in federal district courts. This section was deleted in the November revision.

than had been provided to them in the Elston Act—nevertheless they were selected by each JAG, to serve at his pleasure. Moreover, although the November revision provided that such tribunals were to be "composed of not less than three officers or civilians," the JAG could and in fact has usually appointed only officers to serve on them.[46]

Whatever Morgan's true feelings may have been on the extent to which he had to compromise, he seems to have understood better than many of his fellow attorneys the realities of a military establishment and its requisite command structure. The Morgan who with marked indignation defended Ansell to William Howard Taft in 1919 was not the same Morgan who in 1948–1949 worked in apparent harmony with his committee to fashion the UCMJ. Indeed, one senses a concern on the part of some of the lawyers' associations who had been so critical of military justice in the years prior to 1948—that their complaints and suggestions were receiving something less than proper consideration by Morgan's group.

When, for example, Arthur Ballantine complained to Forrestal that there had been no response concerning his suggestions to Morgan's committee, Larkin hastened to assure Ballantine that the committee "sincerely appreciate[s] your very interesting observations and [is] most apologetic for the oversight in acknowledging their receipt. . . . The Committee appreciate[s] your offer of assistance and is most conscious of your great interest and experience in the field of military justice."[47] On his part, Morgan also tried to discourage what he considered either unreasonable or unrealistic proposals for the code. Thus, on November 29, he wrote to a former student that certain conditions for confinement "and the extent to which disciplinary measures should be used are hardly subject matters for legislation by Congress. They should be taken care of by regulations."[48]

[46] On December 8, the Working Group agreed among itself that the words "or civilians" be deleted from the article dealing with the Boards of Review. *Memorandum to the Judge Advocate General*, December 9, 1948, USCMAP. Apparently this addition had been drafted in Larkin's office, as "neither the Army, the Navy nor the Air Force had recommended or agreed that civilians should be included on the Board of Review." When Morgan's committee considered this change, it split 2–2, with Morgan and Kenney in favor of civilian membership as an option. As of December 1948, it seemed that the question would have to be resolved by Forrestal. It was not, however, among the issues submitted to him. Probably the CUCMJ postponed final action until later and ultimately came to an agreement among themselves. The phrase remained in the draft as submitted to Congress; and it can also be found in the current version of the UCMJ.

[47] LP, November 1, 1948. Similarly, Arthur Keeffe wrote to Larkin "what I would like is a crack at any drafts that are available. I presume as a member of the ABA Committee I will eventually receive them . . . but I would appreciate any information you can give me directly as to your progress[;] and I will, of course, respect any confidence you repose in me." Ibid., November 5, 1948. No reply from Larkin has been located, and it may well be that he did not bother to respond. Apparently, none of the lawyers' groups received specific information about the UCMJ prior to its formal submission to Congress.

[48] MPVU, November 5, 1948. Charles Porter wrote that Forrestal "could have chosen no better

GORDON GRAY'S GRIEVANCE

Even as Morgan's committee moved steadily toward an understanding, if not total agreement, concerning the form of the review system, the topic remained controversial. At the meeting on December 9, Kenney suggested that membership on the judicial council be open to "senior regular and retired officers." Morgan opposed the suggestion, and his remarks help explain why he may have been so willing to accept other changes in his original proposal.[49]

"If," Morgan observed, "both the Army and the Navy . . . want to have either officers or civilians, . . . from my point of view that ruins my scheme, because you may have all officers or you might have a majority of officers. That would still leave the ultimate control in the military, which is the thing that has been strongly objected to. It's the one point in the whole setup that I have been most anxious to preserve."[50] This is why Morgan originally wanted a civilian court, with two civilians—either the president or the secretary of defense—to name the judges who, in turn, would serve "during good behavior." Kenney responded that his proposal might insure a larger pool of available and experienced candidates. "I was merely thinking of it as a manpower problem. . . . I wanted to broaden the base of selection[.] That is all I was thinking of." Before the session ended, Kenney withdrew his proposal.[51]

Also at this meeting, Gordon Gray raised a point "inherent in some of the problems of this Committee." Apparently troubled by his inability to persuade his colleagues to abandon a civilian appellate court for the military, he asked what would happen to a split vote within the committee. Suppose "Professor Morgan makes the recommendation to the Secretary of Defense[, who] adopts a point of view that the Chairman . . . has proposed." Could the other service or services in the minority "not have the privilege of going up before the Congress and opposing it?"[52] Kenney answered that it was up to Forrestal. "If he wants to tell us we can go up and state our position, that's all right, he can, or he can tell us we can't. That's within his authority."[53]

Gray replied "you think it is?" He may well have been surprised to hear

man" for assistance in revamping court-martial procedure. "I can say this with authority for I spent more than four years in the Army[,] and I took your course in evidence." Morgan replied that "no doubt distance lends enchantment to the view of the course on evidence." To a friend he wrote on November 29 that "I have some real hope for at least a few rather fundamental changes in court-martial procedure. Our Committee is excellent and much more liberal than you would expect representatives of the service to be." Ibid., November 29, 1948.

49 These comments are, again, drawn from an excerpt of the December 10 meeting that was found in Gordon Gray's papers.

50 *Transcript, Meeting* CUCMJ, 16–23, December 10, 1948, 17.

51 Ibid., 19–20; LP, *Minutes*, CUCMJ, Meeting, December 9–10, 1948, 3.

52 Ibid., 20.

53 Ibid., 20–21. "He can do it, and I will abide by what-ever he says. If he wants to tell me I cannot go up, . . . I will accept it. That settles it as far as I am concerned."

Morgan observe that "I understood it the way Gordon understands it." The chairman had assumed that an individual service secretary "would be free to oppose the legislation; if he is called up there and [Congress] wants to know what the attitude of the different services is, he tells them what his attitude is."[54] Morgan, of course, immediately realized that his own interpretation might well lead to congressional rejection of his cherished proposal. Whether he conferred with Forrestal is not clear, but on December 22, "Professor Morgan expressed his understanding that Mr. Forrestal had announced his decision that after [his?] approval of the UCMJ none of the armed services would be permitted to oppose or criticize it. He [Morgan] stated that this ban would also apply to himself."[55]

Within two weeks of these CUCMJ meetings, and after talking with Army Secretary Kenneth Royall, Gray contacted two well-known public figures in civilian-military administration, Henry Stimson and Robert Patterson. Stimson, secretary of war under Presidents William Howard Taft and Franklin D. Roosevelt, was living in retirement at the close of a career in public service that had lasted more than half a century. Robert Patterson served as secretary of war after Stimson, and held office during the period when the Elston Act was under consideration in the Congress. Both men were highly respected in the military establishment and well acquainted with James Forrestal. It may have been this fact that led Gray to seek them out.

From the outset, the Morgan committee had agreed that they would not make any provisions of the new code public until after the entire document had been approved by Forrestal and submitted to Congress. Nevertheless, on December 21, after he had set up a meeting with Stimson for December 29, Gray sent the former secretary a copy of Morgan's proposed judicial council, a description of its functions, and Gray's counterproposal. Knowing that his actions were in direct violation of committee policy, Gray asked both men to consider the enclosures classified, "as I am not at liberty to make public the deliberations or findings of the committee in advance of our report to Secretary Forrestal and his decision."[56]

[54] Ibid., 21–22.

[55] *Memorandum to the Judge Advocate General*, December 22, 1948, USCMAP. Since this memo circulated well before the draft of the UCMJ was submitted to Forrestal, it seems reasonable to conclude that the secretary meant his own approval. As will be seen, however, if Forrestal assumed that none of the military would oppose the code—he was mistaken. (As a matter of fact, Forrestal resigned as secretary of defense, and tragically committed suicide before Congress approved the UCMJ.) On the other hand, during legislative consideration, military opposition was much more muted than in previous enactments, and what changes Congress ultimately made in the draft cannot be directly attributed to military agitation or criticism.

[56] Gray to Stimson, December 21, 1948, *Gray Papers*. These documents and Gray's letters to Stimson and Patterson remained in Gray's private papers. After his death, those manuscripts dealing with his army career (which, it might be noted, extended from the rank of private to secretary of the army) were sent to the Army Military History Institute, Carlisle Barracks,

One can only speculate as to why Gray took this highly unusual action. There is no doubt that he strongly believed Morgan's judicial council to be inappropriate, if not illegal. He probably hoped that a few private words from such luminaries as Stimson and Patterson might influence Forrestal to a greater degree than if the current secretary of the army, Kenneth Royall, attempted to do so.

Gray informed Stimson and Patterson of his belief that Morgan's plan "would divest the Judge Advocate General of all power now exercised by him on appellate review. . . , [and] would divest the Secretary of the Army of his present power to determine the legality of court-martial convictions. . . . This plan, if adopted, would effect a radical change in Army appellate review procedure. . . . It would remove final authority from the Judge Advocate General and the Secretary of the Army[,] and lodge such authority in a body of civilians who would have no responsibility for the successful operation of the . . . Army."[57]

Unfortunately, because neither Gray's nor Forrestal's papers contain any response from either Stimson or Patterson, it is unclear what actions, if any, resulted from Gray's efforts. But Gray did more. Besides writing to Stimson and Patterson, the assistant secretary of the army also sent the same material to Army Chief of State Omar Bradley. Bradley responded with a short letter to Gray that remained classified until 1988. Acknowledging that mistakes in military justice had indeed taken place during World War II, Bradley expressed agreement with Gray's "objections and remarks." He was concerned that in attempting to correct these mistakes, "we will go so far as to make what I consider two great errors. First, the people responsible for results will have most of their powers to discipline and their authority over trials taken from them. Second, we will end up with a maximum emphasis on legality and minimum attention to justice. . . . Not only must we give the accused justice, but in so doing we must not go so far as to disregard the rights of his comrades and of his country."[58]

It is doubtful if Morgan ever knew about Gray's actions. There is no doubt, however, that Felix Larkin was unaware of what Gray had done, and he reacted with a sort of amused surprise when informed about it early in 1989. As will be seen, however, Gray's efforts came to naught. Within two weeks of the letters to Stimson and Patterson, Forrestal made his decisions concerning the disputed provisions of the new code. But even after this action, the army continued to resist.[59]

Carlisle, Pennsylvania. Holding a security clearance in 1988, this author was permitted to examine them and successfully secured their declassification.

[57] Ibid., "Comments on the Morgan Plan."

[58] Ibid., December 27, 1948.

[59] Toward the end of his life, Gray recalled his experiences as a member of Morgan's committee. Not surprisingly, of course, he made no mention of his "extracurricular" letter writing. In a 1966 Oral History Memoir, Gray remembered Morgan as "a very able man." He added that "I

The various "adjustments" to Morgan's original proposal for appellate review in response to service objections resulted from Forrestal's decision that a particular provision once agreed upon by the panel or decided upon by him would *not* be subject to further change. The inevitable concomitant of such a policy was a great deal of interaction among the Working Group and the various services, especially when a controversial article was at issue. Forrestal and Morgan understood very well that the new code had to have at least the silent acquiescence of the military if not outright approbation. This meant numerous compromises that would not have been acceptable, had the code been drafted by a committee of civilian lawyers. One example, of course, was the appellate procedure. Another concerned the problem of command influence.

As work on the code moved toward conclusion, Morgan found it impractical to remove the convening authority from the early stages of a military justice proceeding—even though he had been strongly advised to do so by a group of lawyers. On November 22, 1948, Morgan received a nine-page letter from a group of New York attorneys representing several lawyers' associations. They insisted that "command, which controls the prosecution, should not also appoint and control the court and defense counsel. That morale may be maintained without interference with the proper functions of command, requires the appointment of the court and defense counsel by an independent judicial arm of the service."[60]

Of course this argument was not new, and largely as a result of similar comments in 1946–1947, the Elston Act included an amended Article of War that dealt with "unlawfully influencing action of court." It provided that

> no authority appointing a . . . court-martial nor any other commanding officer shall censure, reprimand, or admonish such court, or any member thereof, with respect to the findings or sentence adjudged by the court, or with respect to any other exercise . . . of its or his judicial responsibility. No person subject to military law shall attempt to coerce or unlawfully influence the action of a court-martial or any military court or commission . . . in reaching the findings or sentence in any case, or the action of an appointing or reviewing or confirming authority with respect to his judicial acts.[61]

---

was a strong dissenter as to various points in that report, the only dissenter, I think, and I'm still of the opinion that I was right in my dissents. But in any event, the majority prevailed, and I guess it [is] working reasonably well." Gordon Gray, *Oral History Memoir*, Oral History Research Office, Columbia University, December 7, 1966, 29.

[60] MPVU, November 22, 1948, 4. This memorandum was signed by George Spiegelberg of the American Bar Association, Frederick van Pelt Bryan of the New York Bar Association, Richard Wels of the New York County Lawyers Association, and Arthur Farmer of the War Veterans' Bar Association. All these individuals had been active in military justice issues between 1946 and 1948.

[61] USCMAP, *Memorandum to Mr. Larkin*, November 22, 1948, 1. The memorandum was signed by Marine Corps Col. John Curry, navy representative to the Working Group.

From Morgan's viewpoint, it was necessary to include this provision in the new code, and thus make it applicable to all branches of the military. But the navy disagreed. Its representative informed Larkin that there was no objection to insuring that "the freedom of courts-martial to function must be preserved unhampered by improper influence from command or any other sources." This principle, however, "should not preclude a statement from responsible authority when a sentence is so palpably inadequate as to being a mockery of justice." Col. John Curry had an interesting alternative to the Elston Act excerpt. He proposed that any of the service secretaries "may in his discretion inform the members of any court martial in one of the respective services when in his opinion the sentence adjudged by such court is grossly inadequate for the offense found proved."[62]

From the service viewpoint, Curry's suggestion had some validity. It insured the opportunity for criticism of court action, especially when warranted—and from civilian hands. Thus, it would be difficult to claim that commanders were interfering with military justice matters. On the other hand, common sense indicated that the secretary would probably receive input for such criticism from the commander or some other officer. Moreover, Curry did not resolve the issue, whether comment about a current court-martial case was appropriate from *anyone* in the particular command except a duly constituted appeals tribunal.[63] His assumption that "it is surely unnecessary to prohibit attempts to unlawfully influence" utterly failed to confront the fact that such unlawful attempts did indeed occur.

Ultimately Morgan's committee retained and indeed expanded the language and scope of the Elston amendment, while rejecting Curry's proposed revision. Further, his panel—not satisfied with mere prohibition—voted to make violation of this article subject to punishment.[64] When it came time for Forrestal to resolve the several issues that had eluded settlement, this article was not among them. It may be assumed, therefore, that the CUCMJ handled it internally, probably through compromise and flexibility on other issues.[65]

[62] Ibid., 2. Curry would also have amended the provision against attempting to coerce or influence the outcome of a court-martial by adding "except as expressly provided by law or lawful regulation."

[63] Not content with Curry's comments to Larkin, the Navy JAG informed John Kenney that the wording of the Elston Act provision "might be construed to forbid comment on erroneous rulings of law, grossly inadequate sentences, and action in a proper case against the court or members thereof upon proof that a finding or a sentence was arbitrarily or capriciously arrived at. Restrictions such as these cannot be regarded as furthering the interests of justice." *Memorandum to Mr. Kenney*, December 8, 1948, 5.

[64] However, in the draft as submitted to Congress Morgan's committee added as a "commentary" and *not part* of the article, this sentence: "This article is not intended to preclude a reviewing authority from making fair comment on errors of the court in an opinion which is made in the course of review, or from returning a record for revision of errors, or from taking appropriate action when a member of a court has so misbehaved as to abandon his judicial responsibilities or duties."

[65] The existence of the sentence in the commentary quoted above in n. 64 may be a result of

Each service, as well as Morgan himself, had certain priorities concerning the UCMJ considered so essential that compromise could not be possible. It is not surprising that such issues had to be settled by Forrestal. What is remarkable, however, is that he had to deal with so few. Nevertheless, the secretary had to resolve at least three of them: (*a*) the appellate process, (*b*) the question of enlisted men serving on courts-martial, and (*c*) the role of the law officer. As 1948 drew to a close, and with the UCMJ almost ready for submission to Congress—Larkin undertook to bring Forrestal back into the picture to decide these points.

---

such a compromise. The section dealing with command influence remained as Morgan wished, but an explanatory comment was appended that apparently endorsed the navy position.

CHAPTER 9

Congress, the Code, and the Court, 1948–1949

BY DECEMBER 1948, the essential parts of the Uniform Code of Military Justice were in place. Although Forrestal had yet to meet with Morgan and the committee in order to settle several issues, Larkin was confident that the new code could be submitted to Congress early in 1949. On December 29, he phoned John Adams, a staff member of the Senate Armed Services Committee. Both congressional committees dealing with the armed services had been represented at the Working Group meetings on a regular basis since October. Larkin hoped that such continuous involvement would lessen any political maneuvering that might occur concerning introduction of the proposed statute. So much for Larkin's hopes.

FORRESTAL FORMULATES

In Washington politicians come and go, but politics remains a permanent institution. By November 1948, President Truman had been reelected, and control of Congress had switched back again to the Democrats. This meant that Senator Gurney who, with some justification, may well have considered himself a titular "Godfather" to the UCMJ would no longer be chairman of the Senate Armed Services Committee. Adams, however, told Larkin that "the code should have the color of being Gurney's bill." Further, he thought that "Gurney wants to introduce it in the Senate a few days before it is introduced in the House." Larkin, who had been working closely with Robert Smart from the House Committee, responded that "it would be very bad practice for us to deliver it to the Senate before it goes to the House." He proposed instead that copies be delivered simultaneously to the appropriate officials in both Houses.[1] Adams agreed, and in due course Larkin's plan was followed.

[1] LPPL, December 29, 1948. Adams also told Larkin that while Senate management of the bill depended upon the wishes of the incoming committee chairman, Millard Tydings, "there was absolutely no possibility of joint hearings." Early in January, Adams informed Larkin that he himself would be leaving the committee, and that since Gurney would not push for hearings, "it might be a good idea to let the House pass it first." Ibid., January 10, 1949. With what turned out to be prophetic understatement, Adams warned Larkin that the code "will not get the quick action within the committee that it would have if the [internal] changes had not occurred." More than one year would pass before the UCMJ cleared the Senate.

Both Larkin and Morgan assumed from the outset that the finished code would be guided through Congress under the aegis of the Armed Services Committees. It was for this reason that staff members from these panels had sat in on Working Group sessions. Although Morgan believed that the "centerpiece" of the entire code would be the new judicial council, in reality this provision was only one part of a lengthy compilation of statutes dealing with military law. However, even before the UCMJ had been formally submitted, Adams further informed Larkin that Sen. Patrick McCarran, chairman of the Senate Judiciary Committee, was interested in holding hearings on the proposed UCMJ. He advised Larkin to discuss the matter with Millard Tydings the incoming chair of the Senate Armed Services Committee.[2]

Larkin did so, and although McCarran strongly pushed for his committee's jurisdiction—as will be seen—he lost. Having conceived of the code in nonpartisan terms, Larkin was anxious to get it through Congress as quickly as possible. Internal Senate bickering over committee assignment—with the UCMJ as a potential hostage—was not desirable. Furthermore, he had kept the Armed Services Committees informed on a continuing basis as the code was drafted. From Larkin's point of view, in terms of overall planning it made good sense to keep the proposed statute within their purview. On the other hand, he probably did not appreciate the implications of such a step in terms of later confirming judges for the new council. Whatever strengths the Congressional Armed Services Committees may have, a means for careful and thorough evaluation of judicial candidates has not been one of them. As will be seen in the second volume of this study, this fact would have important implications for the history of the United States Court of Military Appeals.

By early 1949, word was circulating in Washington that the Morgan Committee was almost finished with its work. Thus, for example, the *Washington Post* noted that "several necessary reforms [in military justice] are still to be made. One is a uniform code of military justice . . . something now in preparation by a committee appointed by Secretary Forrestal. A second is the strengthening of the judicial review process. . . . It ought to be possible, without throwing the burden of military cases into regular civilian courts to establish some sort of similar civilian body to supplant the military as a final court of appeals."[3]

Although the specifics of what Morgan's committee had come up with were still confidential, late in January members of the American Bar Association Special Committee on Military Justice tried (in vain) to get Larkin to release a copy of the new code in time for use during the forthcoming ABA convention. Unable to see what the Morgan Committee had prepared, the ABA convention voted that "this Association recommends legislation establishing an advisory

[2] LPPL, January 25, 1949.

[3] *Washington Post*, January 3, 1949, 6.

council in the office of the Secretary of Defense, consisting of nine civilians . . . and three service members representing the legal offices of the three services.'' Appointed by the president, the civilian members would serve without salary, though entitled to some sort of per diem allowance. The council would be required to report annually to the Congress.[4] Among the ABA members signing the report was Cornell Law Professor Arthur John Keeffe. Indeed the resolution just quoted has a striking resemblance to one of the recommendations made in the 1947 analysis on Navy Justice drafted by Keeffe's committee.[5]

On January 5, 1949, Larkin informed Forrestal about the remaining points of difference between Morgan and his own committee. In no instance, he observed, ''is Morgan in single dissent. He is either on the side of the majority in the three-to-one votes, or is supported by one of the Services on the split vote.'' This fact was very important, because Larkin knew that ''inasmuch as you indicated that you plan to look to Professor Morgan for guidance in resolving the differences, we have gone forward and are drafting the disputed provisions based on the side taken by [him.]''[6]

Larkin further reported to the secretary that he had already discussed the new code in detail with the staff of the Budget Bureau, ''in an effort to prevent delay in clearing the bill.'' According to him, ''they are extremely enthusiastic about [it, and] think it is one of the best examples of unification to date, and a progressive and modern penal law[,]'' as well. The Bureau objected, however, ''to the proposal that the civilians on the Judicial Council be appointed by the three [under] Secretaries. They believe that the appointment should be by the President. In addition . . . , all regulations to be promulgated by the three Secretaries should be subject to the approval of the Secretary of Defense.''[7]

[4] Larkin informed Richard Wels, one of the New York attorneys calling for reforms in military justice, that he regretted being unable to send a copy of the UCMJ draft, all the more ''because I knew there were a number of things in it which they would support.'' LPPL, January 24, 1949.

[5] LP, American Bar Association, *Report of the Special Committee on Military Justice*, January 29, 1949, 4–5. Considering how much stronger Morgan's proposed judicial council appeared to be than this advisory panel endorsed by the ABA, the reaction of lawyers like Keeffe, George Spiegelberg, and Richard Wels is of some interest. See below.

[6] LP, January 5, 1949. Had Morgan ever stood isolated three to one, with all the services against him concerning a disputed section of the code, it is uncertain what action Forrestal might have taken. I believe that Morgan was fully cognizant of this fact, and it probably contributed to the skillful merging of adjustment and compromise by which he insured that such a situation never arose.

[7] Ibid., 2–3. The insistence by officials of the Budget Bureau on these changes is yet another example of the tension between the old civilian secretaries of the services, and the new civilian secretary of defense—a tension reflected in Larkin's report and about which Forrestal was only too well aware—that the three services had yet to accept *fully* the conclusion that in terms of initiating policy, by 1949 they were all subordinate to the secretary of defense. In terms of the new appellate procedures, of the three services Gordon Gray and the army remained least willing

Turning to Morgan's plan for appellate review, Larkin reminded Forrestal that the army had a "complex" system with separate reviews by (*a*) the convening authority, (*b*) the judge advocate general, (*c*) a Board of Review, and (*d*) a Judicial Council as set forth in the Elston Act. This council, however, was in reality a "further agency of review which would be staffed by three General Officers," within the JAG department. The navy procedure was "less complicated than the Army . . . , but very much more informal, with the ultimate authority for decision, both as to law and fact, residing in the Secretary of the Navy." Neither the army nor the navy "likes each other's system," and it was the inability to reach a compromise which had led to Morgan's "bombshell."

In terms of procedure, Morgan's plan would have made the various services' lower levels of review virtually identical. He eliminated the army judicial council of three officers, and proposed instead a "Judicial Council in the National Military Establishment, which will act as a Supreme Court *on law only* for the three services."[8] Gray "dissents from the whole plan, although in essence the dissent centers around the single Judicial Council staffed by civilians." Along with his report to Forrestal, Larkin also included a copy of Gray's earlier memorandum to the committee.

On January 7, Forrestal and his key advisors (including Leva and Larkin) met with Morgan and his committee. The secretary heard all the dissents on the disputed articles, and indicated that he would make a final determination shortly. In the meantime another member of Forrestal's staff wrote to Leva that Morgan's judicial council would be an important element in establishing a *uniform* code. Robert Wood observed that without such a body, under the new law "the possibility of varying interpretations by the three [services] is enhanced. With it, [they] have an excellent means of passing upstairs problems which, by attempting to resolve themselves, might well present odious comparisons with similar decisions by their sister services and the consequent unfavorable public reaction."[9]

Morgan's committee next convened on January 14–15, 1949. Forrestal had already been informed by Larkin concerning the Budget Office insistence that appointments to the Judicial Council be made by the president, rather than the three service secretaries. It is not clear if Larkin told his committee about this

to accept the resulting implications of this fact. And, as will be seen, even though Forrestal ruled against him, Gray continued to resist.

[8] It is easy to see why Larkin emphasized this point. The Boards of Review, which would have authority to consider matters of fact *and* law, were to be appointed by the three service JAGS, to serve at their pleasure for terms they would determine. It was this fact, plus Morgan's additional willingness to see the three secretaries name the members of his council that probably led Zuckert and Kenney to support the plan as amended.

[9] LP, January 8, 1949; emphasis in original. Wood added that "Mr. Gray's arguments are, undoubtedly, based on sincere convictions[,] but I feel they do not hold water when looked at from the standpoint of the overall good of the National Military Establishment."

change. At the January 14 meeting, however, Gray asked both Kenney and Zuckert if they would still approve the appellate article "if the membership of the [council] is to be appointed by [some]body other than the Secretaries of the three Armed Forces."[10] Kenney responded that he "would see no great objection to it if it is appointed by the Commander-in-Chief." Whether he knew more than he let on, or was only a perceptive prophet, Gray added "so, that if [the new code] might fall somewhere in the Bureau of the Budget . . . this particular provision would be changed so that the Secretaries of the Departments would have no control of the appointment of the judicial council."[11]

Again, Kenney declined to support his army colleague. On the contrary, he told Gray that "I don't think that is a fair characterization."[12] Gray replied, "So, that you would be satisfied even though a Secretary . . . could not bring about the removal of the members of the judicial council?" Kenney reiterated his assumption that "the Secretaries would always have the right to go to the President . . . to ask for removal." Gray had better luck with Zuckert who insisted that "I would not favor a system where that power [of appointment] was outside of the Secretaries of the Departments."[13]

For his part, Gray—who had already consulted Stimson and Patterson—now asked Larkin to give him "the names of those who work under your direction (other than military people) on research, drafting and editing for the common code of military justice." In particular, Gray wanted to know "the length of time they have actually practiced law, with particular reference to any experience in the State or Federal criminal courts," and "military experience, if any, including any court-martial experience." He assured Larkin that "this information is not for publication and I should be glad to explain why I would like to have it, if you are interested to know." Larkin furnished the requested data on February 2, more than two weeks after Forrestal had decided the disputed articles. He told Gray that he would very much like to know why it was desired. Unfortunately, no further interchange between them

[10] CUCMJ, January 14, 1949, 8. The incomplete excerpt from a transcript of this meeting was found in Gray's papers at the U.S. Army Military History Institute, *Chronologies, '49*. The relevant sentence reads ". . . is to be appointed by nobody other than the Secretaries." I have assumed that this is an error on the part of the stenographer. Comments made a few minutes later indicate that Gray was very concerned about the possibility (as it turned out, the actuality) that this policy would be changed.

[11] Ibid.

[12] Ibid., 8–9. Kenney added that "you do have certain controls even though it is to be appointed by the President." Kenney believed that appointments to the council would be at a high level. On the other hand, if—as Gray seemed to assume—they "would be appointed by the Post-Master general or somebody else without regard to the Secretaries of the Departments, I would agree with you."

[13] Ibid., 10. Zuckert apparently believed that the appellate article as submitted to Forrestal would either be approved or rejected without changes. He appears not to have realized the implications of Gray's comments and, as will be seen, was unhappy with the decision to take the appointing authority away from the secretaries.

on this subject has been located. Given that, as Gray put it, "I disagree with a few of the ultimate decisions and feel personally very keenly about them," it may be that he planned to use the statistics somehow to justify his opposition.[14]

On January 17, 1949, Forrestal informed Morgan that his positions on the three essential areas of dispute are "accepted and should be incorporated into the Code."[15] With that decision reached, all that remained were some corrections and minor clarifications. The provisions of the UCMJ were grouped into coherent sections, such as those dealing with punitive articles, or trial procedures, or review of courts-martial. And, another change was incorporated into article 67, dealing with Morgan's judicial council. A new sentence was added to the end of the article. It stated that "The Judicial Council and The Judge Advocates General of the armed forces shall meet annually to make a comprehensive survey of the operation of this Code and report to the Secretary of Defense and the Secretaries of the Departments any recommendations relating to uniformity of sentence policies, amendments to this Code, and any other matters deemed appropriate."[16]

Larkin then prepared a summary of the code's provisions for submission to Forrestal along with the text of the entire document. He listed eight provisions which were "designed to prevent interference with the due administration of justice."

1. The convening authority could not refer charges for trial until "they are found legally sufficient" by the staff JAG.

2. The staff JAG could communicate directly with the Judge Advocate General without having to go through the commander.

3. All counsel at general courts-martial had to be lawyers and certified by the JAG "as qualified to perform their legal duties."

4. The law officer was to be "a competent lawyer[,]" who would rule on most legal questions.[17]

[14] LP, January 15, February 2, 1949. Gray may have been looking for evidence of inexperience on the part of Larkin's staff as a way of discrediting some key provisions they had helped draft, especially the final form of Morgan's judicial council. In his reply to Gray, Larkin stated that "as you know, although these men had no part in making decisions, they were largely responsible for compiling the excellent Comparative Study."

[15] *Forrestal Papers*, January 17, 1949. It is interesting that in approving Morgan's view of each article, Forrestal listed the names of the other under secretaries who agreed with him. See above, n. 6.

[16] UCMJ, *Text, References and Commentary* (1949), 96–97. This sentence appears to have been an afterthought. It set up the members of the council (or court, as it would soon be called) and the three JAGs as equals on an advisory committee. However, as will be seen in the second volume of this study, the relationship between the court and the JAGs by its very nature is sometimes an adversarial one. In retrospect, this provision has been less than significant in the court's history. Nevertheless, provision for an expanded committee remains in the latest version of the UCMJ.

[17] The exceptions were a motion for a directed verdict, and a ruling on the issue of the accused's

5. The convening authority could not act on a finding or sentence "without first obtaining the advice of his staff judge advocate or legal officer."

6. The Boards of Review were to be established in the JAG office, and thus "removed from the convening authority," to be composed of lawyers empowered to review a trial record for errors in both law and fact.

7. A civilian Judicial Council would pass finally on all questions of law.

8. Defendants appearing before either the Board of Review or the Judicial Council must be represented by qualified lawyers.

Finally, Larkin noted that "censure by a commanding officer of a court martial or any member or officer thereof because of any judicial action of the court or any member or officer is forbidden[,] and any attempt improperly to influence official action in any aspect of a trial or its review is prohibited."[18]

Larkin also included in his summary mention of at least three areas where command function remained undisturbed: (*a*) commanding officers refer the charges in courts-martial and convene them; (*b*) they appoint the members of such courts, including the law officer and counsel for the trial; and (*c*) they retain full power to set aside findings of guilty and to modify or change the sentence. On the other hand, they could neither interfere with a not guilty verdict, nor increase the severity of a sentence duly imposed.[19]

Historical hindsight can blind as well as illumine, and what Larkin saw as major procedural innovations in the new code should not be minimized—especially in the light of developments in military justice since 1951, including several important changes in the UCMJ. Considering what had been in place before, Morgan's committee broke new ground. Furthermore, Larkin had presided over a project that produced the new code in a remarkably short period of time. The Working Group first met on July 9, 1948, and Morgan's own committee did not convene until August 18. By the end of December, most of

---

sanity. Moreover, one of the controversial issues just decided by Forrestal left the law officer much like a judge in a civilian criminal case.

[18] Inexplicably, Larkin failed to include in his summary the fact that the new code not only forbade such conduct, but made it punishable as well. See section 2 of article 98 of the draft. This provision has remained in the UCMJ down to the present day, but this author has been unable to locate *any* case wherein the United States Court of Military Appeals has dealt with any punishments levied upon a commander under this section. As will be seen in the second volume of this study, the court has repeatedly denounced "command influence," but has limited its role to mitigating the abuse, rather than moving against the alleged perpetrator. Moreover, diligent research has turned up only one instance where military authorities have prosecuted a commander under article 98. In his exhaustive treatise on military justice, Homer Moyer, Jr., cites the case of a Marine Corps officer convicted in 1953 under article 98. He was sentenced to forfeit $350 a month for one year, as well as an unfavorable change of position on the service seniority list. Moyer notes that the assistant secretary of the navy later reduced the fine. Concerning article 98 he concludes that "as a sanction against unlawful influence, it is a dead letter." H. Moyer, Jr., *Justice and the Military* (1972), 779–80.

[19] LP, *Summary of UCMJ*, draft of January 26, 1949.

the 140 articles had been completed, and Larkin had already discussed the UCMJ draft with the office of the Bureau of the Budget. Even Gordon Gray who, as will be seen, still smarted from Forrestal's rejection of his proposal concerning appellate procedure could write that "a monumental job had been done."[20]

GRAY GRUMBLES

Prior to the formal submission of the UCMJ to Congress, protocol required Morgan's committee first to present it to Forrestal. Larkin assumed that such a step would be pro forma, and prepared to draft a very short letter of transmittal. In it, however, he wanted to mention the consensus that had been attained in so much of the drafting process. Here, once again, Gordon Gray raised objections. The incident well demonstrated that his disagreement with Morgan did not end with Forrestal's decision. Indeed, Gray's persistence reminds this writer of Ansell's determination to persevere in his cause even after Baker thought the issue had been finally resolved in Crowder's favor in 1918–1919.

On January 31, in his absence, Gray's secretary informed Larkin that "mention should be made in the letter of transmittal to Forrestal that all the decisions on the Code were not unanimous." Later that afternoon, she further told Larkin that "she is sure that he will not sign the redraft of the proposed letter of transmittal. . . . She said Gray wants the specific item in dispute stated, or he wants each member of the Committee to write a separate letter." As if to make the point even clearer, Zuckert sent Larkin a letter supporting Gray's position. This prompted him to phone Zuckert.[21] That the issue obviously troubled Larkin is indicated by the care with which he summarized the conversation.

> I told Zuckert I hoped that he and Gray don't think that I was merely trying to do something the Committee did not desire. . . . I told him I didn't want anyone to think I was pushing my weight around because I have tried all the way through this project to do whatever the Committee wanted. . . . Zuckert said Gray just thought it was pretty cute to make the code appear to be approved unanimously. I pointed out that I could see little purpose in pointing out to Forrestal . . . something he already knows, and Zuckert said that was true except that a copy of the Committee's letter of transmittal to Forrestal might accompany Forrestal's [submission] to Congress[,] and he and Gray wanted to be protected in case that happened.

[20] LP, January 15, 1949.
[21] LPPL, January 31, 1949.

Later that afternoon, Larkin also phoned John Kenney who "said he was not in favor of spelling these things out."[22]

Apparently on January 30, Gray had dictated a letter to Larkin essentially stating his position as noted above. In his proposed draft, Larkin had written that the UCMJ would apply to all the services. "This desirable result has been possible only by the general cooperation of the three Services and the members of the Committee." Gray probably preferred that the three undersecretaries "should each write separate letters stating the extent of their concurrence." As Larkin had drafted it, Gray believed that "the letter is definitely misleading."[23]

Anxious to resolve the issue, if only so that Forrestal could at last officially receive the UCMJ, Larkin redrafted his letter of transmittal. He retained the sentence just quoted, but added two sentences at the end: "The provisions of the proposed Code were unanimously adopted by members of the Committee with the exception of the provisions submitted to you on January 7, 1949. These provisions, on which the members . . . were divided, have been drafted in accordance with your decisions."[24] Back in Cambridge, Morgan's reaction to the controversy over what probably appeared to him as an extremely simple matter, can be gauged from his phone conversation with Larkin on February 1. Morgan "said he is not willing to spell out the points which were not unanimous. . . . If the members of the Committee do not approve the second draft of the letter, Morgan said he will send the first letter and they can write Forrestal anything they please."[25]

Larkin drafted a letter to Gray on February 2, and cited the comment that the first draft "was definitely misleading." He regretted "that you think any such interpretation is possible. I had no intention of making it misleading, and since it is addressed to Secretary Forrestal, it never entered my thoughts that he was being misled."[26] But Larkin never sent this response to Gray, probably because he received a phone call from the assistant secretary that same morning.

> Gray said he wants the areas of disagreement named, not spelled out. He does not want it to appear that they were unanimously adopted[,] and specifically wants the Congress to know it. He said his feeling in the matter stops at the point where the Committee transmits the bill to Forrestal. After that, he plans to do nothing. He

[22] Ibid., 2–3.

[23] *Gray Papers*, January 30, 1949.

[24] LP, January 31, 1949.

[25] LPPL, February 1, 1949. In his covering letter to the other committee members, Larkin stated rather diplomatically that "I have spoken with Professor Morgan, who does not object." He was, however, more candid with Kenney, to whom he summarized Morgan's "take it or leave it" position. Kenney had no difficulty with Larkin's first draft. But Larkin responded that "there is nothing more I can do until the members of the Committee instruct me what to do." Ibid., 2.

[26] LP, February 2, 1949.

said he is sure that Kenney and Morgan want it to appear that the decisions were unanimous. I asked him if what he wanted is the points named and it stated what position each Department took on them, and he said that was correct. . . . I told him Morgan will sign the redraft of the letter, but is not willing to go further than that. . . . Gray said it was all right with him if Morgan wanted to send Forrestal a letter without his (Gray's) signature, but he will not approve a letter that does not state that the decisions were not unanimous. I told Gray I would like to get out from the middle on the matter[,] and suggested that the members of the Committee prepare language on which they agree. Gray said he would draft it.''[27]

One day later, Gray informed Larkin that he and Kenney could not agree about the letter of transmittal. Gray was ''drafting an amendment . . . which he will send me for submission to the committee. He says it will say what I drafted, but will add a dissent from the appellate review system and from the functions of the law officer, with Zuckert (Air Force) dissenting on only the latter. Gray said Kenney does not care to put in his dissent.''[28]

The question arises why Gray was so antisemantic on what appears to be such a minor question of wording. In part, the answer may rest in the fact that the issue of the appellate process was very important to Gray—so important that he had willingly violated his agreement concerning confidentiality of committee decisions. Even more vital from his viewpoint was the extent of Forrestal's authority over his three secretaries. In early 1949, the National Military Establishment (not yet named the defense department) was more a confederation than a unified agency. The three services ''were still largely autonomous organizations with nearly full control over their internal affairs.'' Moreover, powers not specifically ''conferred upon the Secretary of Defense became part of the authority [belonging to] each respective departmental secretary.'' Finally, any of these three individuals could appeal the secretary's decision on a matter relevant to his service directly to either the president or the Bureau of the Budget.[29] Gray's insistence that the letter of transmittal be accurate may well have been a part of positioning in order for his chief, Kenneth Royall, to have grounds for such an appeal.

Larkin received Gray's ''amendment,'' apparently drafted on February 3. He had added a sentence that ''these areas of disagreement and the members of the Committee involved in the dissents are referred to in an attached paper.'' There then followed a statement that Gray ''records a dissent to the appellate system as provided in the proposed articles, particularly with reference to the Judicial Council.'' Both Gray and Zuckert ''record dissents from the proposed article which would prohibit the law member from participating as a full mem-

[27] LPPL, February 2, 1949, 1–2.

[28] Ibid., February 3, 1949.

[29] Steven L. Rearden, *The Formative Years, 1947–1950*; (volume 1 in *The History of the Office of the Secretary of Defense*) (1984), 25.

ber of a general court.'' Finally, Kenney changed his mind and decided to record his dissent ''to the proposed article which would provide enlisted men on general and special courts-martial.''[30]

Larkin and Morgan consulted concerning Gray's ''revisions'' on February 4. The Harvard law professor told Larkin that ''he didn't like it and thought it highly improper[,] and thinks Gray is being unreasonable.'' Larkin may have commented to Morgan about the realities concerning relations between Forrestal and the three services, because Morgan ''did agree to do it that way if Gray insists. He said he would rather have it that way than to have Gray not sign the letter.''[31] So Larkin sent Gray's draft to the other members of the committee. ''I have spoken with Professor Morgan about it,'' Larkin wrote, ''and, although he feels that this kind of letter is unnecessary and unwise, he is willing to sign it in the interest of completing the job.''[32] With probable relief, on February 7 Larkin noted that he visited the three undersecretaries ''to secure their signatures on the letter of transmittal to Forrestal.''[33]

The next day, Larkin personally delivered copies of the code to the appropriate congressional leaders, along with a covering letter signed by Forrestal but drafted by Larkin. Forrestal concluded ''his'' letter by emphasizing that ''in my opinion, the proposed bill is well-designed to protect the rights of those subject to it, will increase public confidence in military justice, and will not impair the performance of military functions. Accordingly, I strongly urge its passage by Congress.''[34] Thus, at the end of the drafting process Forrestal again mentioned the same three points he had raised in his initial instructions to Morgan's committee during the summer of 1948.

[30] LP, February 3, 1949. In this draft, Gray also included a sentence that ''since your [Forrestal's] decisions were communicated to the members of the Committee, there remains only three areas of disagreement in which any members of the Committee continue to wish to record dissents.'' Apparently, Zuckert was uncomfortable with this sentence, believing that it ''sounds like a dissent to Forrestal's decisions.'' His point made good sense. Gray was unhappy not with Forrestal's decision as much as with his colleagues on the Committee for agreeing to the judicial council proposal in the first place. Zuckert talked with Gray, and informed Larkin on February 7 that he ''agrees to cut the sentence in question.'' LPPL, February 7, 1949.

[31] LPPL, February 4, 1949. Larkin also told Morgan that in spite of the difficulties with the letter to Forrestal, all the services had cleared the final draft of the UCMJ. He hoped to submit the bill to Congress during the week of February 7. Morgan ''asked me to send a copy of the bill to Ansell as soon as possible.''

[32] LP, February 4, 1949. The fact that Morgan did not insist on Larkin's original letter may be taken as further evidence of his awareness that the relationship between the secretary of defense and the under secretaries of the three services had not yet clarified. In view of the still tenuous nature of this relationship, one can readily understand why neither Larkin nor Leva felt it appropriate simply to order the under secretaries to sign the letter and be done with it.

[33] LPPL, February 7, 1949. On the same day, Larkin wrote to Frank Pace, Jr., Director, Bureau of the Budget. He enclosed several copies of the UCMJ as the final step prior to formal submission of the draft to Congress. Larkin told Pace that ''confirming my recent conversation with you . . . I have had the Code amended as to reflect your views.'' LP, February 7, 1949.

[34] LP, February 8, 1949.

Larkin also held a press conference announcing the UCMJ. He informed a member of Zuckert's air force staff that at the forthcoming Senate Armed Services Committee meeting on the new proposal, "the only NME [national military establishment] representative would be me."[35] He sent copies of the code to several attorneys, and forwarded one to Samuel Ansell, still practicing law in Washington, with the comment that Morgan "asked me to take particular care to see that you received a copy."[36] He also officially informed Morgan and his committee about a new change in the article dealing with the Judicial Council.

He revealed what Forrestal had resolved—namely, that the Bureau of the Budget had wanted appointing authority for the new council be vested in the president, and *not* in the three service secretaries, as had been decided by the committee. Larkin explained that Pace and Forrestal had discussed the matter, and the secretary "thereafter instructed me . . . to change the text of Article 6[7] to provide that civilian members of the Judicial Council be appointed by the President. I followed Mr. Forrestal's instructions and as a result," the Bureau of the Budget cleared the bill—stating that it was "in accord with the President's program."[37]

Upon receiving word of this change, John Kenney called Larkin. "[H]e feels that Forrestal should have taken up the changes with the Committee. In view of the situation, he asked me to tell Forrestal that he does not now feel that he is bound by the bill." Larkin replied that after consulting with Pace, Forrestal had decided on his own authority to make the requested change.[38] Further, he sent a memorandum to the secretary explaining the background of the issue.

Morgan had proposed a civilian judicial council, "and it was his thought that the members should be appointed by the President for life." Kenney and Zuckert "supported the whole idea and thought it was sound, but insisted that the appointments be by the three Secretaries." Gray objected to the whole idea, but stated that if it was adopted, logic indicated presidential appointments. "In the interest of maximum unity, Professor Morgan compromised his idea of appointment by the President," and the result was a 3–1 vote in favor of his idea as amended. Realizing that Kenney's irritation though unfor-

[35] LPPL, February 8, 1949, 2.

[36] LP, February 8, 1949. As will be seen shortly, Ansell had not lost his interest in military justice. However, based upon examination of Morgan's papers at Vanderbilt and Harvard Law Schools, this author was unable to determine whether Morgan had any contact at all with Ansell during the period when the committee drafted the code.

[37] Ibid. Given the recent episode concerning the letter of transmittal to Forrestal, the defensive tone of Larkin's statement is understandable, as was his timing. Even Gray, surely the most vociferous and persistent critic of the proposed appellate procedure conceded that once the code had been given to the Congress, the role of the committee was ended. Nevertheless, Forrestal's action did not go unchallenged.

[38] LPPL, February 9, 1949.

tunate was also unimportant (Kenney *had already accepted* the idea of the Judicial Council), Larkin merely urged that Forrestal should "send Professor Morgan and the members of the Committee thank-you notes at this time, despite the few dissents. They all worked as a team and achieved maximum unity."[39]

To Morgan, Forrestal (through Larkin) acknowledged "your great contribution." Your "leadership and your personal contributions to the subject are, in large measure, responsible for the accomplishments of the Committee." To the three undersecretaries (each addressed by first name), Forrestal "was very gratified by the amount of agreement achieved by the Committee, and I attribute it to the generous cooperation of your fellow members and yourself." Such "teamwork could have been motivated only by a sincere desire to foster the interests of the National Military Establishment."[40]

Morgan responded with a letter to Forrestal. "I am grateful to you," he wrote, "for giving me the opportunity to contribute to a project which I had not dared to hope would receive official support in my life-time." Moreover, the reason why the committee had successfully completed its work "is to be found primarily in the exceptionally thorough and efficient work of Mr. Felix E. Larkin." Finally, Morgan noted of his three service colleagues that they were "men of fine personality, great ability and tact with the capacity to see and appreciate conflicting points of view."[41]

Whether Morgan would have been as effusive had he known about Gray's efforts to torpedo the new appellate procedure remains a matter for conjecture. On the same day he wrote to Forrestal, Morgan also drafted letters to his three associates, each note revealing something of the way Morgan had worked with them. To Gray he implied that had Gray not been a product of Yale Law School, things might have been different. "I am sorry that I was unable to persuade you of the merits of the proposed appellate system; but I think I appreciate your point of view, even though I attribute it, not to heredity, but to unfortunate environment."[42] To Zuckert, "even though you are a dyed-in-

[39] LP, February 9, 1949. Larkin drafted the notes for Forrestal, enclosed them with his memorandum, and recommended that the secretary sign them—as indeed he did. The confident way in which Larkin dealt with Kenney's "gripe" stands in sharp contrast to the way he had resolved the controversy over the first letter of transmittal. On the other hand, Larkin noted that according to one of Kenney's aides, Kenney "was sore as Hell at me. . . . I couldn't see why . . . because the changes in the Code were not made on my authority." LPPL, February 2, 1949, 2.

[40] LP, February 9, 1949. Forrestal also wrote a note to Larkin. "You have done an outstanding job in connection with this bill, and I want you to know how greatly I appreciate the hard work, good judgment, and legal ability that have gone into the work of Professor Morgan's committee and the much more detailed and arduous labor of the working committee you have headed."

[41] MPVU, February 17, 1949.

[42] Ibid. In due course, Gray responded that "I think I know what you mean. However, for the record at least[,] let me suggest that you should not be so contemptuous of the Yale Law School." Ibid., February 22, 1949.

the-wool Yale man, I have to thank you for the splendid support which you gave my views in a number of important features . . . as well as for your arguments which made me change my mind on a number of others.''[43] To Kenney, he ''reported'' that ''rumor hath it that you and I were in agreement on so many debatable points regarding the proposed code because you had been corrupted in your youth by my course in Procedure.''[44]

MIXED REACTIONS

The official press release heralding the submission of the UCMJ to Congress was distributed to the wire services on February 8, 1949, directly after the statute had been presented to Congress. Reaction from the various lawyers' groups was prompt. George Spiegelberg, chairman of the ABA military justice committee, complained that the ''proposed Forrestal Code, so far as I can see, hasn't changed command control a bit. We strongly advocated the necessity of checking the influence of command over courts-martial[,] and the new proposed code is totally lacking in this.'' From the New York County Lawyers Association, Richard Wels was even more blunt. The new proposal was ''a pretty facade[, one that] is good as far as it goes, but it doesn't go far enough. . . . It doesn't touch the jugular vein where most of the military injustices are hidden.''[45]

In an editorial entitled ''Courts-martial Reform,'' the *New York Times* expanded on Wels's objection. The new code ''includes many improvements. . . . [But] it still does not include the one basic reform urged by every civilian group that the armed services have appointed to advise them—namely, separation of courts-martial from command.'' The editorial writer further noted one ''important reform'' in the code, the judicial council, but added ''there is a question whether, in time of war, it might be overwhelmed with cases.'' Other changes, ''are largely those already adopted.'' The editorial concluded that since ''equal justice under law is so fundamental an American principle[,] . . . no compromise here should be accepted by Congress.''[46]

Both Larkin and Morgan had already talked at some length with Spiegelberg and Wels about the new code, and apparently were unprepared for Wels's dismissal of so much hard work as ''a petty facade.'' Morgan informed Spiegelberg that ''Mr. Larkin and I did our utmost to meet your recommendations;

[43] Ibid., February 17, 1949. Zuckert replied that ''there is not the slightest doubt that the results could not have been obtained without the extraordinary mixture of leadership and flexibility you gave us.'' Ibid., February 24, 1949.

[44] MPVU, February 17, 1949. Kenney received a Harvard Law degree in 1929. Morgan had taught there since 1925.

[45] *New York Times*, February 10, 1949.

[46] Ibid.

and we were both greatly disappointed at the blast which was directed against the Code on its first release.''[47] Morgan had also received a copy of the ABA resolutions, and at Forrestal's request responded to them. His letter is of interest because it shows Morgan's realization that a military commander could not be totally isolated from the operation of military justice.

The ABA had long insisted that the JAGs and *not* the commanders should have the exclusive right to appoint members of courts-martial. Morgan wrote to the ABA secretary that ''it would be entirely impractical to have such appointments made by the [JAG] without the closest cooperation with the commanding officers concerned. This would necessarily mean that the function would be delegated to the local [JAG] representative. . . . It is unthinkable that he could be permitted to dictate to the commanding officer the assignment of duties of officers'' under his authority. Morgan's unequivocal position appears to be very different from what he held in 1919, when he had been a staunch supporter of Ansell. Certainly he had matured in years and experience. But perhaps the most telling reason for the change is apparent from his next sentence. ''This view of the [Committee] members . . . was founded in large part on informed opinions expressed by representatives of the Judge Advocate General's Departments of the several services.''[48]

Morgan and Larkin realized that representatives from the various lawyer associations would make their views known to Congress in due time.[49] But there were other dissenters as well. Another critic, Maj. Paul Davis of the Army JAG Department, objected to the policy whereby the law officer would not be a voting member of the court-martial. This change, he noted, meant that ''the accused would lose the important safeguard of having an informed lawyer present at all times during the deliberations and voting of the court in closed sessions.''[50] Aware of the possible importance of public statements

[47] MPVU, March 1, 1949. ''I cannot believe,'' Morgan added, ''that Mr. Wels gave it any thorough examination before condemning it as a 'petty facade.' ''

[48] MPVU, March 1, 1949, 1–2. In their final form, legislative enactments often tend to be an intriguing amalgam of desired principles that become softened in a context of compromise. Morgan may well have believed that he could gain support for an independent civilian appellate court only if he was ''flexible'' concerning command control. Such a choice may have disturbed Wels and the *New York Times*. Apparently it did not trouble the Harvard law professor.

[49] Had they but known, Gordon Gray was also thinking about testifying before Congress. He wrote to Henry Stimson on February 23, 1949, that ''I regret to say, not for publication of course, that I lost the battle on the two main points I was interested in, the appellate system and the function of the law member. . . . I have no doubt that hearings will soon begin. Officially, of course, I am bound by the National Military Establishment's position. Whether I shall be called upon to express my personal views, I have no idea.'' *Gray Papers*, ibid., February 23, 1949. As far as I have been able to ascertain, Gray apparently did not testify—either on his own behalf or that of the army—concerning the UCMJ.

[50] Newspaper clipping, *Washington Star*, February 22, 1949, in USCMAP. Apparently, Davis did not deem it necessary to add that what he criticized in the new code was common practice in civilian criminal jury trials. From his point of view, in this respect the Uniform Code represented

such as this, even as Congress prepared to begin the process of consideration, Larkin assigned one of his staff to draft a reply.[51]

In the meantime, a nationally televised debate on military justice aired on February 14, 1949. The specific issue "on trial" was command influence. Should military lawyers and judges "be independent of the officer who is responsible for bringing the charges?" Apparently organized with the support of the various lawyer groups interested in military justice, and deliberately timed to air just before Congress took up the new code—the moderator or presiding "judge" was none other than Samuel Ansell.[52] Among the participants as "plaintiffs" were George Spiegelberg of the ABA, and Ernest Gibson, a former JAG officer and at this time governor of the state of Vermont.[53] Col. Frederick B. Wiener, a graduate of Harvard Law School and also a former member of the JAG Corps, represented the traditional military viewpoint.[54]

Spiegelberg again urged that the JAG should appoint members of a military court. Wiener responded by insisting that the proposal to separate military courts from military command was "utterly impractical because it fails to take into account the basic difference between an army and a civilian society."[55] In response to a question by Governor Gibson, Wiener conceded that commanders could abuse their court-martial authority. However, "all power can

---

regression rather than improvement, and uniformity should "not be achieved at the cost of destroying safeguards now existing in the Army . . . system of military justice."

[51] Dated February 28, 1949, it took the form of a six-page letter by Robert Pasley to the editor of the *Washington Star*. In reference to the fact that under army practice, as favored by Davis, "an informed lawyer is present during the deliberations and voting of the court in closed session," Pasley noted that "this is exactly the point. It is the feeling of critics of the Army system that the advice and comments of the law officer should be made in open court in the presence of the accused, and should be set forth in the record." LP, February 28, 1949, 2. See *sup.*, chap. 7 for discussion of this question during the Working Group meetings. The *Washington Star* declined to print Pasley's response because it was too long. LPPL, March 3, 1949.

[52] Transcript of ABC "On Trial." Ansell was extremely careful to be absolutely neutral in his role as "judge." If not familiar with the earlier battles against Crowder, a viewer probably would never have sensed his prior involvement.

[53] In 1948, Gibson had written to Morgan's committee, excoriating command abuses in military justice. He had "an intense, deep, somewhat bitter feeling about this matter—a feeling I promised myself I would someday make perfectly clear to those who should make corrective steps." Indeed, Gibson hoped that "from your study[,]" Morgan's committee "will evolve a system of justice for the armed services that will merit having the word 'justice' attached to it." *Comments on UCMJ*, November 18, 1948.

[54] In addition to a successful career as a lawyer specializing in federal appellate litigation, Wiener has gained a well-deserved reputation as a military legal historian—a field in which he continues to write. As previous chapters have indicated and later ones will also demonstrate, our views on various subjects discussed in this study do not always coincide. Nevertheless, I remain indebted to him both for his interest in my work and his own research that facilitated some of my earlier sections on Ansell and Crowder.

[55] *Transcript*, 8. An army, Wiener added, is supposed "to win wars[,] not just fight them, but win them. They don't pay off on price in a war. And therefore an army has to be so organized that it will lead men obediently against the enemy to their deaths if necessary."

be abused if placed in unworthy hands[;] that does not mean, sir, that the powers should not be placed in some hands.''[56] Gibson reiterated his point that the commander's power over military justice procedure was in reality ''pure dictatorship.'' Wiener's argument of necessity to the contrary, the current practice ''is inhuman. It is un-American and it is dangerous.''[57]

CONGRESS CONTEMPLATES CONSIDERATION

In accordance with usual practice, the chair of the Senate Armed Services Committee selected a subcommittee of three to consider the proposed UCMJ. After this panel's first meeting on February 16, one of its members—Massachusetts Sen. Leverett Saltonstall—informed his good friend Judge Raymond Wilkins of the Massachusetts Supreme Judicial Court that ''the Committee in the House will [hold] full hearings[,] and presumably the Senate will wait until this is done.'' He hoped that Wilkins ''will give the bill a going over and make any comments that you care to when you have had an opportunity to study it.''[58] Wilkins apparently had already discussed parts of the code with Saltonstall's assistant who in turn had drafted a sheet of notes for Saltonstall's use during the first subcommittee meeting—to which Larkin had also been invited to attend. In general, stated one note, the code was a ''big improvement.'' As to the proposed judicial council, ''this may be a good idea but would want to know a lot more about. Would like to have the opinion of Green, the present [Army] JAG. . . . It looks too much like giving three people a job without thinking how it would work out in relation to present authority.''[59]

Once the decision to have a House Subcommittee hold hearings on the proposed code (now listed as H.R. 2498) had been reached, Larkin held several meetings with Robert Smart, a lawyer attached to the House Armed Services Committee and an unofficial participant in a number of Larkin's Working Group sessions. In notes from a meeting on February 23, 1949, Smart asked Larkin to consider, ''Why should the Judicial Council not weigh evidence, credibility, etc.?'' The council ''should not usurp military functions. Al-

[56] Ibid., 12.

[57] Ibid., 15.

[58] *Saltonstall Papers*, Massachusetts Historical Society, box 7, ''Legislation Lex-Nat,'' February 16, 1949. Wilkins went on to a distinguished career as the Chief Justice of the Massachusetts Supreme Judicial Court. Given the multiple demands on a senator's time, it was not at all unusual for Saltonstall to have a lawyer he trusted, such as Wilkins, examine a complex and lengthy statute such as the UCMJ. As will be seen, Wilkins's comments on parts of the new statute would influence Saltonstall to support a key change in the bill, one of vital importance to the later history of the USCMA.

[59] Ibid. Green would have a great deal to do with attempting, for the most part unsuccessfully, to make numerous changes in the code before it became law. These efforts are discussed in a later chapter.

though [it] would do no more than [a] Circuit Court would do, [the judicial council] would specialize in [a] peculiar type of law. One tribunal needed for purposes of uniformity.''[60] One day later, Smart sent Larkin a more detailed set of questions along with a candid letter, explaining why they were important.

''I realize,'' Smart wrote, ''that both you and I already know the answers to most of these questions, however, I am including them in order to insure a proper legislative history.'' Yet, he was a little troubled.

> While you and I know that there is nothing at all sinister in my furnishing you with a copy of these questions, I think it would be advisable to keep this matter confined to those agencies and individuals who are directly involved with the legislation. I would also suggest that departmental witnesses refrain, insofar as possible, from answering these questions in their opening statements. To do so would deprive Mr. [Overton] Brooks [Democrat from Louisiana and chairman of the House Subcommittee] of much of his participation in the hearings. If that should occur, it might prove most embarrassing to me.[61]

Again, Smart called attention to the fact that as drafted, the UCMJ denied the Judicial Council authority that the lower Boards of Review would retain. ''What reasons have motivated this change?'' Moreover, the omission of any mention as to the terms of Council members did not escape Smart's notice. ''What term does the Secretary of Defense recommend—for life, a fixed term or staggered terms?'' Also, ''is it considered desirable that such civilian appointees have some military experience in addition to their legal qualifications?'' On the basis of current case load in each service, could Larkin estimate ''how many cases per month would be reviewable by the Council?'' If too heavy a burden, does the code ''authorize . . . one or two additional members, rather than another Council of three . . . ? [H]ave you considered the possibility of providing one or more commissioners to assist the Council rather than new . . . members?'' As the members of Morgan's council would ''perform substantially the same duties as judge[s] of the United States Courts of Appeal[s], have you considered the advisability of granting the reviewing authority . . . to the Federal Courts of Appeals?''[62]

Larkin instructed representatives from both the army and air force to submit

[60] LP, *Notes on Meeting with Mr. Smart*, February 23, 1949. Why, in other words, should not the council do exactly what Morgan had first proposed that it do? The fact that Smart asked about the altered role of the council indicates that he may not have been aware of Morgan's compromises on this point in order to bring Kenney and Zuckert to support his position. See above, chap. 8.

[61] Ibid., February 24, 1949. It was common practice for staff members to prepare questions for use by committee members. Smart probably concluded that feeding Larkin the questions prepared by the staff of the subcommittee in advance of the hearings could only facilitate the smooth progress of the bill through the committee.

[62] LP, *Questions Pertaining to H. R. 2498*, 8–9. LPPL, February 25, 1949, 2.

answers to Smart's queries in written form suitable for his use in testimony before the House Committee. Stewart Maxey, the air force member of Larkin's original Working Group, focused on the decision to limit the Judicial Council to matters of law. Because it "will be composed of civilians unfamiliar with military procedure and the military service in general, it should not be extended the powers which a court has in weighing evidence taken before them, judging the credibility of witnesses appearing before them[,] and determining the truth from the testimony of such witnesses." Moreover, Maxey believed that "the lack of knowledge of military matters . . . will be a severe handicap to the proper performance of their duties and the interests of the government" Finally, he estimated that approximately 247 cases per month from the air force alone would be reviewable by the council. Because it would cost the accused nothing, "I anticipate practically every man convicted by general . . . or special court-martial whose case is legally reviewable by the Judicial Council will petition for such review."[63]

On behalf of the army, another former member of the Working Group, John Dinsmore, repeatedly emphasized Gordon Gray's dissent to the entire appellate procedure as endorsed by Morgan's committee. He agreed with Maxey that members of the council should have military experience. Dinsmore also noted that while Gray had suggested that appeals from courts-martial be authorized to a federal circuit court "in lieu of the creation of a Judicial Council, . . . no action on this suggestion was taken by the Committee." Dinsmore predicted that in peacetime, the number of army cases reviewable by the council would be "about 1,100 per month, and in wartime about 2,600 per month."[64]

One day after Larkin received the questions from Smart, Judge Matthew McGuire—the jurist who had been so critical of navy justice during World War II—informed Larkin that Congressman Brooks had asked him to testify on the UCMJ. McGuire could not do it, but wrote a letter "which he read to me. I suggested that it would be helpful to us if he would not phrase his letter in such a negative manner, and he agreed that he did not want to scuttle the bill because he actually thought it was very good."[65] McGuire sent Larkin a copy of this letter, and upon examination, it becomes very clear why he urged the jurist to "revise" the text.

[63] Ibid., March 3, 1949. The first report of USCMA, submitted for the period May 31, 1951, to March 1, 1952, listed thirty-nine cases docketed from the air force. U.S. Court of Military Appeals, *Interim Report*, 2–3. These included petitions, certifications from the JAGs, and mandatory review. For the calendar year 1953, 273 air force cases were docketed. Ibid., *Report for June 1, 1952, to December 31, 1953*, 21.

[64] LP, March 4, 1949. For the same periods cited above in n. 62, through March 1952, 372 cases from the army had been docketed. In 1953, 1,638 army cases were submitted.

[65] LPPL, February 25, 1949, 2. McGuire accepted the suggestion, and three days later phoned Larkin to read a revised version, one which Larkin thought "very fair." Ibid., February 28, 1949.

McGuire complained to Brooks that the new UCMJ "still labors under the basic defects of the older systems which have been so critically and bitterly inveighed against." As to Morgan's Judicial Council, "what shall they do in time of peace? And . . . why should they be paid more than the United States District Court judges [such as McGuire] who sit on constitutional courts? Are they to be confirmed by the Senate?" Although McGuire believed that Morgan's committee "should be congratulated for a job well done," his final sentences reiterated potential weaknesses in the UCMJ of which Morgan and Larkin could only have been well aware. "My strictures are levelled against what I consider fundamentals, the absence of which in any system that purports to do justice according to our concepts is fatal. I have no doubt that the Committee agrees—and the end result in this respect being perhaps the result of compromise—where agreement was impossible. But no matter how far reaching are reforms, unless the old vices referred to are completely eradicated, even handed administration of military and naval justice will still remain as elusive as ever, the more so because of the fact that the vicious defects of the old systems still remain—dressed up in new garb it is true, but still as unregenerate as ever."[66]

With hearings on the UCMJ scheduled to begin on March 7, 1949, before the House Armed Services Committee, Larkin sent two memoranda to Forrestal, and also drafted a statement for him to read before the committee as the first witness. He did not "believe that you will be asked any questions, and I think you can refer [any] questions addressed to you to Professor Morgan or to me." Larkin was especially concerned about "the problem of coordinating any testimony that might be given by the members of the committee—that is, Mr. Gray, Mr. Kenney and Mr. Zuckert. . . . I feel very strongly that the Military Establishment should present a united front on this bill[,] and that explanations of dissents should not be phrased in such a way that our witnesses will become engaged in a debate before the Committee."[67] He warned Forrestal that "while I feel that the bill is a very good one and strikes a very fair balance between military command and a system of justice, we have to expect that various items will be criticized by different groups."[68]

[66] LP, March 2, 1949. McGuire's letter to Brooks is dated February 25, 1949. Except for Larkin's phone conversation, I have been unable to find any evidence (*a*) that McGuire redrafted this letter, and (*b*) that *any* communication from him was submitted to the congressional committees that considered the UCMJ. Possibly he did not send it on to Brooks, or the subcommittee chair may not have wished to receive it "officially."

[67] Probably concerned about any comments that Gray might make before the House Committee, Larkin "asked him whether or not he specifically desires to make a statement, and he said he does not want to unless he is called[,] and he is not anxious to be called. . . . He considers the [Morgan] Committee discharged at the point when it submitted the code to Forrestal. He said he feels that appearance by anyone now should be as representatives of their Department." LPPL, March 4, 1949. Later that day, Zuckert took the same position. Ibid., 2.

[68] LP, March 3, 1949.

Two days later, Larkin sent a more detailed explanation of Forrestal's resolution concerning several disputed items on the new code; chief among them being the civilian Judicial Council. In a uniform system, he told the secretary, it is absolutely necessary "to have a final court on the law. Otherwise, the system would be uniform in name only, since lawyers differ on the construction of law and statutes[,] and the Services would undoubtedly construe the provisions of the uniform system in different ways." He explained further that the "civilian aspect of the . . . Council is entirely consistent with the concept of civilian control of the armed forces, . . . and since it would rule on law only, it would not interfere with the discipline and morale factors."

Finally, Larkin stated that Morgan's Judicial Council was "part of an effort by the Committee to restrict command control," which "to the extent that the commanding officer still appoints the court and reviews the case, is retained in the Code." This fact made it all the more necessary "that there should be other measures which would keep such control confined to its proper function." Again, Larkin warned Forrestal that the decision to retain "the commander will be criticized in the hearings by Bar Associations, etc. If you are asked questions on this subject, I think the answer should be that we have left the command with functions which we think appropriate and have added provisions—namely the Judicial Council, law officer, etc.—to keep that control properly circumscribed."[69]

Morgan was perfectly willing to return to Washington and testify, but asked in a private letter to Larkin if he was to appear as a private citizen. "For if I am no longer an employee of the Government[,] I must . . . pay my own expenses. It is a little embarrassing for me to have to ask this question, but it is necessary for me to know in order to make proper budgetary adjustments."[70] Larkin hastened to reassure Morgan that he would appear "as a member" of Forrestal's staff, testifying on his behalf.[71] As he had done for Forrestal, so too Larkin drafted an introductory statement for Morgan. "As I contemplate your role," he wrote to the Harvard law professor, "I think it should be a combination of explaining the broad outline of the bill and a bit of statesmanship."[72] Ultimately, Morgan's "performance" more than satisfied Larkin's criteria.

[69] Ibid., March 5, 1949, 1–2, 4.

[70] Ibid., February 18, 1949. Morgan added that "I hardly see how giving testimony before a Senate Committee can be classified as expert consultant."

[71] Ibid., February 21, 1949.

[72] Ibid., February 23, 1949.

CHAPTER 10

Congress, the Code, and the Court, 1949–1950

LIKE HIS BOSS, James Forrestal, Felix Larkin conceived the work on the UCMJ as nonpolitical, although probably he would have strongly agreed with Forrestal's observation that you can no more divorce government from politics than you can separate sex from creation.[1] He had employed a variety of techniques to keep the proposed code from becoming a vehicle for legislative partisanship. These ranged from inviting representatives of the Congressional Armed Services Committees to sit in as participating (but nonvoting) observers of the Working Group meetings, to cooperating with Robert Smart with answers prepared in advance for key questions to be asked by the House Committee leadership. But Larkin aimed at more than eliminating opportunity for partisan bickering. Both he and Morgan conceived of the new code as a finished entity, one that could benefit from some stylistic corrections or additions—but not from congressional tinkering with its main provisions.

Thus, in advance of the hearings, each member of the Armed Services Committee received a booklet which not only listed each article, but also provided the sources from which it was drawn and explanatory analysis on the way it would work. This *Text, References and Commentary* reflected the complex challenge of shaping various disparate military justice provisions into a uniform single entity. But it also encouraged the perception that the UCMJ had to be "analyzed as an integrated whole," an approach strongly recommended by Forrestal when he testified before the House Committee on March 7, 1949, as the first witness on behalf of the new code.[2]

CONGRESS CONSULTS

Forrestal's brief appearance on Capitol Hill to launch the campaign for swift congressional approval of the UCMJ was one of his last as secretary of defense. His resignation had already been accepted by President Truman, to take effect

[1] *Forrestal Papers*, box 79, October 4, 1948.

[2] *Index and Legislative History, UCMJ*, vol. 1 (1985): 66; hereafter cited as LH, followed by the page listing in the *Legislative History*, rather than the printed committee transcript.

on March 31, 1949.[3] Initially drafted for him by Larkin, Forrestal's short remarks strongly endorsed the proposed legislation. He emphasized that every participant in the UCMJ project "partially compromised his views on a number of points,"—and they all, himself included, "support the many individual provisions with varying shades of enthusiasm." In reality, "the point of proper accommodation between the meting out of justice and the performance of military operations—which involve[s] not only the fighting but also the winning of wars—is one which no one has discovered." But the finished document represented a remarkable consensus. Indeed, he added, "we are striving for maximum military performance and maximum justice. I believe the proposed code is the nearest approach to these ideals."[4]

By prearrangement, Morgan immediately followed Forrestal's remarks with some additional introductory comments, originally drafted for him by Larkin.[5] He summarized the main provisions of the UCMJ including that for a judicial council. "It is apparent," he noted, "that such a tribunal is necessary to insure uniformity of interpretation throughout the armed services." Moreover, it is consistent with the principle of civilian control of the armed forces that a court of final appeal "should be composed of civilians."[6]

Morgan concluded his presentation with some observations concerning certain general assumptions that his committee had kept in mind as it fashioned the UCMJ. The members recognized from the beginning "that a system of military justice which was only an instrumentality of the commander was as abhorrent as a system entirely administered by a civilian criminal court was impractical."[7] Obviously, the new code "cannot ignore the military circumstances under which it must operate[,] but we were equally determined that it must be designated to administer justice." The code provided "functions for command[,] and appropriate procedures for the administration of justice." Echoing Forrestal, Morgan admitted that the draft before the committee

[3] *New York Times*, March 4, 1949, 1, 12. It is not clear to what extent Truman forced Forrestal to resign, as contrasted with the secretary's own desire to relinquish his post. There is no doubt, however, that by March 1949 Forrestal was mentally exhausted, and increasingly distraught emotionally. Less than two months after he left office, the former secretary committed suicide. Ibid., May 23, 1949, 1, 3.

[4] LH, 65. Larkin's draft of Forrestal's comments is in LP, February 23, 1949. The secretary relied heavily on it when speaking before the committee. Forrestal further noted his belief that the new code "does not interfere with appropriate military functions." Ibid., 66.

[5] Introduced to the committee as "Dr. Morgan," the Harvard law professor prefaced his formal testimony with the comment that "first I better thank you for the degree which you have just conferred upon me." Ibid., 67.

[6] Ibid., 72.

[7] Ibid., 74. "I am aware that there are many schools of thought on military justice, ranging all the way from those who sponsor complete military control to those who support a complete absence of military participation. I do not believe either of these extremes represents the proper solution."

"is not exactly what any one of us would have drawn had he been alone and starting without precedent."[8]

Morgan indicated that he would discuss specific provisions of the code in subsequent testimony, but Representative Paul Kilday asked him to clarify the term of membership on the judicial council. Morgan replied that "we felt that Congress would have to determine the term: Whether or not they should go out with the [current] administration." While the draft did not specify, "certainly it is my opinion that these men should be appointed in exactly the same way that the circuit court of appeals judges are appointed. . . . During good behavior, by the President, with the consent of the Senate."[9]

Kilday was not alone in his belief that Congress "would more clearly have to define this office." Although the Senate agreed to delay consideration of the UCMJ until after the House Committee had acted, Senator Saltonstall continued to receive feedback from his advisor, Judge Wilkins, even as the House began its hearings. Wilkins was "not convinced that [the Judicial Council] is a necessary thing, although I don't know that I would vote against it." He visualized the tribunal "as a body—most likely composed of politicians—which would be overwhelmed in war time and, once precedents shall have been established, would have a very soft job at other times, except perhaps on a very few occasions." From what he had seen thus far, Wilkins doubted "that we need any such permanent outfit as this bids fair to be."[10] Shortly before Forrestal and Morgan went before the House Committee, Saltonstall replied to Wilkins that "the Judicial Council rather appealed to me. I agree with you that it should not be a full-time job except in war time."[11]

Larkin and Robert Smart may have expected that after the UCMJ had been introduced by Forrestal and Morgan, the House Committee would begin its consideration immediately, section by section, with Smart reading each article of the code to the committee, followed by discussion based on the questions for which Larkin had previously been prepared. Instead the committee chose to hear from a large number of witnesses—including spokesmen for the several lawyer groups such as George Spiegelberg and Richard Wels—with whose views Morgan's committee was well acquainted. While the speakers praised the UCMJ as a positive advance in general, there were many specific criticisms offered, some of which applied to the proposed appellate process.

[8] Ibid., 74.

[9] Ibid., 78.

[10] SP, March 3, 1949. Wilkins added, "I realize, however, that it is pretty hard to talk against the establishment of an attractive job."

[11] Ibid., March 5, 1949. Saltonstall appears not to have changed this belief. While the House embraced Morgan's idea of full-time service, the Senate insisted on limited terms, originally to be eight years. Whether Saltonstall preferred part-time work on the council, as opposed to full-time activity, albeit for a limited period of years, remains uncertain. The resulting compromise is discussed below.

Not unexpectedly, critics objected to the Morgan Committee's failure to isolate the military commander from the court-martial process. Representing the ABA, Frederick Bryan emphasized that a small correction in the draft could turn it into "a really monumental piece of legislation." All that was needed was to "remove from command the power to appoint [and convene] the court, the power to appoint defense counsel, and the power to make initial review except for clemency or remission of sentence."[12]

For the New York County Lawyers Association, Richard Wels insisted that "there is no question that this bill retains command control in all its ugly aspects."[13] On behalf of the War Veterans Bar Association, Arthur Farmer stated that in the proposed UCMJ, "the elimination of command control from the courts is conspicuously missing."[14] Franklin Riter, a former JAG officer representing the American Legion was not impressed with the safeguards against command influence that Morgan's committee had written into the UCMJ. Making such conduct an offense under article 98 "means nothing." As to the other section which prohibited interference with the court (article 37), "I want you to write into it a jail and fine provision enforceable in the United States district court and indictable under the civil law."[15] George Spiegelberg, also of the ABA, was more of a prophet than he knew when he claimed that "I just cannot realize—and perhaps my imagination is not vivid enough—any officer in a command preferring charges against the commanding officer under article 37. I mean I really cannot."[16]

The proposed appellate procedure generally received support.[17] Bryan cited

[12] LH, 98. Members of a military tribunal should be selected by officers within the JAG's department. "Thus the court will not be appointed by a commander who has complete control over the military future of the men on that court." Ibid., 95.

[13] Ibid., 108. Wels hastened to point out that "we like many things about this bill. Our criticisms are not directed so much at what it does, as to what it does not do. Frankly, we are going to play Oliver Twist and ask for 'more.' "

[14] Ibid., 114. Farmer posed this question to military commanders: "If you don't want to influence [courts], why should you insist on keeping that command influence?" The only way "in which you can prevent command influence on the court is by taking it out of the power of command to do it." Ibid., 119–20.

[15] Ibid., 133. With probably unintentional understatement, Riter added that his proposal "will not be a popular one." If, however, it was adopted, "a general would be a fool with that kind of thing facing him, to go monkeying with it." Congressman L. Mendel Rivers suggested, "You better think that through and look at the practical application of that suggestion." Riter replied, "I have." Ibid., 134.

[16] Ibid., 187. Spiegelberg noted that Morgan had held very strong views on the subject of command influence ever since the Ansell-Crowder controversy. Representative Rivers responded that "well, Professor Morgan is a practical man. When you get into these conferences you cannot always get everything you want, as you know. . . . I am just wondering whether the reason it [referring to a more stringent safeguard against command influence] was not incorporated into this proposal was because he was hitting his head upon a stone wall." Ibid., 188.

[17] There was, however, strong criticism of a little-noticed provision in article 66 dealing with the Board of Review. "Within ten days after any decision by a Board of Review, the Judge

two reasons why "we want a body of qualified judicial officers within the national military establishment of judicial caliber to act as the final court of review. One, in individual cases and two, because with such a body you gradually evolve a system of case law for the military establishment which would be of immeasurable value to all the armed services in the various specific situations that occur."[18]

Here, Bryan correctly anticipated a key goal of the UCMJ: to make the military justice appeals process as similar as possible to its civilian counterpart. He assumed that "you cannot try cases by a code. You have to develop in all law a body of precedents [of case law] which will govern the various situations that arise in . . . military justice."[19] In fact, the United States Court of Military Appeals bases its decisions in large measure upon a body of military common law, consisting of precedents and findings rendered since 1951. Thus, the claim that because military justice is not derived from common law, civil courts can play no part in appellate review of its decisions may be built upon a faulty premise.

If Riter seemed a bit excessive in his suggested remedy for command influence, his comments on article 67 (establishing the judicial council) were equally vigorous. He strongly supported the idea of such a tribunal. But, "that section is badly drafted. I cannot imagine how the draftsmen let that by. The section as it is is [sic] ambiguous."[20] More important, "I want the name changed. I want that called [the] military court of appeals. I do not want it called [the] judicial council because that carries the idea that [it] is another administrative body set up within the confines of the War Department. . . . Let us give it its right name and dignity. And it will have a tremendous influence on the public. Let us call it the military court of appeal—that is what it

---

Advocate General may refer the case for reconsideration to the same or another Board of Review." Bryan called this section "sort of a double-take proposition[,] and I do not think [it] a very salutary provision." Richard Wels concluded that it "destroys the independence and integrity of boards of review, and that it should be stricken." Arthur Farmer saw no reason why the JAG "should be able to peddle the case among other boards of review until he obtains the decision which he desires." Ibid., 92, 110, 118, 193. It is not clear when this provision came to be included in the final version of the UCMJ as submitted to Congress. It apparently was not in Morgan's first draft. Moreover, in his revisions for the appellate review articles, Robert Haydock provided for a "reconsideration or rehearing before such Board of Review." LP, November 26, 1948. The later version went further, however, and adopted the "shopping provision" criticized above. As will be seen shortly, this section may well have been added on to article 66 as an "afterthought"—at the request of the Navy JAG.

[18] Ibid., 93.

[19] Ibid. Bryan also was not troubled by limiting the Judicial Council to matters of law, although as will be seen, other witnesses were against such a step. "If a situation arises in which there are no facts to sustain a conviction, then as I see it that becomes a question of law anyway."

[20] Ibid., 141. Riter was referring to the failure of Morgan's draft to specify the term for the council members, as well as whether or not they would be subject to Senate confirmation.

is—and give it its dignity. . . . I make a special plea that the name be changed.''[21]

A different reaction to Morgan's proposal came from John Oliver, testifying for the Reserve Officers Association. Although the group had requested the opportunity to appear before Morgan's committee, the panel ''did not see fit to accede to our request and we had no opportunity to present our views to them.''[22] Oliver was troubled by the proposed civil review board. If the House Committee deemed such a body appropriate, he suggested that three new judges for the United States Circuit Court of Appeals for the District of Columbia be appointed to consider military justice cases, on both the law and the facts. ''It does not appear to us desirable to create an additional special civilian court operating under the thumb of the Secretary of Defense which would consider only one type of case.''[23] We feel, he added, ''that the sound legal knowledge and the broad experience of our civil appellate judges will bring to the administration of military justice a breath of fresh air at the top that would be extremely desirable. . . . Surely all of the functions of this civilian board could be performed much more adequately by the civilian judiciary of our court of appeals.''[24]

If the Congress insisted on creating the Council, Oliver urged that it should be able to decide matters of law and fact, and more important, that ''hearings should be had [before] the Judicial Council as a matter of right to the accused and not at the [council's] discretion.'' One congressman asked, ''Would that not require more than three judicial officers? In fact, would it not require a tremendous number of them to dispose of all the cases?'' Oliver was emphatic in his response. ''I am much more concerned with the time that a man may serve in a penitentiary or the short drop he gets on the end of the rope than I am with the work load of the Judicial Council.''[25]

A CHORUS OF CRITICS

On March 11, Larkin told Morgan that the ''Committee hearings are going very slowly inasmuch as [its members appear] to be willing to listen at great length to every witness.'' He hastened to reassure ''Eddie'' that ''in the mean-

[21] Ibid., 141. As will be seen in the second volume of this study, Frank Riter's interest in the new court did not end with his testimony.

[22] Ibid., 208. It seems reasonable to assume, given the large number of groups who presented their written views to Morgan's committee, that Oliver's group had failed to take advantage of the opportunity.

[23] Oliver must have been unaware that the UCMJ draft as submitted to Congress had been changed to provide for presidential appointment of council members.

[24] LH, 210.

[25] Ibid., 226.

time, I still think we are doing pretty well.''[26] More witnesses were expected however, and although the panel began its section-by-section analysis one week later, Morgan did not reappear to testify until March 30. In the meantime, the proposed draft received more negative comments.

A spokesman for the National Guard Bureau called Morgan's judicial council ''a diversion from present procedures which would endanger the security of our country in time of war.'' As proposed, it ''would be a hazardous interference with the duties of the proper military authorities,'' as well as ''a deterrent to swift and sure justice in the armed services.'' The witness concluded that if a judicial council was deemed necessary, it should be composed of high-ranking military officers ''with a legal background.''[27] These comments could be dismissed as typical of a conservative military establishment. However, the statements made by a recently retired JAG officer, who practiced law in Washington, while similarly critical were of greater significance.

Frederick B. Wiener, a member of the Army JAG reserve, testified on March 16–17, 1949. An experienced but opinionated observer of military justice, he informed the committee that Morgan's bill ''in my judgment . . . is a distinct retrogression'' and ''a step backwards'' from the Elston Act enacted some months earlier.[28] This conclusion was predicated on three provisions in the new code, all of which had been strongly supported by Morgan. Wiener particularly objected to the proposal that the law member of a court-martial would not deliberate and vote with his colleagues. Such action ''is the most retrograding step in this bill.'' In fact, ''by taking him out[,] you take out of the deliberations the one man who can make the most helpful contribution'' to them. ''I cannot help but think,'' added Wiener, that this provision ''was not the product of anyone who ever sat on a court. . . . It was only ignorance.''[29]

Similarly, the requirement that trial *and* defense counsel had to be lawyers

[26] MPVU, March 11, 1949. Larkin also enclosed a copy of another missive received from Gordon Gray. He reminded Larkin that since the UCMJ draft as submitted to Congress contained some changes not ''considered or in some respects approved'' by the CUCMJ, ''I think it should be made clear that in any of your relationships with Congressional Committees or any other people you are the representative of the Office of the Secretary of Defense'' rather than the committee on the uniform code. Concerning this memorandum from ''our friend Gordon,'' Larkin wrote that ''it looks to me as though he is now trying to dance on a pinpoint.''

[27] LH, 240–41. Maj. Gen. Kenneth Cramer urged that the words ''civilian life'' be deleted from article 67, and replaced with ''qualified general or flag officers from the Army, Navy and Air Force.'' Ibid., 241.

[28] LH, 250.

[29] Ibid., 252–53. Congressman Rivers responded, ''You do not deny that commanding officers have deliberately injected themselves into the results of trials . . . and openly demonstrated their dislike for the decisions rendered in many, many cases?'' Wiener acknowledged, ''I have heard a great deal of testimony to that effect from people whose probity and credibility I have great confidence in, and I believe them. I can only say that it never happened in any of the places that I served.'' Such an admission on Wiener's part may have undercut the effectiveness of his initial criticism.

was "worse than unnecessary, it is impractical." Moreover, in time of peace such a requirement would be "utterly impossible," because "you won't get the lawyers."[30] Congress would "have to appropriate an awful lot of money to supply the lawyers that will be necessary to [argue] the simple cases, desertions, and the small larcenies, and the disobedience cases, if this bill goes through."[31]

Wiener reserved his harshest criticism for Morgan's cherished judicial council. "I don't think it is sound; I don't think it is necessary; and I think it is wholly self-defeating.[32] In the first place, "and I think we should face it frankly—the appointments to the specialized courts of our judicial system haven't attracted the same sort of talent that the courts of general jurisdiction have attracted."[33] Furthermore, "I think it is terribly important to have some sort of provision which is not present here that the people on this judicial council have military experience." Wiener was troubled by what he saw as an attempt to "drive a wedge between civilians and military people." What was needed, he implied, were outstanding judges, and there was no justification for the implied conclusion that they were available only in civilian life. Why should we seek to interpose civilians "for decision matters that are basically military?"[34]

Among the final witnesses to appear was a future president of the United States, Gerald Ford—at that time a Michigan congressman. He recalled hearing conversations among members of courts martial during his several years in the navy "along this line: What does the Old Man [an old but still current navy term referring to the ship's commander] want us to do?" Ford concluded

[30] Ibid., 257–58. Wiener much preferred the requirements of the Elston Act which mandated lawyers "if available," and also required that if "you have a lawyer on the prosecution, you have to balance the thing and make the odds fair by having one for the defense." Ibid., 260–61.

[31] Ibid., 262.

[32] Ibid.

[33] Wiener's point was prophetic, and remains valid to this day, as will be discussed in the second volume of this study. Without anticipating those comments, it can be said that the quality of the judges who are named to federal courts depends in large measure upon the care and importance that the president attaches to making their selection. It is less the particular court and more the talents of the judge that make the difference. Again, as will be seen, only President Harry Truman seems to have had a special interest in selecting the first three judges of this court. This is not to deny, however, that politics certainly played a role in his choices.

[34] Ibid., 264. On the other hand, taking sharp issue with numerous other lawyers who had already testified, Wiener insisted on the absolute necessity for keeping the power to convene a court-martial *within* the command. "We make a man a multistarred commander. He is generally trained at public expense; he is sent to service schools at public expense; and we give him a command of several millions of men; and he gives the signal to go; and as a result of that signal, thousands of men lose their lives and thousands more are maimed or blinded. . . . Yet when it is proposed that [this] same general, with those incalculable powers of life and death over fellow citizens, be permitted to appoint a court for the trial of a soldier who has stolen a watch, oh no, we can't have that; we have to have a panel. Doesn't make sense, does it?" Ibid., 268.

that all too often such individuals were concerned less with determining guilt or innocence, than "with what the captain of a ship, or the commanding officer of a station, wants done with the man. . . . I also participated in various courts martial; and the whole system is fundamentally wrong; and I am particularly pleased to see something being done about it."[35]

It is not clear how closely Morgan followed the testimony offered between March 8 and March 30, 1949, when he returned to Washington. He was probably not surprised at the nature of the criticism. Indeed, Larkin had already warned Forrestal that the proposed UCMJ would be attacked both by those who felt it to be a needless intrusion upon a fundamentally good military justice system, and observers who believed that in reality the code represented less than effective reform. If Wiener typified the former, Arthur John Keeffe well personified the latter. What united both witnesses was the certainty if not stridency of tone with which they articulated their opinions. Keeffe did not testify, but sent a long statement which was the final "opinion" read into the committee records on March 18, the day the panel began detailed analysis of the UCMJ.

Referring to Morgan and Larkin as "the ablest of lawyers and the finest of fellows," Keeffe denounced the proposed code as "a sorry substitute" in place of the 1920 Chamberlain bill "for which Professor Morgan once fought so hard."[36] He pointed to the mistake of not providing for an advisory council, an error compounded "by sending this code to the Congress without clearing it with the American Bar Association and other representative lawyer and veteran groups." He disliked the idea of having "three civilian judges buried in the Department of Defense." Also, there was "no advisory council created for the same reason that the drafting of this code was not done by such an advisory council. The armed services want a minimum of civilian control, preferably none. I don't blame them."[37]

Keeffe next turned to the judicial council's authority, which he described as "badly limited." Everyone, regardless of rank "should have his case automatically heard before this top civilian judicial council. . . . I say expand the [council] to five judges and give review to every one alike." He labeled Morgan's provision for petition for cause as "a phony[, one] for the wicked and well connected, not for GI Joe."[38] Even worse was the failure to provide for

[35] Ibid., 293–94. It is interesting that later as president, upon recommendation by his staff, in 1975 Gerald Ford would appoint a judge with minimal military experience to the United States Court of Military Appeals, Albert Fletcher, Jr., whose tenure would be among the most controversial in the court's entire history. The episode will be discussed at some length in the second volume of this study.

[36] Ibid., 306.

[37] Ibid., 307–8.

[38] Ibid., 310. "This method of providing an appeal by petition will result in the wrong kind of cases going to the judicial council and the right kind being buried in the Board of Review in the office of the Judge Advocate General." Keeffe added, correctly, that Morgan's code "does not

a chief defense counsel. "Such an officer, and not the Judge Advocate General should have the responsibility of appealing cases to the top civilian court."[39]

To top off all these weaknesses, Keeffe pointed to the limited scope for the judicial council.[40] Morgan's code "limits [it] to review of questions of law and chains the judicial council to the facts as found by command. This is not the kind of civilian review that we ought to have." The proposed code reflected an unpleasant fact. "The hope of those in the armed services who oppose reform is that those of us who are informed and interested will lose interest and tire out. It is a severe personal sacrifice for busy lawyers and busy men to take the time that is necessary to present the civilian point of view on reform to the Congress."[41]

One can dismiss Keeffe's anger in part because of his understandable frustration at being isolated from the process by which the code had been drafted. But there was more to his comments than mere personal pique. Morgan's panel had a number of policy choices it could have made concerning the appellate review system. Keeffe may or may not have known how badly the committee was divided over this issue, but his criticisms of its final choices have considerable merit. For what they deemed good and sufficient reasons, Morgan's committee opted to limit judicial review. Keeffe's position as contrasted with his Harvard colleague's reflected a continuing tension between the presumed needs of military justice, and the perceived requirements for civilian due process.

THE HOUSE AND THE CODE

On March 18, 1949, Robert Smart, the staff member to the House Armed Services Subcommittee, told the panel that "I think you have heard all the general statements you want. It is time to get down to business now."[42] "Business" meant a reading of the entire code, article by article, allowing time for discussion, comments, and changes. By the time the group completed this procedure, Morgan had returned to testify again. Kenney, Zuckert, and vir-

insure appeal to the United States Supreme Court for GIs and Gobs." Not until 1984, and then under very limited conditions, did Congress provide for direct appeal from decisions of the Court of Military Appeals to the High Court.

[39] Ibid., 310.

[40] For some, even the limited role of the council was too much. On March 15, Raymond Wilkins wrote again to Senator Saltonstall. "I talked at some length . . . with [former] Secretary of War Patterson. He can see no value whatsoever in the Judicial Council proposition and he says that Gen. Eisenhower, if asked a direct question, would say the same thing. I do not know what any high navy officials might think[,] but I would be surprised if they favored it either." SP, March 15, 1949.

[41] LH, 311.

[42] Ibid., 314.

tually all of the original Working Group also participated. However, the bulk of the analysis was provided by Larkin, whose comments on every article were often prompted by Smart's questions. Examination of the transcript makes it possible to consider the extent to which the subcommittee accepted the changes urged upon them by witnesses such as Bryan, Wels, Farmer, Wiener, Keeffe, and others.

Wiener had strongly criticized the proposal to make the law officer a non-voting member of the military court. Larkin admitted that "it is a difficult problem. There's no question about it." Army officials "feel that the law member is of great assistance when retiring with the court and instructing them in closed session. They feel it is a protection for the accused, as a matter of fact." Having accurately restated Wiener's position, Larkin destroyed it with equal facility. "Inasmuch as no one knows what goes on, however, behind the closed doors[,] and the elements of the crime and the law of the case are not preserved for the record, it is impossible to tell whether erroneous law is given or not."[43] With minimal discussion, and no recorded dissent, the subcommittee approved the article as drafted.[44]

Although it had heard consistently from several distinguished lawyers that the proposed UCMJ retained the undesirable potential for command influence, before taking any action the subcommittee waited to hear from Morgan who returned to testify on March 30, 1949.[45] He stated that the "panel idea is one that theoretically is very attractive. I think it will not work practically." In wartime, he added, "I suppose that it is absolutely impossible for a commander to know in advance what men he could spare for a panel."[46] One of the basic goals of the code was that it be *uniform* in not only that it apply to *all* armed services, but that it apply at *all* times, during peace and war. Morgan explained again the various steps his committee had taken to contain command influence, "as far as that is humanly possible." However, he added, "it is true whether you have the panel system or any other system, if the commanding officer is determined to beat it he can beat it."[47] The panel accepted the

[43] Ibid., 621. "The opponents . . . felt that it was most valuable to have the instructions . . . preserved on the record so that they could later be scrutinized and reviewed to determine whether or not the law was accurately given to the court so that you could be sure that its verdict was based on the accurate instructions."

[44] One member of the panel observed that there might well be a member of the court who also was an attorney, so that there could be legal guidance available to the court in closed session. Larkin agreed, but reminded the panel that a trial jury can go out and pay no attention to its instructions whatever. "But that is something over which no one has any control in any tribunal." Ibid., 622.

[45] Spiegelberg had already submitted nine pages of proposed amendments, dealing with use of a panel as the basis for selecting the court, rather than the choice of the commander. LP, March 14, 1949.

[46] LH, 501–2.

[47] Ibid., 502.

UCMJ's original proposal, and left the commander with initial authority to select the court.[48]

Lawyer critics had better success with their objection to the provision in article 66 which permitted the JAG to "shop around" in that he could bring a verdict from one Board of Review to another which he had constituted.[49] As worded, this practice apparently could go on indefinitely. Although Larkin explained that the provision was intended to help not hinder the accused, on April 1, 1949, the subcommittee voted to limit the JAG option to one additional board of review. But apparently its members were not completely comfortable even with this change. Their doubt may be reflected in the manner in which Congressman Brooks announced the vote on the amendment—"The ayes seem to have it."[50] One day later, Brooks took the unusual step of asking his colleagues to reconsider the question.[51]

As some subcommittee members expressed their opposition to "shopping around," representatives of the army and air force quickly moved to disassociate their services from such a policy.[52] Colonel Dinsmore stated, "I am sure that the [Army] Judge Advocate General has never sent a case from one board of review to another, that it is not his practice to do so, and that he does not feel it is the proper thing to do."[53] Nor did the army object to an amendment prohibiting such action by any JAG. A representative for the Air Force JAG stated that "even with the statutory authority[,] he doubted whether he would ever use it."[54] If such was the case, why had the section been incorporated into the article at all?

Larkin stated that the navy had desired the provision, and its JAG later explained why. Up to the present, that service had not established a board of review. What, he wondered, would happen under the proposed UCMJ if a Navy Board of Review affirmed a harsh penalty against an accused, based on the

[48] It is interesting to note that the code still retains this provision. However, since 1968 at least one armed service—the army—has experimented with the use of panels in convening courts-martial within its various commands.

[49] It will be recalled that article 66 also provided that civilians could be appointed to the Boards of Review. This provision was inserted into the article at the request of the Coast Guard. Its representative was careful to emphasize, however, that the service was "in no way advocating civilians for any other armed force[,] . . . and the request was made in the nature of an exception for the service because of existing practice." Ibid., 663. Earlier, Larkin had observed that in the past, both the Coast Guard and the navy had utilized civilian lawyers who "were extremely competent." Ibid., 657. But neither he nor the spokesman for the Coast Guard pointed to the desirability of having civilian judges because they might improve the quality of military justice.

[50] Ibid., 663.

[51] Ibid., 669. "I personally feel that is one part of the bill that we cannot properly defend on the floor of the House. I have thought a good deal about it."

[52] Representative Elston was typical. "I agree with the chairman that it is a dangerous provision and I think we will have trouble with it on the floor." Ibid., 670.

[53] Ibid.

[54] Ibid., 674.

facts of a case, and he found himself in disagreement. He could not appeal to the Judicial Council because his objection was on the facts not the law. "I have no desire to shop around. What I am afraid of is the case won't get as good a review as it gets now. . . . We have as many as eight or nine officers review an important case or a close case right now. If we are only going to have three people doing it and that is going to be final, I am just afraid of it."[55]

As it happened, Admiral Russell—the Navy JAG—made these comments to the subcommittee after it had already voted to delete the entire section on referral to another board of review from the bill.[56] One member later explained to the admiral why they had reconsidered:

> You have a board of review here who might say a man is innocent. All right. You don't think their decision is correct, for some reason. You refer it to another board of review and they come out with a different decision. . . . There you have two boards of review, each with equal authority, not one higher than the other. The board has declared him guilty on the facts. And the court of appeals can't review those facts except where they are just insufficient as a matter of law to constitute a conviction. . . . So you have two boards with equal power, one of which has declared him innocent and the other has declared him guilty. Now, he is declared guilty because that one happened to pass on it last and yet the other one has just as much authority. That was the thing we were confronted with.[57]

On April 4, 1949, the subcommittee held the last of its public hearings, and took up article 67, dealing with the Judicial Council. It made no major changes in the scope of this proposed appellate court, thereby rejecting the various suggestions that its mandate be broadened to include matters of fact. Nor did the panel directly confront the implications of Wiener's perceptive comment about attracting outstanding judicial talent. The panel did, however, discuss some possible changes, and its members made sufficient remarks about the new tribunal to indicate how seriously they considered its role in military justice.

The subcommittee assumed that although the council was "not a constitutional court," the terms of its members should be "for life, subject only to good behavior."[58] Representative Rivers further suggested that the "terms

[55] Ibid., 773.

[56] Ibid., 674–75.

[57] Ibid., 774.

[58] At least one member of the panel, Representative Rivers, was concerned about the flip side of the life tenure option. "Let us fix it where you can get rid of these people at such and such an age because some of these old boys. . . ." (at which point Rivers went "off the record"). Ibid., 744. Both Rivers and Congressman Brooks stated that the judges should be appointed by the president "by and with the advice and consent of the Senate," Brooks noting further that "whether we put it in there or not, I am satisfied that the Senate is going to write it in there." Ibid., 740–41. As will be seen, the Senate was less concerned with advice and consent than with the issue of life tenure.

should be staggered so as to always have a man on [the] Judicial Council who knows about the makeup of the court.'' Congressman Brooks added that ''I feel very strongly that the success or failure of the whole thing is going to lie in the Judicial Council, and it seems to me that you ought to have a strong court, whether you call it a Judicial Council or otherwise makes no difference.''[59] Moreover, there was consensus among the lawmakers that rather than bipartisan, the judges ought to be ''non political and non partisan.'' As Congressman Elston put it, ''I want it certain that this court[,] which is going to be an exceedingly important court[,] is not filled by political appointments.''[60]

The panel also had some difficulty with understanding the term ''from civilian life.'' Larkin noted that this clause ''would exclude officers of the Regular components and retired Regulars. A retired Regular, I should say, would be eligible if he resigned. If he just retired, he wouldn't be.'' This statement is one of the very few from Larkin that may have confused rather than clarified, and he immediately added that ''the notion specifically was to make this as civilian as possible, otherwise perhaps the court would consist of nothing but Regular officers who have resigned for the purpose of taking the job[,] and in effect you would have it more military than civilian.''[61] Morgan had intended that a judge on the court should be a civilian ''as distinguished from a military officer who is either on Regular service now or is a retired Regular who is still, of course, an officer of the United States. But it would not exclude a Reserve on inactive duty, or would not exclude anybody who has military service, of course.''[62]

As the subcommittee continued discussion on the appellate tribunal, it became clear that General Riter was not the only one who disliked the term ''Judicial Council.'' Larkin explained that since the Elston Act had used this name, ''we just picked it up and carried it along.'' Actually, ''we have no pride of authorship at all.''[63] Robert Smart suggested that ''you should adopt some judicial terminology and get away from this 'Council,' which suggests to me one of the usual basement operations here in Washington.''[64] Elston

[59] Ibid., 740. ''It ought to be a strong court, because it is going to have control of the whole system and is going to make recommendations to the Congress from time to time; and, unless it is a strong court, your system is not going to be responsive to the recommendations.''

[60] Ibid., 742.

[61] Ibid., 744.

[62] Ibid., 745. Larkin's statement resulted in the following exchange between himself and the chairman of the subcommittee, Overton Brooks. Brooks: ''Well, a retired officer is still part of the Regular [Military] Establishment, isn't he?'' Larkin: ''That is right. . . . He is not from civilian life.'' Brooks: ''Therefore, he would be automatically excluded from the meaning of that term.'' Larkin: ''That is right.''

[63] Ibid., 745.

[64] Ibid. The fact that during this entire discussion about an appropriate name for the panel no one recalled either Riter's name or any mention of his testimony, may be indicative of how closely the subcommittee listened to its earlier witnesses.

agreed. "That sounds too much like a city council." Larkin added that "it sounds like a round table, instead of a court."[65] After minimal discussion, the subcommittee settled on "The Court of Military Appeals."[66]

With the hearings completed, the subcommittee went into executive session on April 5. Smart informed Larkin that "they want me and only me to be present . . . to testify on the [UCMJ]."[67] Because no records have been located for the session, there is no way of knowing exactly what Larkin discussed. In his papers, however, there is a typed version of article 67, dated April 5, and because it incorporated the changes discussed during the open hearings—it seems reasonable to assume that this draft served as the basis for his comments concerning the Judicial Council now renamed the Court of Military Appeals. Several changes had been approved: (*a*) the revision provided for exactly three judges—the original draft had called for "not less than three"—appointed by the president from civilian life; (*b*) the appointments required Senate confirmation, and the term of each appointment was "during good behavior." These two stipulations were not found in the original article; (*c*) Morgan had proposed that each judge had to be "a member of the bar admitted to practice before the Supreme Court." During the hearings, this requirement had been transformed into "No person shall be eligible for appointment to [this court] who is not a member of the bar of a federal court or of the highest court of a state"; and (*d*) finally, the earlier draft provided compensation and allowances equal to those received by a federal appeals judge. The later version called for "compensation, allowances, perquisites and retirement benefits" of such a jurist.

The subcommittee had failed to resolve one final issue before its members unanimously reported the revised draft of the UCMJ (now called H.R. 4080) for favorable consideration to the full House Armed Services Committee. Ohio Representative Elston and others on the subcommittee had wanted appointments to the new court to be nonpolitical and nonpartisan. When the full committee met on April 27, Elston stated that originally he had even intended to propose amending article 67 to include a section that "Not more than two judges of such court shall be appointed from the same political party."[68] The committee chairman, Carl Vinson, now endorsed this amendment. Because

[65] LH, 746.

[66] At first, Elston suggested the "Supreme Court of Military Appeals," because "if you say 'Court of Appeals,' it might imply that there is a supreme court above that." Elston withdrew his proposal because "of course, there isn't." Ibid., 746–47. However, this issue was more complicated than Elston's statement implied, and it has become even more complicated today. As earlier chapters have indicated, from time to time—albeit rarely—the United States Supreme Court has involved itself in military justice. And in 1984, Congress amended the UCMJ to provide for direct appeal from USCMA to the High Court under specified conditions.

[67] LPPL, April 5, 1949.

[68] LH, 1885, 1890.

"this is a new military court of civilians, it is nothing but right and proper that it be a non partisan court."[69]

It is, admittedly, difficult to follow the reasoning behind Elston's and Vinson's support for this change. There was no provision in existing law that federal courts be bipartisan. But Elston claimed that "this is a special court." Granting this premise, the question can be asked how it becomes nonpartisan in nature when two of its three judges can be from the same political party.[70] Moreover, if the committee had truly desired to make the new court nonpartisan, it would have been just as easy to stipulate in article 67 that specific party affiliation should not be the basis for judicial appointment. To put it another way, if this tribunal was to be like other federal appeals courts—except in its scope of jurisdiction—why should it be necessary to provide such a stipulation here, but not for these other judicial bodies? At any rate, on April 27, 1949, the committee unanimously approved the amendment, and with another unanimous vote sent the UCMJ to the full House. Under the House "rule" which cleared the bill for legislative action, only three hours of general debate were scheduled—clear evidence that the leadership assumed the entire code would be approved in one session.[71] In what turned out to be an extremely impressive display of legislative choreography, the leadership proved to be correct.

LEGISLATIVE LOVE AT FIRST CITE

On May 5, 1949, almost three months to the day since James Forrestal and Edmund Morgan had addressed the Armed Services Committee, the House took up the UCMJ. Considering the importance of the proposed legislation, the debate was short, surprisingly superficial, and characterized more by excessive amounts of self congratulations among the leadership of the committee than by systematic exegesis of key provisions in the code.[72] Prior to introducing Congressman Brooks, the Louisiana Democrat who had chaired the subcommittee, Vinson reminded his colleagues that the bill was based on five weeks of careful study by a subcommittee that unanimously supported the bill as did the full committee. Moreover, the bill was endorsed and recommended by the bureau of the budget, approved by the National military establishment, and supported by Truman's administration.[73]

[69] Ibid., 1886.

[70] Vinson added that this amendment if adopted "makes it nonpartisan and shows the whole tendency of the armed services to be a nonpartisan organization all down the line." Ibid., 1390.

[71] Ibid., 1900.

[72] Allowing for the pages devoted to the reprinting of the revised bill, this first 1949 House debate on the UCMJ appears to fill less than thirteen pages in the *Congressional Record*.

[73] LH, 1903. In introducing House Resolution 201, which was the "rule" under which the UCMJ would be debated, Representative Adolf Sabath called the proposed code "an extremely important

Representative Brooks summarized the key provisions of the proposed code, much as Morgan had done early in March. He also explained the few changes made by the subcommittee from the original proposal. Moreover, he discussed the slightly revised article 67, which created the Court of Military Appeals. This article, according to Brooks, "contains the most revolutionary changes which have ever been incorporated in our military law." As to the number of seats on the new court, "we have concluded that it would be sounder to limit the number to three until such time as the facts may warrant an increase."[74]

Carl Vinson told his colleagues that "I am sure you will all agree that the technical provisions of a bill of this character are about as difficult and uninteresting as the formula for atomic energy."[75] Preparation of such a statute "has involved efforts that can best be characterized as plain drudgery" for the "eight lawyers and three laymen of the [House] subcommittee."[76] Another member of that subcommittee, Representative Philip Philbin, added that "this measure has been given exhaustive and most diligent and painstaking consideration." This subcommittee, he stated, "has among its membership some of the very best lawyers in the Congress." Its chair possessed "penetrating judgment, wisdom, patience and sagacity," as well as "a keen analytical, legal mind."[77]

Philbin described Representative Elston as not only "one of the ablest civilian lawyers in the Nation, but also a specialist and outstanding expert in the field of military law." The other lawyers "are all of commanding legal ability," while the nonlawyers "are all men of learning, broad experience, and conspicuous ability and are without exception thoroughly versed, deeply interested, and exceptionally well informed on the problems of military justice."[78] But there was more. "I am happy to state to the House, our subcommittee has been most fortunate in that we have enjoyed the advice, opinions, and assistance of experts and eminent lawyers and specialists, highly qualified to grapple with these problems." And, "at all times, of course, we have had the benefit of the farsighted, mature judgment of our own most distinguished and capable chairman, a man of broad knowledge and outstanding patriotism."[79]

---

bill, but the most important part, to my mind, is the section providing for a special Court of Military Appeals." Ibid., 1902.

[74] Ibid., 1904. In 1989, Congress voted to increase the size of USCMA to five judges. The reasons for such a change, the first in the court's history, may have had as much to do with political considerations as with judicial necessity.

[75] The implication behind Vinson's point seemed to be that the difficult and uninteresting aspects of the bill made it unnecessary for the House to spend much time on its consideration. Instead, it should rely on the collective wisdom of Vinson's committee.

[76] LH, 1907.

[77] Ibid., 1908.

[78] Ibid.

[79] Ibid., 1909.

Philbin expounded enthusiastically to his colleagues about the merits of the new code. "It regulates and checks arbitrary, capricious, and whimsical action of commanding officers at every level and every point."[80] Furthermore, "we have carefully combed every possible way by which the rights of the accused have been or could be violated and have closed up any gap which we have been able to discern by which any member of the armed forces might be denied equal and full justice under the law."[81] A key link in this process was the proposed Court of Military Appeals.

It was to be a tribunal similar to the federal circuit courts of appeal. Forgetting that from the very beginning Morgan had assumed that the new court would be "in the National Military Establishment," Philbin emphasized its independence. "This court will be completely detached from the military in every way. It is entirely disconnected with the Department of Defense or any other military branch, completely removed from any outside influences. It can operate, therefore, as . . . a great, effective, impartial body sitting at the topmost rank of the structure of military justice and insuring as near as it can be insured by any human agency, absolutely fair and unbiased consideration for every accused."[82]

Representative Harold Gross asked if the new appeals court would have "at least one member . . . [as] a former enlisted man." Vinson responded that the president "has the right to appoint any type of man he sees fit to appoint," including "a former enlisted man. He can appoint any lawyer, even though he has never had any military experience. . . . However, military service may be a factor in selecting him."[83]

Aside from the House members who had participated in the hearings, only seven additional representatives joined in the debate on the UCMJ. Due possibly to the effective presentation by the committee leadership which may well have discouraged many congressmen from raising questions about a complex code with more than 140 separate articles, interest in the legislation appears to have been so desultory that not all the time allotted for discussion was

[80] Ibid. Members of the House who listened to Philbin might have wondered how he could make such a claim in the light of Brooks's admission only a few minutes before that explained the decision *not* to remove the commander's authority to convene courts-martial and select their personnel as one resulting from a desire to "avoid the enactment of provisions which will unduly restrict those who are responsible for the conduct of our military operations." Ibid., 1905. At least one member, Foster Furcolo from Massachusetts, told his colleagues he did not think that the article dealing with influencing the court "will amount to a hill of beans. I know it is put in there and it says a lot of things, but I do not think it is going to amount to too much." Ibid., 1911.

[81] Ibid., 1909.

[82] Ibid. To this day, the court claims total independence from the Pentagon, except in matters of fiscal administration. But, as will be seen in the second volume of this study, the court functions under the very large shadow cast by the awesome size of the American military establishment. The subtle result of being inextricably connected to it can only affect the way the judges perceive their mission.

[83] Ibid., 1911.

needed.[84] All of the numerous technical amendments presented by the committee were approved by voice vote. Foster Furcolo, later to become governor of Massachusetts, proposed three additional amendments. Two were rejected after Vinson reminded his colleagues that "the bill is highly technical, and we don't want to throw it out of balance."[85] Without even a roll call, the House passed the bill.[86]

Even before this step, the Senate had turned to its consideration of the UCMJ. As in the House, the chair of the Senate Armed Services Committee appointed a subcommittee to examine the bill. Many of the same witnesses who had already spoken presented their views at the earlier hearings now returned for a repeat performance. Although he had reason to be pleased with the UCMJ's progress through the House, Larkin assumed that the Senate would have its own agenda. He was right. More than another year was to go by before the UCMJ became law.

[84] Ibid., 1913.

[85] Ibid., 1926. Furcolo's third amendment giving some flexibility to a court-martial concerning the scope of punishment under one article was accepted. Vinson's comment was further indication—seen also in the committee's repeated emphasis on the length of subcommittee time devoted to the bill, and the number of experts involved—of the leadership's successful desire that the House make virtually no changes whatsoever in the UCMJ as reported to them by Vinson's committee. The practice of discouraging open debate on major legislation by pointing to its complexity and the number of competing interests that support it is, of course, nothing new. But more than forty years later, the skill employed by Brooks, Philbin, and Vinson in using this technique remains impressive.

[86] Ibid., 1927.

CHAPTER 11

Creation of the Court, 1949–1950

THE SENATE SCENARIO

ALTHOUGH there seems to have been an informal agreement that the Senate would defer consideration of the UCMJ until after the House had acted, the upper house actually began its proceedings before the House Armed Services Committee unanimously sent the revised bill to the floor. When compared with the earlier House Subcommittee hearings, the Senate action revealed several differences. In the first place, the Senate spent much less time on the proposed code than its House counterpart. Brooks's panel had consumed at least twenty days in consideration of the UCMJ, with its sessions—as well as those of the full committee—spread out over more than five weeks. By contrast, the Senate Subcommittee devoted only three days to public hearings, with a fourth and final session reserved for further discussion with Morgan, Larkin, and his assistant. The House panel included more than a dozen participants, while for most of its public hearings the Senate Subcommittee consisted of only two members, Kefauver and Saltonstall.[1]

Moreover, the House Subcommittee conducted its business at a leisurely pace. By comparison, Kefauver, a newly elected Democrat from Tennessee, urged each speaker to limit himself to twenty minutes. He asked Wiener, for example, "to make your points fully, but try not to get into any extraneous matters."[2] Finally, at the House hearings in addition to Morgan, two of his colleagues—Kenney and Zuckert—also testified. None of the JAGs came before the panel. The situation was reversed for the Senate Subcommittee. Not one of the service undersecretaries testified, but the three JAGs were invited to speak—and all duly appeared.[3]

[1] Sen. Millard Tydings had appointed a five-member subcommittee including himself, Kefauver as chair, Saltonstall, Wayne Morse, and Richard Russell. As far as I have been able to ascertain, Morse attended only two sessions, while Tydings and Russell appear not to have participated in the subcommittee hearings at all.

[2] LH, 1019. To another witness Kefauver stated, "Frankly, the way we are going, I am afraid the summer will catch us before we get around to reworking and the consideration of this bill. So, I do hope all the witnesses will assist the committee. We want to cover all the points, but please do so as briefly as possible." Ibid., 1091.

[3] Kefauver took care to note in the record that the Judge Advocates were appearing at the request of his committee. Gordon Gray had declined to appear before either panel, although as

Kefauver's decision to call the three senior military justice officers concerned Larkin. He was all too well aware that for the most part, the major modifications in the code had been accepted to accommodate their needs. Larkin feared that the invitation might open the door to additional changes. "I do not know," he wrote to Leva, "what impels Senator Kefauver to call [the JAGS] at this time[,] or who persuaded him to do so." He urged Leva to discuss [Army JAG] Green's testimony with Gray. More important, "I think a decision should be made as to whether General Green will speak as the official army representative expressing the army views or whether he will give his own personal views."[4]

With the exception of the JAGS, most of the witnesses before Kefauver's panel were content to reiterate and indeed in some cases merely repeat verbatim earlier statements made to the House Subcommittee. Not unreasonably, attention tended to focus on the articles that had generated controversy since they were first considered. Three of these were of special importance to military justice: (*a*) the problem of command influence, (*b*) the role of the law member, and (*c*) the new appellate process. The committee's staff prepared a summary of the conflicting views on these points, including what had been said before both panels, as well as action taken by the House. Before reporting the bill to the full Senate Committee, Kefauver determined to bring Morgan and Larkin back for a final session to comment specifically on these several issues.

Kefauver received other information about opposition to some of the articles as well. Thus, an unsigned memo in his file on Military Justice noted that barring the law member from deliberation with the other court members "deprives the court of the benefit of legal learning and experience during the most critical stage of the proceeding."[5] Furthermore, the discretionary authority of the boards of review to reduce sentences was "extremely unwise. It would authorize them to substitute their judgment on military policy for that of responsible commanders or even the Secretary of the Army." Nor was there any need for "civilian review by a civilian court. Its members will not have the experience necessary to consider military questions which are so closely related to questions of law that they cannot be separated. In effect the court will be another administrative board and not a court at all."[6]

Another unsigned memorandum concluded that the proposed UCMJ "is no

---

will be seen shortly, his resentment concerning the decisions reached by Forrestal about several disputed articles in the UCMJ had not yet abated.

[4] LP, May 6, 1949. As will be seen, Larkin had good reason to be concerned with Green's testimony although, given Gray's consistent opposition to the proposed appellate review system, that Gray's own representative would also oppose it cannot have surprised him.

[5] *Kefauver Papers, Military Justice File*, hereafter cited as KF. This memorandum is undated as well as unsigned.

[6] Ibid.

improvement'' over the recently enacted Elston Act. Like some other suggested changes, the proposed court of military appeals will ''simply add expense, without improving efficiency.''[7] The writer advised Kefauver to avoid ''hasty enactment of legislation on such an important and far reaching subject.'' It would be better to see how the changes prescribed under the Elston Act (which went into effect in February 1949) worked out in practice.[8]

One of the ''new'' witnesses who appeared before Kefauver's subcommittee was William Hughes, Jr., president of the Judge Advocates Association. He testified that the proposed UCMJ ''civilianizes a thing that is basically noncivilian in character, namely the discipline of the Army. It does this by toning down and minimizing the military control and exaggerating the civilian control.'' The flaw with Morgan's proposed court was that ''in serious cases the discipline of the Army is in the hands of civilians, and no longer in the hands of the Army.''[9] Hughes also presented a summary of answers to a questionnaire concerning the new code that he had submitted to the members of the Association. Many responses opposed the principle of civilian control concerning military justice.[10]

> Military justice is a means instead of an end[,] anyway. It's too bad we have to have it at all and if we ever have lasting world peace we can abolish it all. But until we reach that state of security[,] let's keep our military establishments military. . . . Let's just admit that the military can't do as good a job of justice as the civil authorities, but the military can do a better job of fighting and since military justice is a necessary part of the fighting machine we will have to keep it.[11]

But the anonymous comments on the proposed Uniform Code were by no means uniform in their reactions to it. Another response argued that ''ultimate [judicial] recourse should be civilian, because the ultimate government and

[7] KF, *Memorandum, S. 857,* [undated] 1, 2.

[8] Ibid., 4. In contrast with these two memoranda, the summaries put together by Larkin and Senate staff member Mark Galusha for Kefauver's subcommittee were accurate, well balanced, and judicious in tone. See LP, *Issues before the Senate Committee on Armed Services*, in particular I, ''Command Control''; II, ''Law Officer''; and III, ''Boards of Review and Courts of Military Appeals.'' After noting army opposition to a civilian court, the summary repeated Morgan's contention that ''it is necessary if the substantive and procedural law of the Uniform Code—which applies to all persons in the Services—is to be uniformly interpreted.'' Those agreeing with Morgan also saw ''a need for a final authority on the law[,] and feel the present system—whereby the Secretaries of the Departments or the President are called upon to decide questions of law—is completely inadequate.'' Finally, ''they believe that a court of this character, with the prestige of a United States Court of Appeals, will do a great deal to insure public confidence in the fairness of military justice.'' Ibid., III, 3.

[9] LH, 1115.

[10] ''This is a code obviously drawn up by some fuddy-duddy who never saw a day in the field with troops and certainly no combat. . . . [It is] too technical to work.'' LH, 1119.

[11] Ibid., 1118. Another respondent wrote that ''a soldier is not a civilian and a civilian is not a soldier, and never the twain shall meet.'' Ibid., 1119.

law of the land are civilian. Soldiers, as such, do not lose their citizenship. Citizenship is a civilian capacity and should not be impaired with ultimate civilian supervision.''[12] And at least one member of the Association echoed Farmer, Wels, Spiegelberg, and Keeffe in their less than unrestrained enthusiasm for the new statute. ''I am for the uniform code even though it is a single, faltering, inadequate step—yet it is a movement in the right direction.''[13]

GREEN'S GRIPES

Of the three JAGs who testified *seriatim* on May 9, 1949, Army Maj. Gen. Thomas Green was most critical of the proposed civilian appellate process.[14] Military justice, he argued ''is a field . . . which requires not only a thorough familiarity with criminal law, but also experience and training in military matters.'' The civilian high court proposed by Morgan should, according to Green, consist of ''those military lawyers who are most highly experienced and trained both from a military and judicial viewpoint: both as soldiers and as judges.''[15] Echoing Wiener, Green insisted that these individuals were already available within the JAG Corps; there was no need to have civilians on such a tribunal.

Hence it followed that no real necessity for a *civilian* high court existed. In reality, this panel ''would be at best an administrative board.''[16] A more desirable alternative would be the type of judicial council mandated in the Elston Act. It consisted of three general officers, appointed by Green himself, ''each of whom has more than thirty years experience in the Army.'' Moreover, ''this panel operates without the benefit of any civilian corps to supervise it.''[17]

[12] Ibid., 1121.

[13] Ibid., 1122.

[14] As Larkin had desired, Green made it clear to Kefauver's panel that ''he was here at the request of the committee and with the approval of the Department of the Army; and the views I am expressing are my own personal ones and not necessarily those of the [service].'' Ibid., 1146.

[15] LH, 1150.

[16] Ibid., 1154.

[17] Ibid. Green's opposition to civilian participation in military justice predated consideration of the UCMJ in 1949. During much of World War II he had served as ''essentially the czar of civilian life and criminal law enforcement'' in the Hawaiian Islands, while they were under martial law. By December 1942, his autocratic conduct as ''Executive, Office of the Military Governor'' had received sufficient criticism for President Roosevelt's attorney general, Francis Biddle, to write privately to the president describing Green as ''a stuffy, overzealous, unyielding martinet'' who should ''be replaced at once.'' Scheiber, ''Constitutional Liberty in World War II,'' 347, 362, 365. Within a few months, Green was transferred to another post, and in 1945 became Army JAG. He retired in November 1949. It will be recalled that early in the deliberations concerning preparation of the UCMJ, Green had refused to meet with Larkin's Working Group, insisting that he would be available only to Morgan's committee. ''As to General Green's suggestion,'' noted

Yet the Army JAG conceded the need for coordination among the services in both the administration and application of military justice. Thus, he too proposed a court of appeals; one that was far from what Morgan had in mind. It would consist not of judges drawn from civilian life, but rather the three JAGs themselves, joined by a senior official from the treasury department who would represent the Coast Guard—Green's sole concession for a civilian dimension to the court, and one that could always be outvoted by the majority.

Finally, Green—as had Keeffe—called for creation of an advisory council *within* the military establishment, to consist of not more than five lawyers. They were to be drawn from civilian life, but would be appointed by the secretary of defense, not the president. Unlike Keeffe's council, however, this one would have no authority over military justice. Instead, it could provide for "a continuing study on the administration of military justice by a body of eminent jurists in conjunction with" the JAGs.[18]

Although Admiral Russell also suggested some amendments, he voiced no complaint about Morgan's proposed Court of Military Appeals.[19] Similarly, Air Force Major General Harmon not only supported the new tribunal, but saw "no particular objection to having civilians serve on the board of review if they are men of sufficient experience in the administration of military justice to act."[20] Yet Harmon also believed that Morgan's court should not be limited only to civilians. "I certainly think they should have military experience, whether they are military or civilian, on that court." The criterion "should turn on the question of qualifications. The test should be the qualifications of the man rather than the suit he happens to be wearing."[21]

GRAY'S GRUDGE

During the Senate Subcommittee hearings on the UCMJ, Gray's lingering irritation with Forrestal's decision to support a civilian appellate court surfaced again. As with the earlier episode, it appeared to be based on a trivial incident, and yet it demonstrates anew the extent to which Gray was willing to go to win his point. On April 19, he wrote an angry letter to Larkin objecting to

Morgan, "I can tell you confidentially that he was uncooperative from the beginning although he had a representative of his office sitting in at all sessions." MPVU, October 22, 1951.

[18] LH, 1155, 1162–64. Green submitted his suggestions in the form of specific amendments to the UCMJ as passed by the House. They provided for no civilian judicial supervision of any sort within the military justice system. Green even did away with the option of naming civilians to the boards of review.

[19] Ibid., 1178.

[20] Given Harmon's initial opposition to the UCMJ in 1948, as well as his somewhat negative comments in his interview almost forty years later, these statements to Kefauver's subcommittee probably did not reflect his own opinions. See above, chap. 8.

[21] Ibid., 1180, 1182.

language that Larkin had used in an article "Unifying the Code of Military Justice," appearing in the April issue of *Army Information Digest*.

Gray stated that Larkin's language "conveys the impression that the committee arrived unanimously at decisions which were the complete basis for the [UCMJ]. . . . This we all know is not correct." Gray believed that any public statement about the code must indicate "that committee decisions were not unanimous, and in fact, that even in a couple of instances the committee itseif was overruled. I must insist that when information concerning the activities of the committee is made public[,] care must be taken to assure that it will not be misinterpreted. I feel that in the event of recurrences of this nature I must . . . take action publicly to correct possible misunderstandings resulting therefrom."[22]

Larkin immediately drafted a reply that bristled with irritation. "I resent," he wrote, "a great quickness on your part to impute to me an attempt to convey an erroneous impression on the question of unanimity." The editor of an army journal in Gray's own department had requested the article, and then had deleted a sentence of Larkin's draft which "I went out of my way to include in recognition of your position." Moreover, Larkin had not even received the courtesy of being informed about the change of the paragraph in question. If Gray wanted to take action publicly, "I must reserve the right to do the same in connection with any public statements which might be construed as affecting me personally."[23]

But Larkin never sent this letter. Instead he spoke to Marx Leva, one of Forrestal's assistants who had stayed on when Louis Johnson became secretary of defense. Leva in turn wrote to Gray suggesting that "on this particular point, I think . . . we have reached the stage at which it becomes a little fruitless to pile up controversy on top of controversy. . . . I would suggest that the subject be dropped."[24]

Larkin also wrote to Morgan. "As you see, Gordon is still dancing on his pinpoint, and my patience with him is worn thin." Larkin added that he had drafted "an answering memorandum which was considerably more forthright than Marx's, but [Leva] urged me not to send it and took up the cudgels himself."[25] Morgan now sent his own comments to Gray. He could "appreciate your desire to have it appear clearly that the report of the Committee was not unanimous, . . . but do you not think it would be unwise to appear to emphasize the dissent, unless the situation calls for comment upon the specific issues?"[26]

22 LP, April 19, 1949.

23 Ibid., April 20, 1949.

24 Ibid.

25 Ibid., April 21, 1949.

26 Ibid., April 25, 1949. In his original draft which was handwritten on the top of Gray's letter

Gray responded to all three letter writers. He did not apologize to Larkin. Rather, he admitted that "under the circumstances I do not feel that my letter to you should have been couched in such strong terms. I trust that you will understand that it was written in ignorance of what had happened."[27] To Leva, Gray acknowledged that he had not known of the editorial omission. "However, even the language originally submitted by Felix fails to make it clear that there were important disagreements." Gray felt "so strongly about a couple of the issues involved that considerations of self respect make it imperative for me to guard against official indications that I was a willing party to some of the decisions reached."[28]

Gray reminded Morgan that "I declined the invitation to appear before the House Committee[,] when my presence would very probably have inevitably resulted in rather sharp emphasis on the dissent." Nevertheless, "there is no inclination on my part to prolong the discussions. As far as I am concerned, the memorandum to Felix Larkin stated my position, and I don't expect to have anything more to say about it, either to him or to the other members of the committee."[29]

What Gray did not write to Larkin, Leva, and Morgan, was that even as he waxed indignant over this issue, he again sought the intervention of a senior official on his behalf—as he had in 1948. This time it was through the secretary of the army, Kenneth Royall. On April 25, Royall wrote to Defense Secretary Louis Johnson, reminding him that Gray had "differed radically with the Committee report on one or two vital matters, including particularly the establishment of a civilian review board. My views were entirely in accord with those of Mr. Gray." Royall suggested "that you personally discuss this matter with Mr. Gray with a possible view to reconsideration of the position of the National Military Establishment. Even if your decision is not changed, I would like you to consider permitting Mr. Gray to express his personal views in this matter in the event he is called upon to testify before Congressional Committees."[30] The impetus for Royall's letter came from Gray, who wrote upon the copy he had received from Royall that "this was written in response to a request from me."

Johnson turned Royall's letter over to Larkin, who submitted a memorandum to the new secretary explaining the background of the controversy. He also enclosed a draft of a suggested reply to Royall. In it, he emphasized the unanimous vote in favor of the UCMJ by the House Armed Services Com-

---

to Larkin, Morgan had originally used this sentence: "I cannot help feeling that you are a bit too sensitive about this matter." He later deleted it.

[27] Ibid., April 22, 1949.

[28] *Gray Papers*, April 21, 1949.

[29] MPVU, April 28, 1949.

[30] Ibid., April 25, 1949. As if to make the matter even clearer, Gray signed his name to the sentence he had appended to Royall's letter.

mittee, as well as the endorsement received by the Bureau of the Budget, thus making the bill "an administration measure." Finally, Larkin recommended that the new secretary write, "I shall be glad to speak to Mr. Gray and would like Professor Morgan and the other available members of the Committee present when I do so."[31] Johnson signed the letter, thus apparently ending Gray's final attempt to reverse support for Morgan's civilian court. There is no indication that either Royall or Gray ever accepted Johnson's invitation.

McCARRAN'S MACHINATIONS

As Kefauver's panel proceeded with the hearings, another Senator, Nevada Democrat Patrick McCarran, offered his views on military justice and the UCMJ. They took the form of a thirty-five page letter to Kefauver, one which McCarran specifically requested to be made a part of the subcommittee's record on the bill.[32] He described his missive as an "intensive study" of the proposed code. McCarran probably had much more on his mind than merely an interest in military justice, and there may have been a number of reasons for this rambling if not confused analysis.

The Nevada senator was chairman of the Senate Judiciary Committee, and his letter, replete with numerous complaints and suggestions for changes in the code perhaps was the first step in an effort to insure that his committee rather than the Armed Services panel controlled the bill once it reached the Senate floor.[33] As will be seen later, this issue was resolved with McCarran the loser. However, several of his comments about the proposed system of appellate review warrant brief discussion here.

McCarran implied at the outset that Morgan's committee had been dominated by the military, thus furnishing all the more reason for *his* Senate Committee to take jurisdiction of the bill. He went on to ask two questions about Morgan's appellate system: (*a*) is the judicial council "a court"? and (*b*) if so, can it be set up within the military? McCarran argued that "used in the general sense, this is a court; however it is not a court in the strict constitutional sense in that it does not derive its power from Article III of the Constitution," but

[31] LP, April 29, 1949. Having made his point, Larkin added that Gray was "of course, free to give his personal views to Congress, if he desires." He also reminded Royall that Johnson had designated Morgan to speak on his behalf before the Senate Committee. Gray chose not to appear before Kefauver's panel.

[32] It duly appears in LH, 993–1011. Also, another copy is in Kefauver's papers.

[33] A colorful, conservative, and controversial political figure, in 1949 Sen. Patrick McCarran was preparing to seek reelection to a fourth term. As chairman of the Senate Judiciary Committee, he claimed a sort of proprietary interest in any bill related to the judiciary. By the late 1940s, he had managed to broaden the scope of his committee to the extent that 40 percent of all national legislation came within its purview. See "Patrick A. McCarran" in *Dictionary of American Biography* (Supp. 5), 443–44.

rather from Article I which, among other things granted plenary authority to Congress concerning enactment of "rules for the government and regulation of the land and naval forces."

Accepting McCarran's premise, two conclusions followed. First, that Morgan's judicial council did not belong to the judicial branch, but to the executive.[34] Second and more important, though it might have the trappings of an appellate court, in fact the council findings "are subject to executive or administrative action of the President or the Secretary of the [military] department." McCarran concluded that the "proposed tribunal is in the final analysis nothing more than an agency of the executive department."[35]

These assertions were merely a reiteration of the traditional view put forth by Winthrop, and debated at great length during the Ansell-Crowder controversy. McCarran believed, as had Crowder, that somehow the presidential authority as commander in chief affected judicial independence. Rather than confront this conviction, Morgan's approach had been simply to ignore it as irrelevant. He assumed that power to create military courts did indeed come from Congress, vis-à-vis Article I. Such authority, however, included congressional discretion over both jurisdictional parameters and the terms of its judges. Nothing, in other words, except its own inclination prevented Congress from giving life tenure to the judges of a court created under Article I.

For Morgan, the issue of presidential control over military courts had been a brick without straw. The president could always mitigate a sentence or pardon the defendant. Presumably, he could also pardon any criminal defendant in a federal court. As far as the functioning of the military appeals court was concerned, it made no difference. Morgan believed, correctly as later history would reveal, that this tribunal would operate as did any other federal appellate court, subject to the specific limitations set forth in the proposed statute.[36]

Maintaining that the proposed court would be "merely another administrative agency . . . rather than a military supreme court," McCarran recommended the use of existing federal courts as a final forum in which to resolve issues of military justice. These decisions would emanate from an Article III judicial panel, and would be more creditable than findings handed down by a "military tribunal appellate in character."[37] The same proposal had been made by other witnesses before the congressional panels considering the UCMJ. Besides rejecting the premise upon which McCarran based this suggestion, Larkin and Morgan had other objections.

[34] LH, 1004.

[35] Ibid., 1005–6.

[36] In this context, attention is called to article 76, which provided that judicial actions taken under the UCMJ were binding "upon all departments, courts, agencies, and officers of the United States." Presidential authority was exempted from this article. McCarran's interpretation of it is discussed below.

[37] LH, 1007, 1009.

Given the size of the military justice system and the admitted need for uniformity, how could separate federal district courts operate efficiently in this area? Also, if one tribunal outside the military justice system—such as the Court of Appeals for the District of Columbia—was selected, how would it interact with the JAGS and the judges of Morgan's proposed court, all of whom were required to confer together and make recommendations with respect to the military justice system? Finally, "the complex military matters involved in many of the offenses" required a specialized Court.[38]

MORGAN'S PENULTIMATE POINTS

Although Kefauver had declared the public hearings on the UCMJ concluded with the evidence offered by the three JAGS on May 9, the subcommittee was unable to meet until May 27, when Morgan returned for a final appearance.[39] While he focused on all the controversial issues that had to be resolved by the panel, three of them are of special interest here: command influence, the law member of the court, and the military appellate process. Although the senators had listened sympathetically to those witnesses urging changes beyond the provisions enacted by the House, after meeting with Morgan the alterations they actually approved turned out to be very few—due in part, perhaps, to Morgan's powers of persuasion.[40]

Virtually all of the witnesses, including Morgan, had conceded the undesirable potential for command influence when that official was permitted to select members of the court-martial. Emphasizing that the UCMJ had to be practical as well as practicable, Morgan reminded the senators of the specific safeguards against command influence that had been incorporated into the proposed draft, that is, making such conduct an offense and providing for its punishment. He further noted that if a commander is determined to use "undue influ-

[38] LP, May 10, 1949. In this memorandum to Larkin, his assistant Robert Haydock (recently graduated from Harvard Law) examined twenty-five of McCarran's objections, proposals, and comments—rejecting every one of them. McCarran, however, was not yet finished with the UCMJ.

[39] According to Kefauver, "considerable time has elapsed since we completed hearings . . . because it has been difficult to find a time when we could all get together." LH, 1194.

[40] Shortly after Morgan's meeting with the Senate Panel, he received a letter from Robert Smart, the staff member of the House Armed Services Committee. "I got a little disturbed by the proceedings before the Senate Subcommittee and felt they should send for the old master, meaning you, of course. . . . I have remained completely aloof from the Senate proceedings, knowing they will act in their own sweet time. I can only hope that they don't emasculate the product of your long and earnest efforts without the cogent reasons which I know they cannot produce." MPVU, June 2, 1949. In addition to Morgan's skill as chairman of the CUCMJ, to say nothing of his reputation as a distinguished elder statesman of legal scholarship, his network of former law students was quite extensive. Thus, Kefauver cited "a very pleasant recollection of the days when Professor Morgan taught evidence at Yale University. I am glad that Harvard hasn't—" Morgan immediately interrupted with the comment that "it hasn't corrupted me too much." LH, 948.

ence, . . . he can use it on men of his command who are selected by the JAG just as well as if he selected them himself.''[41] Kefauver and Saltonstall, the only two senators present for this final session, agreed to leave the matter of command control untouched, but to ''put the services on notice that . . . we are watching to see whether there is going to be undue influence.''[42]

Turning next to the question of the law officer voting with the other members of the court, Morgan observed that the issue of having lawyers on military courts was not new. During World War I, commanders had not wanted attorneys as members of the court because of their fear that lawyers ''would bitch up the thing by telling them some law.''[43] Again, the senators agreed with Morgan that the law officer who, under the UCMJ now had to be a lawyer, should not participate in the deliberations of the court.

Several witnesses had objected to the proposed power of a Board of Review to reduce sentences, arguing that it interfered with authority of the JAG. Morgan commented that the problem of excessive sentences ''is one of the places where there has been . . . tremendous criticism of the [armed forces].'' He recalled that during World War I, ''I happened to sit for 6 weeks as chairman of the clemency committee, and I know we remitted 18,000 years in 6 weeks. The sentences are just fantastic at times.''[44] Without further discussion, Saltonstall and Kefauver decided to make no change.

Kefauver opened discussion on the Court of Military Appeals (Morgan's old ''judicial council'') with the point that several witnesses, such as Wiener, had urged that previous military experience be required for the civilian judges. Morgan replied, ''Well, I ask you, after you saw Colonel Wiener here, he is a civilian, would you like to have him on a court of military appeals?''[45] One would like to know the response of the senators to Morgan's question. Unfortunately, right at this point there was ''discussion off the record.'' Both senators, however, determined not to impose a requirement of prior military experience.

Saltonstall then turned to the one area where he proposed a real change in Morgan's court as it had been drafted by the House. His prior thinking on the question of terms for the judges has already been discussed in his correspondence with Raymond Wilkins. Now, Saltonstall told Kefauver and Morgan that ''my feeling would be to establish this civilian court, but not give them life tenure on good behavior, but make it for a period of years.''[46] Kefauver added that there should be initial terms of three, five, and seven years—with future terms for reappointed judges set at either seven or nine years. ''We

[41] Ibid., 1197.

[42] Ibid., 1198.

[43] Ibid., 1200.

[44] Ibid., 1202.

[45] Ibid.

[46] Ibid.

want,'' he said, ''to see how this court is going to operate and what kind of personnel we are going to get. . . .''[47]

Assuming (wrongly, as it turned out) that the court could begin operation in March 1950, Larkin noted that three-, five-, and seven-year terms ''would scatter pretty well,'' missing presidential elections in each case.[48] Morgan stated that ''I have no objection to whatever term you fix, just so the thing is not made a football of politics. I am just as anxious as you are, Senator, that they shall not have a lot of lame ducks running around here.'' Perhaps with insights gained from actual experience as a politician, Kefauver immediately added ''unless they are good lame ducks.''[49]

One can only speculate as to why Morgan was so quick to endorse this change, even though it represented a major shift away from the type of tribunal he had envisaged. Perhaps he was more concerned with getting the appellate court established, something that obviously required Senate support. He may also have been aware of Saltonstall's consistent inclinations against life tenure. Whatever the reason, the Senate decision to go with fixed-year terms was the most significant alteration made in the House version of the UCMJ. Inevitably, both congressional and presidential politics played a role in judicial appointments to the court. Moreover, this action insured a frequent turnover of judges, resulting in a future source of judicial instability during much of the court's subsequent history—probably to its overall detriment.[50]

With his labors on the new code now concluded, Morgan drafted letters of appreciation to Leva and Larkin. ''My work on the Code is finished,'' he wrote to Larkin; adding with unintentional understatement that ''you still have quite a job on your hands.'' Morgan did not exaggerate when he praised Larkin's ''extraordinary administrative ability in a situation that required not only thorough study and comprehensive planning[,] but also smooth and speedy accomplishment. If I have deserved a Certificate of Merit, [something Morgan received at the behest of Larkin] you ought to get two.''[51]

In a letter to Leva written the same day, Morgan acknowledged his gratitude for securing ''the opportunity to take part in this important project. It was especially welcome because of my experience in 1919–1920, when I supported General Ansell in his heroic losing battle with General Crowder.'' As

47 Ibid., 1203. Saltonstall had already noted that ''we have got to gamble that the President is going to appoint good men. That is a gamble and there will be some good and some bad.'' The court's subsequent history seems to have vindicated his prediction. Later, after the revised bill had been unanimously reported to the full Senate, Kefauver wrote to a member of the House that ''I have no deep convictions about the length of time appointments should be for. The idea of the Committee was that if the original appointments were made for a shorter time than life, this would give us an opportunity of having another look at how the Court works.'' KP, October 3, 1949.

48 Ibid., 1204.

49 Ibid.

50 These developments are discussed in the second volume of this study.

51 MPVU, May 31, 1949.

for Larkin, "it has been a joy to work with him. He is proof positive that not all first-class lawyers and administrators come from the first string law schools."[52]

Speaking for the Armed Services Committee, Kefauver favorably reported the UCMJ by a unanimous vote to the Senate on June 10.[53] He emphasized that the appeals court "is established in the National Military Establishment for the purpose of administration only, and will not be subject to the authority, direction, or control of the Secretary of Defense." The panel had ultimately fixed on eight-year terms, and "the judges are to be highly qualified civilians. . . ."[54] Under Senate rules, the bill would take its place on the consent calendar, and when called up could pass without debate, *provided* there was no objection. If, however, senators objected, not only could the bill be subject to debate and amendment, but its place on the calendar would depend on other business before the Senate.

SENATORIAL SWIPES

Even as Kefauver presented the proposed code to the Senate, he had already received a warning that its immediate and uneventful passage would be unlikely. New Hampshire Republican Sen. Charles Tobey informed him that if the House bill was reported substantially without changes by Kefauver's committee which, as has been shown, is just what happened, "I shall consider it my duty to bring the facts to the attention of the Senate by introducing the bulk of the Amendments proposed by [the JAG] of the Army and discuss them thoroughly upon their merits."[55] Since Green had suggested more than twenty-five of them, Kefauver's concern was understandable. He immediately asked Larkin "to have little talks prepared for him on the amendments."[56]

Larkin received word from a staff member of the Armed Services Committee on June 21, that Oregon Republican Wayne Morse had objected to the UCMJ on the calendar call, and that other senators including Joseph R. McCarthy were also ready to object. Why the Wisconsin senator opposed it, "he

[52] Morgan also wrote Gordon Gray who had just been named secretary of the army. "It is heartening for an old Mugwump like me to see an appointment to important public office made strictly on merit." Adding that he had sent Gray a telegram, Morgan noted that "I should have sent it to the President on his good luck and his—somewhat delayed—good sense. . . . If this keeps up I shall soon be convinced that occasional manifestations of sound judgment cannot be ascribed to mere accident." Ibid., June 10, 1949.

[53] According to Larkin, the actual vote was taken on June 8, and would not have been unanimous had Sen. Wayne Morse been on time. "He wanted to vote against it, but he came in too late[,] and it didn't go on record." LPPL, June 9, 1949.

[54] LH, 1256.

[55] KP June 2, 1949.

[56] LPPL, June 2, 1949.

doesn't know, but said no one pays any attention to him.''[57] Discussing Morse's action later that day with Morgan, Larkin echoed his committee source, Mark Galusha, about McCarthy. ''I am unable to find out, as of this writing, what he has in mind, and, generally, would write him off as unimportant.'' Morse, unfortunately, was another story.[58] Apparently he had decided to support the ABA proposal to solve command control by using a panel for the selection of court-martial members.

Larkin assured Morgan that he would try to see Morse, but ''I don't believe I will be able to convince him. . . . [I]t appears to me that he has now publicly committed himself in such a way that he would be reluctant to back down. It is vastly annoying to find that he is such a demagogue in those matters, particularly when it is perfectly obvious that he knows nothing about the bill, command control[,] or the implications of the panel.''[59] Larkin asked Morgan to write to Morse directly. ''A few choice words about the panel, the unwieldy labyrinth it provides[,] and the fact that it will be no more effective in eliminating command control than present provisions—all might be helpful.''[60]

Upon receipt of Larkin's letter, Morgan wrote to Morse on June 24, expressing sorrow ''that you were unable to be present at the meetings of the Sub-Committee of which you were a member.'' He explained again why the panel idea was impractical, and pointed to the new provisions in the UCMJ as the best means to provide against command influence. ''I trust,'' he concluded, ''that you will give personal attention to this letter, and not be satisfied with a word from your personal secretary as to its content.''[61]

Morse responded to ''Dear Eddie'' with a friendly but firm rejoinder. ''I am sure,'' he wrote, ''that I've given the matter as conscientious study as those members . . . who did attend the meetings.'' He objected to quick approval of the UCMJ in part because he had not completed ''to my own satisfaction my study and analysis of the issue,'' and also ''because I am satisfied that legislation as important as this should not be passed in the Senate of the United

[57] LPPL, June 21, 1949, 3. Given the national role that McCarthy shortly assumed, this observation is of some interest.

[58] At the age of 31, Wayne Morse had been appointed dean of the University of Oregon-Eugene. Prior to this post, he taught ''argumentation'' at the University of Wisconsin. First elected to the Senate in 1944, he served four terms, two as a Republican, two as a Democrat. A well-known political maverick, Morse resigned as a Republican during the 1952 presidential campaign, charging that ''reactionaries were running a captive general'' [Eisenhower] as Republican candidate. William O'Neil, *American High* (1986), 186. Later, Morse broke with President Lyndon Johnson over the Vietnam conflict. He was defeated for reelection in 1968, but captured the democratic nomination again in 1974. His unfortunate death during the ensuing campaign deprived Oregon voters of the opportunity to return him for a fifth term.

[59] Larkin may have been overly harsh in his criticism of Morse, who, when the bill finally came up for Senate debate, offered some very cogent criticisms of the UCMJ. See below.

[60] LP, June 21, 1949.

[61] MPVU, June 24, 1949.

States by unanimous consent.'' Finally, ''I am not going to vote for the proposal until I am thoroughly convinced on it.''[62]

As Larkin's office hastily prepared separate responses to each of Tobey's amendments, Millard Tydings, chairman of the Armed Services Committee, received a not unexpected letter from his colleague, Patrick McCarran. Aware that Kefauver's subcommittee had demonstrated little interest concerning the points raised in his lengthy ''analysis'' of the UCMJ, McCarran informed Tydings that ''I intend to move that the bill . . . be taken from the Senate Calendar and referred to the Committee on the Judiciary.'' He cited several ''compelling instances'' which he felt should have the scrutiny of *his* committee. The Nevada Democrat criticized in particular the provisions of article 76, which made decisions reached through the military justice system ''final and binding upon all departments, courts, agencies and officers of the United States.'' Failing to cite the clearly stated exemption for presidential authority, McCarran attacked the validity of this section on constitutional grounds. ''It is questionable whether an Act of Congress could rob the Supreme Court of appellate jurisdiction. I do not believe all civilian courts should be closed to anyone with respect to all matters which may have been tried before a military tribunal or administratively determined by the military. I question the wisdom of conferring absolute finality upon the decisions of an alleged 'court,' the members of which are subject to removal by an administrative officer.''[63]

Drafted by Larkin's office on July 6 and 9, Tydings's letter of July 13 rejected the premises upon which McCarran had attacked the UCMJ. He reminded McCarran, for example, that the reports of both the House and Senate concerning the code ''specifically state that article 76 does not foreclose the right to habeas corpus in the federal courts.'' More important was the fact that for the last fifty years at least, ''all matters on [military justice] have been considered as falling within the jurisdiction of the Committee on Armed Services or their predecessor committees.'' Specific legislation dealing with military justice had been before this panel in 1912, 1913, 1916, 1919, 1937, 1942, 1947, and 1948–1949. Tydings concluded by citing the desire of the secretary of defense that the bill be passed in the ''present session of Congress. My present feeling is that it should go forward at this time and, for that reason, I would not like to be required to oppose your motion.''[64]

[62] Ibid., July 5, 1949.

[63] LP, July 1, 1949, 1–2. McCarran failed to cite one very plausible justification for giving jurisdiction of the bill to his committee, and this was the fact that traditionally all federal judicial appointments were scrutinized first by the Senate Committee on the Judiciary. Morgan's committee had skirted the issue of whether or not the status of the proposed appellate judges under article I blocked consideration of the appointments by the Judiciary Committee; although Senate approval had been required in the House version and retained by the Senate. Nor did McCarran raise the point in his rebuttal to Tydings; see below. It may well be that McCarran saw the issue more as one of turf jurisdiction, rather than an important issue both in political and philosophical terms.

[64] LP, July 13, 1949.

Larkin kept Morgan closely informed about the developments threatening prompt consideration of his code. "Morse is not going to be nearly so difficult as he otherwise would have been if it weren't for the fact that you are in the picture." As for McCarran and his claim of jurisdiction, "Kefauver is in favor of meeting the issue head-on and vigorously opposing McCarran. That, of course, is just the position I want. . . . I suspect that McCarran will change his mind, and if he doesn't, I feel confident that we can beat him with the Parliamentarian and on the Floor, if necessary." More worrisome was the fact that "the Senate is so far behind and there are so many important measures still to be taken up."[65] These included time-consuming debate over changes in the National Labor Relations Act [the Taft-Hartley law], and the newly created North Atlantic Treaty Organization [NATO].

McCarran responded with another letter to Tydings that demonstrated his not inconsiderable skill in appearing to concede points without retreating on the primary issue. He denied any challenge to the jurisdiction of the Armed Services Committee. "All I am doing is asserting that the bill includes subject matter clearly within the jurisdiction of the [judiciary] Committee, and asking that now, after [Tydings's Committee] has had its say, the bill may be referred to the [Judiciary] Committee for consideration of those matters which do lie within [its] . . . jurisdiction." McCarran reminded Tydings that the Judiciary Committee retains jurisdiction over "judiciary proceedings, civil and criminal, generally, and over civil liberties. Where the rights and liberties of civilians are concerned, I believe that the jurisdiction of the [Judiciary] Committee should stand unquestioned; and there is no doubt that such rights are involved in the [proposed UCMJ]." Finally, McCarran assured Tydings that "if the bill is referred . . . it will be considered most promptly, and most promptly reported back to the Senate."[66]

As long as the UCMJ draft remained on the Senate Calendar, McCarran could do nothing. But his efforts to take the bill from Armed Services represented only one in a series of obstacles that arose as spring of 1949 turned into summer and fall. Besides McCarran's machinations, Morse had invited members of the ABA to prepare an amendment for him along the lines strenuously endorsed by George Spiegelberg, one that would set up a panel within the JAG Corps for appointment to courts-martial. Tobey had submitted more than two dozen amendments embodying the changes that had been proposed by Army JAG Thomas Green. And if all this wasn't sufficient, now Missouri Sen. James Kem proposed an expansion of what he had undertaken in 1948—to

[65] MPVU, July 13, 1949.

[66] LH, July 19, 1949, 1795–96. Larkin discussed "the advisability of replying further to McCarran" with one of Tydings's staff members, "and Galusha thought that if we did, McCarran would just come back with some other point." LPPL, July 26, 1949. Because McCarran could do nothing until the UCMJ was called up for Senate consideration, his attempt lay pending, as did the measure itself.

make the provisions of the Elston Act applicable to all the armed services, not just the army. As for the UCMJ, the senator saw no need for it at all.

In the Senate on July 29, 1949, Kem argued that "one of the main purposes of unification was simplification."[67] Incredibly, he described the UCMJ as a code that would "abolish all existing rules and start with a completely new set . . . a complication that is entirely unnecessary." The "simple, direct and satisfactory way" to bring about uniform court-martial procedure would be to "make this improved system [now in effect for the army] applicable to all three services. We will than have the unification desired."[68]

Larkin was less than impressed with Kem's proposal. As he wrote to Morgan, "the delay in bringing the UCMJ up for debate has created a few extra problems, because it has given some of the busybodies a little more time." Leading the list was Kem, "the latest nuisance, [who] now comes up with the wholly ridiculous idea that the best way to unify the court-martial system is to subject the Navy to the Articles of War. . . . This idea is so bad that I don't worry about it."[69]

Possibly at Kefauver's request, Larkin drafted a tactful, but thorough reply to Kem. It extended to fifteen pages, explained the origins and main features of the UCMJ, and pointed to the impossibility of the navy operating under the Articles of War. One reason the UCMJ had been so carefully drafted was because of a recognition that the two services had different needs. The letter concluded that "I feel our aims are identical. We both desire a uniform system. We want one that preserves the advances made by your amendment of last year and one that incorporates as many new advances as possible. I think the Uniform Code does this admirably well and merits our support."[70]

With one exception, discussion of all the Tobey amendments is unnecessary here. Larkin and his staff went to a good deal of trouble to fashion "mini-briefs" for Saltonstall and Kefauver to use on the floor. As it turned out, Tobey ultimately refrained from pushing his proposals. Brief comment, however, both on his suggested appellate procedure and Larkin's response is appropriate. Like Green, Tobey would have followed the existing army process, with appellate review confined primarily to the JAG department. As had Green, Tobey also criticized the excessive power vested in boards of review,

[67] LH, 1672.

[68] Ibid.

[69] LP, September 16, 1949.

[70] LP, August 10, 1949, 15. Writing to Kefauver, Larkin stated—quite accurately—that the arguments against Kem's proposal "could extend almost indefinitely, but I believe the suggested draft may persuade him to abandon his idea and support our bill as presently written." Ibid., August 10, 1949. In response, Kefauver called Larkin's letter "wonderfully prepared[,] and I am sending it to him." Ibid., August 22, 1949. Whether Kem was influenced by the Larkin-Kefauver message is not clear. However, in February 1950 when the Senate finally took up the UCMJ, he made no attempt to attach his amendment to the bill. Kem voted, unsuccessfully as will be seen, to refer the measure to McCarran's committee.

but endorsed the "judicial councils" that had been created by the Elston Act. Further, the Army JAG had recommended a court of appeals to consist of the three JAGs plus a civilian official from the treasury, representing the Coast Guard. Tobey disagreed, calling instead for cases to be heard by the U.S. Court of Appeals for the District of Columbia. This was "a court in whom all concerned can have confidence." He denounced the idea, reflected in the UCMJ, that Morgan's court should be "constituted on the basis of political considerations. I have never before heard of a proposal . . . that not more than two of the judges of such court shall be appointed from the same political party. Political considerations have no place in the appointment of a judicial body for the armed forces."[71]

Larkin's rebuttal emphasized the unwieldy character of the existing appellate system as generally "unintelligible[,] . . . probably unworkable . . . and uneconomical of men, time and money." A more serious flaw with Tobey's amendment was that it could not guarantee "uniformity of [judicial] interpretation or construction of the Code." No service was obligated to follow the holdings of a judicial council from another service. Nor were the appropriate officials required to certify a case to the District Court of Appeals—"even if that case had been decided in a manner diametrically opposed to a decision on a similar case" in a different branch of the armed forces.

Furthermore, the UCMJ "gives the accused the right to appeal to a supreme civilian court on matters of law," something Tobey would deny. Finally, Larkin suggested a reminder from Kefauver that "civilian control of the armed forces is a fundamental principle of our government." It was true that Tobey's proposal would allow for a possibility of a civilian review from the service secretaries. But historically, such review has "of necessity, been perfunctory and largely dependent upon the advice of assistants. The [UCMJ] transfers the duty of reviewing these cases on the law to a single body of experts, and that duty will be their fulltime job."[72]

Morse's action, Kem's proposed amendment, McCarran's jurisdictional ploy—together with Senator Tobey's introduction of twenty-seven separate amendments—left Senate consideration of the UCMJ up in the air.[73] Regretfully, Larkin informed Morgan on June 30, that "there is no fixed date for the

[71] LH, 1716. Tobey would have limited jurisdiction of this court to matters of law only. Moreover, only the president, secretary of defense, or a JAG could certify a case to it. Unlike Morgan's, this tribunal had no discretionary powers of certiorari. Ibid., 1721. Thus, unless one of these three high officials wanted otherwise, the appellate process for most defendants would end with the Board of Review, whose members were, of course, appointed by the JAGs.

[72] LP, "Proposed Statement, Articles 66–71—Amendments L-1 and L-2—Senator Tobey." The draft is undated, but was undoubtedly prepared either in June or July 1949.

[73] "My net feeling about all of them," wrote Larkin to Morgan concerning these obstacles to Senate passage, "is that they represent more of a nuisance value, rather than anything else, and that we can take care of them if we can ever get a debate on the Floor." LP, September 16, 1949.

debate on military justice.''[74] By September 16, he suspected that the bill ''may go over to the 2nd session.''[75] One month later nothing had changed, and ''the uniform code rests peacefully on the Senate Calendar.''[76] Although Larkin remained optimistic, in fact there would be no debate until the 81st Congress convened for its second session beginning January 2, 1950.[77]

Not until February 1, 1950, did the Senate turn to the UCMJ. Kefauver formally presented the bill, with a section-by-section analysis that had, of course, been prepared for him by Larkin's office. Indeed, at Kefauver's request, the Senate permitted Larkin and his assistant, Robert Haydock, to sit with Kefauver on the Senate floor during debate on the code. When Kefauver took up the appellate process, he told his colleagues that ''since the court represents a new concept in military law, it was advisable to provide the appointment of the judges for a term of years, rather than for life.''[78] Senator Kem questioned whether the ''court would have enough to do . . . to keep three men busy throughout the year, in time of peace.'' Kefauver answered ''that was one of the questions which . . . caused the Senate committee to recommend that the terms of the three judges be not for life, but for a certain number of years.''[79]

The Senate spent February 2 on other issues, with only desultory comment on the UCMJ. Sen. Wayne Morse noted, however, that on February 3, McCarran would propose that the bill be referred to the Judiciary Committee. Morse added that he would support McCarran's motion. ''It is my opinion that the bill should never have been referred to the Armed Services Committee'' at all. He could ''see no reason why questions as to judicial right[s] on the part of men in the armed services should be considered by any committee other than'' the Judiciary Committee. Morse sensed, correctly, an implication in the UCMJ that military justice differed in key essentials from its civilian counterpart. ''I happen to be one,'' he concluded, ''who believes we should not draw

[74] MPVU, June 30, 1949.

[75] Ibid., September 16, 1949.

[76] Ibid., October 12, 1949.

[77] Larkin so informed Morgan on November 23, 1949. ''We are initiating plans to have it brought to the Floor . . . in the first few weeks of the 2nd Session, and I am sure that when we get it to the Floor we will secure its passage.'' Part of Senate failure to consider the UCMJ can be attributed to legislative logjam. But politics may have played a role as well. Tydings had entrusted the bill to the care of a freshman senator from Tennessee, Estes Kefauver who, for reasons irrelevant to this study, was regarded with marked hostility by the senior senator from his state, one Kenneth McKellar who had been in office since Wilson's administration, and was a high-ranking member of the conservative southern clique that effectively ran the upper chamber. The consistent refusal of the Senate Majority Leader to bring the UCMJ to the floor may have been due in part to McKellar's preferences, rather than Kefauver's priorities. See Charles L. Fontenay, *Estes Kefauver* (1980), 154–55, 161. Fontenay wrote of McKellar that ''his bailiwick was the United States Senate, and he was its dean.'' Ibid., 106. McKellar, it should be noted, voted to refer the UCMJ to McCarran's committee.

[78] LH, 1976.

[79] Ibid.

the type of curtain between civilian and military justice that is drawn by this bill.''[80]

When Saltonstall pointed to the heavy weight of precedents favoring the Armed Services Committee considering military justice, Morse responded that ''I do not quarrel with the citation of precedents. I quarrel with the advisability of following those precedents. . . . It is high time—in fact it is long overdue—that we bring about a uniformity of principle in the administration of criminal justice, covering both civilians and military personnel.''[81] Here, Morse raised a fundamental, and possibly insolvable, issue. On the other hand, numerous witnesses had argued these questions before both congressional committees. The UCMJ had accepted the premise he rejected, a duality of the two justice systems. But Morgan's committee had taken several important steps to render military justice as close to its civilian counterpart as feasible. Also, it was very late in the legislative game for Morse to bring up these points, all the more as the Senate Majority leader had informed his colleagues that the vote would be taken on the next day, February 3.[82]

True to his promise, McCarran duly moved to have the bill referred to his committee. The ensuing debate essentially reiterated the points made in earlier correspondence between McCarran and Tydings. McCarran noted the less than rapid pace with which the bill had been considered by the Senate, and asked ''Why deny [his] committee jurisdiction? Are Senators afraid of the 13 men of whom the able Senator from Tennessee [Kefauver] is one?''[83]

Kem added that it ''is difficult for me to understand why any harm can be done to the public interest by having the subject deliberately considered by the Senate [Judiciary] Committee.''[84] McCarran further argued that, given the complaints received by his committee concerning military justice, ''I say to the Senate that it cannot afford not to refer this bill to the Judiciary Committee.'' Military courts, he concluded, ''are reeking with injustice, if we are to believe the charges which have been made.''[85] Finally, McCarran inquired, ''Is it desired that Senators who, like myself, favor something of the kind designed by the bill shall vote against [it]? I certainly shall vote against it if it comes to a vote and my committee is denied the right of review.''[86]

[80] Ibid., 1982.

[81] Ibid., 1983.

[82] ''I wish to advise Senators that the session will run rather late.'' Ibid., 1984.

[83] Ibid., 1986.

[84] 78. Ibid., 1988. Earlier, Kem could not resist inquiring ''why [passage of the UCMJ] becomes a matter of the utmost urgency at this time, when it has been pending for months and when no effort has been made . . . on the part of the majority to bring it to the attention of the Senate.'' Ibid., 1986.

[85] Ibid., 1987.

[86] Ibid., 1988. McCarran's insistence that the UCMJ be considered by his committee may have been due more to concern with his power over that committee, than with principles of military justice. McCarran's biographer notes that when in January 1951 Kefauver had proposed a Senate

When the vote was taken, the Senate defeated McCarran's motion, 33 in favor, 43 opposed, with 20 abstaining. Among those supporting McCarran were Kem, McCarthy, Morse, and Michigan Sen. Homer Ferguson, for whom the future held both defeat for reelection in 1952, and appointment to the very court soon to be created by the UCMJ. Had Tobey been present, he also would have voted with McCarran. With this motion lost, with both Kem and Tobey making no effort to move on their proposed amendments, the only remaining obstacle appeared to be Wayne Morse, who immediately claimed the floor after the Senate returned to consideration of the bill.

Morse's lengthy speech in support of the ABA-Spiegelberg amendments to the UCMJ was noteworthy for his release of a letter from Arthur Farmer (another New York attorney), severely critical of Morgan's opposition to the panel idea. The Harvard law professor had been "sold a bill of goods by those who advocated retention of command control . . . made possible because he is not familiar with the practical workings of either military justice or the Army line of command." He shows "an extraordinary and lamentable failure" to understand the proposed plan. Because Morgan lacked "complete familiarity with the processes of military justice," he was "at a tremendous disadvantage when faced by the Judge Advocate General or others equally experienced."[87]

Morse also had some comments about the Court of Military Appeals. Emphasizing that such a tribunal "must be free of the slightest imputation of political or military pressure," he argued that the Senate decision to reduce the terms from life or during good behavior to eight years was "inadvisable." Moreover, limiting tenure in this manner could well cause individuals with outstanding qualifications to decline appointment. Finally, and most important, Morse chided his own subcommittee for inconsistency. It wanted the new court to be on a par with United States Courts of Appeals, but it refused to give the judges that security and tenure common to their federal counterparts.[88]

---

investigation into organized crime (later to make him famous as chairman of the nationally televised Kefauver Hearings), "the resolution was amended to create a special Senate committee, partly because of fears that McCarran might dominate a purely Judiciary Committee inquiry." See Jerome E. Edwards, *Pat McCarran: Political Boss of Nevada* (1982), 149, 151. During one of my visits with him in 1987, Felix Larkin commented that he and his staff had feared that if McCarran "got hold of the code," at best it would be delayed, and at worst probably changed to such an extent as to make it unacceptable to the individual services. Morgan recalled that "I think no one took very seriously Senator McCarran's objections in his efforts to get the bill referred to his Committee. . . . The implications, despite his protests, were a bit too clear." MPVU, October 22, 1951.

[87] LH, 1994.

[88] Ibid., 2002–3. Morse urged that the bill be put off for a week, so that the Senate could consider the ABA amendments. "I think they are entitled to a much more careful consideration

Larkin's reaction to Morse's comments, some of which were perceptive and accurate, remains unclear. He did, however, note one amusing side light. Arthur Keeffe had objected to much more in the UCMJ than just the compromises dealing with command control. Yet the ABA had focused its attention exclusively on this one issue. Keeffe angrily dissented from the ABA resolution, accusing the ABA committee chairman—none other than George Spiegelberg—of demonstrating "the most perfect example of command influence I have ever seen."[89] Larkin commented to Morgan that "Keeffe is as wild as he usually is, but at least we may get some benefit from it." To another correspondent he wrote, "I was particularly amused to see that he attributes to Spiegelberg command influence in the operation of the Committee[,] and points out that one thing Spiegelberg is worried about is command influence in military justice."[90]

By the time Morse concluded his remarks, Kefauver probably knew that the votes to pass the UCMJ were well in hand. He reiterated the point that the command influence issue had been discussed and debated many times over, and always with the same results. Because Morse had to leave the floor to meet a prior appointment, Kefauver even agreed to move the amendments on his behalf. They were rejected without a roll call, and late in the afternoon of February 3, 1950, the Senate passed the bill, 62 in favor, 9 opposed, 25 abstaining. True to his threat, McCarran voted against the measure, as did Morse and Tobey.[91]

CONGRESS COMPLETES THE CODE

Although the Senate had added a number of amendments to the House bill, the only one of major importance was the change in terms for the judges on the new Court of Military Appeals. Larkin wrote to Morgan that since the bill cleared the Senate, the House Armed Services Committee had been holding hearings to determine if the Senate changes were acceptable. "I testified at three of those hearings, and was able to persuade them to take forty-four out of the forty-five amendments." One, however, was put off for a future hearing, "and, of course, they held it the day after I left town, and, contrary to

than can possibly come to them in the short few minutes they will receive this afternoon if the Senate now rushes into a vote."

[89] LP, "Dissenting Report of Arthur John Keeffe," September 1949, 2.

[90] LP, September 16, 1949. Ibid., September 14, 1949. Although Morgan probably never saw Farmer's letter to Morse, he had already made his position clear to Larkin. "My notion is that the only way to remove that influence [of command] is by setting up a civilian department of military justice; and at present and in the foreseeable future, that would receive no legislative support." Ibid., September 26, 1949.

[91] LH, 2006.

my expectation, decided that they would not adopt it and, hence, the bill must go to Conference.''[92]

Larkin added that the committee had settled for a fifteen-year term, rather than the eight as decided by the Senate. Because the lower chamber had accepted the principle of a finite term rather than life tenure, he saw ''the whole thing as inconsequential, and more as a delaying maneuver on Vinson's [the chairman of the House Armed Services Committee] part than anything else. According to Larkin, this was because Vinson ''wants to wait until April to pass the bill so that members of this Congress will be eligible for the Court,'' which could not come into formal existence until 1951—after Congress had adjourned. One week later, Robert Smart informed Larkin that Vinson now believed that the first terms should be on a staggered (five-, ten-, and fifteen-year) basis. ''He said that Kilday [a Texas Democrat and member of the House Committee] is Vinson's candidate and he wants him to get the fifteen-year term''[93]

Larkin may well have been correct in his implication that practical politics rather than philosophic principles lay behind the decision to send the bill to conference. The conferees agreed to the fifteen-year term, both Houses accepted their recommendations without a roll call, and on May 6, 1950, President Truman signed the Uniform Code of Military Justice into law. In urging his colleagues to accept the compromise, Representative Brooks stated, ''It was my idea that this court would correspond as nearly as could be made to that of the Federal courts of appeal.'' To be sure, we have ''to some extent fallen short of this goal; but the tenure agreed upon . . . is sufficiently long to insure a stability and a permanence to the court which will serve to inspire confidence in its vitality and integrity.''[94] Whether Brooks was as good at predicting the future as his friend Carl Vinson appeared to have been can be seen in the first three decades or so of the new court's history—a subject to be taken up in the second volume of this study.

[92] LP, March 17, 1950. Diligent inquiry both to the National Archives and the staff of the House Armed Services Committee has failed to turn up any trace of these hearings. If any transcript was produced, it apparently remains unpublished.

[93] LPPL, March 24, 1950. In terms of prognostication, on this matter Vinson performed rather well. Congress ultimately accepted the staggered term concept, and not in 1951 but rather in 1961 the first Democratic president since Truman—John F. Kennedy—did in fact appoint Paul Kilday to the court.

[94] LH, 1933.

Epilogue

THE ESTABLISHMENT of the Court of Military Appeals in 1950 resulted both from a culmination of incidents as well as a confluence of interests—the most important of which have been discussed in earlier chapters. From the Revolutionary era to the present, the American legal system has recognized the unusual needs of military justice. Yet acknowledgment of this fact left other related problems unresolved. To give military justice the special tools necessary for it to function within a unique environment was one thing, but to isolate it from any type of civilian/judicial oversight was quite another.

Early patriots such as John Adams and Thomas Jefferson readily accepted the claim that military necessity required a set of judicial procedures very different from the civilian world. The unusual controversy in 1815 between a federal judge and Gen. Andrew Jackson raised but did not resolve issues concerning the extent to which a commanding general's actions were subject to civilian judicial review. As early as 1843, James Fenimore Cooper concluded that military justice was too important to be left only to the military. He inveighed against the navy in the *Spencer* case not so much because of the captain's conduct but because, apparently, no effective mechanism existed within the military for reviewing this officer's conduct *before* several executions had taken place at sea. Cooper argued that, even when allowances were made for the type of review that the commander in chief might undertake of court-martial cases, examination by an independent judicial source, outside the military, was still necessary.

Although Abraham Lincoln probably reviewed more court-martial records than any of his predecessors, pressures of time lessened his overall effectiveness. Lincoln's political role as chief executive, to say nothing of his additional burdens as commander in chief during four years of civil war did not give him the opportunity for judicial reflection required by appellate review. On the other hand, this conflict produced some change in civilian review of military justice. For the first time in its history, the Supreme Court acted to limit the authority of military tribunals, but only over civilians and only under carefully defined conditions.[1] The question of appellate review for the military, whether exercised within or by an external tribunal, remained unresolved.

As retired Army JAG George Prugh stated in 1975, the JAGs ''are not going

[1] A thorough study of military commissions utilized during Lincoln's presidency that unfortunately was unavailable during my research for this volume is Mark E. Neely, Jr., *The Fate of Liberty* (1991).

to be the originators of ideas that are going to change the military justice system, at least not very often."[2] One explanation for this fact may be in the continuing tension that existed between line officers and staff officers. Indeed, the history of attempted change in military justice during World War I and immediately thereafter demonstrates the validity of Prugh's insight. That a World War I staff officer (such as Army JAG Enoch Crowder) avoided open confrontation with a line officer (such as Gen. John Pershing) concerning military justice is very understandable.

The unusual conditions resulting in Ansell's failure to bring major reforms in military justice need not be reexamined here. As an insider, the "self criticism" he applied to certain practices was unusual. In retrospect—given the personal antagonisms involved, political disputes, and genuine disagreement both over the appropriate place for military appellate review and by whom it should be exercised—the outcome of this episode is not surprising. How different were the conditions in 1948–1950!

The magnitude of American involvement in World War II produced extensive interest and concern in the way military justice was administered. After the war ended, the armed services were unified, although not by choice, and not without severe internal friction. Both the decision to unify, and the concomitant step to promulgate a uniform code of military justice were inspired by civilians and mandated by Congress. Moreover, it was a civilian James Forrestal as secretary of defense who formed the Morgan Committee, instructed the various services that ultimately they would be bound by its decisions, and decided on the final form of proposed articles where Morgan's panel could not reach agreement. When the UCMJ was submitted to Congress, again it was civilians such as Forrestal and Morgan who spoke on behalf of the "Defense Establishment." Although the three JAGs appeared before Kefauver's subcommittee, they apparently could offer only their personal views. The difference in approach between Forrestal in 1949 and Newton Baker in 1919 is striking.

Twenty years after the UCMJ went into effect, retired Army JAG Kenneth Hodson recalled in 1971 concerning the creation of the code that "the military departments were pretty much out of the picture with respect to [the UCMJ]. . . . we were given several opportunities to comment on the draft . . . , but our comments were not always given very much weight by . . . Mr. Larkin and Mr. Morgan and by the various congressional committees. Once in a while we would point out an absolute error, and they would make a change. But for the most part the whole concept, the philosophy of the Code, remained pretty much as it was when it was drafted by professor Morgan and Mr. Larkin. In other words, it was pretty much a civilian effort."[3]

[2] George S. Prugh, *Oral History Interviews* (1975), U.S. Army Military History Institute, 15.

[3] Kenneth Hodson, *Oral History Interviews*, ibid. (1971), III-69-70.

Actually, Morgan's committee made far greater allowance for military preferences than Hodson realized, or at least remembered. The limitation on jurisdiction for the court, the expanded powers for the intermediate courts (the Boards of Review which were to be appointed by the JAGs themselves), retention of basic command authority to convene courts-martial and to select their members—all are examples where UCMJ provisions were drafted or altered to meet objections raised by the military. Finally, the congressional decision to limit terms of the judges can be seen in part as a compromise between those who favored a court as much like a federal appeals tribunal as possible, and those who believed such a court to be unnecessary.

Important questions concerning the new court, some of which had already been raised by witnesses testifying before Congress, could only be answered in the future. Could the court be truly independent of the military establishment? Would it receive the type of cooperation from the JAGs necessary for its operation? Would its presence inspire increased public confidence that command influence could not affect the quality of justice administered by American armed services?

These questions were more than important: they were troublesome. Never before had Congress created a civilian appellate court for the military. Nor had the new code provided a clear demarcation between the JAGs and the court concerning supervision of military justice. Thus article 6 of the UCMJ mandated the JAGs to make "frequent inspections in the field in supervision of the administration of military justice." Yet it was probable that an appellate tribunal, one that had already been labeled by various congressional speakers as "the supreme court of the military" would claim for itself ultimate supervisory jurisdiction of military justice. The new code mandated cooperation between the judges and the JAGs, but the appellate jurisdiction given the court inevitably meant that on occasion there would be friction between them.

Finally, the success of the court would depend largely upon the legal and, to a great extent, the diplomatic skills of the new judges. However, compromise and political considerations affected the final form of the court. They would also affect selection of the judges to sit on its bench. It may be appropriate to end this volume with mention of a letter by Donald Dawson, Truman's administrative assistant in charge of personnel. On August 29, 1949, he wrote to the chairman of the Democratic National Committee reminding him that while the UCMJ had not yet passed the Senate, "it would be well for us to line up the Judges to be appointed."[4]

[4] HST, box 995, August 29, 1949.

Bibliography

Manuscript Collections

Newton D. Baker Papers, Library of Congress
Tasker Bliss Papers, Library of Congress
George E. Chamberlain Papers, Oregon Historical Society
Enoch Crowder Papers, University of Missouri
Felix Frankfurter Papers, Library of Congress
Gordon Gray Oral History, Columbia University
Gordon Gray Papers, Military History Institute
Gordon Gray Papers, University of North Carolina
Kenneth Hodson, Oral History, Military History Institute
Judge Advocate General of the Army Department Files, Judge Advocate General's School, University of Virginia
Judge Advocate General of the Army Records, National Archives, and National Archives Records Center
Estes Kefauver Papers, University of Tennessee
Felix Larkin, Oral History, Truman Library
Felix Larkin Papers, in temporary custody of author
Marx Leva, Oral History, Truman Library
Edmund Morgan Papers, Vanderbilt University, and Harvard Law School
George Prugh, Oral History, Military History Institute
Leverett Saltonstall Papers, Massachusetts Historical Society
Henry Stimson Papers, Yale University
William Howard Taft Papers, Library of Congress
Harry Truman Papers, Truman Library
Millard Tydings Papers, University of Maryland
John Henry Wigmore Papers, Northwestern University

Government Documents

Committee on a Uniform Code of Military Justice, *Uniform Code of Military Justice: Text, References and Commentary*, 1949.

U.S. Air Force, *Oral History Program. Interview of Major General Reginald C. Harmon*, 1987.

U.S. Army, *Oral History Program. Interview of Major General Kenneth Hodson*, 1971.

U.S. Army, *Oral History Program. Interview of Major General George S. Prugh*, 1975.

U.S. Congress, *Journals of Congress*, 1786.

U.S. Congress, *Abridgement of the Debates of Congress* 14, 1842–1844.

U.S. Congress, *Congressional Record* 57, 1919.

U.S. Congress, *Congressional Record* 49, 1948.

U.S. Court of Military Appeals, *Interim Report*, 1952.

U.S. Court of Military Appeals, *Report*, 1953.

U.S. House of Representatives, Subcommittee of the Committee on Military Affairs. Hearings. *Courts-Martial, Amendments to Articles of War*. 69th Cong., 2d sess., 1920.

U.S. House of Representatives, Committee on Military Affairs. *Report, Judicial System, United States Army*. Report No. 2722, 79th Cong., 2d sess., 1946.

U.S. House of Representatives, Subcommittee of the Committee on Armed Services. *Hearings to Amend the Articles of War*. 80th Cong., 1st sess., 1947.

U.S. House of Representatives, Committee on Armed Services. *Report, Amending the Articles of War to Improve the Administration of Military Justice*. Report No. 1034, 80th Cong., 1st sess., 1947.

U.S. Navy, Office of the Judge Advocate General. *Legislative History-Uniform Code of Military Justice*, 1950, 1985.

U.S. Senate, Committee on Military Affairs. *Hearings on Trials by Courts-Martial*. 65th Cong., 3d sess., 1919.

U.S. Senate, Subcommittee of the Committee on Military Affairs. *Hearings on [The] Establishment of Military Justice*. 66th Cong., 1st sess., 1919.

U.S. War Department. *Proceedings and Report of Special War Department Board on Courts-Martial and Their Procedure*. Washington: Government Printing Office, 1919.

Periodicals

Anderson, Thomas. "Is a Court-Martial a Criminal Court?" *United Service* 6 (1882): 297–301.

"Andrew Jackson and Judge D. A. Hall." *Louisiana Historical Quarterly* 5 (1922): 538–570.

Ansell, Samuel. "Military Justice." *Cornell Law Quarterly* 5 (1919): 1–17.

———. "Some Reforms in Our System of Military Justice." *Yale Law Journal* 32 (1922): 146–55.

Association of the Bar of the City of New York. *Report on Pending Legislation for the Revision of the Army Court-Martial System*. New York, 1948.

Bogert, George Henry. "Courts-Martial: Criticisms and Proposed Reforms." *Cornell Law Quarterly* 5 (1919): 18–47.

Brown, Terry W. "The Crowder-Ansell Dispute: The Emergence of General Samuel T. Ansell." *Military Law Review* 35 (1967): 1–45.

Connor, William M. "The Judgmental Review in General Court-Martial Proceedings." *Virginia Law Review* 32 (1945): 39–88.

Cox, Walter T. III. "The Army, the Courts, and the Constitution: The Evolution of Military Justice." *Military Law Review* 118 (1987): 1–30.

Droddy, J. D. "King Richard to Solorio: The Historical and Constitutional Bases for Court-Martial Jurisdiction in Criminal Cases." *Air Force Law Review* 30 (1989): 91–133.

Fairman, Charles. "The Law of Martial Rule and the National Emergency." *Harvard Law review* 55 (1942): 1253–1302.

"Free Speech in the Military." *New York University Law Review* 53 (1978): 1102–23.

Hansen, Donald W. "Judicial Functions of the Commander." *Military Law Review* 41 (1968): 1–54.

Henderson, Gordon. "Courts-Martial and the Bill of Rights: The Original Practice." *Harvard Law Review* 71 (1957): 293–324.

Holtzoff, Alexander. "Administration of Justice in the United States Army." *New York University Law Review* 22 (1947): 1–18.

Keeffe, Arthur John. "Universal Military Training With or Without Reform of Courts-Martial?" *Cornell Law Quarterly* 33 (1948): 465–87.

Margulies, Herbert F. "The Articles of War, 1920: The History of a Forgotten Reform." *Military Affairs* 43 (1979): 85–89.

New York Herald, 1882.

New York Times, 1917–1920, 1945–1946, 1948–1950.

New York Tribune, 1919.

New York World, 1919.

Pasley, Robert, Jr., and Felix Larkin. "The Navy Court Martial: Proposals for its Reform." *Cornell Law Quarterly* 33 (1947): 195–234.

Prugh, George S. "Introduction to William Winthrop's *Military Law and Precedents*." *Revue de Droit Penal Militaire et de Droit de la Guerre [Review of Military Justice and the Law of War]* 27 (1988): 437–59.

Royall, Kenneth T. "Revision of the Military Justice Process as Proposed by the War Department." *Virginia Law Review* 33 (1947): 269–88.

Scheiber, Harry and Jane. "Constitutional Liberty in World War II: Army Rule and Martial Law in Hawaii, 1941–1946. *Western Legal History* 3 (1990): 340–78.

Sherman, Edward F. "The Civilianization of Military Law." *Maine Law Review* 22 (1970): 3–103.

Van de Water, Frederick. "Panic Rides the High Seas." *American Heritage* 12 (1961): 20–23, 97–99.

Washington Herald, 1919.

Washington Post, 1918–1920, 1948–1950.

Wiener, Frederick Bernays. "American Military Law in the Light of the First Mutiny Act's Tricentennial." *Military Law Review* 126 (1989): 1–88.

———. "Book Review." *Cornell Law Review* 59 (1974): 748–58.

———. "Courts-Martial and the Constitution: The Original Understanding." *Harvard Law Review* 72 (1957): 1–49, 266–304.

———. "The Seamy Side of the World War I Court-Martial Controversy." *Military Law Review* 123 (1989): 109–28.

White, Robert J. "The Background and the Problem." *St. John's Law Review* 35 (1961): 197–214.

Books

Adams, John. *Diary and Autobiography*. Ed. L. H. Butterfield. New York: Atheneum, 1964.

Army Lawyer: A History of the Judge Advocate General's Corps, 1775–1975. Washington: Government Printing Office, 1975.

Ashton, J. Hubley, ed. *Official Opinions of the Attorneys General of the United States*. Washington: W. H. & O. H. Morrison, 1869.

Auerbach, Jerold. *Unequal Justice: Lawyers and Social Change in Modern America*. New York: Oxford University Press, 1976.

Bassett, John S. *The Life of Andrew Jackson*. New York: Doubleday, Page & Co., 1931.

Bates, Edward. *Diary*. Ed. Howard Beale. Washington: American Historical Association, 1930.

Beaver, Daniel R. *Newton D. Baker and the American War Effort, 1917–1919*. Lincoln: University of Nebraska Press, 1966.

Buell, Augustus. *History of Andrew Jackson*. New York: Charles Scribner's Sons, 1904.

Chambers, John Whiteclay II. *To Raise an Army: The Draft Comes to Modern America*. New York: The Free Press, 1987.

Coffman, Edward M. *The Hilt of the Sword: The Career of Peyton C. March*. Madison: University of Wisconsin Press, 1966.

———. *The Old Army: A Portrait of the American Army in Peacetime, 1784–1898*. New York: Oxford University Press, 1986.

———. *The War to End All Wars: The American Military Experience in World War I*. New York: Oxford University Press, 1968.

Cooper, James Fenimore. *Letters and Journals*. 4 volumes, ed. James F. Beard. Cambridge: Belknap Press, 1964.

Crackel, Theodore J. *Mr. Jefferson's Army: Political and Social Reform of the Military Establishment, 1801–1809*. New York: New York University Press, 1987.

Cramer, C. H. *Newton D. Baker: A Biography*. New York: World Publishing Co., 1961.

Davis, Burke. *Old Hickory: A Life of Andrew Jackson*. New York: Dial Press, 1977.

Edwards, Jerome E. *Pat McCarran: Political Boss of Nevada*. Reno: University of Nevada Press, 1982.

Fairman, Charles. *Reconstruction and Reunion, 1864–1888, Part I*. New York: Macmillan, 1971.

Fontenay, Charles L. *Estes Kefauver*. Knoxville: University of Tennessee Press, 1980.

Frankfurter, Felix. *Felix Frankfurter Reminisces*. New York: Anchor Books, 1960.

Friedman, Lawrence M. *History of American Law*. 2d ed. New York: Simon and Schuster, 1985.

Fry, James B. *Military Miscellanies*. New York: Brentano, 1889.

Gayarre, Charles. *History of Louisiana*. New York: Armand Hawkins, 1885.

Generous, William T., Jr. *Swords and Scales*. New York: Kennikat Press, 1973.

Grossman, James. *James Fenimore Cooper*. New York: William Sloan Associates, 1949.

Hayford, Harrison. *The Somers Mutiny Affair*. New York: Englewood Cliffs: Prentice Hall, 1960.

Ives, Rollin. *A Treatise on Military Law*. 4th ed. New York: D. Van Nostrand, 1886.

Jackson, Andrew. *Correspondence*. Ed. John Bassett. Washington: Carnegie Institution, 1927.

Jones, Howard Mumford. *The Pursuit of Happiness*. Cambridge: Harvard University Press, 1953.

Klement, Frank L. *The Limits of Dissent: Clement L. Vallandigham and the Civil War*. Lexington: University Press of Kentucky, 1970.

Kohn, Richard. *Eagle and Sword, the Federalists and the Creation of the Military Establishment in America, 1783–1802*. New York: The Free Press, 1975.

Lane, Jack. *Armed Progressive: General Leonard Wood*. San Rafael: Presidio Press, 1978.

Lewis, Walker. *Without Fear or Favor*. Boston: Houghton Mifflin, 1965.

Lieber, G. Norman. *The Justification of Martial Law*. Washington: Government Printing Office, 1898.

Lincoln, Abraham. *Collected Works*. Ed. Roy Basler. New Brunswick: Rutgers University Press, 1953.

Lockmiller, David A. *Enoch H. Crowder: Soldier, Lawyer and Statesman*. Columbia: University of Missouri, 1955.

Meador, Daniel J. *Criminal Appeals: English Practices and American Reforms*. Charlottesville: University Press of Virginia, 1973.

Millett, Alan R., and Peter Maslowski. *For the Common Defense: A Military History of the United States of America*. New York: The Free Press, 1984.

Moyer, Homer F., Jr. *Justice and the Military*. Washington: Public Law Education Institute, 1972.

Neely, Mark E., Jr. *The Fate of Liberty*. New York: Oxford University Press, 1991.

O'Neil, William L. *American High: The Years of Confidence, 1945–1960*. New York: The Free Press, 1986.

Parrish, Michael. *Felix Frankfurter and His Times*. New York: The Free Press, 1982.

Philbrick, Thomas. *James Fenimore Cooper and the Development of American Sea Fiction*. Cambridge: Harvard University Press, 1961.

Pitman, Benn. *The Assassination of President Lincoln and the Trial of the Conspirators*. New York: Funk and Wagnalls, 1954.

Polenberg, Richard. *Fighting Faiths: The Abrams Case, the Supreme Court, and Free Speech*. New York: Penguin Books, 1987.

Proceedings of the Naval Court-Martial in the Case of Alexander Slidell Mackenzie. New York: Henry G. Langley, 1844.

Pound, Roscoe. *Criminal Justice in America*. New York: Da Capo Press, 1930.

Remini, Robert. *Andrew Jackson and the Course of American Empire, 1767–1821*. New York: Harper & Row, 1977.

Rearden, Steven L. *The Formative Years, 1937–1950*. Vol. 1 of *The History of the Office of the Secretary of Defense*. Ed. Alfred Goldberg. Washington: Government Printing Office, 1984.

Roalfe, William R. *John Henry Wigmore: Scholar and Reformer*. Evanston: Northwestern University Press, 1977.

Schlesinger, Arthur. *War and the Constitution: Abraham Lincoln and Franklin D. Roosevelt*. Gettysburg: Gettysburg College, 1988.

Smith, Page. *John Adams*. New York: Doubleday, 1962.

Turner, Thomas. *Beware the People Weeping: Public Opinion and the Assassination of Abraham Lincoln*. Baton Rouge: Louisiana State University Press, 1982.

Welles, Gideon. *Diary*. Boston: Houghton Mifflin, 1911.

Weigley, Russell F. *The History of the United States Army*. Rev. ed. Bloomington: Indiana University Press, 1984.

Winthrop, William. *Military Law and Precedents*. 2d ed. Washington: Government Printing Office, 1920.

Index

Italicized page numbers indicate photographs.